The
Oxford Dictionary of
English
Christian Names

The
Oxford Dictionary of
English
Christian Names

BY

E. G. WITHYCOMBE

SECOND EDITION

OXFORD UNIVERSITY PRESS
LONDON   OXFORD   NEW YORK

Oxford University Press

OXFORD LONDON NEW YORK

GLASGOW TORONTO MELBOURNE WELLINGTON

CAPE TOWN IBADAN NAIROBI DAR ES SALAAM LUSAKA ADDIS ABABA

DELHI BOMBAY CALCUTTA MADRAS KARACHI LAHORE DACCA

KUALA LUMPUR SINGAPORE HONG KONG TOKYO

ISBN O 19 881302 3

First edition 1945
Second edition 1950
First issued as an
Oxford University Press paperback 1973

*Printed in Great Britain
at the University Press, Oxford
by Vivian Ridler
Printer to the University*

PREFACE TO THE SECOND EDITION

THE present edition contains some fifty names not included in the original issue, but the main work of revision has consisted in a multitude of small corrections, additions, and emendations, which affect almost every article, and for the greater number of which I am indebted to the kindness and learning of correspondents, unfortunately too numerous to name here. It would seem, judging by their letters, that my readers, hitherto, have all been amiable, witty, and well informed, and the pleasure which I have derived from their letters has more than compensated for the tediousness of revision. Though it is not possible to make acknowledgement of all such help, I must express my particular gratitude to Professor G. R. Driver, Professor Idris Foster, Professor Max Förster, the Very Rev. Dean Reidy of Tralee, Dr. C. Suffern, and Professor J. A. Twemlow, for the time and trouble they have spent on the book, though it would be impertinent in me to speak of the value of their help and advice.

It will be noted that pronunciation has been indicated whenever it is doubtful.

E. G. W.

ST. PHILIP'S AND ST. JAMES'S DAY
1949

PREFACE TO THE FIRST EDITION

SOME apology, or at least explanation, may be expected for the addition of yet another to the list of books on this subject, which is already very long and is added to in almost every publishing season. It must, however, be stated frankly that they are for the most part almost valueless. There has been little change in this respect since the Rev. R. S. Charnock wrote in 1882, in the preface to his *Praenomina*: 'I cannot say I have been greatly edified by the perusal of many [books on the subject]. The unworthiness of works on this subject is caused by the fact that one author copies from another, and but few writers have more than a superficial acquaintance with two or three languages.' These strictures are still valid (*Praenomina* itself, incidentally, was no better than its predecessors). At the time when Charnock wrote, the primary source was still the lists of names with etymologies which form part of Camden's *Remaines* (1605), and these amusing but completely fanciful explanations were still solemnly put forward. Edward Lyford, a pious young man, of whom it is stated in the preface to his work that in six weeks he learned enough Hebrew for the purpose, in 1655 published a little book entitled *The True Interpretation of Christian Names*, the purpose of which he explains: 'I wish therefore, that all Christians were more seriously exhorted, not so much to use those Barbarous and Strange names, as Saxon, Sabin, and German names, which are now introduced amongst us, but rather, that as we are Christians, so we would use such names that become Christians (I mean) those Scripture names whose Interpretations and Etymologies might be suitable to our several estates and conditions.' Lyford copied the etymologies of non-Hebrew names almost word for word from Camden, and his own Hebrew etymologies are some-what wild. His book was probably not much read, but Mrs. Thrale had a copy of it, and planned and partly executed a a work which she named *Lyford Redivivus*, which has never been printed.

The first attempt at seriously tackling the subject was made by Charlotte M. Yonge, the novelist, who in 1863 brought out a work in two volumes entitled *A History of Christian Names*; a revised edition in one volume was issued in 1884. This has ever since remained the standard work on the subject in English, and practically the whole substance of later books has been based on it, their authors, sometimes openly and sometimes tacitly, using it as a quarry. Before pointing out the deficiencies of this work it must be emphasized that it was a great deal better than anything which had gone before and, indeed, than most of its successors. Having regard to the author's equipment, to the sources then available, and to the fact that few at that time had any conception of apply-ing historical methods to linguistic studies, it is indeed a remarkable achievement and assembles a great deal of miscel-laneous information in a very readable form. Miss Yonge's modesty prevented her from philological flights of fancy, except when all her authorities failed her, but it also led her to adopt uncritically the pronouncements of those authorities, particularly the Germans. The etymological part of her book is to-day almost valueless, but it contains a mass of anecdotes and facts about the history of names, which are still of interest and value.

The next landmark in English studies of nomenclature was the posthumous publication in 1901 of *A Dictionary of English and Welsh Surnames* by Canon C. W. Bardsley, who had already published in 1873 a short work on the subject, and in 1880 *Curiosities of Puritan Nomenclature*. Bardsley's book was the fruit of thirty years' study and is a measure of the revolution which had taken place in linguistic studies in England during that period, which had witnessed the establishment, for example, of the Early English Text Society and the Rolls Series, and the launching of the *Oxford English Dictionary*. The necessity of an historical basis for philological speculations was now generally recognized by scholars, though the old army of happy guessers was still fighting a stiff rearguard action, and is indeed by no means extinct to-day, particularly in the field of place-name study. The foundation of Bardsley's work was an enormous mass of material collected by himself from both published and unpublished sources. Though his subject was surnames, he incidentally provides a most valuable corpus of material illustrative of medieval christian names, upon which the present work has drawn freely.

Of equal importance is Förstemann's monumental *Altdeutsches Namenbuch* which has likewise been of the greatest use for all names of Germanic origin.

The principal original sources of which use has been made will be found in the list of abbreviations, but a very much greater number of works have been consulted. The earliest recorded forms of each name are given. It will be noted that a majority of these are in Latin, and the rarity of early records in English is one of the chief difficulties in elucidating the history of difficult names. For the later history of uncommon names, Burke's *Peerage*, the *Baronettage*, and the *Landed Gentry* are invaluable.

There was an obvious difficulty at the outset in deciding which names to include in a book of this kind. The standard adopted is roughly that a name should have survived in use after the end of the fourteenth century (or been revived later). At the other end, it has not been felt possible, or even desirable, to deal with the flood of newly invented names in use at the present time in the United States of America, many of which have already crossed the Atlantic. Some of the commoner Irish and Welsh names have been included, since they are of obvious interest and are often used in England.

I wish here to express my gratitude to Dr. Onions and to both the late and present Secretary to the Delegates of the Press for their help and encouragement in the preparation of this book, and also to the late Sir Allen Mawer, but for whose teaching and example it would never have been written.

E. G. W.

ST. FRIDESWIDE'S DAY
1944

CONTENTS

LIST OF ABBREVIATIONS

ASC	Anglo-Saxon Chronicle
Ass	Assize Rolls
Bardsley	C. W. Bardsley, *Dictionary of English and Welsh Surnames* (pub. 1901)
Black	G. F. Black, *Surnames of Scotland*, 1946
Burke	Burke's *Peerage, Baronetage*, and *Landed Gentry*
C	Century
Cal Gen	*Calendarium Genealogicum*
Camden	Camden's *Remaines*, 1605 (pub. 1623)
Chester	Child-marriages, &c. in the diocese of Chester, 1661–6 (E.E.T.S. 108)
Chester Wills	Wills at Chester, 1545–1720
Cl	Close Rolls
Clerkenwell	Cartulary of St. Mary, Clerkenwell
CMY	Charlotte Mary Yonge, *History of Christian Names*, 2 vols., 1863. Revised ed. 1884
Cornhill Reg	Church Registers of St. Peter's, Cornhill
Cornish Reg	Cornish Church Registers
Cov	The Coventry Leet Book
Cur	Curia Regis Rolls
DB	Domesday Book
Exch R	Exchequer Rolls
f.	feminine
FA	Feudal Aids
FF	Feet of Fines
Förstemann	E. Förstemann, *Altdeutsches Namenbuch*
14th C Legendary	Early S. English Legendary, 14th C (E.E.T.S. 87)
GEC	G.E.C. *Complete Peerage*
Godstow	English Register of Godstow Nunnery, *c.* 1450 (E.E.T.S. 129–30)
HR	Hundred Rolls
Huntspill	Parish registers of Huntspill, Somerset
IPM	Calendar of Inquisitions Post Mortem
Keighley Reg	Church Registers of Keighley
Lancs Wills	Lancashire Wills (1531–1760)
Langland	William Langland, *Piers Plowman*
Linc	Lincoln Diocese Documents (E.E.T.S. 149)
Lond Marr Lic	Allegations for Marriage Licences issued by the Bishop of London, 1520–1828

Lyford	Edward Lyford, *The True Interpretation of Christian Names*, 1655.
m.	masculine
Magd.	Muniments of Magdalen College, Oxford.
N & Q	*Notes and Queries*
Notts P Reg	Nottinghamshire Parish Registers
OED	*Oxford English Dictionary*
Oseney	English Register of Oseney Abbey, *c.* 1460 (E.E.T.S. 133-4)
Ox Univ Reg	Register of Oxford University
Pat	Patent Rolls
Pipe	Pipe Rolls
Poll Tax	Poll Tax of West Riding of Yorkshire, 1379
Privy Purse Exp	Privy Purse Expenses of Henry VIII and Elizabeth
Prompt Parv	*Promptorium Parvulorum*
QW	Placita de Quo Warranto
Reg	Regesta Regum Anglo-Normannorum
St. Antholin	Church Registers of St. Antholin, Budge Row, 1538-1754
St. Columb Major	Church Registers of St. Columb Major
St. Dionis	Church Registers of St. Dionis, Backchurch, 1538-1754
St. Geo. Hanover Sq	Church Registers of St. George's, Hanover Sq., 1725-1809
St. Jas. Clerkenwell	Church Registers of St. James's, Clerkenwell, 1551-1754
St. Mary Aldermary	Church Registers of St. Mary Aldermary, 1558-1754
St. Mary at Hill	Records of St. Mary at Hill, 1420-1559 (E.E.T.S. 125-8)
Testa de Neville	Testa de Neville, or Book of Fees, temp. Hen. III–Edw. I
TRE	Tempore Regis Edwardi (In the Reign of Edward the Confessor)
Werburga	*Life of St. Werburga*, transl. 1573
Whitby Cart	Cartulary of Whitby Abbey
Yorks Recusants	A list of the Roman Catholics in the County of Yorks in 1604
Yorks Visit	Visitation of Yorkshire

INTRODUCTION

'EVERY person had in the beginning one only proper name', writes Camden, adding in his pleasant gossiping way, 'except the savages of Mount Atlas in Barbary, which were reported to be both nameless and dreamless.' Whatever be the truth about the savages of Mount Atlas, it is certainly true of the two main sources of English personal nomenclature, which are respectively Hebrew and Indo-European, that, with a few exceptions, they were originally based on the theory of one name for each individual.

SEMITIC NAMES

Semitic names, for the most part, consisted of two elements, so combined as to have an intelligible meaning, usually religious. The true meaning of the Hebrew names in the Old Testament is revealed by comparing them with those in the cognate Semitic languages, and these show that the explanations offered in the Old Testament are often only pieces of folk etymology; thus *Moses* has nothing to do with 'drawing up', nor 'Samuel', with 'hearing'.

The divine name was *Yaweh*, of which only the first element was used in making up personal names. The full name was too sacred to be uttered except in the high-priestly blessing on the Day of Atonement; either *'ădônāy* 'my lord' or *'ĕlôhim* 'God' was substituted for it. In course of time the vowels of these words were substituted for those of *Yahweh*, producing the absurd *Yehovah*, first in writing and then in speaking. This was written in European books with the Latin *j* for *y*, yielding *Jehovah*, which was pronounced with the sound of the English *j*. Further, *Yah-* was shortened to *Yô-* at the beginning of names, so that we get such pairs of names as 'Ēlîyāh (English *Elijah*) = 'God (is) Jehovah' and *Yô'ēl* (English *Joel*) = 'Jehovah (is) God'.

The primitive Semitic doctrine seems to have been that a man's name was in some way an expression of his personality and that any one name could therefore apply to only one individual. In historic times, however, a limited number of these names had been adopted (chiefly those of patriarchs and their families) and were given to children instead of newly coined names. The ambiguity arising from the use of only a comparatively few names was obviated by the adoption of patronymics (e.g. Matt. xvi, *Simon Bar-Jonah*, i.e. 'Simon son of Jonah'). A boy received his name at his circumcision, and the giving of a christian name at baptism was probably derived from this Jewish custom.

Indo-European Names

Of the great Indo-European family of languages the general principle was also that of one name for each individual, the majority of names being compounded of two elements chosen from a stock of special name-words. Such elements were naturally for the most part words of good augury, but they seem, in most languages, to have been combined with no particular regard for meaning. As Professor Stenton writes:[1] 'Most compound names can be translated, but the translations often make nonsense. The men who coined the names *Frithuwulf* "peace-wolf", and *Wigfrith* "war-peace", were not concerned about their meaning. These are ancient names and they prove that at an early time the sense which a compound name bore was a matter of little importance . . . in most cases personal or family reasons determined the choice of a name, and speculation as to its meaning, if it came at all, came as an afterthought.' Sanskrit, Greek, Slavonic, Germanic, and Celtic names were all of

[1] *Introduction to the Survey of English Place-names*, p. 168.

this type, but there are also shorter names formed from the compound ones; examples of such pairs are Sanskrit *Indra-ketu*, *Indra*, Slavonic *Bogu-slav*, *Bogoj*, Greek Νικο-κλῆς, Νίκων, Celtic *Catu-rix*, *Catoc*, Scandinavian *Sig-urd*, *Siggi*, Old German *Hari-bald*, *Herilo*, Old English *Ceol-ric*, *Ceola*. These short names arose at an early date and established themselves in independent use, often superseding the longer compound names.

The special name-words of which personal names were composed were originally ordinary significant words, but with the passage of time some of them fell out of use in the spoken language, and others underwent phonetic and semantic changes to which personal names were not always subject. An example of this is the word *Os*, 'a god', which was often used as an initial element in Old English personal names, but is hardly ever found in independent use, having become obsolete at an earlier date than any written records of the language.[1] A modern French writer[2] says of such names: 'Fossiles de la langue, épaves de couches historiques submergées par les apports successifs des sédiments lexicaux, ils permettent de reconstituer des formes et des types disparus du parler courant.' The Frankish monk Smaragdus, who wrote at the beginning of the 9th century, shows that even as early as that there was no longer a clear understanding of the formation and meaning of Germanic names: thus he translated *Uuilmunt* ('will'+'protection') as 'volens bucca' (willing mouth), and *Ratmunt* ('counsel'+'protection') as 'consilium oris' (counsel of the mouth), confusing *mund* 'protection', with *mund* 'mouth'. The short uncompounded names were naturally even less comprehensible than the compounded ones; Redin[3] lists 736 such names in Old

---

[1] It occurs once, in the plural, in the Charms.
[2] Dauzat, *Les Noms de Personnes*.
[3] Redin, *Uncompounded Names in Old English*.

English, of which he classes 338 as intelligible and 398 as
unintelligible.

GREEK NAMES

In Greece a child was given its name on the seventh or
tenth day after birth. The father chose the name and could
change it later at his will. The eldest son was usually given
the name of his paternal grandfather, later children those of
other relatives. Thus Sositheus, a client of Demosthenes,
named his eldest son after his own father, the second after
his wife's father, the third after another relative of his wife,
and the fourth after his own maternal grandfather. Sometimes, though rarely, a son bore the same name as his father,
e.g. the orator *Demosthenes*; or a derivative of the father's
name, e.g. *Phocion* son of *Phocos*; or a compound name with
one of the same elements, e.g. *Philotheus* son of *Philocles*. If
two persons bore the same name, and confusion was likely
to be caused, ambiguity was avoided by adding the name of
the father, either in the genitive case (e.g. Δημοσθένης Δημοσ-
θένους) or with the suffix -ίδης or -ιάδης;[1] or by indicating
their place of origin, the name of the tribe or deme being
added for persons of the same town (e.g. Δημοσθένης Δημοσ-
θένους Παιανιεύς, i.e. *Demosthenes* son of *Demosthenes* of the
deme of *Paiania*), and the name of the country or town for
foreigners (e.g. Ἀγησίλαος Λακεδαιμόνιος, *Agesilaus of Lace-
daemon*). Women's names were formed in the same way as
men's, but with feminine terminations; an unmarried woman
was designated as her father's daughter, a married woman as
her husband's wife, and a widow as her son's mother. Slaves
were given short, often neuter, names. Nicknames, added to
or substituted for the genuine name, were common, the most
famous example being the philosopher Plato, who was named

---

[1] In Aeolic there was a patronymic in -ιος (e.g. Αἴας Τελαμώνιος, *Ajax*
son of *Telamon*) which corresponds to the Latin names in -*ius*.

Aristocles after his grandfather, but received from his gymnastic master the nickname Πλάτων (from πλάτυς, broad), which practically superseded his real name. When such names were in general use they were written after the original name, preceded by the words ὁ ἐπικαλούμενος or ὁ καί.

CELTIC AND SLAVONIC NAMES

The Celtic system of nomenclature seems to have been much the same as the Greek, and it survived long after a system of regular surnames had been established in the rest of Europe.[1] It is noteworthy that a very large proportion of Greek personal names are composed of words denoting moral and intellectual qualities, while Celtic names have a preponderance of those concerned with physical attributes. Slavonic names were also very largely composed of two elements. The use of patronymics arose early in Russia, and they continue to be used down to the present day, though proper surnames came into use in the Middle Ages. Thus a Russian always has three names, the christian name, patronymic, and surname. The first two are generally used in addressing anyone who is known to the speaker; thus *Lef Nikolaivitch Tolstóy* would in general be addressed as *Lef Nikolaivitch*. The patronymic is regarded as honorific and is not used, e.g., in signing one's name, when the christian name and surname alone are used.

ROMAN NAMES

The Romans evolved a quite different system of nomenclature, which in its classical form consisted of three names, the praenomen (e.g. Marcus), nomen (e.g. Tullius), and cognomen (e.g. Cicero), and two other designations (the name

---

[1] Hereditary surnames were not generally used in Wales until the 17th century, and the names of the Highland clans were hardly used as surnames in the full sense of the word until the 18th century.

of the father and of the tribe): thus a full, formal appellation would be in the form *Marcus Tullius, Marci filius, Cornelia tribu, Cicero*. In very early times a man seems to have been known by a single name together with his father's name in the genitive case, e.g. *Marcus Marci*; but the name of the *gens*, or family, developed early. Finally, the cognomen, originally a personal nickname, then the name of a *familia* or branch of the *gens*, acquired importance and became the name by which a man was usually known in familiar speech, though until the time of Sulla only two names were recognized by the law, i.e. the praenomen and nomen (name of the *gens*) followed by the designation of the father, e.g. *Publius Cornelius Lucii filius*. The cognomen was first used in patrician families, which were distinguished from the plebeian by the use of three names. The general adoption of the system for all free men came towards the end of the Republic. The praenomen and nomen for the most part consisted of simple stems with the suffix *-us* or *-ius*, which correspond to some of the contracted forms in other languages (e.g. Celtic *Tontius* from *Tontio-rix*, Greek *Zeuxias* from *Zeuxippos*, &c.).

The praenomen was the name given to a male child nine days after his birth, and enrolled in the official list of citizens when he assumed the *toga virilis*. There are 36 known praenomina, though there may originally have been more. Varro (116–27 B.C.) gives a list of 32, of which 14 had by then fallen out of use. The 18 which remained were *Appius, Aulus, Decimus, Gaius, Gnaeus, Kaeso, Lucius, Mamercus, Marcus, Manius, Numerius, Publius, Quintus, Servius, Sextus, Spurius, Tiberius, Titus*. The number in general use was further reduced by the fact that some of these names were confined to certain patrician families (e.g. *Appius* to the *Claudii*, *Mamercus* to the *Æmilii*), that some families renounced the use of a certain praenomen which had been disgraced by one of their name, and that yet other families used only one or two (the

Domitii Aenobarbi, for instance, used only *Lucius* and *Gnaeus*).[1] It was, moreover, a common practice to give brothers the same praenomen. The Senate (A.D. 6) decreed that the eldest son alone should bear his father's praenomen. It was inevitable that such a system should lead to the wide use of nicknames to distinguish identically named members of a family, and in this way the cognomen arose. But though, e.g., *Publius Cornelius Scipio* might in later life be distinguished from his brothers or cousins as *Africanus*, we do not know how he was addressed in his youth and by his family. The imagination, indeed, retires baffled before the prospect of a Roman patrician nursery where all the boys might have the same name and the girls none at all.

The nomen belonged to all members of a *gens* and to all those attached to it (women, clients, and freedmen included). Almost all these names are adjectival in form, derived from some other personal or place-name, usually by the addition of the suffix *-ius*, *-aeus*, *-eius*, or *-eus*; Gauls used the suffix *-acus*, Etruscans *-nas* or *-na*, Umbrians *-enus*, *-ienus*.

The cognomen was originally a nickname or surname given to an individual by his friends or the public, which afterwards came to be used by a whole branch of a *gens*. The cognomen is usually more intelligible than the far older gentile name, being formed directly from names of places, events, physical characteristics, or else from praenomina or some other cognomen by the addition of the suffix *-inus* or *-ianus*. The *gens* could admit a new cognomen either for an individual or for a whole branch, and it was thus possible in the course of time for one person to bear several cognomina. Thus the Cornelian *gens* had a branch named *Scipio*, from which was later formed another named *Nasica*, and one consequently finds such names as *P. Cornelius Scipio Nasica Corculum* (the last being his personal cognomen). But in the best period people used only one

[1] A few of the plebeian families had praenomina of their own.

or at most two cognomina, and the occasion of a second was usually some feat of arms or an adoption; an adoptive son usually took all three of his adoptive father's names together with a derivative in *-anus* of the name of his own *gens*.

Women originally bore the name of the father's *gens* with another name placed before it; this, which often formally resembled the masculine praenomen, seems actually to have been more in the nature of a cognomen; thus besides *Gaia, Lucia, Publia*, &c., we find *Rutilia, Murrula, Rodacilla, Tertia, Secunda, Prima*, &c. These names went out of use about the middle of the Republican period, and women were known simply by the name of the *gens*. At the beginning of the Empire they took to personal names again, placing them after instead of before the name of the *gens* (e.g. *Iunia Tertulla*). Later there were fresh changes; two names were still used, but these were either the father's nomen and cognomen put into a feminine form (e.g. *Aemilia Lepida* daughter of *L. Aemilius Lepidus*), or the nomen of the father plus that of the mother (e.g. *Valeria Attia*, daughter of *L. Attius Atticus* and *Valeria Sextina*). These variations seem to have been chiefly a matter of fashion. Married women are often designated by their own names followed by that of the husband in the genitive case (e.g. *Agrippina Germanici Caesaris*).

Slaves originally had no official names of their own, but simply took their owner's praenomen in the genitive case followed by the suffix *-por* (= *puer* boy), e.g. *Marcipor, Publipor, Quintipor*. Later they were given Greek (often neuter) names followed by the owner's name in the genitive case. Freedmen used their own name as cognomen, the nomen of whoever freed them, and any praenomen they fancied.

During the later centuries of the Empire no strict rule was observed, and the number of names which a member of a great family could bear was very large. It was the fashion to use many cognomina in order to display the illustriousness of one's ancestry. Sometimes we find a man with two prae-nomina, two or more nomina, and a considerable number of cognomina. Moreover, the order in which the names were arranged became quite arbitrary, and it is often difficult to tell by which of them a person was usually known. Finally, there arose, particularly in the army and lower classes, a new kind of surname, called *signum* or *vocabulum*, which was at first a nickname but later became a genuine surname. The introduction and spread of Christianity seems not to have affected the existing usage in the matter of names.

It is difficult to judge how far the Roman system of nomen-clature was adopted in the various parts of the Empire, but it is certain that at all events the upper classes in the more thoroughly romanized parts adopted it; examples are *L. Aurelius Augustinus*, a Numidian, better known as *St. Augustine*, and the 5th-century Gaul *C. Sollius Modestus Apollinaris Sidonius*. The hordes of barbarians who overran the Empire, however, obliterated the Roman system, and even in such countries as Gaul and Spain, where the Franks and Goths adopted the language of their victims, they for the most part kept their own names. For instance, Dauzat, speaking of France, says that in the 9th century, out of a hundred names chosen at random, one will find five or six of Latin origin such as *Honoré* or *Loup*, three or four Biblical ones, and all the rest Germanic. Conversion to Christianity made little difference in this respect, for though the Church has always favoured the use of the names of saints and deprecated purely heathen names, and was partly able to enforce its preference in the later Middle Ages, it seems not to have taken any strong line in earlier times. Heathens seem mostly to have retained their old names on baptism, though sometimes they were given a new one in its place (e.g. *Ceadwalla*, King of Wessex, after his abdication, went to Rome in 689 and was baptized by Pope Sergius in the name

Peter); but sometimes the new name was no more Christian than the old (e.g. the Dane *Guthrum*, who became Alfred's son by adoption at his baptism, was given the name Æthelstan, which was in the old tradition of the West-Saxon royal family).

OLD ENGLISH NAMES

The Germanic-speaking peoples had a simple system of nomenclature, with general features the same amongst them all, though with minor variations of detail. It may be said in general that cognate forms of most names exist (or may be presumed to have existed) in Old German (and its derivatives), Old English, Gothic, and Old Scandinavian. As with the Greeks and Celts, there is a single name for each individual, and the names are usually made up of two elements taken from a stock of special words used in name-making. Some of these words could be used only as a first element in a name (e.g. Old English *Æthel-*, *Ead*), others only as a second element (e.g. Old English *-weard*), while others could be used in either position (e.g. Old English *ric, beorht*). Men's names usually had a second element of masculine gender and women's names one of feminine gender, but there are some exceptions. In addition there were a number of short names which are of two kinds: (1) genuine independent names derived from a single root-word, (2) hypocoristic or pet-names formed from compound names, e.g. *Cutha* from *Cuthwulf*, &c., which sometimes acquired the rank of independent names. The available evidence seems to show that uncompounded names were relatively common both in England and on the Continent in the Migratory period, but became less so later. It should, however, always be remembered that the material for study of early names is almost entirely derived from lists of witnesses to charters, &c., and that such people were necessarily for the most part members of the ruling classes. There is some evidence that the uncompounded names continued to be used by the lower classes after they had been discarded by the upper. There is, e.g., a group of 11th-century English manumissions where a high proportion of the serfs bear uncompounded names; and surname material suggests that such names survived among this class long after the Norman Conquest: *Bugg* and *Wragg*, for instance, of which Matthew Arnold eloquently complains,[1] are almost certainly derived from the Old English personal names *Bugge* and *Ragge*, and there are a number of similar examples. But these names, with a very few exceptions (e.g. *Hilde*) did not survive as christian names after the 13th century, have not been revived since, and so do not concern us here.

Except in Scandinavia and Iceland, where patronymics and nicknames acquired a wide currency at an early date, the Germanic-speaking peoples used but a single name, family connexions being indicated chiefly by the devices of alliteration and variation. Alliteration (i.e. the use of names beginning with the same letter for members of a family) is of very early date, traces of it being found in Tacitus. It was particularly common in the Old English kingdoms, from the earliest recorded genealogies down to the Norman Conquest. Vocalic alliteration was commonest, but consonantal was also practised (e.g. SS. *Mildthryth*, *Mildburh*, and *Mildgyth*, daughters of *Merewald*). Alliteration was definitely of Germanic origin, but variation probably arose before the Germanic languages were differentiated from the main stock (traces of it are found, for instance, in Greek); it consists in giving to the child or children a name or names of which one element is the same as one in the name of the father (or occasionally mother) and the other is different. Variation could be either of the first element (e.g. *Eadmund* son of *Alkmund*) or of the second element (e.g. *Eadgar* son of *Eadmund*). In England end-

[1] *The Function of Criticism.*

variation was rather the commoner. Very rarely both elements represented parts of the parents' names, as in the classic example of St. *Wulfstan*: 'Pater Æthelstanus, mater Wulfgeua nominati . . . puero Wulfstanus vocabulum datum ex anteriore materni et ex posteriore paterni nominis compositum.'[1] But this never became a general fashion. In the East Saxon royal family *Sige-* was the commonest initial element, in Bernicia *Os-*, in Kent *Eormen-* or *Æthel-*, and in Wessex *Æthel-*, *Ead-*, and *Ælf-*.

A third method of showing family connexions was by the repetition of names, usually in alternate generations (e.g. naming a child after his grandfather). This was a late development and seems, indeed, to have been prohibited in early times, perhaps for religious reasons. It was practised in England to some extent in the 10th and 11th centuries, and there are a few examples of repetition between great-grandfather and great-grandson in the 7th century.

Women, in the Old English period, were named on precisely the same system as men with due regard to alliteration and variation on the names of the father's family.

The Danish invasions had no great effect on the general system of nomenclature in England, though the Danes and Norwegians, of course, used their native names. These were usually cognate with Old English names, but some specifically Norse ones, such as *Knud*, *Thorkill*, *Sweyn*, were introduced. They do not, however, seem to have become current outside the Danelaw, and were in any case reinforced later by the much greater influence of the Normans, many of whose names were of Norse origin.

EFFECTS OF THE NORMAN CONQUEST

With the Norman Conquest a great change came over the personal nomenclature of the English. So far as the upper

[1] *Vita Wulfstani* (11th C.).

classes are concerned, it is almost true to say that the Old
English names (with a few exceptions) had disappeared
within two or three generations, and though, as we have
seen, there is some reason to suppose that some of the uncompounded Old English names remained in use amongst
the peasantry, they, too, had disappeared by the end of the
13th century. For example, in a list of 800 names of jurors
and bailiffs in the Eyre of Kent 1313-14, the only Old English names found are two *Edmunds*, one *Edward*, one *Hereward*, and one *Aylwyn*. In a Poll Tax roll for the West
Riding of Yorkshire in 1379 there is hardly a single Old
English name. Those few names which did survive usually
did so for one of two reasons: either they were names of
saints (e.g. *Edward, Edmund, Hilda, Mildred*) or they were
the names of former kings of the house of Wessex (e.g.
Alfred, Edgar, Ethelbert); the first of these classes is the
more numerous. The change was facilitated by the fact that
the Norman names were largely drawn from the same ultimate sources as the English, being for the most part gallicized
forms of Old German names, most of which had cognates in
Old English, or else gallicized forms of Norse names, many
of which were also familiar in England. Such Old English
names as did remain in use were subject to a gallicizing process, the chief effects of which were: (1) *th* was either omitted
(e.g. *Aylward, Aylwin* for *Æthelweard, Æthelwine*) or became
t (as *Turbett* for *Thurbeorht*) or *d* (as *Adlin* and *Edlin* from
Æthelwine); (2) final -*eald* became -*auld*, -*aud*, or -*old* (e.g.
Reynebaud, later *Rainbow*, from *Regenbeald*); (3) *w* tended to
become *v* before *a, e,* or *i,* and to disappear before *o* and *u*
(as *Harvard* for *Hereweard, Ayloffe* for *Æthelwulf, Reynold*
for *Regenweald*); (4) final *h* was replaced by *k*, and later by
-*ge* (e.g. *Elphick, Alphege* from *Alfeah*). Some of these, however, were probably merely Norman *spellings*.

But these survivals are few and hardly noticeable among

the flood of *Williams, Richards, Roberts, Ralphs, Odos, Hughs, Walters,* which fill the records of the period. The Normans also brought with them a certain number of names of Latin and others of Breton origin (e.g. *Ives, Sampson, Alan*).

GROWING INFLUENCE OF THE CHURCH

Down to this time the Church in western Europe had had little influence on the names of its members. It is true that various Fathers and ecclesiastical writers and some synodal decrees had from time to time exhorted the faithful to give their children only the names of canonized saints or of angels, but their admonitions had not been much heeded, and in fact it was not until the Council of Trent (1545–63) that the Roman Catholic Church absolutely required the use of such names in baptism. By the end of the 12th century, however, the growing power of the Church to influence every aspect of life is reflected in the greatly increased use of the names of saints. To take only scriptural saints as an example, it may be observed that *Matthew, Peter, John,* and *Andrew* each occur once in Domesday Book, and are rare until the end of the following century; *Luke, Bartholomew, Philip, James, Paul, Simon, Michael,* are first recorded between 1185 and 1200, *Barnabas* in 1201, and *Mark* not until 1303. At the end of the 12th century the commonest man's name in the records is still *William* (15%) followed by *Robert* (11%), *Ralph* (10%), *Richard* (8%), *John* accounting for only 2 per cent. A hundred years later *William, Robert,* and *Richard* represent respectively 14, 11, and 10 per cent. of recorded names, but *John* has jumped to first place with no fewer than 25 per cent., and other scriptural names are well established. The change was even more noticeable in the case of women's names, the old Germanic names being almost entirely replaced by the names of scriptural and legendary saints. *Mary* is first found recorded as a christian name about 1203, *Anne* in 1218, *Joan* in 1189, *Elizabeth* in 1205, while of the names of the three great virgin saints, *Agnes, Catherine,* and *Margaret,* the first two are recorded in 1189 and 1196; *Margaret* came into use rather earlier owing to St. *Margaret,* sister of Edgar Atheling, who had Hungarian connexions, *Margaret* being used from an early date in eastern Europe.

CHANGES IN THE 12TH AND 13TH CENTURIES

The first effect of this change in fashion was greatly to increase the number and variety of names; in the late 12th century and early 13th century there were probably more christian names in use than at any subsequent period until the 20th century. Some of the Old English names were still in use, there was the rich Norman stock with a sprinkling of Breton, in addition to the newly adopted saints' names which were drawn from Hebrew, Greek, Latin, and other tongues. But even this wealth of material seems not to have satisfied the eclectic taste of the period, and the oddest names are to be met with in late-12th-century records, e.g. *Aliena, Antigone, Camilla, Cassandra, Celestria, Extranea, Grecia, Hodierna, Idonea, Ismenia, Juvenal, Italia, Lavina, Leda, Melodia, Norma, Oriolda, Paris, Pavia, Pharamus, Splendor.* It will be noted that these are mostly feminine, and they no doubt represent the same love of novelty as led Mrs. Kenwigs to invent the name *Morleena* 'for the special distinction of her eldest child, in case it should prove a daughter', and still sways the minds of potential stars of stage and screen in their search for professional names. But as the 13th century advanced, the stock of names shrank rapidly, and of those still in use a comparatively small number were borne by an increasingly large proportion of the population. The five names *Henry, John, Richard, Robert, William* together accounted for 38 per cent. of recorded men's names in the

12th century, for 57 per cent. in the 13th century, and for 64 per cent. in the 14th century. The same tendency is to be observed in France; it has been calculated that in Paris at the end of the 13th century the names *Jehan* and *Jehane* were at least twice as frequent as the next commonest, *Guillaume* and *Marie*. This tendency continued until at least the end of the 18th century, though interrupted by temporary fashions, such as the use of Biblical names in the 17th century. It is easier to illustrate after the compulsory registration of baptisms begins, as is shown in the following tables which give percentages of total baptisms.

Commonest Men's Names

	1550–99	*1600–49*	*1650–99*	*1700–49*	*1750–99*
William .	22·5	15·5	18·5	20·0	20·0
John .	15·5	19·0	28·0	24·5	19·0
Thomas .	13·5	16·0	16·0	10·0	16·0
Total .	51·5	50·5	62·5	54·5	55·0

Commonest Women's Names

	1600–49	*1650–99*	*1700–49*	*1750–99*
Elizabeth .	25·0	14·5	22·0	19·0
Mary . .	17·0	20·5	20·0	24·0
Anne . .	10·0	11·5	14·0	14·0
Total . .	52·0	46·5	56·0	57·0

RISE OF SURNAMES

To return to the 13th century, it is evident that such a limitation in the number of christian names must have led to a considerable amount of confusion, and this had no doubt some influence on the fairly general adoption of surnames in the 13th and 14th centuries. Surnames had been in use to some extent among the Norman nobility since the Conquest, though even by them they were not used consistently and were often not real hereditary surnames. A good example is the genealogy of the Fitzhugh family, which was founded by one Bardolph, the succession being Akaris Fitz-Bardolph, Hervey Fitz-Akaris, Henry Fitz-Hervey, Randolph Fitz-Henry, Hugh Fitz-Randolph, Henry Fitz-Hugh (fl. 1321). But the bearing of a surname of some sort became common in all classes of English society in the late 12th and early 13th centuries. A large number of these were patronymics; even more were place-names indicating the residence or place of origin of the bearer; others were names of trades or callings, and yet others were nicknames, sometimes descriptive, sometimes derisive. A man might very well be known at different times or in different places by different names (in the Battle Abbey Deeds, for example, the same man is referred to indifferently as John Hervy, John Fitz Hervie de Sudwerk, and John de London), and it was long before the custom of keeping to a single hereditary surname became general. The compulsory keeping of parish registers (from 1538) probably completed the process in England. In Wales even the gentry bore no hereditary surnames until the time of Henry VIII, who strongly advised the heads of Welsh families to conform to English usage; their use by other classes in Wales was by no means universal even in the 18th century. Borrow has a story of a Welsh 18th-century poet Twm o'r Nant (Tom of the valley) whose father's name was Evan Edwards, and who accordingly was in the habit of calling himself Thomas Evans, until it occurred to him that this might be taken as meaning that he was a bastard, after which he called himself Thomas Edwards. There are even parts of England (notably Yorkshire and Staffordshire) where, within living memory, the poorer classes seldom used their surnames except in legal documents, &c., men being known by such appellations as 'Tom o' Dick o' Mary's'.

LEGAL ASPECT OF NAMES

It is, indeed, by no means clear what a man's name legally is, or, indeed, whether there is such a thing as a legal name. The Church recognizes only the name given in baptism,[1] and there is some division of opinion whether a second name can be added to or substituted for the baptismal name at confirmation. Monks and nuns always take a new christian name in religion, and priests can change their christian name at ordination. Before the Reformation the unauthorized change of a christian name was a grave offence. It is recorded in the consistorial acts of the Bishop of Rochester that on 15th October 1515 one Agnes Sharpe appeared and confessed that she had 'of her own motion and consent, voluntarily changed at confirmation the name of her infant son to Edward, who was when baptized named Henry, for which she submitted to penance'. A beneficed clergyman of the Church of England is obliged to perform the ceremony of baptism when required to do so by a parishioner, and to give whatever names the godparents select; but, although the rubrics do not expressly say so, it is generally assumed that he may object to any name on religious or moral grounds. A Roman priest is authorized to add a saint's name to those chosen by the godparents, if these are unchristian or non-christian and circumstances are such that discussion and dissuasion are impracticable or impolitic. The Registration of Births Act (1874), though it makes provision for the insertion of a christian name, does not require such insertion, which remains permissive, not compulsory. Chief Justice

---

[1] e.g. in the rites of baptism, confirmation, and holy matrimony. Bishops sign only their christian names, followed by the name of their dioceses. Another vestige of this is to be found in the signatures of royal personages, e.g. *George R.*

Coke (1552–1634) says: 'It is requisite that a purchaser be named by the name of baptism and his surname, and that special heed be taken to the name of baptism, for that a man cannot have two names of baptism as he may have divers surnames'; and again: 'It is holden in our antient books that a man may have divers *names* at divers times, but not divers Christian names.' Sir Joseph Jekyll, Master of the Rolls, in 1730 in the case of *Barlow* v. *Bateman*, remarked: 'I am satisfied the usage of passing Acts of Parliament for the taking upon one a surname is but modern, and that anyone may take upon him what surname, and as many surnames, as he pleases, without an Act of Parliament.' This decision, however, was reversed by the House of Lords, and it is now usually assumed that a man's legal appellation is the christian name given him in baptism by his god-parents (or, alternatively, inserted in the registration of his birth) and the surname of his father or, in the case of an illegitimate child, of his mother.

NICKNAMES

The adoption of surnames was not in itself enough to prevent the ambiguity caused by the extensive use of a very few christian names, particularly as it was by no means uncommon in the 13th to 15th centuries to give more than one living child in the same family the same name; in particular it is quite usual to find brothers named John (e.g. the two sons of John Paston, Sir John Paston the elder (1442–79) and Sir John Paston the younger (died 1503)). Examples from 15th-century wills are bequests to 'Isabel and Isabel my daughters', and to 'Besse my daughter and Elizabeth my daughter'.[1] The difficulty was partly solved by the use (as in

---

[1] It has been suggested that one reason for giving the same name to more than one son was the custom of granting leases for three lives, i.e. to John Doe and his sons John and William; if one son died, there would still be one of the same name left to hold the lease.

the last-quoted example) of diminutives or pet-names; thus the common name *Bartholomew* appears variously as *Bat, Bate, Batty, Bartle, Bartelot, Bartelet, Batcock, Batkin, Tolly.* The French diminutive suffixes *-el, -on, -in, -ot, -et* are earlier than the English *-kin* and *-cock* and were used by all classes of the community, whereas the English ones are found only among the lower classes. The French diminutives were used either singly or in combination with each other and are found from the early 12th century; thus the Norman name *Hamo(n)* developed the diminutive forms *Ham-el, Ham-el-in, Ham-el-et, Ham-el-ot, Hamon-et.* They were used for both men's and women's names, but survived longer in the latter case; thus *Philpot, Wilmot, Marriot, Emmot* are found as women's names in the 16th and 17th centuries, and even later in Cornwall, long after such forms had ceased to be used by men. *-on*, which is always feminine in French and usually in English (e.g. *Alison, Marion*), was also sometimes used for men (e.g. *Gibbon* from *Gib*, a pet-form of *Gilbert*).

The vernacular suffixes *-cock* and *-kin* are first recorded about the end of the 13th century. *-kin* was possibly of Flemish origin, having been in use in the Low Countries from the 10th century. It is usually masculine, though occasionally feminine (e.g. *Malkin* or *Mawkin* from *Mary*), the earliest recorded examples being *Janekin, Malekin, Watekin,* and *Wilekin* which are found in 1250. It was most common in the second half of the 14th century. *Piers Plowman* (1362) has *Malkin, Perkin, Hawkin,* and *Watkin*; Chaucer uses *Jankin, Malkin, Perkin, Simkin,* and *Wilkin*; in 'The Tournament of Tottenham' (*c.* 1450) occur *Dawkyn, Hawkyn, Jeynkyn, Perkyn,* and *Tymkyn.* It will be noted that most of these are derived from the commoner christian names, and the same is true of compounds of *-cock*, examples of which are *Adcock* (from *Adam*), *Batcock, Hancock* (from *Jehan*), *Hitchcock, Simcock, Wilcock.* The origin of this suffix is obscure,

but it seems probable that it is the Middle English *cok*
(= French *coq*), used in the sense 'good fellow' (cf. modern
slang 'old cock', &c.), though this sense is not recorded until
much later than the first occurrence of the suffix in personal
names (*c.* 1275). Christian names in *-kin* and especially *-cock*
are rare after about 1450, though they survive in numerous
common surnames.

There was another kind of pet-name, that formed by
apocope or syncope from the original name, as *Will* from
William, *Sim* from *Simon*, *Gib* from *Gilbert*, *Wat* from *Walter*; and these in turn gave rise to other, rhyming, forms, as
Dick and *Hick* for *Ricard*, *Hitch* for *Richard*, *Hob* and *Bob*
for *Robert*, *Hodge* for *Roger*. *Dick* is one of the earliest of
these names to be recorded (*quidam Dicke Smith* Curia Regis
Rolls 1220), and many of them are still in use, though it is
curious to note that the once common forms with initial *H*,
e.g. *Hob*, *Hodge*, *Hick*, *Hitch*, *Hudd* (for *Richard*, see Bardsley s.v. *Hudd*), *Hibb* (for *Ib* from *Isabel*), have all died out.
There can be little doubt that the majority of peasants in the
13th to 15th centuries went by these rather uncouth names,
which so nearly resembled the Old English uncompounded
names which had been general among their forefathers before
the Norman Conquest and had lingered on in occasional use
until the 13th or 14th century. The *locus classicus* for these
pet-names in literature is Gower's *Vox Clamantis*, where the
poet describes the peasant's revolt of 1381:

> *Watte* vocat, cui *Thomme* venit, neque *Symme* retardat,
> *Betteque*, *Gibbe* simul, *Hykke* venire jubent;
> *Colle* furit, quem *Geffe* juvat, nocumenta parantes,
> Cum quibus ad dampnum *Wille* coire vovet.
> *Grigge* rapit, dum *Dawe* strepit comes est quibus *Hobbe*,
> *Lorkyn* et in medio non minor esse putat:
> *Hudde* ferit, quem *Judde* terit, dum *Tebbe* minatur,
> *Jakke* domosque viros vellit et ense necat.

These forms were mainly a plebeian usage, a sign of which is the later use of many of them as common nouns, e.g. *hodge* for a country labourer, *jack* and *dick* meaning 'man', 'fellow', and such phrases as *every Tom, Dick, and Harry*. In the 14th century there was scarcely a name in common use which had not one or more of such diminutives. After the Reformation, with the advent of Biblical names, the old French and English diminutive suffixes fell out of use, but the habit of using shortened forms of names for familiar use went on and still persists.[1]

It is instructive to note how age throws a cloak of respectability over names of plebeian origin. Thus the medieval *Jack, Tom, Dick, Bob, Will* are now used by all classes; the 17th-century *Sam, Ben, Joe* were freely used by the middle classes in the 19th century and would doubtless still be so used, but for the fact that their originals have gone out of fashion; but the modern *Les, Reg, Bert* have not yet had time to rise in the social scale.[2]

Use of Men's Names for Women

One other result of the increasing use of saints' names in the later Middle Ages was the adaptation of men's names to the use of women. In some cases a similar name was taken to be the equivalent; *Joan*, for instance, was given to girls whom it was wished to put under the patronage of St. *John*. In French the formation of feminines was perfectly easy, and these became, and have remained, common in France. Latin records of the 13th to 15th centuries show that the custom of giving masculine names to girls was also common in England; they appear in Latin with feminine endings,

[1] Cf. Mr. Samuel Weller's comment on the name of Mr. Job Trotter: 'And a wery good name it is—only one I know, that ain't got a nickname to it.'

[2] *Reggie* and *Bertie*, for some obscure reason, have a much higher social standing than *Reg* and *Bert*.

e.g. *Philippa, Nicholaa, Alexandra, Jacoba,* but it is clear that girls so named were in fact baptized and called *Philip, Nicholas, Alexander, James,* &c. For further details see under these names. Other names which were commonly used for girls were *Gilbert, Aubrey, Reynold, Basil, Eustace, Giles, Edmund, Simon, Florence. Nicholas* was particularly common as a girl's name in Scotland, where it was still current at the end of the 17th century. An interesting reference to this custom occurs in a 12th-century tract by Maurice of Kirkham to Gilbert of Sempringham, quoted by M. R. James ['The Salomites', *J. Theological Studies,* 35, 1934 (287–97)]. The writer was concerned to refute the heretical opinion that *Salome* was a man's name (i.e. that in *Mark* xv. 40 and xvi. 1, *Mary* and *Salome* represent not two, but one person 'Mary wife of Salome'). The Salomites, he says, make use of the vulgar argument that women often borrow men's names ('plerasque mulieres a viris sibi nomina solere mutuari'), giving as examples Alexander, Thomas, Eustace, and William. He then describes how he had crushed a scholar who was defending this opinion. ' "Were you never present in a baptistry when infants were being baptized?" "Yes, often." "Did you ever on such an occasion hear a boy named Beatrice or Gunnilda or Matilda or Godiva?" "Certainly not." "Then why should you suppose that the Jews should be in the habit of giving feminine names to males? Women's names or nicknames are given to lazy, slothful, effeminate persons, not in their baptism, but on account of their vicious life, as, for example, we formerly knew a Robert who for his infamous character was called Godiva." '

The Scots in the 18th century were very fond of making feminine forms of masculine names, quite regardless of euphony, possibly under French influence. Examples are *Abrahamina, Adamina, Æneasina, Alexina, Angusina, Clementina, Davidina, Forbesia, Jacobina, Jamesina, Johnina, Philippina, Roberta, Robina, Stewartina, Vallentina, Williamina.* A few of these survive, but most of them have, happily, disappeared.

NAMES REFERRING TO CIRCUMSTANCES OF BIRTH

Before we leave the pre-Reformation period there are one or two details which may be noted. Children were often christened with names referring to the day of their birth: *Christmas, Nowell, Easter, Pask, Whitsun, Pentecost, Epiphany, Theophania* or *Tiffany, Loveday,* and others were all used as christian names. It was the custom for a midwife to christen quick children before birth when it was feared that they might not be delivered alive. They were given neuter names such as *Vitalis, Creature, Chylde-of-God.*

THE REFORMATION

The change in nomenclature which followed the Reformation was second in importance only to that caused by the Norman Conquest. Up to that time the number of Biblical names in use was comparatively small, consisting for the most part of those made familiar by the mystery plays, as *Adam, Eve, Noah, Sarah, Abraham, Isaac, Jacob, Joseph, Daniel, Sampson, David, Absalom, Susanna, Judith, Anna, Hester, Tobias, Jonah.* There were also a few names brought back by the Crusaders, such as *Baptist, Jordan, Elias,* and the names of the apostles, particularly *John, James, Simon, Peter, Bartholomew, Matthew, Philip, Thomas, Barnabas; Paul* and *Timothy* were also used, but were not common. With the Reformation all the names of non-scriptural saints fell into disgrace and were for the most part speedily disused. *Austin, Basil, Bennet, Blase, Brice, Christopher, Clement, Crispin, Denis, Fabian, Gervase, Hilary, Martin, Quentin, Theobald, Valentine, Viel* were some of those which almost disappeared in the 16th century, and some of the apostles (e.g. *Simon Peter*) fared little better. The effect was even greater on the naming of women, for some of the favourite women's names were those of unscriptural saints, e.g. *Agnes, Cecily, Barbara, Katherine, Margaret, Ursula*. Since the disgrace of the calendar coincided in time with the dissemination of the English Bible, it was naturally to the Bible that people looked for new names, and since the names of the apostles had long been in use and were felt to savour somewhat of popery, it was the Old Testament names which now began to be used. Cartwright, writing in 1565, advised that 'They which present unto baptism ought to be persuaded not to give those that are baptized the names of God, or of Christ, or of Angels, or of holy offices, as of baptist, evangelist &c. nor such as savour of paganism or popery: but chiefly such whereof there are examples in the Holy Scriptures, in the names of those who are reported in them to have been godly and virtuous.'

Puritan Names

The next innovations were made by the Puritans, who, wishing to mark their children off from what they regarded as the godless masses, found that the more manageable of the Old Testament names were already in use. They accordingly took to such names as *Renovata, Donatus, Beata, Renatus, Rediviva, Desiderius, Desideratus, Deodatus*, all of which are recorded in the 16th century. Later they began to coin corresponding English names. Thus *Desiderius, Donatus*, and *Amor* are matched by *Desire, Given*, and *Love*, and as time went on many strange names were invented, of which the classic example is *Praise-God* Barebones. It is sometimes stated that these Puritan names are a mere myth, but that is because the mistake has been made of consulting parish registers of the second half of the 17th century, whereas the time when they were most rife was from about 1580 to 1640. Thus Thomas Heley, minister of Warbleton, called his children (born between 1583 and 1589) *Much-Merceye, Increased, Sin-denie,* and *Fear-not*; a contemporary Presbyterian minister called his *Persis, Renewed,* and *Safe-on-high.* Camden in his *Remaines* (1605) writes:

'If that any among us have named their children *Remedium amoris, Imago saeculi,* or with such like names, I know some will think it more than a vanity, as they do but little better of the new names, *Free-gift, Reformation, Earth, Dust, Ashes, Delivery, Morefruit, Tribulation, The Lord is near, More triall, Discipline, Joy again, From above, Acceptance, Thankfull, Praise-God* and *Livewell,* which have lately been given by some to their children with no evill meaning, but upon some singular and precise conceit.'

The more responsible religious leaders did not encourage this fashion: Cartwright, as we have seen, merely recommended the use of the names of virtuous persons mentioned in the scriptures, but his condition of *virtuous* was not always heeded, and during the 17th century there was hardly a name in the Bible which was not used, regardless of its associations, as a christian name, and the more thoughtful were scandalized by such names as *Antipas, Cain, Dinah, Tamar, Sapphira,* as well as pained by the cacophonies of *Bezaleel, Ezekiel,* or *Habakkuk.* Camden, who probably represented the normal point of view, wrote:

'In times of Christianity, the names of most holy and vertuous persons, and of their most worthy progenitors were given to stir up men to the imitation of them, whose name they bare. But succeeding ages (little regarding S. Chrysostom's admonition to the contrary) have recalled prophane names, so as now Diana, Cassandra, Hippolitus, Venus, Lais, names of unhappy disaster are as rife somewhere, as ever they were in Paganism.[1] Albeit in

---

[1] Camden was probably thinking primarily of France, where the fashion of using classical names was very general among the nobility. It was also prevalent in Italy and Germany. Such names as *Lucrezia, Cesare, Alessandro, Olimpia, Diane, Hercule, Aurore, Achille* are examples. In England they were less common, but *Diana* was establishing itself, and

our late reformation, some of good consideration have brought in
Zachary, Malachy, Jozias &c. as better agreeing with our faith,
but without contempt of countrie names (as I hope) which have
both good and gracious significations.'

The judicious Calamy, writing his account of the ejected
ministers at the end of the 17th century, says: 'This was a
course that some in those times affected, baptizing their
children *Reformation, Discipline* &c. as the affection of their
parents stood engaged. For this they have sufficiently suffered
from Profane Wits, and this worthy person [Sabbath Clark]
did so in particular.' Anyone interested in these eccentricities
may refer to Bardsley's *Curiosities of Puritan Nomenclature*,
where he will find much information and entertainment.
Here there is only room for a few detached remarks. There
is no doubt that a fanatical minister had much influence in
the matter of names: thus while Thomas Heley, mentioned
above, was minister of Warbleton (1585–9) the parish registers show at least 100 eccentric names including *Sorry-for-
Sin* and *No-merit*. One Edmund Snape, curate of St. Peter's,
Northampton, in 1590 refused to christen a child Richard
(after its grandfather) because it was not a scriptural name,
but this seems to have been an exceptional case. Some
typical Puritan families are those of Robert Pound of Canterbury, whose children (born between 1564 and 1592) were
baptized *Abdias, Barnabas, Ezekiell, Philemon, Repentance*,
and *Postumus*; and of Michael Nichollson of St. Peter's,
Cornhill, who between 1589 and 1599 had *Bezaleel, Aholiab,
Sara*, and *Rebecca*. Later examples are Zachary Crofton
(d. 1672), whose sons were named *Zachary, Zareton, Zephaniah, Zelophehad*, and *John*; and *Jonathan* Grant (d. 1681),
who had by his wife *Obedience* children named *Jedediah*,

there are occasional others such as *Apollo* Pepys (d. 1644), the great-
uncle of Samuel Pepys. One of Camden's examples, *Cassandra* (q.v.),
had been in general use in the Middle Ages.

Jonathan, Deodate, Elizabeth, Hadassa, Charity, Hannah, and *Sarah.* Foundlings were obvious subjects for the ingenuity of Puritan ministers, and they were freely given such names as *Helpless, Repentance, Lament, Forsaken, Flie-fornication*; perhaps the climax of this kind of name was reached in the case of a poor little foundling girl baptized in 1644 at Baltonsborough, Somerset, in the name *Misericordia-adulterina.*

The more extravagant of these names died out gradually after the Restoration, and the permanent addition made to the stock of christian names in general use was (1) the large class of Biblical, especially Old Testament, names, (2) names such as *Faith, Hope, Charity, Prudence.* Of the Old Testament names, some became truly acclimatized and common, e.g. *Samuel, Benjamin, Joseph, Jacob, Sarah, Susan, Hannah.* Others, such as *Elijah, Amos, Zachary, Ebenezer, Caleb,* and many others, continued to be used by the sectaries and later by Wesleyans and Evangelicals in the Church of England, and died out only towards the end of the 19th century; examples still linger on, as for example three brothers recently still living in a Devon village, who were named *Shadrach, Meshach,* and *Abednego.* The permanent effects of Puritan nomenclature were greater in America. The settlers of the 17th century were very largely sectaries, and there was therefore an unusually high proportion of these names among them; *Preserved* Fish (1766–1846), for instance, could hardly have received such a name at that date in England. Besides the common Old Testament names there are others which have taken firm root in America, such as *Ira, Seth, Jedediah, Elihu*; and the commoner ones, *Benjamin, Samuel, Daniel,* &c., which are now rare in England, are still in general use in the U.S.A.

SURNAMES AS CHRISTIAN NAMES

An interesting post-Reformation development was the use of surnames as christian names. One of the earliest examples noted is Lord *Guildford* Dudley, son of the Duke of Northumberland and husband of Lady Jane Grey, whose mother's maiden name was *Guildford*. The fashion became fairly general among the landed gentry in Elizabeth's reign, and apparently gave rise to some criticism. Camden writes (1605):

'Whereas in late years Surnames have been given for Christian names among us, and no where else in Christendome; although many dislike it, for that great inconvenience will ensue: nevertheless it seemeth to proceed from hearty good will, and affection of the godfathers to shew their love, or from a desire to continue & propagate their own name to succeeding ages. And is in no wise to be disliked, but rather approved in those, which matching with heirs generall of worshipfull antient families, have given these names to their heirs, with a mindful and thankful regard of them, as we have now, *Pickering Wotton, Grevill Varney, Bassingburne Gawdy, Calthorp Parker, Pecsall Brocas, Fitz-Raulf Chamberlaine*, who are the heirs of *Pickering, Bassingburne, Grevill, Calthorp* &c.'

He continues in virtuous indignation:

'Neither can I believe a wayward old man, which would say, that the giving of Surnames for Christian Names first began in the time of King *Edward* the sixt, by such as would be Godfathers, when they were more than half fathers, and thereupon would have persuaded some to change such names at the Confirmation. Which (that I may note by the way) is usuall in other Countries, as we remember two sons of King Henry the second of France, christened by the names of *Alexander* and *Hercules*, changed them at their Confirmation to *Henry* and *Francis*.'

Fuller in his *Worthies of England* (1662) has the following passage on the subject, s.v. *Besilius Fetiplace*:

'Reader, I am confident an instance can hardly be produced of a surname made Christian, in England, save since the Reformation; before which time the priests were scrupulous to admit any at the font, except they were baptized with the name of a scripture or legendary Saint. Since, it hath been common; and although the

Lord Coke was pleased to say he had noted many of them to prove unfortunate, yet the good success in others confutes the general truth of the observation.'

These names were occasionally given to girls, e.g. *Essex*, daughter of Lord Paget (1609–78) and granddaughter to an Earl of Essex, and, in the 18th century, Johnson's friend Miss *Hill* Boothby; in such cases they were sometimes given a feminine termination, e.g. *Jermyna*, *Althama*. The fashion was confined to the nobility and landed gentry until the 19th century when it was imitated by the middle classes. Some of the more aristocratic surnames, e.g. *Percy*, *Sydney*, *Neville*, *Russell*, *Howard*, have now become genuine christian names, i.e. they are used without any family connexion. At the present time, though family names are still very generally given as a second or middle name, they are less frequent as first names. The use of surnames as christian names is now much more common in the U.S.A. than in England. It has been calculated that three out of four eldest sons of American families of any pretensions bear their mothers' maiden names either as first or as middle names. Compare the Spanish practice of combining the paternal and maternal surnames. Many surnames, for various historical reasons, have also become generally used in America as christian names, e.g. *Calvin, Chauncey, Dwight, Elmer, Jackson, Grant, Lee, Jefferson, Lincoln, Luther, Washington, Wesley*.

USE OF TWO OR MORE CHRISTIAN NAMES

Another fashion which became general in the 17th century was that of giving more than one christian name. Very rare, isolated examples have been noted earlier, e.g. John William Whytting, vicar of Egdean 1389–1432; John Philip Capel of Fineham 1363. But it is not until the beginning of the 17th century that the number of such names becomes noticeable. Camden, writing in 1605, says:

'But two Christian names are rare in England, and I only remember now His Majesty [James I], who was named Charles James, as the Prince his son Henry Frederick, & among private men Thomas Maria Wingfield [Rector of Warrington 1527–37] and Sir Thomas Posthumus Hoby.'

A few other early examples are Robert Browne Lilly, born 1593, son of John Lilly, his mother's maiden name being Browne; Arthur Rous Russhe, born 1564; Charles Maria Chute, born 1610; Gulielma Maria Postuma Springett, born 1640. It will be noted that the second name is usually either a surname or one chosen for religious or other obvious reasons, e.g. *Maria, Postumus*. The general spread of the fashion was probably due to the French influence first of Queen Henrietta Maria and later of the Court of Charles II. Charles II's natural daughter by Lady Shannon, who was born 1650 and later married the Earl of Yarmouth, was named Charlotte Jemima Henrietta Maria. In the 18th century this type of name was widely used, especially for girls, who were given three or more names, usually in latinized forms. Goldsmith was laughing at this kind of thing when he invented Miss Carolina Wilhelmina Amelia Skeggs, and at the use of romantic names in general in the Vicar's remarks on his daughters' names:

'Our second child, a girl, I intended to call after her aunt Grissel; but my wife, who during her pregnancy had been reading romances, insisted upon her being called Olivia. In less than another year we had another daughter, and now I was determined that Grissel should be her name; but a rich relation taking a fancy to stand godmother, the girl was, by her directions, called Sophia: so that we had two romantic names in the family; but I solemnly protest I had no hand in it.'

The double names *Mary Anne* and *Anna Maria* are found only after the Revolution of 1688, and seem at first to have been given in honour of Queens Mary and Anne. These and similar combinations, such as *Mary Jane*, *Sarah Jane*, &c.,

were treated as a single name and commonly used in addressing a person so named well into the 19th century, gradually becoming confined to the poorer classes, and eventually dying out. In the Southern States of America this fashion is still common. Examples of the accumulation of many names are Maria Ann Isabella Margaretta Beatrix, wife of R. Venn, died 1762, and the son of Charles Stone a tailor of Burbage, Wilts, who in 1781 received the names Charles Caractacus Ostorius Maximilian Gustavus Adolphus. The worst offenders in this tasteless piling up of names have been the royal and noble houses both in this country and on the Continent, but in the mid-19th century the middle classes set themselves to imitate them in this as in so many other ways. The great Victorian novelists, Dickens, Thackeray, Trollope, constantly laugh at the fashion, which reminds one forcibly of that, already mentioned, which was current in the later years of the Roman Empire.[1]

Revival of Obsolete Names

On the whole, however, the 18th century did not display any very great change in nomenclature beyond two limited fashions; one being that already noted of preferring the Latin forms of women's names (e.g. *Anna, Maria, Sophia, Olivia, Evelina, Cecilia, Juliana*, &c., instead of *Anne, Mary, Sophy, Olive, Aveline, Cecil, Julian* or *Gillian*); the other being a certain revival of Old English or medieval names,

---

[1] There is a difference of usage in Great Britain and the U.S.A. in the matter of initials when there is more than one christian name. The American generally gives the first name in full and the second only as an initial, e.g. Franklin D. Roosevelt, Elihu P. Root. The corresponding usage in England would as a rule be either Franklin Delano Roosevelt, or F. D. Roosevelt, or (with suppression of the middle name) simply Franklin Roosevelt. There was a correspondence on the subject in *N. & Q.* 1856; the American practice was then quite unfamiliar in England, and some correspondents suggested that the initial was merely inserted for distinction, and did not stand for a real name.

which was connected with the general interest in the 'gothic'; examples are *Edgar, Edwin, Alfred, Galfrid, Emma, Matilda*. This second tendency was much accelerated in the 19th century when a whole host of old-fashioned and long obsolete names came back into use as the result of several movements, both religious and literary. The first of these was the Romantic movement, and particularly the great influence of Scott's novels, which reintroduced such names as *Wilfrid, Guy, Roland, Nigel, Quentin, Amy,* &c.; the second was the Tractarian movement which revived the names of long-neglected saints such as *Aidan, Augustine, Alban, Theodore, Benedict, Bernard,* &c.; finally the medievalism of Tennyson and the Pre-Raphaelites brought back into use such names as *Lancelot, Hugh, Walter, Aylmer, Roger, Ralph, Ella, Alice, Mabel, Edith*. The fashion has continued ever since, every ten years or so producing new favourites—either names which had become altogether obsolete such as *Joyce*, or obsolete forms of names still in use such as *Gillian*.

MODERN ECLECTICISM

In the present century the taste in names has become more and more eclectic, and there are few European languages which have not been laid under contribution. This has been a natural development in the U.S.A. whose population is drawn from every European country, and to some extent that example may have influenced this country. There can be no doubt that at the present time one of the most powerful influences on the masses in this country, in this, as in so many other ways, is that of the American films. The names of American film actors and actresses (frequently fancy inventions of their own) are freely bestowed on the children of their 'fans'. Thus the registrar for Tottenham in 1938 stated that at least 20 per cent. of the parents of Tottenham chose 'cinema names' for their offspring, *Gary* and *Shirley* being the favourites. Other common names from the same source are *Carol, Maureen, Marlene, Myrna, Merle*. The great number and enormous circulations of cheap story magazines, the characters in which usually have somewhat fanciful names, has also, no doubt, had much the same effect. On the whole the names of boys remain simpler than those of girls, and in any case the old favourites, *John, Thomas, William, Henry, Richard, Mary, Elizabeth, Anne, Joan*, still retain first place.

Though in this country and the U.S.A. there is no legal restriction on the taste of parents in naming their children, many European countries have laws, more or less operative, with the object of regulating the matter. Thus in France the Revolutionary Law of 11 Germinal XI (1 April 1803), which is still in force, decrees that names shall be chosen only from those of persons known in ancient history, or in use in the various calendars. Good revolutionaries were averse to using names from christian calendars and availed themselves largely of the permission to use names from ancient history which was interpreted to include a good deal of mythology. Such favourite French names as *Marcel, Jules, Aristide, Achille* came into use at this time. The rule is not now very strictly applied, but still has a restrictive effect. The law in Germany is that a name must not be used which cannot be proved to have been used before. Such regulations as these, even though they are not always rigidly applied, have, on the whole, had the effect of saving European continental countries from the flood of neologisms which has swept over U.S.A. and, to some extent, over Great Britain.

There is still, however, a strong conservative tendency, at least among readers of *The Times*, and a correspondent writing to that paper (11 Jan. 1950) states that the relative popularity of the ten commonest names for boys and girls respectively, as shown by announcements of births, in *The Times* during 1949 was as follows:—*John* (207), *Richard* (126), *Peter* (114),

David (108), *Charles* (100), *Michael* (96), *William* (81), *Robert* (79), *Christopher* (77), and *James* (77) for boys; and *Ann(e)* (144), *Mary* (141), *Elizabeth* (132), *Jane* (101), *Susan* (83), *Margaret* (72), *Sarah* (57), *Caroline* (44), *Jennifer* (40), and *Frances* (38). In the previous year also, 18 of these names were in the first 20, but *William* has taken the place of *Anthony* and *Jennifer* of *Penelope*.

A

Aaron (m.): the name of the brother of Moses, first High Priest of Israel. It may be Egyptian, but the meaning is unknown. There was a Celtic saint named *Aaron*, but that was probably a different name. *Aaron* has been used occasionally as a christian name since the Reformation. Bardsley says he did not meet with a single English *Aaron* in medieval times, though it sometimes occurs as the name of a Jew; but there is mention of one apparently English *Aaron* in the Curia Regis Rolls for 1199.

Abel (m.): the 2nd son of Adam and Eve; the meaning of the name is obscure, but it is possibly the accusative of *ablu* 'son'. It was a favourite christian name in the 13th C and gave rise to various surnames, such as *Abel(l)*, *Abelson*, *Able*, and *Nabb(s)* (from the nickname *Nab*, cf. *Abel* in Jonson's *The Alchemist*, who is called *Nab*), *Ablet(t)* from the dim *Abel-ot*. It had some revival in the 17th C. It is still in use in France.

ABEL Cur 1205–6, 1207–9, HR 1273.
ABELOT HR 1273.

Abigail (f.): Hebrew signifying 'father rejoiced'; for *'ăbîgāl* with *ā* changed to hypocoristic *ai* for a girl; the name of the wife of Nabal and afterwards of David (1 Sam. xxv). It came into use in England in the 16th C and was common in the 17th C. From a character so named in Beaumont and Fletcher's play *The Scornful Lady* (1616) it became a slang term for a lady's maid and gradually went out of fashion, though it never became obsolete. CMY suggests that it may also have suffered through being the name of Queen Anne's unpopular favourite, Mrs Masham. In Ireland it was formerly used as an equivalent of the native Celtic name *Gobnait*. *Abbey* was the usual abbreviation of it.

Abner (m.): Hebrew 'the [divine] father (is) light'; the name of the cousin of Saul and commander of his army. One of the many

Old Testament names adopted after the Reformation, and still occasionally used in the USA.

Abraham (m.): Hebrew. The name of the patriarch was originally *Abram*, 'high father', but was changed to *Abraham*, 'father of a multitude'. *Abraham* occurs as the name of a priest in DB, and was in general though not frequent use in the 13th C. It was revived after the Reformation and was particularly popular in the Low Countries in the forms *Abram*, *Bram*. It is now commoner in the USA than in England (partly, no doubt, owing to its being Lincoln's name), and is there often abbreviated to *Abe*.

ABRAHAM DB 1086, Cur 1189–1207 *passim*, 1294 QW.
HABREHAM (a Jew) Magd. 1230–40.

Absalom (m.): Hebrew 'the [divine] father (is) peace'. The name of the unhappy son of David and Michal was a favourite in the 12th and 13th C, usually in the French form *Absolon*, and was given by Chaucer to the lively young clerk in his *Miller's Tale*. It has not been much used since about the end of the 14th C.

ABSALOM Cur 1189–1207.
ABSOLON Cur 1197, 1200, 1210, 1213–15.

Acelin (m.): diminutive of Old French *Asce*, *Ace* from Old German *Azzo*. *Ezzelin* was the form in which it took root in Italy. There was another diminutive *Acelet*, and a f. form *Ascelina* also occurs in Latin records. Common in the 13th C, it gave rise to various surnames, e.g. *Aslin*, *Ashlin*, *Asling*, *Acelet*.

AZELINUS DB 1086.
ASCELINA Cur 1207.
ASCELYN HR 1273.
ACELIN HR 1273.
ASSELIN HR 1273.

Achilles (m.) [ăkĭ'lēz]: Greek Ἀχιλλεύς. The etymology of the name is obscure (it is possibly allied to the name of the river Ἀχέλωος.) This Homeric hero, unlike his rival Hector, was not a favourite in the Middle Ages and his name never came into general use. But there was a 3rd-C St. *Achilleus*, the apostle of Vienne, and consequently *Achille* has been not uncommon in France, where it is still used. The revival of classical names at the Renaissance led to an occasional use of *Achilles* by German princes, and it has been used, very rarely, in England.

Ada (f.): imported from Germany at the end of the 18th C. An early example is the name of Byron's daughter, *Augusta Ada*. It became very popular in the 19th C, but has now fallen out of favour. *Ada* is probably a pet form of some name in *Adal*, but there was an Old German m. and f. name *Eda*, *Æda*, *Etta*, *Ætte*, cognate with Old English *Eadda*, *Eadu* (see EDEN). The Hebrew *Adah* (an ornament) has been used occasionally since the 16th C, especially in America, and it may sometimes have been confused with *Ada*, cf. *Ada Nowell*, baptised at Feering, Essex, in 1573. *Ada* is also sometimes a pet-name for *Adelaide* (q.v.).

Adam (m.): Hebrew 'red', from the colour of skin. In medieval Latin the name was declined as though it were a noun of the first declension (e.g. nominative *Ada*). When it was used for a woman (as it frequently was) the Latin form was *Adama*. St. *Adamnan*, the 8th-C Irish saint, whose name means 'little Adam', is one of the earliest bearers of the name. It occurs once or twice in England before the Conquest, but always as the name of a monk. In DB it is the name of one tenant-in-chief and some sub-tenants, and its popularity increased rapidly in the 12th C. In 13th-C records it is one of the two or three commonest names (it is the name of Chaucer's Scrivener) and was a particular favourite in the North and in Scotland (e.g. *Adam* Bell, *Edom* o' Gordon). It gave rise to a multitude of surnames such as *Adam(s)*, *Adamson*, *Adcock*, *Addis(on)*, *Adkin*, *Atkin(son)*, and *MacAdam*. *Ade* and *Adekin* were pet-forms of the name. Like many of the favourites of the 13th C it lost ground in the 14th C, but came back into use after the Reformation and continued to be popular with the poorer classes down to the end of the 19th C. It has recently had some revival.

ADAM (genitive *Ade*) DB 1086, Cur 1187–1212 *passim*, Ass 1218–19 *passim*, HR 1273 *passim*, Exch R 1306.
ADECOCK IPM 1311.
ADEKIN Exch R 1306.
ADINET Exch R 1306.

Adela (f.): Old German *Athala, Adila, Edila,* &c., from *athal* 'noble'. The name was introduced into England by the Normans; it was borne by the 4th daughter of William I, who was named after her maternal grandmother, a daughter of Robert of France. The continued use of the name in France and Flanders was helped by veneration of St. *Adela,* daughter of Dagobert II, and Abbess of Pfalzel near Trèves, but it was never common in England. It was revived in the 19th C, probably in imitation of modern French *Adèle.*

Adelaide (f.): Old German *Adalhaid* or *Adalheidis,* compound of *athal* 'noble' and *haidu* 'kind', 'sort' (= English -*hood*). This became in Norman-French *Adelais, Adeliz, Aaliz, Aliz* (whence English *Alice* q.v.). *Adelaide* is the modern French version of German *Adelheid,* and is now the usual form of the name all over the Continent. The popularity of William IV's queen, 'Good Queen Adelaide', led to its general use in England in the 19th C, when it was often abbreviated to *Ada* or *Addy.*

ADELIZ SEU ADELIZA DB 1086.

Adeline (f.): another derivative of Old German *athal,* 'noble', introduced into England by the Norman Conquest. It was common in the Middle Ages in the forms *Adelin, Edelin* (cf. surnames *Adlin, Edlin*). A sub-tenant in DB is *Adelina joculatrix.* Lyford, 1655, gives *Adelin* as a f. christian name, but it must have been very uncommon at that date. *Adeline,* like *Adelaide* and *Adela,* came back into favour in the 19th C. See also ALINE.

ADELINA JOCULATRIX DB 1086.
ADELIN Cur 1201–3.
ADELINA, EDELINA Cur 1210–12.
EDELINA Cur 1213–15.
EDOLINA Magd. 1246–7, 1268–70.
ADELENA Magd. *c.* 1280–90.

Adolphus (m.): Old German *Athalwolf,* compound of *athal* 'noble' and *wolfa* 'a wolf'. The equivalent Old English *Æthelwulf* died out after the Conquest. *Adolphus* is a latinized version of the German form *Adelulf,* which was adopted in the 17th and 18th C by various German royal families and brought to England by the

Hanoverians. It was sometimes abbreviated to *Dolly* in the 19th C. *Adolf* is the usual form in German to-day and *Adolphe* in French.

Adrian (m.): Latin *Hadrianus*, 'of the Adriatic'; the name of a Roman emperor and of several popes, one of whom, Adrian III, was beatified. It has never been a popular name in England, but occurs from time to time from the end of the 12th C. The earliest example noted occurs in the Curia Regis Rolls 1189. It is possible that the introduction of the name into England may have been due to its adoption by Nicholas Brakespear (died 1159), the only English pope, who took the name Adrian IV.

ADRIANUS Cur 1189–1205.
ADRANUS, ADRIEN Clerkenwell 13th C.

Adriana (f.): (French *Adrienne*), f. form of *Adrian* (q.v.), used very rarely. The name occurs in Shakespeare's *Comedy of Errors*.

Aeneas (m.): the name of the Trojan hero was occasionally used in Italy and elsewhere after the Renaissance (e.g. Aeneas Sylvius Piccolomini (born 1405), Pope Pius II). But its chief use has been in Ireland and Scotland to translate the Gaelic *Aonghus* (Old Irish *Oeng(h)us*) or *Angus* (q.v.) (cf. the similar use of *Terence*, *Cornelius*, *Penelope*, &c.). The Clan Macdonell, for instance, have used *Aonghus* since at least the 15th C, and the Glengarry branch still use it and spell it *Aeneas*.

Agatha (f.): (French, German *Agathe*, Russian *Agafia*), from Greek ἀγαθός 'good', the name of a 3rd-C Sicilian martyr honoured in both Eastern and Western Churches. Her cult was very widespread and her name still appears in the Anglican Calendar; there are four English churches dedicated to her. *Agatha* was the name of the mother of Edgar Atheling, a daughter of the Emperor Henry II, and also of one of the daughters of William the Conqueror. The medieval French form of the name was *Agace*, and *Agacia* is usual in Latin records of the 13th C. Prompt Parv (c. 1440) and Godstow (1450) give *Agase* and *Agas* respectively as the English for *Agatha*, and Bardsley gives several examples to illustrate the surnames *Agasson, Agace, Aggas*. It appears as *Aga-thie* in 1652. It is often abbreviated to *Aggie*.

AGATHA Cur 1186–1215 *passim*, FA 1303.
AGACIA HR 1273.
AGACE 14th C Legendary.
AGASE *Prompt Parv c.* 1440.
AGAS Godstow 1450.

Aglaia (f.): Greek Ἀγλαία, 'splendour', 'beauty', the name of one of the three Graces. It was also the name of a legendary saint, whence its use in France as *Aglaë*. It has been used very occasion-ally in England, probably directly from the Greek.

Agnes (f.): (French *Agnès*, Italian *Agnese, Agnete*, Spanish *Iñez*) from Greek ἁγνός, 'pure', 'chaste'. The original Latin form of the name was *Agnes (-etis)*, but in the Middle Ages a form *Agneta* was commonly used. St. *Agnes*, a 3rd-C saint, was one of the most popular virgin martyrs and her cult was very widespread. Many legends gathered round her name, and unmarried girls celebrated the eve of her festival with semi-magical rites. There are five churches dedicated to her in England. From the 12th to 16th C *Agnes* was one of the com-monest English f. names; in the 16th C it was one of the first three, the others being Joan and Elizabeth. The usual forms of the name were *Annis, Annys, Annais*; Prompt Parv (*c.* 1440) gives it as *Anneyce*. The common medieval *Annot* was almost certainly a diminutive of *Annis* and not of *Ann*, for it was very frequent at a date when *Ann* was still scarcely used in England. (It may, how-ever, sometimes be for *Annora* (q.v.)) The names *Agnes* and *Ann* became confused at a later date, and in the case of King *v*. King (42 Eliz.) it was argued that they were 'all one name', though the court unanimously decided that they were 'several names'. Again in the case of Griffith *v*. Middleton (15 James I) it was held that 'Joan and Jane are both one name, but Agnes and Anne, Gillian and Julian are different'. Since Agnes was habitually pronounced, and usually spelt, *Annis*, the confusion was natural. A child was christened *Anese* as late as 1870 at Ducklington, Oxon., and *Anis* is still used as a gipsy name. In Welsh the name became *Nest* or

Nesta, and it was used in Ireland as an equivalent of the Gaelic *Una* (q.v.) After the 16th C its popularity waned together with that of most of the non-scriptural saints, but it remained current among the poor, especially in the West country, until its revival in the 19th C. *Taggy* and *Taggett* were formerly nicknames for *Agnes*, but have now given place to *Aggy*. The Latin *Agneta* is also occasionally used.

AGNES Cur 1187–1215 *passim*, HR 1273 *passim*.
ANNAIS Ass 1218.
ANNEYS(E) 14th-C Legendary.
ANNYS *Prompt Parv c.* 1440.
ANNES FA 1450.
ANNISE *Pills to Purge Melancholy* 1684.

Agneta, see AGNES.

Aidan (m.): Old Irish diminutive of *aid*, 'fire'; the name of a 7th-C Irish monk of Lindisfarne, the apostle of Northumberland, which appears in Old English as *Æthan*. Revived by the Tractarians in the 19th C.

Aileen (f.), see EILEEN.

Ailie, see ALISON.

Ailith, see ALDITH.

Aine, Aithne (f.) [ã'në]: Old Irish *Aodhnait*, f. diminutive of *Aodh*, 'fire', modern Irish *Eithne*, was a favourite name in Ireland for centuries, sometimes semi-anglicized as *Ena* (q.v.) and often translated as *Anna* or *Hannah*. With the revival of Celtic names it is coming back into use in Scotland as well as Ireland.

Al(l)an, Allen (m.): A Celtic name of doubtful etymology. The name of a popular early Welsh and Breton saint, Bishop of Quimper. It was introduced into England at the time of the Norman Conquest, notably by *Alain* Fergéant, Count of Brittany, and *Alain* le Roux, 1st Earl of Richmond, companions of the Conqueror, and soon became common. In French it was *Alain* and *Alein*, and the spellings *Allan* and *Allen* have both been used in England. *Alan* is the commonest form at the present time. From the 14th to 16th C it was usually *Aleyn(e)*. It has always been most popular in the north and especially in Scotland (where it was perhaps confused with the old Gaelic name *Ailéne* or *Ailin*) and has given rise to a number of surnames. *Alain* is still a favourite in Brittany, but is not much used in the rest of France.

ALANUS Reg 1071–5, DB 1086, Cur 1189–1212, FA 1284.
ALEYNE 15th C *Brut*.
ALEYN *Prompt Parv c.* 1440.

Alard (m.): Old German *Adalhard*, compound of *athal* 'noble' and *hardu* 'hard'. *Adalhard* was the name of a 9th-C saint, cousin to Charlemagne. The equivalent Old English *Æthelheard* was also the name of a saint, an Archbishop of Canterbury (died 805), and *Alard* may represent a survival of this as well as of the German name, which was introduced into England by the Normans and continued in use until the 16th C.

ADELARDUS DB 1086.
ATHELARD Cl 1272, Kirton Parish Reg 1519.
ADELARD HR 1273.
ADERLARD HR 1273.
AYLARD HR 1273.
ALARD 13th-C documents *passim*.
ADELARD or ALARD Ox Univ Reg 1505.
ADLARD Gedney Parish Reg 1596, 1610.
ALART Privy Purse Exp 1530.

Alaric (m.): Old German *Alaricus*, compound of *ala* 'all' and *ric* 'ruler'; the name of several kings of the West Goths, notably Alaric I who sacked Rome in A.D. 410. Occasionally used as a christian name since the beginning of the 19th C.

Alastair, see ALEXANDER.

Alban (m.): Latin *Albanus* 'of Alba'. The name of the first British martyr has never been a favourite, but it occurs in the 13th C and survived the Reformation, e.g. *Alban* Hill died 1595. The name was used until the middle of the 17th C by the Thrale family of Sandridge Bury, Herts., no doubt from association with the neighbouring town of St. Albans. It was revived in the 19th C by the

Tractarians, along with other names of pre-Augustinian saints, e.g. Aidan. Bardsley gives examples of a name *Albany* in the 17th C, which he regards as the same as *Alban*. It is still sometimes used. There was also a fourth-century French saint named *Albinus*, and the name *Albin*, still in use in Germany, was not uncommon in the thirteenth century and gave rise to several surnames.

ALBANUS Cur 1201.

Alberic (m.): Old German *Albirich*, compound of *alfi* 'elf' and *ric* 'ruler', the equivalent of Old English *Ælfric*, was introduced into England by the Normans in the form *Alberi*, *Auberi*, and in due course developed into *Aubrey* (q.v.). The Latin form of the name was *Albericus*, and in the 18th C the back-formation *Alberic* was made; it is still sometimes used.

Albert (m.): Old German *Adalbert*, compound of *athal* 'noble' and *berhta* 'bright', equivalent of Old English *Æthelbeorht*. The name, either in the Latin form *Albertus* or the French *Aubert*, is not uncommon in the 12th and 13th C, and it occurs in DB. It is impossible to be quite sure whether this points to a survival of the Old English name or to an importation of the continental form of it, but on the whole the latter is the more likely. The surnames *Albert*, *Albright*, &c., were formed from it. In the form *Halbert* the name survived in the North country until the 17th C and is still common on the Scottish borders. *Albert* was reintroduced from Germany in the 19th C on the marriage of Queen Victoria, and soon became very popular, especially among the poorer classes with whom it is still common. The Queen's own name never had anything like the same measure of popularity. *Albert* is commonly abbreviated to *Bert* in England and *Al* in America.

ALBERTUS DB 1086.
ALBERT Cur 1189–1205.
AUBERT Cur 1189–1205.
AYLBRICHT HR 1273.

Alberta, Albertine: f. of *Albert* (q.v.). Occasionally used in the 19th C during the period when *Albert* was in fashion. A writer to

N & Q (4.10.1930) mentions the occurrence of the name *Albertine* in a dairy kept in Lincs. 1865–93. *Alberta* may sometimes be the name of the Canadian province rather than a simple f. form of *Albert.*

Albin(i)a (f.): *Albinus* was a Latin cognomen, derived from *albus* 'white'. *Albina* was the name of a 3rd C saint. The name *Albina* or *Albinia* (common in Italy) was apparently first given in England to *Albinia* Cecil, born 1604. It has been retained in use to the present day in many families descended from her. See *The Albinia Book, being the History of Albinia Cecil, & others who have borne her name, with a new and particular account of the celebrated Albinia Bertie, Countess of Bucks and her immediate descendants,* by Albinia Lady Cust, 1929. The name now usually appears as *Albinia,* but *Albina* was frequent in the 17th and 18th C. The Italian name is often spelt *Albigna,* and *Albinia* is probably a phonetic rendering of that.

Albreda (f.): Old German *Alverat, Alvered, Alberad, Albrad,* compound of *alfi* 'elf', *radi* 'counsel', the equivalent of Old English *Ælfred,* was used both as a m. and as a f. name, and it is the f. use which seems to have survived in the name which appears in medieval records as *Albreda.* It was no doubt introduced into England by the Normans, and in the vernacular became *Aubrey.* Bardsley gives an example of *Albray,* and *Albreda* is common in 12th- and 13th-C Latin records. The use of the name (for women, but see AUBREY) seems to have come to an end before the 15th C.

ALBREDA Ass 1218, Cur 1187–1215 *passim.*
ALBRAY Yorks Poll Tax 1379.

Alda (f.): Old German *Alda,* 'old'. *Alda* or *Aldabella* was the name of the wife of Orlando and sister of Oliver in the Charlemagne romances, and the French form of the name, *Aude,* was not uncommon in England in the 12th C, and survived at least until the 14th C.

ALDA, Cur 1199, FA 1303.

Aldhelm (m.): Old English *Ealdhelm,* compound of *eald* 'old' and *helm* 'helmet'. *Eald* in compounds of this kind seems to have had the sense 'great'. It was the name of a Bishop of Sherborne (? 640–709), later venerated as a saint. It did not survive in use after the Norman Conquest, but was revived by the Tractarians in the 19th C.

Aldith (f.): Old English *Ealdgyth*, compound of *eald* 'old' and *gyth* 'battle', 'strife'. It survived the Conquest and was not uncommon until the beginning of the 14th C. In Latin records it usually appears as *Alditha*. Old English *Æthelgyth* also survived for some time in the form *Ailith*.

ÆLDIET, ÆLDIT, ÆLDID, ELDIT, ELDID, ALDGID, ALDIET, ALDID, ALDED DB 1086.
ADELID, AILIET, AILITH, AILID, ALITH, ALID DB 1086.
ALDITHA Cur 1189, 1200, 1210, Ass 1313.
ALDITH HR 1273.

Aldous (m.): *Aldus*, *Aldis*, or *Aldous* has been used as a christian name in England since at least the 13th C. It seems to have been almost confined to East Anglia, where it is still occasionally used, and where the surnames *Aldous*, *Aldis(s)*, *Aldhouse*, &c., are common. Its earlier history is obscure, but there can be little doubt that it is the same as the Old German *Aldo* 'old', which corresponds to the Old English *Ealda*. *Aldo* took firm root in Italy and was often latinized as *Aldus* (cf. *Aldus Manutius* the famous printer of 'aldine' editions of the classics). There were two saints of the name, *Aldo* or *Aldus*, an 8th-C hermit of Bobbio whose relics are preserved at Pavia, and *Aldo* Count of Ostrevant, an 8th-C Benedictine of the monastery of Hirson in Belgium.

ALDUS HR 1273.

Aldred (m.): Old English *Ealdred*, compound of *eald* 'old', 'great', and *ræd* 'counsel'. A fairly common pre-Conquest name which survived the Conquest, though not in wide use, and gave rise to the surnames *Aldred* and *Eldred*. *Eldred* occurs as a christian name as late as 1850 in Bucks. and is still used in the Lincolnshire half-blood gipsy family of Brown.

EALDRED Reg 1066–9.
ÆLDRED(US), ÆLDRET, ELDRED, ALDRET, ALDRED DB 1086.
ALDRED(US) Cur 1189, HR 1273.

Aldwin (m.): Old English *Ealdwine*, compound of *eald* 'old', 'great', and *wine* 'friend'; it survived the Conquest and was not uncommon in the Middle Ages in the form *Aldwin, Aldin*; cf. the surnames *Aldin, Alden,* &c.

ELDUIN, ALDUIN DB 1086.
ALDEYN, ALDUN, ALDYNE HR 1273.
AUDOENUS Exch R 1306.

Alec, see ALEXANDER.

Alethea (f.) [ălethē'a]: Greek ἀλήθεια, 'truth', came into fashion as a christian name in the 17th C. The Spanish Infanta wooed by Charles I as Prince of Wales was named *Maria Aletea.* Lyford 1655 gives the name as *Alethia.* In 1670 Charles Savile married *Alethia* Mellingham, and the name has continued to be used in the Savile family. The spelling has always been liable to variation; thus Jane Austen writes the name of her friend sometimes as *Alethea* and sometimes as *Alithea* Bigge, and the name is also sometimes spelt *Aletheia. Alethea* is sometimes confused with *Althea* 'wholesome', the name of the mother of Meleager, which was used by Lovelace in his well-known poem 'To Althea from Prison'.

Alexander (m.): (French *Alexandre,* Italian *Alessandro, Sandro,* Gaelic *Alasdair*). Greek Ἀλέξανδρος, 'defending men', originally one of the epithets of Hera, and often applied as an alternative to Paris. It acquired general use at a later date as the name of the Macedonian conqueror. The immense popularity of the Alexander Romance in the Middle Ages helped to make it a favourite christian name. An early example is *Alexander* of East Marcham, who distinguished himself in the wars during the reign of Stephen. In England it usually appears in the French form *Alysaundre,* and Prompt Parv (1440) gives *Alesaunder* as the English for *Alexander.* It was often shortened to *Saunder* or *Sander* and the surnames *Saunder(son), Sa(u)nders, Sander(son)* as well as *Alexander* testify to its popularity. It has always been a particular favourite in Scotland, where it was probably introduced by Queen Margaret, sister of Edgar Atheling, her 3rd son being *Alexander* I of Scotland.

The long reigns of *Alexander* II and III, which covered the period 1214–85, no doubt helped to consolidate its position, and ever since then it has been one of the commonest names in Scotland. In a list of inhabitants of Inverness in 1894 there were 584 Johns, and the next most frequent name was *Alexander* with 363. It is often shortened to *Alec*, *Alick*, or *Sandy*. It was early adopted into Gaelic as *Alasdair* (now often spelled phonetically *Alastair*, &c.).

ALEXANDER Cur 1189, HR 1273, FA 1284, 1316.
ELEXANDER, ELYSANDRE FA 1284.
ALESAUNDER *Prompt Parv c.* 1440.
ALIZAUNDER Oseney 1460.
ALISAUNDER 15th-C Brut.
ALISANDRE AL. SANDRE HR 1273.
SANDER, SAUNDRE, SAUNDER HR 1273.
SAUNDER *Cocke Lorelle's Bote c.* 1515.

Alexandra (f.): this and *Alexandrina*, both f. forms of *Alexander*, are mainly Russian, and were popularized in England by the marriage of Edward VII when Prince of Wales to the Princess *Alexandra* of Denmark. But *Alexandra* is found in England in 1205 and *Alexandria* in 1218, and these may have been named after a 4th-C martyr, though they are more likely to be mere latinizations of *Alexander* used as a girl's name. The use of m. names for girls was far from uncommon up to the 15th C, especially when there were no sons in a family. Lyford 1655 gives *Alexander* as a f. name, and an early-14th-C English legendary gives *Alisaundre* as the name of the mother of St. Thomas of Canterbury. See also SANDRA.

Alexis (m.): Greek Ἀλέξιος, 'helper', 'defender', the name of a 5th-C Roman saint. It has always been used more in the Eastern than the Western Church, and is particularly common in Russia. The 20th-C fashion for Russian names has led to its being sometimes used in this country.

Alfred (m.): Old English *Ælfræd*, compound of *ælf* 'elf' and *ræd* 'counsel', was the name of *Alfred* the Great (849–901). The name *Ealdfrith* ('old' or 'great peace') borne by a 7th-C king of North-

C

umberland, also sometimes appears as *Alfrid*. *Alfred* was latinized as *Aluredus* (= *Alvredus*), and from that came the French forms *Alveré*, *Auveré*, whence the Middle English *Alvery*, *Avery*, which seem to have superseded the native form of the name. *Alvery* survived until the 18th C; it was the name of one of the brothers of Robert Dodsley the bookseller and is still used in that family. *Alfred* was restored to favour with other Old English names in the 18th C. *Alured*, which has been used from time to time since the late 18th C, is a modern back-formation from the medieval Latin form of the name, of the same kind as Alberic, Galfrid, Hugo, Nigel, Reginald (qq.v.). *Alfred* is vulgarly abbreviated to *Alf*.

ALUEREDUS Reg 1086.
ALURED(US), ALURET, ALUERAD, ALUERD, ALUER, ELURET DB 1086.
ALVREDUS, ALUREDUS Cur 1189–1205.
ALUREDUS, ALFRIDUS FA 1285.
ALUREDUS, ALVREDUS FA 1303.
AUVERAY HR 1273.
AVEREY HR 1273.
AVERE Ox Univ Reg 1608.

Algar (m.): Old English *Ælfgar*, compound of *ælf* 'elf' and *gar* 'spear'. It survived the Conquest and gave rise to the surnames *Algar*, *Elgar*.

ALGAR, ÆLGAR, ÆLGER, ALGER DB 1086.
ALGAR FF *c.* 1160, HR 1273.
ALGOR HR 1273.
EYLGAR HR 1273.

Algernon (m.): Norman-French, meaning 'with whiskers' or 'moustaches'. William de Percy, companion of William the Conqueror and founder of the Percy family, bore this nickname (most Normans of that time were clean-shaven); cf. also Eustace II, Count of Boulogne, who was called *aux Gernons* or *als Gernons*, to distinguish him from his father, Eustace à l'œil. In the Whitby Cartulary William de Percy is called 'cognomento *Asgernuns*' and his son is 'filius Willielmi de Percy *Ohtlesgernuns*'. It was not until 400 years later that the sobriquet *as* or *al Gernons* was bestowed as a christian name upon his descendant, Henry *Algernon* Percy, 5th Earl of Northumberland (1478–1527). From that time it was

commonly used in the Percy family, and transmitted by marriage
to other families (e.g. *Algernon* Sidney's mother was a Percy). It
has remained a mainly aristocratic name. It is sometimes abbreviated to *Algy*.

Alice (f.): from Old French *Aliz* < *Aaliz* < *Adaliz* < Old German
Adalheidis (see ADELAIDE). By the 12th C it was being latinized as
Alesia, Alicia, and was a very common name in England as well
as France, its popularity being partly due to the influence of the
literary type of '*Bele Aaliz*' in contemporary romances. It is still
used in France in the form *Alix*. The Curia Regis Rolls of 1219–20
give a good example of the development of the name; one woman
appears there in different places as *Athelesia, Aelesia, Aeleis le
Neweman*. In England it was usually *Alys*, and was in time
contracted to *Alse* (Lyford 1655 '*Alice* or *Alse*, abridged from
Ade-liz'). By the middle of the 17th C it was regarded as an old-
fashioned, country name and fell into general disuse, until its
revival in the middle of the 19th C by the romance writers, often
in the latinized form *Alicia*. CMY says of it (1863) 'now with
Constantia and Edith a favourite fancy name'. The publication of
Alice in Wonderland in 1865 no doubt contributed to its further
popularity. It is sometimes abbreviated to *Ally*, cf. Brome's
A Mad Couple Well Match'd (1653). See also ALISON.

ALICIA Cur 1189–1215, FA 1303.
ALESIA Cur 1200.
AELEIS, AELESIA, ATHELESIA Cur 1219–20.
ALICE, ALISE HR 1273.
ALYS 15th-C Brut.

Alick, see ALEXANDER.

Aline (f.): very common from 12th to 15th C, usually appearing
in the Latin form *Alina, Alyna*. It is almost certainly a development from *Adeline* similar to that of *Alice* from *Adalheidis*, but it
was sometimes treated as a diminutive of *Alice*.

ALINA Cur 1187–1215 *passim.*
ALYNA, ATHELYNA FA 1346.
ALINE FA 1428.

Alison (f.): a pet-name for *Alice* (q.v.), formed by the addition of the suffix *-on* to the French *A(a)lis*. It was common in France from the 13th C and was often treated as an independent name. It was still common in England in the 17th C, especially in the North country, where it often appears as *Alicen*. It is now mainly confined to Scotland, where it is sometimes abbreviated to *Ailie*. The *locus classicus* is the Middle English poem with the refrain 'From alle wymmen my love is lent, Ant lyht on Alisoun'.

ALISON Chaucer *Canterbury Tales c.* 1386.
ALISCEON, ALISON Yorks Wills 15th C.
ALISONE, ALYSON, ALSON Lincs Wills 1450–3.
ALICEN, ALLISON Yorks Recusants 1604.

Alma (f.): This name had a temporary vogue, following the battle of *Alma* 1854. The battle took its name from the river *Alma* in the Crimea. No doubt the name was sometimes associated, in the minds of those giving it, with the Latin adjective meaning 'loving', 'kind', &c.

Almeric (m.): Old German *Amalricus*, compound of *amal* 'work' and *ric* 'ruler'; introduced into England at the Norman Conquest in the French form *Americ*, *Emeric*, and later common as *Aimeri*, *Amaury*, *Amery*, which gave rise to many surnames. *Almeric* is a modern back-formation from *Almericus*, a latinization of the German by-form *Almeric(h)*. The first example noted is in the will of Lord Kinsale, 1699, which is signed *Almarick* de Courcy.

AMALRICUS DB 1086.
AMAURI, AMAURY Cur 1189–1205, 1213–15.
AMERICUS HR 1273

Aloysius (m.) [ălōē′zēus]: see LOUIS. The name of a popular 16th-C Spanish saint, used in Britain only by Roman Catholics. A f. name, *Aloisia*, occurs in the 16th and 17th C in the parish registers of Hinton Charterhouse. This may be a f. form of *Aloysius*, or a latinized form of *Helewise* (q.v.).

Alphonso (m.): Old German *Adalfuns*, compound of *athal* 'noble' and *funsa* 'ready', 'apt'. It was carried to Spain by the Visigoths, and was borne by a series of kings of Asturias and Leon who in the 8th and 9th C fought successfully against the Moors.

From that time *Alfonso* or *Alonso* has been a favourite name in Spain and has been borrowed occasionally in other countries.

Althea, see ALETHEA.

Alured, see ALFRED.

Alvery, see ALFRED.

Alwyn, see AYLWIN.

Amabel (f.) [ă'mabĕl]: this is apparently the Latin adjective *amabilis*, 'lovable'. It appears in Latin as *Amabilis*, *Amabilia*, *Amabilla*, and in the vernacular as *Amabel*, *Amable*, *Amiable* from the 12th C onwards. An early example was one of the three co-heiresses of William Earl of Gloucester (died 1183). *Amabel* was later shortened to *Mabel* (q.v.), and was gradually superseded by it. It was uncommon between the 14th and the 19th C when it was revived, with other medieval names, by the writers of romances; but in the 12th and 13th C it was a very common name. See also ANNABEL(LA), ARABEL(LA).

AMABILIS Cur 1189, 1219.
AMABILIA Cur 1218, FA 1284.
AMABILLA FA 1316.
AMABLE HR 1273, D'Urfey *Pills to Purge Melancholy* 1684.
AMABIL, AMABLE, AMIABLE Testa de Neville 13th C.

Amanda (f.): Latin 'fit to be loved', seems to be a 17th-C literary invention. It occurs in a Notts parish register of deaths for the year 1805, but was probably in use earlier than that.

Amaryllis (f.): Latin, from Greek Ἀμαρυλλίς, used by Theocritus, Ovid, and Virgil as a name for a country girl, and borrowed by English poets (e.g. Milton). Sometimes used as a christian name in recent times.

Ambrose (m.): (Latin *Ambrosius*, French *Ambroise*, Italian *Ambrogio*); Greek ἀμβρόσιος, 'pertaining to the immortals'. It became popular in the West as the name of St. *Ambrose* the 4th-C Bishop of Milan. It occurs twice in DB and from time to time in the

12th and 13th C, and is given in Prompt Parv 1440 as an English name. In 1604 it occurs in a list of Yorkshire recusants, and it has been in regular though infrequent use during the last three centuries. The fairly common Welsh name *Emrys* is said to be a Welsh form of *Ambrosius*, and to go back to *Ambrosius Aurelianus*, the semi-historical 5th-C prototype of King Arthur.

AMBROSIUS DB 1087, Cur 1189–1213.
AMBROYS HR 1273.
AMBROSE *Prompt Parv c.* 1440.

Ambrosine (f.): a f. form of *Ambrose* (q.v.), borrowed from the French. It has been first noted in 1888.

Amelia (f.): (German *Amalie*, French *Amélie*), a hypocoristic form of an Old German name in *amal-*, such as *Amalburga* the name of an 8th-C Burgundian saint. Many Gothic royal names were compounded with this element, which may mean 'labour'. The name became confused quite early in Germany with *Aemilia*, from the name of the well-known Roman *gens*. It was not much used in England until the Hanoverian period, when it became very popular and was often anglicized as *Emily* (q.v.). Thus Princess *Amelia*, the youngest daughter of George III, was usually called Princess *Emily*. In the Curia Regis Rolls for 1205 there occurs the name *Amilia, Amellia* which may be an early use of *Amelia*.

Amery, see ALMERIC.

Amfrid (m.): Old German *Anafrid*, compound of *ano* 'ancestor' and *frithu* 'peace'. It was introduced into England by the Normans and survived at least until the 14th C.

AMFRIDUS Cur 1189–1213.

Amice (f.) [ă'mis]: this name, very popular from the 12th to 15th C and surviving into the 16th C, appears in Latin as *Amisia, Amicia*. *Amisius* is also found, and *Amis* was certainly a m. name in French (e.g. the romance of *Amis and Amiloun*). There was a St. *Amicia* whose relics were highly venerated in the Cathedral of St. Pol-de-Léon. The origin of the name is obscure, and it is often confused with AMY (Latin *Amata* or *Amia*) (q.v.). Bardsley gives two entries from a Lincs. record of 1273 which come close together and almost certainly refer to the same person: *William fil. Amye* and *William fil. Amice*. The latest example he gives of the name is *Ameis* Austen died 1540. The surnames *Ames*, *Amies*, *Amis(s)*, *Aymes*, *Amison*, &c., probably derive from *Amice* rather than from *Amy*, which was much less common in the surname period.

AMICIA Cur 1187–1215, FA 1346, HR 1273.
AMIS Testa de Neville 13th C.

Amos (m.): Hebrew 'carried'. The name of one of the minor Old Testament prophets, occasionally used since the Reformation and especially common in the USA.

Amphelisia (f.): the first occurrence of this name which has been noted is *c.* 1190, when Alan of Leigh gave land to Godstow together with his daughter *Amphelisia* to be a nun. The Abbess of Godstow from 1216 to 1230 was also of this name (and possibly the same person); she appears variously as *Felicia*, *Aunphelice*, *Amphelice*, *Felice*, *Amyfelyse*, *Anfelise*, *Amfelice* (the forms *Felice*, *Felicia* were no doubt attempts at replacing an unfamiliar by a familiar name). *Amflisa* Comyn is mentioned in 1303. Several examples have been noticed in the 16th C, spelt *Amphelicia*, *Amphelice*, *Amfelice*, *Amphillis*; *Amphillis* is found in 1770 at North Repps, and a writer to N & Q 1898 stated that *Amphelisia* and *Amphillis* were then still current in some families. No etymology can be offered; Charnock's suggestion of ἀμφίλαλος, 'speaking two languages', is not convincing.

AMFELISIA Magd. *c.* 1230.
AMFLISIA HR 1273.
AMFLIS Testa de Neville 13th C.
AUNFLIS HR 1273.

Amy (f.): this is Old French *amée*, Modern French *aimée*, past participle of the verb *aimer*, 'to love'. In England it was sometimes latinized as *Amata*, more often as *Amia*. Prompt Parv (*c.* 1440) gives *Amye* as the English, *Amia* as the Latin form. There was a

13th-C St. *Amata* of Bologna who may have helped to popularize the name, which does not seem to occur before about 1270. It was sometimes confused with *Amice* (q.v.). The best-known bearer of the name was *Amy* Robsart, the ill-fated wife of Robert Earl of Leicester, but it was not uncommon in the 17th C. Lyford, 1655, gives both *Amata* and *Ainie*. It seems to have fallen out of use in the 18th C, and its return to favour in the 19th C may have been due to the popularity of *Kenilworth* (1821), and later *The Heir of Redclyffe* (1853).

AMYA HR 1273, Poll Tax 1379, FA 1346.
AMIA Testa de Neville 13th C.

Amyas (m.) [ā'mēas]: the etymology of this name is obscure. There was a m. name *Amis* (Latin *Amisius*) corresponding to the f. *Amice* (Latin *Amisia*) (q.v.), and there was also a French *Amé* (Latin *Amatus*), the name of a popular saint. The diminutive *Amiot* which occurs in England in the 12th and 13th C was probably formed from *Amé* or from the more common f. *Amée* (see AMY). *Amyas* or *Amias* may likewise be derived from *Amé*, though the formation is irregular. *Amias* is found as early as 1199 (Curia Regis Rolls) but was never common. Camden (1605) says 'We do now use *Amias* for this (i.e. *Aimé*) in difference from *Amie* the woman's name'. Kingsley's use of it for the hero of *Westward Ho!* (1855) was doubtless responsible for the modern revival of the name. *Amias* has sometimes been misread in old records and printed *Ananias*. See also ESMÉ.

AMIAS Cur 1189–1213, HR 1273.
AMIOT, AMISIUS Cur 1199.

Anastasia (f.): this and the m. *Anastasius* represent adjectives formed from the Greek ἀνάστασις, 'resurrection'. *Anastasius*, common in the Greek Church, was seldom used in the West, but *Anastasia*, the name of a 4th-C martyr mentioned in the Canon of the Mass, became a general favourite, and in medieval legend was attached to the Virgin's midwife. It is found in England from the 13th C, and Bardsley gives 16th- and 17th-C examples of *Anstey*, *Anstice*, *Anstes*, *Anstis(s)* all as christian names. Lyford 1655 gives the name as *Anastase*, and in the 18th C it regained its full stature and became *Anastatia*. It has been a particular favourite in Ireland, where it was used, amongst others, to translate the native *Aine* (q.v.).

ANESTASIA, ANASTASIA Cur 1219, 1220.
ANASTAS FA 1303.
ANNESTAS Magd. 1447.

Ancel (m.): Old German *Ansila*, a derivative of *ansi* 'a god'. A favourite Norman name, with diminutives *Ancelin* and *Ancelot*. It was sometimes confused with *Anselm* (q.v.). See also LANCELOT.

ANSELL' Testa de Neville 18th C.
ANSELLUS HR 1273.
AUNSELLUS HR 1273.
ANSELL St. Dionis 1545.

Anchoret (f.): is usually explained as being simply the word *anchoret*, 'an anchorite', but it does not occur on the Continent, and there is no parallel to a name formed in this way from a common noun. CMY was probably right in suggesting that *Ancret* (which is the earliest form) was an anglicization of the Welsh *Angharad*. This is strongly supported by the fact that the earliest occurrences of the name are in Welsh Marcher families such as the Le Stranges; or are Welsh, such as *Ancreta* daughter of Rhys ap Gruffudd, Prince of South Wales, who married a Lord of Kylsant in the 12th C. *Angharad* is found in Herefordshire in 1207. *Angharad* is the name given in the *Mabinogion* to Peredur's lady. The name may mean either 'much loved' or 'unloved' (the prefix *an* may have an intensive or a negative force), but the former is the more likely. Later examples of it are *Ankerita* 1528, *Ancret* 1660, *Ancrett* 1791. Lyford 1655 gives it as *Anchoretta*. *Ingaretta* occurs in a 17th-C visitation of Cambridge and *Ingaret* is recorded in Shropshire in 1904.

Ancilla (f.): (Latin *ancilla*, handmaid), occasionally used as a christian name from the 17th C. It is found in Devon in the 17th and 18th C., and in Oxfordshire in the 19th. *Annzella*, which occurs at Eynsham (Oxon.) in 1824 may be a form of this name, or possibly a late survival of *Ancel* (q.v.).

Andrea (f.): the use of this name is comparatively modern and infrequent, though *Andrée* has long been a common name in France. It is simply a f. form of *Andrew* (Latin *Andreas*). *Andrea* occurs occasionally in medieval Latin records, but probably represents the ordinary m. name *Andrew* applied to a girl, i.e. the person in question was called *Andrew* in the vernacular and only acquired the distinctively f. ending when her name was turned into Latin. See ALEXANDRA for further discussion of this point. The earliest example noted of *Andrea* as a genuine christian name is *Andrea* Beeston, who appears in a list of Middlesex recusants in 1617.

Andrew (m.): (Latin *Andreas*, French *André*, Italian *Andrea*, Spanish *Andres*, German, Dutch *Andreas*, Russian *Andrei*); Greek Ἀνδρέας, from ἀνδρεῖος 'manly'. The name of the first disciple called by Jesus, the brother of Simon Peter, and patron saint of Scotland and of Russia. Ἀνδρέας is a genuine Greek name, found in papyri, but it is unlikely that St. *Andrew* had a Greek name, and in his case it was probably a translation of a Hebrew name. The great popularity of St. *Andrew* in the Middle Ages is shown by his having 637 churches dedicated to him in England alone (it is the fourth most frequent dedication), and is partly accounted for by an apocryphal history of St. Andrew and St. Matthew, which was declared heretical as early as the 5th C, but versions of which were widely read for many centuries; it was translated into Old English verse and prose. *Andrew* is not found in England applied to a native before the Conquest, but there is a sub-tenant called *Andreas* in DB. From the 12th C it became a general favourite and gave rise to many surnames such as *Andrew(es)*, *Anderson*, *Dandy*, *Tandy* (the last two from nicknames). It has naturally been particularly common in Scotland. The usual pet-form now is *Andy*.

ANDREAS DB 1086, Cur 1189–1213, HR 1273, FA 1302.
ANDREU HR 1273.
ANDEREWE Yorks Poll Tax 1379.
DANDI HR 1273.
DANDY QW 1292.

Aneurin (m.) [ănëï'rin]: the name of a Welsh bard, supposed to have flourished about A.D. 600. Probably derived from Latin *Honorius*. It is still a common name in Wales. The older and better spelling is *Aneirin*.

Angel (m.): Greek *ἄγγελος* 'a messenger', used in the Septuagint to translate the Hebrew *mal'āk yĕhōwah* messenger of Jehovah, and adopted in most European languages as the name of these celestial visitors. *Angelos* was first used as a personal name in Byzantium, whence it spread to Sicily where there was a 13th-C saint of the name. *Angelo, Agnolo* has since been a fairly common name in Italy, *Ange* has been occasionally used in France, and *Angel* in England, where it occurs from 16th C onward, especially in Cornwall, as a man's name. Probably the best-known example of its use is in Hardy's *Tess of the D'Urbervilles* for Tess's husband *Angel* Clare. In the 17th C *Angel* was also sometimes used instead of *Angela* (q.v.).

Angela (f.): a f. form of *Angel* (q.v.). St. *Angela* Merici (d. 1540) founded the Ursuline Order of teaching nuns, and her name has been used occasionally in Italy and France (*Angèle*). CMY says 'occasionally used by lovers of ornamental names', and that *Angel* and *Angela* are sometimes found in the 17th C. It remained uncommon until the end of the 19th C. It was possibly Tractarian influence which led to its revival in the first place, for there is evidence of the name having been given to children born on the eve of St. Michael and All Angels. Lyford 1655 gives a name *Angeletta*, but there is no further evidence for its use.

Angelica (f.): f. of Latin adjective *angelicus*, 'angelic'. The name of the lady beloved by Orlando in the poems of Boiardo and Ariosto. Occasionally used in England, France, and Germany since the 18th C. The most celebrated bearer of the name was the painter Angelica Kauffman. *Angélique* is not uncommon in France.

Angelina (f.): a diminutive of *Angela* (q.v.), occasionally used in 19th C. Not uncommon in Italy, where there have been three saints of the name.

Angharad, see ANCHORET.

Angus (m.): this common Scottish name is identical with the Irish *Aonghus*, from Old Irish *Aengus*, 'one choice'. It was the name of a 9th-C saint, Bishop of Clonenagh, as well as of a legendary hero. See also AENEAS.

Anketil, see ASKETIL.

Ann, Anna, Anne, Annette, Annie (f.): (French *Anne, Annette, Nanette*, German, Italian, &c., *Anna*, Spanish *Aña, Anita*). The usual Western form of the Hebrew *Hannah* (q.v.). The name is not given to the mother of the Blessed Virgin in the Bible, but appears in various apocryphal gospels. Her cult did not take hold until the 14th C, and it was not until after the Council of Trent (1545) that the observance of her festival was imposed upon the Roman Catholic Church. The name was a favourite in the Byzantine Empire, and was carried to Russia by the marriage in 988 of *Anna*, daughter of the Emperor Romanus, to Vladimir, Prince of Kiev. Her granddaughter *Anna* married Henri I of France (1031–60) and so introduced the name into the West. It occurs first in England about the beginning of the 13th C (1218 is the earliest record), but it was rare until the beginning of the 14th C, when it began to come into more general use, perhaps partly owing to the influence of *Anne* of Bohemia, queen of Richard II. Its popularity grew steadily after the beginning of the 16th C, and by the beginning of the 17th C it was one of the commonest English names, a position it retained for at least two centuries. There was an early tendency to confuse it with *Agnes* (q.v.). *Anna*, the Latin form of the name, came into fashion in the 18th C. The early diminutives were *Nan* and *Nanny*, but they came in time to be used as a term for a loose woman, and were replaced in the 18th C by *Nancy*. *Nan* has recently come into use again. In the 19th C the diminutive *Annie* was frequently used as an independent name. The French *Annette, Nanette* and Spanish *Anita* are occasionally used in England as independent names. The very common medieval *Annot*, which survives in Scotland and the North, was probably a diminutive not of *Ann* but of *Agnes* (q.v.).

Bardsley remarks that one out of every ten Yorkshire girls was named *Annot* at a time when *Anne* or *Anna* is never found. The spellings *Ann* and *Anne* were used indifferently until recent times when spelling became more rigid. *Anne*, like *Marie*, was sometimes added to men's names in France. Lord *Anne* Hamilton (1709-48) was named after his godmother, Queen *Anne*. In the 18th and 19th C it was often joined with Mary, and both *Mary Anne* and *Anna Maria* were common.

Annabel(la) (f.): this puzzling name has always been primarily Scottish and was apparently not known on the Continent until modern times. One of its earliest occurrences is as the name of a daughter of Duncan, Earl of Moray, who in 1158 carried it into the Lucy family. Robert III of Scotland in 1367 married *Annabel* Drummond, who became mother of James I of Scotland. The name appears variously as *Annabel*, *Anabel*, *Anabill*, *Anabul*, *Annable*, *Annaple*, and is latinized as *Annabella*. It was in general use in Scotland at a time when *Anne* was practically unknown in Great Britain, and there is almost certainly no connexion between the two names. The most probable explanation is that *Annabel* was derived by a process of dissimilation from *Amabel* (q.v.). It is in favour of this explanation that *Amabel* seems not to occur in Scotland, in spite of its popularity with the Anglo-Normans in England. Poe's poem 'Annabel Lee' has caused some revival in the use of this name in America and England and has even introduced it to France.

ANABEL Cl 1311.
ANABILLE Cl 1386.
ANABUL Cl 1379.

Anne, Annette, see ANN.

Annis, see AGNES.

Annora, see HONOR(I)(A).

Anselm (m.): Old German *Ansehelm*, compound of *ansi* 'a god' and *helma* 'a helmet'. The name was chiefly used by the Lombards and was brought to England by St. *Anselm* (1033-1109),

Archbishop of Canterbury, a Lombard by birth. It was never popular in this country, though it occurs from the 12th C onwards, sometimes spelt *Ancelm* through confusion with the common name *Ancel* (q.v.); conversely *Ansellus* of Laon is called *Anselmus* of Laon. *Anselm* was revived in the 19th C by the Tractarians.

ANSELMUS Reg 1078-85, Cur 1189-1213, FA 1284.
ANCELMUS FA 1284, 1303.

Anthea (f.): the f. of the Greek adjective ἄνθειος, 'flowery' (an epithet of Hera at Argos). It was used by pastoral poets in the 17th C (e.g. Herrick's poem 'To *Anthea*, who may command him anything') and passed into currency as a genuine, though never common, christian name. CMY does not mention it, but a writer to N & Q (23.12.1922) says: 'I know two families in which for several generations it has been usual to call a daughter *Anthea*.'

Antigone (f.) [ănti'gŏnē]: Greek compound of ἄντι 'contrary', 'against', γόνος 'born', the name of the heroic daughter of Oedipus. The name occurs in a Curia Regis Roll of 1219 as *Antigonia* and Humphrey Duke of Gloucester (1391-1447) had an illegitimate daughter named *Antigone*. *Ismene*, the name of the sister of *Antigone*, is also found at about the same date. The story of Oedipus and his children was probably familiar from the tragedies of Seneca.

Antoinette, Antonia (f.) [ăntwahnĕt', ăntō'nĕa]: these are respectively the French (diminutive) and the Italian f. forms of *Antony* (q.v.). Both were occasionally used in England in the 19th C and are still so used. There was a 3rd-C Byzantine saint *Antonia*, and a 3rd-C Portuguese saint *Antonina*, and some *Antonia*s and *Antonina*s may be named after them rather than after *Antony*.

Antony, Anthony (m.) [ăn'tonē]: (Latin *Antonius*, French *Antoine*, Italian *Antonio*, German *Anton(ius)*, Slav *Anton*); the name of a Roman *gens*, the most famous member of which was 'Mark *Antony*', the triumvir Marcus *Antonius*. The etymology is unknown. The later popularity of the name was due to St. *Antony* the Great, the Egyptian ascetic, whose cult was diffused in the West at the time of the Crusades. The Temptation of St. *Antony* was one of the favourite subjects of medieval art. He was regarded as the patron of swineherds, and a *St. Antony* or *Tantony* pig was one of the many names for the smallest of a litter; erysipelas was called St. *Antony's* Fire after an outbreak in 1089 when many were said to be cured after making intercession to him. The name *Antony* *(Antoine)* was particularly common in France after the relics of the saint were translated to Vienne. At a later date St. *Antony* of Padua (1195–1231), a favourite saint, no doubt contributed to the popularity of the name. (It is he, and not St. *Antony* the Great, who is invoked to find lost property.) *Antony* was fairly common in England from the 12th C, and has continued steadily in use. It was also common in Scotland and appears as *Anton* in Middle Scots. The intrusive *h* in the spelling *Anthony* was a late development, and seems not to appear before the late 16th C. It may have been the result of false etymologizing, for Camden (1605) derives the name from Greek ἄνθος. The *h* is, of course, silent, but there is some danger nowadays of a spelling pronunciation (already in use in USA), and the older spelling is to be preferred. The usual abbreviation of the name is *Tony*, which is found from the 17th C (e.g. in Brome's *Weeding of Covent Garden* 1658).

ANTONIUS Cur 1207–13. HR 1273.
ANTONY *Prompt Parv c.* 1440.

Aphra (f.): this was a not uncommon name in the 17th C, the best-known example of it being the woman dramatist *Aphra Behn* (1640–89), whose name is variously spelt *Afra, Aphra, Ayfara.* An earlier example is *Aphra Hawkins,* who died in 1605 aged 25. The name originated in a misunderstanding of a verse of the Book of Micah: 'In the house of *Aphrah* roll thyself in the dust', where *Aphrah* is in fact a word meaning dust.

Appoline (f.): Greek Ἀπολλωνία, 'pertaining to Apollo'. This was the usual English form of the name of St. *Apollonia*, a 3rd-C Alexandrian martyr who was said to have been tortured by having her teeth broken, and hence was invoked against the toothache.

Bardsley says it was a favourite name before the Reformation and gave rise to the surname *Ap(p)lin*, but he gives no early examples of it, his first being 1593 (*Apeline*), 1609 (*Apoline*), and a later *Aplin*. It appears as *Appolonia* in Shropshire in 1787 and as *Abbelina* in New England in 1827. An old lady of 85 named *Appolina* died in 1938.

April (f.): the name of the month, used as a christian name in recent times (cf. *June*).

Aquila (m.): Latin *aquila* 'eagle', a cognomen in several Roman families. This was the name of the tent-maker with whom and his wife Priscilla St. Paul stayed at Corinth. It came into use in the 17th C, both as a man's and a woman's name, e.g. *Aquila* Moor (a man) 1695, and *Aquila* Burge (a woman) 1793, both in Huntspill parish register, and *Aquila* Cruso, Rector of Sutton, Sussex, 1633.

Arabel(la) (f.): this name, like *Annabel* (q.v.), was originally Scottish and is apparently unknown on the Continent. The earliest example noted is one *Orabilis*, daughter of Ness, Lord of Leuchars, and sometimes said to be a granddaughter of William the Lion, who married Robert de Quincy about the middle of the 12th C and became mother of Saer de Quincy, 1st Earl of Winchester. In 1255 Magdalen Laver was held by *Arabella* wife of John de Montpynçon. The name occurs in the 13th C in the forms *Arable, Orable, Orabell*. The Lady *Arabella* Stuart (1575–1615) was commonly called *Arbell* by her contemporaries, and Lyford 1655 gives both *Arbella* and *Orabilis* (which he derives from the Latin *orabilis*, 'easy to be intreated'). The probabilities seem to point to the derivation of this name from *Annabel* by a process of dissimilation (cf. the development of *Durham* from *Dunholm*). But there can be no certainty, and there is another factor to be considered. In the *chansons de geste*, *Orable, Oriabel, Oriabiaus* occur as a m. name; *Orable* is also given as the name of a queen of Arabia; and the name of Arabia is variously rendered *Arabe, Arrabe, Arable, Arrable, Errabe, Esrabe, Erable, Araboi, Arabloi*. It is doubtful whether there can be any connexion between these and the 12th-C Scottish name, but the possibility cannot be altogether ruled out. *Arabel* and especially its latinized form *Arabella* came into fashion again in the late 18th and early 19th C, but it is not now much used.

Archelaus, see HERCULES.

Archibald (m.): Old German *Ercanbald*, compound of *ercan* 'genuine', 'simple', and *bald* 'bold'. Like other names in *ercan* (see Förstemann) it developed *A*-forms which were influenced by the supposed analogy with Greek names in *Archi-* (cf. *Theodoric*), and such forms as *Archembald, Archimbalt* appear at an early date. The name was brought to England at the Norman Conquest and appears in DB as *Arcebaldus, Arcenbaldus, Erchenbaldus,* while later versions are *Erkenbaud, Erchebald, Herchembaut.* There was a corresponding OE name *Eorconbeald* in use in the East Anglian royal family, many of whose members bore names compounded with *eorcan,* and some of the post-Conquest examples may represent a survival of it. St. *Eorkonweald* (died 693) is sometimes at a later date referred to as St. *Archibald. Archibald* survived in occasional use in England, especially in the North, and gave rise to the surnames *Archbell, Archbold.* But it was only in Scotland that it took permanent root and became really common. It has always been a particular favourite with the Campbells and Douglases. The usual abbreviation is now *Archie,* but *Baldie* still survives in Scotland. Like *Algernon* (q.v.) it is taken by comic writers as a typical aristocratic name. In the Highlands *Archibald* has commonly been used as a translation of Gaelic *Gillespie.* This has been explained as due to the mistaken notion that *-bald* in the former name = hairless, and was therefore the equivalent of Gaelic *gille* 'servant', 'shaven one', 'monk'.

ARCEBALDUS, ARCENBALDUS, ERCHENBALDUS DB 1086
ERKENBAUD Cur 1201–3.
ERCHEBALDUS FA 1303.
ARCHEBALD or ERCHENBALD Lyford 1655.

Aretas (m.): Greek Ἀρέτας for Ἀρέθας, Arabic *Hāritā,* the name of a series of kings of the Nabataeans. *Aretas* IV is mentioned in 2 Cor. xi. 32, being King at Damascus at the time of St. Paul's escape from there. The name was made use of in the 17th C, like many names occurring in the Bible, without much regard to its associations. The daughter of *Aretas* Seton, Governor of the Leeward Islands, married at the beginning of the 18th C Edmund Akers, ancestor of the present Lord Chilston, and from that time the name has been in regular use in the Akers (now Akers-Douglas) family.

Ariadne (f.): the Greek heroine Ἀριάδνη probably conceals an earlier Cretan goddess, and her name signifies 'the very holy one'. The name was borne by an obscure Phrygian martyr, and in the forms *Arianna*, *Ariane* has been used in Italy and France respectively. It has been used occasionally in England of late years, probably with no reference to the saint.

Armigil, see ERMYNTRUDE.

Armin, see HERMAN.

Arminel (f.): a rare name which seems to be confined to Devon, where it is still in use. There was an *Arminel* Cording in that county in 1797. It looks like a diminutive of *Armine*, the English form of French *Armand*, German and Dutch *Herman* (q.v.). *Armin* (m.) and *Armine* (f.) were both current in Norfolk in the 17th and 18th C.

Arnold (m.): Old German *Arenvald*, compound of *arin* 'eagle' and *vald* 'power'. It early became *Arnoald*, *Arnald*, and finally *Arnold*. The Normans brought it to England in the French form *Arnaud* or *Arnaut*, which accounts for the common Middle English *Arnott*. The occasional *Ernald*, *Ernold* which are found in the 11th and 12th C may represent a survival of the corresponding Old English name *Earnweald*. The modern form *Arnold* is probably a comparatively late back-formation from the Latin *Arnoldus* (cf. the supersession of *Harry* by *Henry*). It was a very popular name in the 12th and 13th C and gave rise to a number of surnames (e.g. *Arnold*, *Arnoll*, *Arnot(t)*, *Arnould*, *Arnald*, *Arnall*, *Arnell*, *Arnet(t)*. Later it fell out of use. Camden (1605) seems to regard it as a rare name, but mentions that 'it hath been common in the old family of the Boyses'. Bardsley, writing about 1870, says 'of course *Arnold* is now practically forgotten as a personal name in England'. That is far from being true to-day, when *Arnold* is once more a comparatively popular name.

ERNALDUS DB 1086.
ARNOLDUS Cur 1189–1213.
ARNALD or ARNAUD HR 1273.
ERNALD HR 1273.
ARNET HR 1273.

Artemisia (f.): Greek Ἀρτεμισία, 'belonging to Artemis'; the name of a queen of Caria in the 4th C B.C., who built the Mausoleum at Halicarnassus. The name has been in use since the middle of the 18th C in the family of Philipps of Picton, and has been carried by marriage into other families. A writer to N & Q (15.12.1934) states that there are a number of instances of its use in the neighbourhood of Lewisham, Greenwich, and Bermondsey.

Arthur (m.): the etymology of this name has been the subject of much speculation: it has been variously derived from Celtic *artos* 'a bear', Irish *art* 'a stone', and other Celtic words. It is more probably of Latin origin. There seems to have been a Roman *gens* named *Artorius*; Tacitus mentions an *Artoria Flacilla*, and Juvenal an *Artorius* (some MSS have *Arctorius* or *Arcturius*). There are other examples of Latin names naturalized and surviving in Wales (e.g. *Cai* or *Kai*, Arthur's seneschal = Caius; *Emrys* = Ambrosius), and it is significant that Gildas says that the leader of the Britons against the Saxons was a man of Roman race, Ambrosius Aurelianus.

The earliest recorded example of the name *Arthur* occurs (as *Arturius*) in Adamnan's life of St. Columba, where it is the name of an Irish prince killed in 596; the earliest mention of King *Arthur* is in Nennius (fl. 796). *Artor* and *Artur* are the names of tenants in DB. In the 13th C and thereafter it is usually *Artur(us)* until the 16th C when *Arthur, Arther, Artheur*, &c., are usual, though *Arter* is found as late as 1630, and the vulgar abbreviation *Arty*, which is still sometimes heard, may represent a survival of this. Never very common (until the 19th C), *Arthur* is most often found, in the Middle Ages, in counties bordering on Celtic districts, Cumberland, Yorkshire, Somerset, for example. It may be noted that the two early examples of its use for royal persons are also the result of Celtic connexions: *Arthur* Duke of Brittany, the unfortunate nephew of King John, was a Breton on his mother's side, and *Arthur* Tudor, elder son of Henry VII, was a Welshman. The name first appears in Scotland in the 13th C in the Galbraith family, whence it was carried by marriage to the Hamiltons. In the 19th C *Arthur* became very popular, chiefly, at first, on account of *Arthur* Wellesley, Duke of Wellington (he was named after his maternal grandfather, *Arthur* Hill, Viscount Duncannon, whose family had used the name since the 17th C). Apart from his general influence, Wellington had a number of godsons named after him, among them the Duke of Connaught, youngest son of Queen Victoria. Tennyson also, no doubt, had something to do with the revival of the name, both by his *In Memoriam* (commemorating his friend *Arthur* Hallam) and by his *Idylls of the King*. It is sometimes abbreviated to *Arty* (e.g. in *The Newcomes* 1854, *Kipps* 1905).

Artur(us) DB 1086.
Artor DB 1086.
Azer, Azor(ius), Azur DB 1086.
Arthurus Cur 1189–1213, HR 1273.
Artur, Acur, Azur Cur 1189–1213.

Asenath (f.): '(woman) belonging to (Egyptian god) Neith.' The name of the Egyptian wife of the patriarch Joseph. It was occasionally used in the 17th C, and there was an *Asenath* Angel in Shropshire in 1798. *Assenath* occurs in 1813 at Leasingham, Lincs. The gipsy name *As(h)ena* may be derived from it.

Asketil, Anketil (m.): Old Norse *Asketil*, compound of *áss* and *ketal*. The corresponding elements in Old English were *ós* and *cytel*. Both are found chiefly in compound proper names; the first signifies 'god' or 'divinity', the meaning and derivation of the second are doubtful but probably have nothing to do with the common word kettle; it may be cognate with Old German *Kacili*, *Chacili*, *Chazili*, which Förstemann derives from a root *Caz-*

cognate with *Cuth*. Old English *Oscytel* and Norse *Asketel* were both common in England before the Norman Conquest, and *Aschetil, Osketel, Askell, Astell, Oskell* are found as late as the thirteenth century. In the main, however, they were superseded by the Norman forms *Ansketil, Anketil,* and the still commoner *Anketin*. This once popular name fell into disuse in the course of the fourteenth century, but continued to be used in a few families. Camden (1605) says of *Anskettell* 'used much in the ancient house of Mallories', and *Anchitel* was used in the family of Grey (Earls of Stamford), e.g. *Anchitel* Grey, son of the 1st Earl born *c.* 1625, and the Rev. *Anchitel* Grey, son of the 5th Earl (1774–1833).

ARCHETEL, ARCHEL, ARCHIL DB 1086.
ANSCHITILLUS Reg 1087–94.
ANSCHETILLUS Lincs Survey 1109.
ANKETEL Cur 1189–1213, HR 1273.
ANKETIL HR 1273.
ASCHETIL, ASCHETIN, ASKETIN, ASCHETEL, ASTELL (one man) Whitby Cart 13th C.
ASTILL, ASTELL HR 1273.
ANKETIN QW 1273.

Aspasia (f.): Greek ἀσπασία 'welcome'; the name of the celebrated mistress of Pericles, and used by Beaumont and Fletcher for a principal character in their play *The Maid's Tragedy* 1619. It was occasionally used as a christian name in the 17th C. CMY has a story of finding the name in use for a village child, whose mother explained 'Her name's *Aspasia*, but us calls her *Spash*'.

Astrid (f.): a Norse name, corresponding to the Old German *Ansitruda*, compound of *ansi* 'god' and *drudi* 'strength'. It was the name of the mother of Olaf Trygvesøn, King of Norway, and of the wife of St. Olaf, and has been used ever since in the royal families of Scandinavia. Of recent years it has been used occasionally in England.

Athelstan (m.): Old English *Æthelstan*, compound of *æthel* 'noble' and *stan* 'stone', the name of a King of Wessex (925–40) son of Edward the Elder. It was a common Old English name, but seems not to have survived the Norman Conquest. Lord Herbert of Cherbury, in his autobiography, mentions a cousin named *Athelston* Owen, but this seems to be an isolated example. It was revived in the 19th C, perhaps as a result of Scott's use of it in *Ivanhoe*.

ÆTHELSTAN, ACHESTAN, ATHESTAN, ADESTAN, ADSTAN, AISTAN, ALESTAN DB 1086.

Athene (f.) [ăthē′nĕ]: the name of the Greek goddess Ἀθήνη is very ancient, and no explanation of its meaning is possible. In modern times it has occasionally been used as a christian name in this country.

Aubrey (m.): from *Auberi*, the French form of *Alberich* (see ALBERIC). Introduced into England by the Normans, it was fairly common during the Middle Ages, sometimes in the form *Albery*. It has been used in the family of de Vere since the house was founded by Albericus de Vere, one of the Conqueror's companions, and they continued to bear it after it had fallen out of general use and before its restoration to favour in the 19th C. See also ALBREDA.

ALBERICUS DB 1086.
AUBRI HR 1273.

Aude, see ALDA.

Audrey (f.): a reduction of the Old English *Æthelthryth, Etheldreda* (q.v.), until the 17th C used as a pet-name for it, but now usually an independent name. St. *Etheldreda* appears as St. *Audry* in the early-16th-C life of St. Werburga, and *Audrey, Awdrie, Audrye,* &c., appear as christian names from about the same period. No doubt this pronunciation was current long before it was recorded in writing. It was in the 16th C that the word *tawdry* arose, at first to describe the necklaces sold at St. *Etheldreda's* fair, and later for any cheap garish goods. *Audrey* was mainly used by the poorer classes, as is shown by Shakespeare's use of it for the country wench in *As You Like It*. It has had a revival of favour in the present C and is probably commoner now than at any time in the past.

Augusta (f.): f. form of *Augustus* (q.v.), first used by the German princes who had taken to using *Augustus* in the 16th C. It was introduced into England by the Hanoverians (one of George III's daughters was named *Augusta* Sophia) and became common in the 19th C, often shortened to *Gus* or *Gussie*. It is now quite out of fashion.

Augustine, Austin (m.): (French, German *Augustin*, Italian *Agostino*, Spanish *Agostin*): Latin diminutive of *augustus* 'venerable', 'consecrated'. The name was very common in England in the Middle Ages (it is not found before the Conquest) usually in the syncopated form *Austin*. It was probably the 6th-C St. *Augustine*, 1st Archbishop of Canterbury, as often as the 4th-C Bishop of Hippo, who was the sponsor of the English *Austins*. *Austin* has remained in use until the present day, though it lost much of its popularity after the Reformation and is now more familiar from the common surnames *Austin, Austen*. The full form *Augustine* has been used with some frequency in the last 100 years; it was one of the names revived by the Tractarians.

Austin(us) Cur 1189–1213, HR 1273.
Astin HR 1273.
Augustinus Poll Tax 1379.
Austyn Poll Tax 1379.

Augustus (m.): Latin *augustus*, 'venerable', 'consecrated'. *Augustus* was adopted as a second name by some of the German princes after the Renaissance in imitation of the Roman emperors, and it soon became an ordinary christian name among them. It was introduced into England by the Hanoverians and was popular in the 19th C. It was often shortened to *Gus* or *Gussy* in familiar use. *August* is common in Germany and *Auguste* in France.

Aulay (m.), see OLAF.

Aurea (f.): Latin *aurea* 'golden'. *Aurea* Otway married a Lambarde of Sevenoaks in 1789, and the name has been used in the Lambarde and Battiscombe families ever since.

Aurelia (f.): the name of a Roman *gens*, a derivative of *aurum* 'gold'. There was an 11th-C French saint of the name, and *Aurélie* has been used in France for that reason. *Aurelia* has been used occasionally in England since the 17th C, probably directly from the Latin. Lyford 1655 gives *Aureola* as a f. christian name, giving its meaning as 'little pretty golden lady', but there seems to be no instance of its use. *Auriol* has recently come into use, presumably with some reference to *aurum*.

Aurelian (m.): Latin *Aurelianus*, a derivative of *Aurelius*, the name of a Roman *gens* (see AURELIA). The name of a 3rd-C Roman emperor of obscure origins, and also of a 6th-C saint, a Bishop of Arles. It was revived at the time of the Renaissance and has been used occasionally since, e.g. *Aurelian* Townshend the 17th-C poet.

Aurora (f.): the Latin name for the goddess of the dawn. Since the Renaissance occasionally used in England, Germany, and France (*Aurore*). It was the name of the Countess von Königsmark, sister of Count von Königsmark and mother of Marshal Saxe (b. 1696).

Austin, see AUGUSTINE.

Aveline, see EVELINA.

Avenel (m.): this name, not uncommon in the 12th and 13th C, first appears in England in DB. It appears to be a m. equivalent of *Aveline* (see EVELINA), from the same stem *Ava* and with double diminutive, in *-en* and *-el*.
AVENEL DB 1086, Cur 1189–1213.

Averil (f.) [ă'verĭl]: *Everild* (Latin *Everildis*), the name of a 7th-C Yorkshire saint, is probably a compound of Old English *eofor* 'boar', *hild* 'battle'. There is a well-attested cognate Old German *Eburhilt* (other forms are *Eburhild, Eberhild, Eurohildis, Eurildis*). *Everild* was not uncommon in the Middle Ages and was in use as late as the 17th C; it is still occasionally used in Yorkshire and *Everilda* survives as a gipsy name. But the usual form of the name is now *Averil*. *Averell* appears in 1604 in a Yorkshire list of recusants, side by side with the form *Everild*.

Avice, Avis (f.) [ā′vĭs]: this name seems to have been introduced into England by the Normans. It may be from Old German *Aveza*, a derivative of *Avi* (a common element in personal names) which is recorded by Förstemann. It was fairly common from the 12th to 14th C, and is found occasionally in the 16th to 18th C. Bardsley speaks of it as just coming into fashion again after two centuries of neglect, but a writer in N & Q at about the same time (1872) says: '*Avice*, if it is the same as *Avis*, is certainly not obsolete, for I have known more than one.' *Avis* is also a gipsy name. The surnames *Aves, Avis, Avison* are derived from it.

AVICIA Cur 1196–1219.
AVICE HR 1273, St. Columb Major 1600.
AVIS Stepney Register 1590.
AVICE Lyford 1655.
AVEIS Binsey Church 1711.

Aylmer (m.): Old English *Æthelmær*, compound of *æthel* 'noble' and *mære* 'famous', was a common name before the Conquest, and the medieval *Aylmer* may sometimes represent a gallicization of it. But there was also a common Old German name *Agilmar*, which early appears as *Ailemar, Eilemar*, and this was brought to England by the Normans. *Aylmer* (e.g. Tennyson's Sir *Aylmer* Aylmer) was common in the Middle Ages and has never died out altogether. It gave rise to several surnames, including that of *Elmer* (q.v.), which has gained independent currency as a christian name in the USA, being the surname of two New Jersey brothers who played an active part in the American Revolution.

AYLMER(US) Reg 1066–70.
ÆGELMAER Reg 1066–70.
AELMAR, ÆILMAR, AILMAR, ALMER, AILMER, EILMER, ÆLMER, ELMAR, ELMER DB 1086.
AYLMER Cur 1207–9.
AYMAR HR 1273.

Aylwin, Alwyn (m.): both Old English *Æthelwine*, from *æthel* 'noble', *wine* 'friend', and Old English *Ælfwine* from *Ælf* 'elf', *wine* 'friend', could give a gallicized *Alwin* or *Aylwin*. The names survived the Norman Conquest and have never been altogether

disused, though not common since the 12th C. They gave rise
to the surnames *Alwin, Aylwin, Elwin,* and others.

ADELUIN, AILUIN, ÆLUUIN, ÆLUIN, ALUUINE, ALUUIN DB 1086.
AILWIN(US), ALWIN(US) Cur 1189–1213.
ALEWYN, ALWYNE HR 1273.

Azariah (m.): Hebrew 'whom Jehovah aids', the name of a king
of Judah. Occasionally used by Puritans in England and America.

B

Babette, see ELIZABETH.

Babs, see BARBARA.

Baldie, see ARCHIBALD.

Baldric (m.): Old German *Baldarich,* compound of *balda* 'bold'
and *ricja* 'rule'; introduced into England at the time of the Norman Conquest. It remained popular in the 12th and 13th C,
usually in the French form *Baldri, Baudri; Baudrey* occurs as
late as the 15th C.

BALDRICUS DB 1086, Cur 1187–1219.
BAUDRE FA 1284.
BAUDRI FA 1346.
BAUDREY FA 1428.

Baldwin (m.): Old German *Baldavin,* compound of *balda* 'bold'
and *vini* 'friend', and the cognate Old English *Bealdwine* are joint
sources of this name. In DB there is mention of actual tenants of
this name and also of tenants TRE. *Baldwin* was a particular
favourite in Flanders, and it was probably Flemish influence
which was responsible for the popularity of the name in England
in the 12th and 13th C. The surnames *Baldwin, Bawden, Boden,
Bowden* (the last three from French *Baudoin*), and *Bodkin* (from

the diminutive *Baudkin*) are from it. Though less common in later centuries, it has never been altogether disused.

BALDEWYNE Reg 1066–70.
BALDUIN, BALDEWIN DB 1086, Cur 1187–1219.
BALDWYN, BALDEWYN, BALDEWYNE HR 1273.
BAUDUIN Testa de Neville 13th C.
BAWDEN Cornish Registers 1550.
BODWINE Clerkenwell 1694.

Balthasar (m.) [balthaz'ar]: *Belshazzar* ('Bel protect the king') appears in the Vulgate in the form *Baltassar* and in the Septuagint as βαλτασάρ. *Balthasar* is the name, in medieval legend, of one of the Magi. As early as the 2nd C it was believed that they were three in number and were kings, and by the 11th C the names *Balthasar*, *Caspar* (see JASPER), and *Melchior* had been attached to them. In 1164 Rainald of Dassel brought their supposed relics from Milan to Cologne, which thenceforward became a great place of pilgrimage and the centre of a widely diffused cult. *Baldassare* became a fairly common name in Italy, but *Balthasar* has rarely been used in England; Shakespeare gives it to a servant in *Much Ado about Nothing* and it is sometimes found in the 17 C.

Baptist (m.): Old French *baptiste*, Latin *baptista* from Greek βαπτιστής, 'one who baptizes'. This name, which is much used in Roman Catholic countries, usually with John (e.g. French *Jean-Baptiste*, Italian *Giambattista*) but also by itself and as a f. as well as a m. name (e.g. Italian *Baptista*), is uncommon in England, and seems not to have been used earlier than the Reformation; examples are Baptist Hicks, 1st Viscount Campden (1551–1629) and Baptist Wriothesley Noel (1798–1873). The f. form *Baptista* sometimes occurs in the 17 C, e.g. *Baptista Jones* who is recorded in 1619.

Barbara (f.): (French *Barbe*, Russian *Varvara*); f. of Greek βάρβαρος 'strange', 'foreign'. St. *Barbara*, a 3rd-C Syrian saint, was one of the four great virgin saints, and though her name never became as common as those of the others (Margaret, Agnes, Katharine), yet it was fairly popular from the end of the 12th C onwards. She was the patroness of architects and engineers, and

invoked against thunder and lightning. The English form of the
name was *Barbary*, and CMY says it was still so pronounced by
poor people in her time. The French form *Barbe* and its diminutive *Barbot* also occur in medieval records, and both gave rise to
surnames. It was still fairly common in the 16th C, but, like other
names of non-scriptural saints, it tended to drop out of use after
the Reformation. Bardsley writing *c.* 1870 says it is 'now of rarest
use'. It was revived with other medieval names at the beginning
of the 20th C. The usual modern abbreviation is *Babs*, which
has been used at least since the 17th C.

BARBOT Cur 1203-5.
BARBATA, BARBOTA Cal Gen 13th C.
BARBERY St. Antholin 1581.
BARBERRY Cheshunt Church Reg 1692.

Bardolph (m.): Old German *Berhtolf*, compound of *berhta*
'bright', and *wulfa* 'wolf'. The cognate Old English *Beorhtwulf*
was not very common, and the name was introduced into general
use in England by the Normans, giving rise to several surnames,
e.g. *Bardolph, Bardell.* Now obsolete, it is chiefly remembered for
Falstaff's roistering companion in *Henry IV*, *Henry V*, and *The
Merry Wives of Windsor.*

BARDOLPHUS Cur 1205.
BARDOLF alias BARDOL Cal Gen. 1261.
BARDULPHUS Testa de Neville 13th C.

Barnabas (m.): Hebrew 'son of exhortation or consolation'. The
name of St. Paul's companion on many of his missionary journeys
—'Joses, who by the apostles was surnamed *Barnabas* (which is,
being interpreted, The son of consolation).' It is found in use as a
christian name in England from about 1200. The English form of the
name, *Barnabe* or *Barnaby*, survived in use until the early 19th C
(e.g. Dickens's *Barnaby Rudge*), and has recently been revived.

BARNABAS Cur 1201.
BARNABE 14th C Legendary.

Barnard, Barnet, see BERNARD.

Barret(t) (m.): Old German *Beroald*, compound of *bera* 'a bear',
wald 'rule', later became *Berold, Berolt*, and in that form was

introduced into England by the Normans; the Middle English form *Barrett* is a similar development to *Arnett* from *Arnold*. It was not uncommon in the surname period, but died out later.

BEROLDUS Pipe Roll 1159.
BARAT, BARET HR 1273.

Barry (m.): Irish *Bearrach*, a derivative of a word meaning 'spear'; until recent years confined to Ireland, but now not uncommon in England and the USA. The name of the poet Barry Cornwall was an invention of his own—a partial anagram of his real name, Bryan Waller Procter.

Bartholomew (m.): Hebrew 'son of Talmai' ('abounding in furrows'); the patronymic of the Apostle *Nathanael* (q.v.), by which he is commonly known. It is not found in use in England before the Conquest, but it was very common from the 12th C onwards. The cult of St. Bartholomew was popular (there are 165 church dedications to him in England) and his relics were widely diffused. *Bartholomew*, with its diminutives *Bartle(t)* and *Bat*, gave rise to a number of surnames such as *Bartholomew, Bartle, Bartlet(t), Bate(s), Bateson, Bateman, Batcock, Batkin, Batt(s), Batson, Batty*. In Ireland *Bartholomew* is used as an equivalent of Irish *Portholan*.

BARTHOLOMEUS Cur 1196, HR 1273, FA 1303.
BARTHOLOMEW HR 1273.
BARTELMEU HR 1273, 14th C Legendary.
BARTEL, BERTOL, BARTLY HR 1273.
BARTELOT HR 1273.
TOLY, THOLY HR 1273.
BERTYLMEW Coventry Mysteries 15th C.

Basil (m.): Greek βασίλειος 'kingly', the name of one of the great doctors of the Church, St. Basil the Great (329–79), brother of St. Gregory. The name has always been more common in the East than in the West, but it is found in England from the end of the 12th C. The Tractarians revived its use in the 19th C. See also BASILIA.

BASILIUS Cur 1196.
BASIL HR 1273.
BASILL St. Mary at Hill Reg 1486.

Basilia, Basilie (f.): now obsolete, but very common in England and France in the 12th and 13th C. It may be a f. form of the name *Basil* (q.v.), formed at a comparatively late date, or may have been taken from the name of an early Saint *Basilla*; but as *Basil* was at no time a common name in the West, and as St. *Basilla* was a very obscure saint whose cult was never of any great importance, the popularity of *Basilia* remains something of a mystery. The usual English form of the name was probably *Basil*, though the French form *Basilie* sometimes occurs (cf. *Denis*, *Denise*). *Basilia* occurs only in Latin documents. The surnames *Bassil*(*l*), *Bazell*, *Basley*, *Basely*, *Bazley*, are derived from it and testify to its former popularity.

BASILIA Cur 1187–1220 *passim*, HR 1273 *passim*.
BASSILLY Clerkenwell 1665.

Bastian, see SEBASTIAN.

Bat, see BARTHOLOMEW.

Bathsheba (f.): Hebrew 'daughter of satiety', 'voluptuous', the name of the wife of Uriah and afterwards of David. It occurs occasionally as a christian name in the Middle Ages in the form *Barsabe*, and more frequently after the Reformation, often as *Bathshua*, the form of the name in the Authorized Version of the Book of Chronicles.

Beata (f.) [bēā′ta]: f. of Latin *beatus* 'happy'. There was a St. *Beata* martyred in France under Aurelian, and it was possibly after her that the name was occasionally used in England from the 12th to the 18th C, when it seems to have died out.

Beatrix, Beatrice [bē′atriks, bē′atris] (f.): (French *Béatrix*, Italian *Beatrice*, *Bice*, Spanish *Beatriz*); Latin 'bringer of joy', the name of a 4th-C Roman saint. It occurs as the name of a sub-tenant in DB, and was fairly common from the 12th to 13th C. The two forms of the name are relics of the old French *cas-sujet Béatrix*, and *cas-régime Béatrix*; both occur in England, but the second was the commoner; in 1487 it appears as *Beautrice*, a little later as *Betteresse* and in 1604 as *Bettris*. *Bettrys* is still the Welsh form. The diminutives *Beatty*, *Beton* were common in the Middle Ages and gave rise to various surnames. *Beaten* occurs in Cornwall as late as the 17th C. The name went quite out of fashion in the 17th and 18th C, and its revival in the later part of the 19th C was probably due to its many literary associations—Dante's *Beatrice* Portinari, Shakespeare's *Beatrice* in *Much Ado about Nothing*, and Thackeray's *Beatrix* Esmond. The name is not now generally abbreviated; when it is, it is usually to *Bee* or *Trix(ie)*; occasionally, in the Italian mode, to *Bice*. It is interesting to note that the vulgar modern pronunciation of the name as a disyllable, and abbreviation of it to *Beat*, closely correspond to the medieval vernacular pronunciation.

BEATRIX Reg 1076–84, Cur 1187–1215, FA 1346.
BEATRICIA HR 1273.
BEAUTRICE St. Mary at Hill 1487.
BETRYS, BETTE Coventry Mysteries 15th C.
BETE or BETUNE *Prompt Parv c.* 1440.
BETON Yorks Poll Tax 1379.
BEATEN Cornish Reg 1637.
BETTRICE *Pills to Purge Melancholy* 1684.

Bedelia (f.): this obscure name is used in Ireland as a genteel substitute for Bridget [see also DELIA], and is also used in the USA.

Bee, see BEATRIX, BRIDGET.

Belinda (f.): Old German *Betlindis*; the second element is the Old German *lindi*, 'a snake', which formed the second element of a very great number of f. names; the meaning of the first element is uncertain. The name was perpetuated in the Charlemagne romances as that of Orlando's wife, but was not taken into ordinary use. Pope's use of it for the heroine of his *Rape of the Lock*, and Tate's in *Dido and Aeneas*, started a literary fashion, and it was occasionally used as a christian name in the 18th and 19th C (e.g. Maria Edgeworth's successful novel *Belinda* 1801).

Bell (f.): used from the 13th C onwards as a pet-name for *Isabel* (q.v.).

Bella (f.): an abbreviation for *Isabella* (q.v.).

Benedict, Bennet (m.): (French *Benoît,* Italian *Benedetto,* Spanish *Benito*). Latin *benedictus* 'blessed', the name of St. *Benedict,* the founder of the Benedictine Order (490–*c.* 542). It is not found as a christian name in England before the Conquest, but it soon afterwards became common, and a measure of its popularity is to be found in the number of common surnames derived from it, such as *Benn, Benson, Bennet*(*t*), as well as the rarer *Benedict.* The usual form of the name from the 12th to the 18th C (e.g. Dr. Johnson's friend *Bennet* Langton) was *Bennet* from the Old French *Beneoit, Benoi*(*s*)*t,* and Prompt Parv gives *Benet,* and Godstow *Bennet* as the English form of *Benedict.* There is also some evidence for an English form *Benedick,* derived directly from the Latin, e.g. the surnames *Benedick, Bendixson,* and Shakespeare's *Benedick* in *Much Ado about Nothing.* In modern times *Bennet* has fallen out of general use, but *Benedict* is occasionally met with, especially among Roman Catholics.

BENEDICTUS Cur 1167, HR 1273, Poll Tax 1379.
BENEDICT or BENETT HR 1273.
BENEYT HR 1273.
BENEDICUS HR 1273.

Benedicta (f.): (French *Benoîte,* Italian *Benedetta,* Spanish *Benita*); f. of Latin *benedictus* 'blessed'. Probably as a rule simply a f. form of *Benedictus,* the man's name, though there are one or two obscure saints *Benedicta.* It is found in England from the beginning of the 13th C. In Latin documents it appears as *Benedicta,* but in English ones it is the same as the m. name, i.e. *Bennet.* Lyford 1655 gives *Benet* or *Benedicta,* and *Bennitt* is found as a woman's name as late as 1690. The Latin form of the name was revived at the end of the 19th C, and lately the Spanish *Benita* has been introduced by way of America.

BENEDICTA Cur 1205, FA 1316.

Benjamin (m.): the youngest son of Jacob was originally named *Benoni* 'son of my sorrow', but later *Benjamin,* literally 'son of the south', interpreted as 'son of the right hand' (Gen. xxxv. 18). The name occurs very rarely in the Middle Ages, but came into general

use in England after the Reformation. It was very common from
the 17th to 19th C, but suffered a decline, like other Biblical
names, at the beginning of the present century. It is a name which
lends itself naturally to abbreviation, and *Ben* has at all times
been the form of the name in ordinary use. *Benny* seems to be
exclusively Jewish. In Ireland *Benjamin* frequently represents
Berihert, the name of a Saxon saint whose cult flourished in
Ireland. It is well established in certain families.

Bennet, see BENEDICT, BENEDICTA.

Berengaria (f.): f. of *Berenger* (q.v.). The queen of Richard I
was named *Berengière*, which was latinized as *Berengaria*. The
name did not take root in England, but there have been children
named *Berengaria* in Southampton in the present century after
the well-known transatlantic liner of that name.

Berenger (m.) [bĕr'enjĕr]: Old German *Beringaer*, *Beringer*, compound of *berin* 'a bear', *ger* 'a spear'; the name of one of the
paladins in the Charlemagne romances. *Berengerius* occurs in DB,
and it was in fairly common use throughout the 12th and 13th C,
usually in the form *Bereng(i)er*, but the shortened form *Benger* occurs
as early as 1201. The name died out in general use after the 14th C,
but has been used down to the present day in a few families.

BERENGERIUS DB 1086.
BERENGARIUS Pipe Roll 1159.
BERENGER Cur 1201, HR 1273.
BERENGERUS FA 1285.
BENGER Cur 1201.

Berenice (f.) [bĕrenī'sĕ]: Macedonian form of Greek Φερενίκη,
'bringer of victory'. The name was borne by a 4th-C Syrian
martyr, but was not used in England until after the Reformation,
when it was occasionally employed on account of its occurrence
(in the form *Bernice*) in Acts xxv. 13. See also VERONICA.

Bernadette (f.) [bĕrnadet']: French f. diminutive of *Bernard*
(q.v.), which has gained wider currency from St. *Bernadette*
Soubirous (1844–79) of Lourdes. The name is sometimes used in
England by Roman Catholics.

D

Bernard (m.): Old German *Berinhard,* compound of *berin* 'a bear', *hard* 'stern'. The cognate Old English name was *Beornheard* (Old English *beorn* having acquired the sense brave, noble). *Bernard* was introduced into England at the Norman Conquest, and occurs in DB as the name of one tenant-in-chief and several sub-tenants. It is also given as the name of two tenants holding TRE, and though these may have been English *Beornheards,* it is more probable that they were of continental origin. It was a common name from the 12th C onwards, often in the English forms *Barnard, Barnet,* which were usual until the 15th C. For the development of *Barnet* cf. *Arnet* from *Arnold, Barret* from *Berold.* The influence of St. *Bernard* of Clairvaux (1091-1153) may have had something to do with the popularity of the name, but it was well established on the Continent before his time. Its use declined after the Reformation though it survived in some families. Camden says: 'It hath been most common in the house of *Brus,* of *Connington* and *Exton.*' It was revived in the 19th C, probably by Tractarian influence. The diminutive *Bernie* is used in America.

BERNARDUS DB 1086, Cur 1186-1219.
BARNARD 15th C Brut.
BERNARD HR 1273.

Bert, Bertie (m.): the somewhat plebeian *Bert* is the usual diminutive of *Albert* (q.v.). *Bertie,* on the other hand, is more often from *Herbert* or *Bertram* (qq.v.), but both may be used for any name ending in *-bert,* e.g. *Cuthbert.*

Bertha (f.): (French *Berthe,* German *Bertha,* Italian *Berta*); primarily a Frankish name, a pet-form of some of the many names in *berhta* (Old English *beorht*) 'bright'. It was a favourite with the Carolings, having been the name of the mother of Charlemagne. The only occurrence in England before the Norman Conquest is *Bercta,* daughter of Charibert and queen of *Æthelbert,* King of Kent. After the Norman Conquest it was in regular though not frequent use, often appearing in the form *Berta.* It does not appear to have been much used after about the beginning of the 14th C, though Lyford 1655 gives it in his list of christian names. It came back into use with other old names in the 19th C,

one of the earliest to use it being the poet Southey, one of whose
daughters was named *Bertha*.

BERTHA, BERTA Cur 1205–15.
BERTA Werburga 1513.

Bertram (m.): (Latin *Bertramus*, German *Bertram*, French
Bertrand, Spanish *Beltran*); Old German *Berahthraben*, compound of *berhta* 'bright' and *hraben* 'raven'; introduced into
England at the Conquest (*Bertrannus* occurs in DB). The French
form of the name, *Bertran(d)*, is much less common than *Bertram*,
Bartram, which occur from the end of the 12th C. For the form
Bartram, which survives as a surname, cf. *Barnard* from *Bernard*.
Bertie is the usual diminutive.

BERTRANNUS DB 1086.
BERTRAM Cur 1198–1215.
BERTERAM HR 1273.
BARTREM Poll Tax 1379.
BERTRAN Lyford 1655.

Beryl (f.): Greek βήρυλλος (of doubtful etymology, see OED s.v.),
the name of a precious stone. Its use as a christian name seems to
be modern; CMY does not give it and no earlier example has
come to light.

Bessie, Beth, Betsy, Betty, see ELIZABETH.

Bethia (f.) [bĕthĭ'ă]: Hebrew *bith-yah* 'daughter (i.e. worshipper)
of Jehovah', the name of a daughter of Pharaoh and wife of Mered
(1 Chron. iv). The name appears in the Septuagint as βετθία, in
the Vulgate as *Bethia*, and in the Authorized Version as *Bithiah*.
It is found in use as a christian name from the 17th C, being most
popular in Scotland, possibly from its likeness to the Gaelic
Beathag, a derivative of *beath* 'life'.

Bevis (m.) [bē'vis]: Frankish *Bobo*, *Bovo* (cognate with Old
English *Bobba*) became French *Beuves* (cf. *Eudes* from *Eudo*, *Ives*
from *Ivo*) by the addition of a final *s* to mark the nominative case,
and in England, where the name was introduced at the Norman
Conquest, it became *Beves* or *Bevis*, and was not uncommon in

the 12th and 13th C. The popular romance of Sir *Bevis* of Hampton no doubt helped to keep it in use. Lyford 1655 gives a characteristically fanciful etymology '*Beavis*, Beautifull, Fr. as some will have it'. Richard Jefferies's novel *Bevis, the story of a boy* (1882) has been responsible for a slight revival of the name.

Bianca, see BLANCH(E).

Bice [bĕ'chĕ], see BEATRICE.

Biddy, see BRIDGET.

Bill(y), see WILLIAM.

Blanch(e) (f.): French f. of the adjective *blanc* 'white'. There were several saints *Candida*, and *Blanche*, which seems to have originated in Navarre and Castile, represents a translation of the Latin name. Candida was in some cases a translation of a Celtic name, e.g. *Guenolé*. There is, in the same way, some evidence that St. Candida was known in England as St. *Whyte*; thus Whitchurch Canonicorum was said to take its name from a chapel dedicated to St. *Whyte* (the fact that this is a false etymology is not relevant here). Similarly Chaucer says of his Duchess *Blaunche* 'And gode faire *Whyte* she hete'. One of the earliest examples of the name was *Blanca* of Navarre who married Sancho III of Castille (died 1156); her namesake and granddaughter (died 1252) married Louis VIII of France and became the mother of St. Louis. Her name, in the form *Blanch*, became fairly popular in France, and her granddaughter *Blanch* of Artois carried it to England, when she married Edmund, Earl of Lancaster (died 1296). Chaucer's *Duchess Blaunche*, the wife of John of Gaunt, was a great-granddaughter of *Blanch* of Artois. The name has never been common in England, but *Blaunch* occurs in the 15th C, and Lyford 1655 gives *Blanch* or *Blanchia*. Charles Lamb, writing about 1808, says '*Blanche* is out of fashion', and his sister bestowed it on the subject of a Cinquecento painting. They evidently regarded it as old-fashioned and romantic, and with other such names it had a revival of use during the 19th C. The Italian form *Bianca* is occasionally used in England.

Blase (m.): the etymology is obscure; there was a cognomen *Blasio* current in the Cornelian *gens*, and also one *Blaesus* in the Sempronian *gens*. *Blaesus* is Latin *blaesus*, 'splay-footed', 'deformed', 'stuttering', and *Blasio* may possibly be cognate with it. The cult of St. *Blasius*, Bishop of Sebaste, martyred in 316 and patron saint of wool-workers, was widely diffused in the Middle Ages, and was naturally popular in England where the wool trade was of so much importance. The only relic of the trade in Romsey, Hants (once a wool staple), is an inn called the *Bishop Blaise*. *Blase* or *Blaze* survived the Reformation and is found occasionally in the 17th C. The French form of the name was *Blaise* (e.g. *Blaise* Pascal) and the Spanish *Blas* (e.g. Gil *Blas*).

Blodwen (f.): a Welsh name from *blod-yn* 'flower' and *gwen* (m. *gwyn*) 'white'.

Bob(by), see ROBERT.

Bonamy (m.): French *bon ami* 'good friend', a not uncommon surname in France. Peter Dobrée of Guernsey in 1751 married Rachael *Bonamy*, daughter and heiress of Peter *Bonamy* of that island. Since that time *Bonamy* has been regularly used as a christian name in the Dobrée family and in others connected with them by marriage, e.g. *Bonamy* Price, the Victorian economist. [*Ex inf.* Prof. Bonamy Dobrée.]

Boniface (m.): Latin *bonifacius* 'well-doer', the name of a 3rd-C saint martyred at Tarsus, and adopted by a series of popes, beginning with Boniface I (418–22); it was given by Pope Gregory II, in 719, to St. Winfrid or Winfrith (680–755), the Apostle of the Germans. It occurs in England as a christian name from the 13th C, but did not long survive the Reformation, the latest example noted being *Bonyface* Tateham whose name occurs in a list of Roman recusants 1604. It became a surname and was given by Farquhar to the innkeeper in his play *The Beaux' Stratagem*, 1707, whence it was taken into use as a general term for an innkeeper. It may be noted that the name *Bonchurch* in the Isle of Wight, which is sometimes stated to be an abbreviated form of

Boniface church, has nothing to do with this name; it was Old English *bana cerce*, the first element probably being Old English *bana* 'murderer'.

BONIFACIUS Cur 1207, HR 1273.
BONYFACE Cornhill Reg 1543.
BONEFACE Ox Univ Reg 1456.

Boris (m.) [bŏ'rĭs]: a favourite Russian name, said to signify 'fight'; occasionally used, like other Russian names, in England in the present century.

Botolf (m.): Old German *Bodoloff*, *Bodenolf*, *Bodolev*, an uncommon name of doubtful, possibly Slavonic, origin. St. *Botolf* or *Botulf* (died 680) is said to have first introduced the Benedictine rule into England, though it did not take root until three centuries later. *Boston* Lincs. is *Botulf's stone*, and *Botolphs* Sussex is also named after the saint. It is of rare occurrence as a christian name. *Botolfe* Thomas was baptized at Trull (Som.) in 1551.

Brenda (f.): this is a Shetland name, possibly a f. form of the common Norse *Brand*, which is still current in Iceland and was in use in England until the 12th C. The present wide diffusion of the name *Brenda* is probably due to Scott's use of it for one of the two heroines of his novel *The Pirate* (1821). In Ireland it is nowadays regarded as a f. form of *Brendan*.

Brendan (m.): the name of a 6th-C Irish saint, frequently used in recent times in Ireland. The modern Irish spelling *Brenainn* indicates the pronunciation. Professor Max Forster derives it from Old Irish *brēn* 'stinking' and *find* 'hair'.

Brian (m.): a pet form of some name compounded with British or Irish *bre* 'hill' (cf. 9th-C Breton names *Brior*, *Brian*, *Briunal*). *Brian* or *Bryan* has from early times been a favourite in Ireland on account of the national hero *Brian Boroimhe*; but it was, during the Middle Ages, equally popular in England, where it was introduced from Brittany at the time of the Norman Conquest. *Brian* is the name of 2 sub-tenants in DB, and for several centuries it was a favourite, as the many common surnames derived from it testify (e.g. *Brian(t)*, *Bryan(t)*, *Briand*, *Bryanson*). It survived in Yorks., Westmorland, Cheshire, Lancs. until the 18th C, but gradually fell into disuse and came to be regarded as an exclusively Irish name. It is still used in Brittany and has come back into use in England during the present century.

BRIENUS DB 1086, Cur 1199.
BRIANUS Cur 1199–1219.
BRIAN HR 1273.

Brice (m.): St. *Britius* or *Brice*, Bishop of Tours 444, was responsible for the vogue of this name in England and France in the Middle Ages. It is probably of Celtic origin. *Brice* and the diminutive *Bricot* were fairly common in England in the 13th and 14th C and have left traces in the surnames *Brice*, *Bryce*, *Bryson*, *Brisson*, *Bricot*.

BRICE HR 1273.
BRICEUS FA 1316–46.

Bride, see BRIDGET.

Bridget (f.): the English form, derived through the Old French *Brigette*, from latinized *Brigitta*, adapted from Old Irish *Brigit*, later *Brigid* (modern Irish *Brighid* pronounced *brī'id*). The etymology of the name is a primitive Celtic *briganti 'the high one'. *Brighid* was the name of a Celtic fire goddess, and many of her attributes were incorporated in the legends which gathered round the name of the historical St. *Brighid* (453–523). The cult of St. *Brighid* was very popular in England as well as in Ireland. In English she was usually called *Bride* or *Bryde*, which represents the Irish *Brighde*, the genitive case of *Brighid*; thus a 14th-C Legendary has *seinte Bride*, Godstow 1450 gives *Bryde* as the English of *Brigida* (cf. also *Bridewell* in London). The earliest occurrence which has been noted in England as a christian name is in 1563 (*Brigitte*), and it does not seem to have come into common use in Ireland until the 17th or 18th C. St. *Brighid* was known as 'the Mary of the Gael', and it is possible that her name, like that of the Blessed Virgin, was considered too sacred for ordinary use.

It is significant that *Mary* came into general use in Ireland at about the same time as *Brighid*. They are now and have long been the two commonest names in that country. The common pet-form *Biddy* displays the same process of formation as *Fanny* from *Frances*, *Kit* and *Kester* from *Christopher*. The name of the Swedish St. *Brigitte* or *Birgitte* (1303–73), which is usually translated *Bridget* in English, was an independent Swedish name. French and German *Brigitte* may represent either the Irish or the Swedish name, as the cults of both saints had a considerable extension.

Brilliana (f.): Sir Edward Conway, 1st Lord Conway, and for some time governor of the *Brill* in Holland (held by the English 1585–1616), named one of his daughters (born *c.* 1600) *Brilliana* after the seat of his office. She later married, as his 3rd wife, Sir Robert Harley, and her name was used for several generations in the Harley family and spread by marriage into others. It occurs as late as 1844, and may still be in use. Lady Harley's sister was also given a name, *Helegenwach* (Dutch = Saints' lane), commemorative of her father's service in the Netherlands. She married Sir W. Smyth of Hill Hall, Essex, and had children, but it is not surprising that her very uneuphonious name should not have been perpetuated as her sister's more pleasing one was.

Britannia (f.): occasionally used as a woman's name in the 18th C.

Bronwen (f.): Welsh, 'white breast'; a common Welsh woman's name.

Bruce (m.): the use of this as a christian name in Scotland and to some extent in England appears to be of recent growth; CMY does not mention it. It is the surname of Robert de Bruce (1274–1329), liberator and King of Scotland. The family of *de Bruce* or *de Braose* took its name from *Braose* (now *Brieuse*) near Falaise in Normandy. It was spelt in various ways during the Middle Ages, when the family was a powerful one with branches all over England; some of the surviving forms are *Bruce, Browse, Brewis*.

Brunhild, Brynhild (f.) [broon'hild]: the name of one of the Valkyries in ancient German legend, probably a compound of Old German *brunnia* 'corslet' and *hild* 'battle'. It was introduced into England in the last century by the cult of Wagner.

Bruno (m.): Old German *brun* 'brown'; has survived in Germany, probably on account of St. *Bruno*, Archbp. of Cologne 953–65, and of *Bruno* of Cologne (1030–1101), founder of the Carthusian Order. *Bruno* occurs in England from time to time (e.g. *Bruno* Ryves, Dean of Chichester 1646), probably always as a borrowed name. But the cognate Old English *brun* was also used as a christian name both before and after the Norman Conquest until at least the end of the 13th C, and was probably the ancestor of some examples of the surname *Brown* (most of which, however, come from the common nickname *le brun* 'the brown') and certainly of the less common *Brownson*.

Bryan, see BRIAN.

Brynhild, see BRUNHILD.

C

Cadwallad(e)r (m.): Welsh *cad* 'battle' and *gwaladr* 'leader', in use in Wales from at least the 7th C.

Caesar (m.) [se'zar]: a cognomen in the Julian *gens*, of which the most famous member was Caius Iulius Caesar, after whom the name *Caesar* was borne as a title, first by all Roman emperors and later by the heirs apparent to the emperors. The German *Kaiser* and Russian *Czar* are both derived from it. Various etymologies have been suggested; Pliny derives the name 'a caeso matris utero', Julius Caesar having been delivered by the operation now known as *Caesarian* section, but this obviously is no explanation of a name which was already in use. Another early explanation was that it was from *caesaries*, a fleece or head of hair, whilst a third connects it with *caesius* 'bluish-grey'. It is not improbable that the name is in fact not Roman but Etruscan in origin. *Caesar* has been used occasionally as a christian name since the revival of classical nomenclature at the Renaissance. *Cesare* was fairly common in Italy in the 15th C (e.g. *Cesare* Borgia), and *César* has been used fairly often in France. There were two or three saints named *Caesarius* who may be partly responsible for its use in Latin countries. The earliest example noted in England is *Cesare* Adelmare (1558–1636), a Venetian who became physician to Queen Elizabeth and later dropped his patronymic, adopted the christian name of Julius, and in due course became *Sir Julius Caesar* and founder of a long line of physicians. A clergyman named *Cesar* Walpole died in 1613. *Caesar* Williamson was a Westminster scholar in 1627. Bardsley gives an example of a baby born in 1799, who was brought into the world by Caesarian section and bore, during his short life of 17 months, the names of *Julius Caesar* Thompson.

Caius, see GAIUS.

Caleb (m.) [kā'leb]: Hebrew 'bold', 'impetuous'. Used as a christian name after the Reformation (e.g. *Caleb* Willis, a Westminster scholar in 1585), and survived till the 19th C. It is still used in Scotland and the USA.

Camilla (f.): possibly of Etruscan origin; the name of the Queen of the Volsci, killed in battle by one of the followers of Aeneas (Virgil's *Aeneid* bk. vii). The name occurs in a Curia Regis Roll under the date 1205, but has not been noted between that date and the late 18th C. Mme D'Arblay's novel *Camilla* (1796) may have contributed to its later use.

Candace (f.): *Candace* appears to have been a dynastic title of the Queens of Ethiopia (cf. Pliny vi. 29, 'regnare feminam Candacen, quod nomen multis iam annis ad reginas transiit'). It occurs in Acts viii. 27 and has been used occasionally as a christian name since the 17th C. Mr. Collett of Woodbridge, in whose family the name has been used for at least 250 years, tells me that it was spelled *Candase* in 1675, and is pronounced *can'dis*.

Candida (f.): Latin 'white'; the name of a 1st-C Neapolitan saint supposed to have been cured by St. Paul. See further under BLANCH(E). The name does not appear to have been used in England until recently, after its use by G. B. Shaw for the heroine of his play *Candida* (1898).

Canute, see KNUD.

Caradoc (m.): Welsh *Caradawg* 'amiable'. The British name was *Caratācos* of which '*Caractacus*' was a latinized form. A favourite christian name in Wales (cf. the surname *Craddock*). The equivalent Irish name *Carthac(h)* is often rendered in English by *Carthage*.

Carl (m.): = German *Karl*, see CHARLES. *Carl* is fairly common in USA where it is now used by people of all races.

Carmel (f.): Hebrew 'the garden', the name of a mountain in Palestine. The church and convent on the mountain, founded by St. Louis, are dedicated to the Blessed Virgin who, according to legend, frequented the neighbourhood with her infant Son. *Carmel* (*Carmen* in Spanish) is used as a christian name by Roman Catholics (cf. *Loretta*, *Lourdes*, &c.).

Carol (m.): Anglo-Irish for Irish *Cathaoir* and *Cathal*, the latter of which is also often anglicized as *Charles*. Also an anglicization of Czech *Karel*, Dutch *Carolus* (see CHARLES); very common in USA and now becoming naturalized in England.

Carol (f.): this name, a favourite in the Southern States of the USA, is now, probably through the influence of the cinema, spreading to England. It is presumably a shortened form of *Caroline* (q.v.), but see also CAROL (m.).

Carola (f.) [kǎ'rŏlǎ]: one of the f. forms of *Charles* (see also CAROLINE and CHARLOTTE). A *Carola* Harsnet is recorded in 1670. It was probably coined by Royalists in the middle of the 17th C. It has never become common.

Caroline (f.): originally an Italian f. form (*Carolina*) of *Charles* (*Carlo*), which spread to south Germany and was introduced to England by George II's queen, Caroline of Brandenburg-Anspach. It became a favourite English christian name in the 18th C. The usual diminutive is *Carrie*, but *Caro* (e.g. Lady *Caroline* Lamb) and *Lina* are also used. There is an isolated example of its use as a man's name; the Rev. *Caroline* Robert Herbert was a godson of Queen Caroline. The spelling *Carolyn* has recently come into fashion.

Casimir (m.): Polish *Kazimir*, 'proclamation of peace'. The name spread from Poland, by intermarriage, to some of the German royal houses, and *Casimir* is not infrequent in France. It was sometimes, like *Ladislas*, used in England in the 19th C when there was much sympathy for the national aspirations of Poland.

Caspar, see JASPER.

Cassandra (f.): Greek Κασσάνδρα, the name of the prophetic daughter of Priam and Hecuba. The Trojan war was a favourite theme of medieval poets and romancers, and medieval sympathies seem to have been entirely with the Trojans; we thus find *Cassandra*, like *Hector* (q.v.), a common christian name in the 13th and 14th C. It is first recorded about 1207, and though it became less common in the 15th and subsequent centuries, it never quite died out. In the 17th C it is found in Lincs, sometimes in the form *Cassandry*. The most notable later example is *Cassandra* Elizabeth *Austen*, the elder sister of Jane Austen, who was named after her mother, *Cassandra* Leigh of Stoneleigh, Warwick, in whose family it had been used from at least 1690. Dr. R. W. Chapman suggests that the popularity of La Calprenède's romance *Cassandre*, which was translated in the 17th C, may have helped to keep the name in use. The surnames *Cash*, *Cass*, *Case*, *Casson* are derived from the diminutive *Cass*.

CASSANDRA Cur 1207, 1210–13, FA 1302–3, HR 1273.
CASSE HR 1273.
CASSANDER Poll Tax 1379.

Catharine, Catherine, see KATHARINE.

Catriona, see KATHARINE.

Cecil (m.): Latin *Caecilius*, the name of a Roman plebeian *gens*, from the root of *caecus* 'blind'. There was a 3rd-C saint *Caecilius*, and *Cecil* was not uncommon in England in the Middle Ages, though much less common than the corresponding f. name. The present widespread revival dates back only to the end of the last century, and is a use of the family name of the Marquis of Salisbury.

Cecil (f.), see CECILIA.

Cecilia, Cecily, Cicely (f.): (French *Cécile*, German *Cäcilie*); Latin *Caecilia*, f. of *Caecilius* (see CECIL). St. *Cecilia*, martyred *c.* 177, was a Roman and presumably belonged to this family. She is mentioned in the Canon of the Mass and was regarded as the patroness of music; her name became a favourite one in the Western Church. It was introduced into England at the Norman Conquest (the Conqueror had a daughter of the name, Abbess of Caen), and soon became a favourite. The usual English form of the name was *Cicely* or *Sisley*. Lyford 1655 gives *Sisley* as an equivalent of *Cicely*. It was also sometimes abbreviated to *Cecil* (e.g. *Cecil* Matthews who in 1709 married the 1st Lord Talbot, and whose name has continued in use amongst her descendants). *Celia* is also sometimes an abbreviation of *Cecilia*, and *Sela, Sely* occur in 1221. The Latin form *Cecilia* was adopted in the late 18th C, probably in part on account of Mme D'Arblay's novel of that name (1782). *Sis, Ciss* were the diminutives of the name in the days of its general popularity (cf. Corbet's 'When Tom came home from labour, or Cis from milking rose'). See also CELIA, SHEILA.

CECILIA Cur 1197–1219, HR 1273, FA 1428.
CECILLE HR 1273.
CECELYA FA 1303.
CECILLIA FA 1346.
CECILIE Godstow 1450. CYCALYE, CYCLY, SYCILY Yorks Rec 1604.
SISCELLA 1656.

Cedric (m.) [sĕ'drik]: this now not uncommon name seems to have been invented by Sir Walter Scott for one of the characters in *Ivanhoe*, '*Cedric* the Saxon'. It was probably a mistake of Scott's for *Cerdic*, the name of the traditional founder of the West Saxon kingdom. *Cerdic* is itself a puzzling name, for it has the appearance of a Celtic rather than a Teutonic word and may be from *Caratacos* (see CARADOC). *Cedric* came into fashion as a christian name after the publication in 1886 of *Little Lord Fauntleroy* (it was the christian name of the hero of that book), and seems to have settled down to permanent use, unlike the hero's clothes, which were also once popular.

Celeste (f.): Latin *caelestis* 'heavenly'. There was a St. *Celesta*, who no doubt sponsored the name, which is not uncommon in France. *Celestine*, which also occurs, is probably a diminutive of *Celeste*, and not taken from the papal name *Celestinus*. *Celeste* and *Celestine* are occasionally used in England. The m. name *Celestine* was formerly used to render the Gaelic *Gillespie*.

Celia (f.): the Italian name *Celia* is from the name of the *Caelian gens* and from it was derived the French *Célie*, used chiefly in romances. The English name *Celia*, however, is probably as a rule a form of *Cecilia* (q.v.). Shakespeare's use of it for the cousin of Rosalind in *As You Like It* is responsible for its modern vogue as an independent christian name. See also SHEILA.

Ceridwen (f.) [kerĭd'wen]: Welsh goddess of poetic inspiration, a not uncommon name for girls in Wales. Professor Max Förster derives it from *ceiridd* a by-form of *cerdd* 'poetry', and *gwyn* (f. *gwen*) 'white', 'fair'.

Charis (f.) [kă'ris]: Greek χάρις 'grace'; its use as a christian name is subsequent to the Reformation (cf. *Alethea, Sophia*). Spenser's *Charissa* in the *Faerie Queene*, a latinized form of *Charis*, is also occasionally used.

Charity (f.): Old French *charité*, from Latin *caritatem*. Like other names of abstract qualities this came into use as a christian name after the Reformation, and was fairly common in the 17th C.

Faith, *Hope*, and *Charity* were sometimes given as names to triplets. *Cherry* is sometimes used as a pet name for *Charity* (e.g. in *The Beaux' Stratagem* 1707, and *Martin Chuzzlewit* 1843).

Charles (m.): (Latin *Carolus*, French *Charles*, Italian *Carlo*, Spanish *Carlos*, German, Scandinavian *Karl*, Dutch, Slav *Karel*): Old German *carl* (Old English *ceorl*) 'a man'. *Karl* or *Carl* was latinized as *Carolus*, whence the French *Charles*. The great popularity of the name in France and Germany was chiefly due to the renown of the Emperor *Charles* the Great, or *Charlemagne*. *Charles* was introduced to England by the Normans, but did not become common, though it is occasionally found from the 12th C, often in the form *Carle*, and gave rise to the surnames *Charles* and *Charlet* (from a diminutive). Prompt Parv gives it as *Charlys*. The use of the name in the house of Stuart did something to increase its popularity amongst Royalists in the 17th C and Jacobites in the 18th C, but it was not until the 19th C that it became really common, often in the pet-form *Charlie*. It was hardly used in Ireland until the 17th C, when it began to be used to translate various native names such as *Cathal* and *Cathaoir*. It is also used to translate Gaelic *Teàrlach*, the same name as the Irish *Turlough* (see TERENCE).

KAROLUS Cur 1205, 1207.
CARLE Cur 1205, 1210.
CHARLES HR 1273.

Charlotte (f.) [sharl'ot]: Italian *Carlotta*, f. form of *Carlo* (*Charles*); first given as a name to *Carlotta* (French *Charlotte*) of Savoy, wife of Louis XI of France. *Charlotte* was introduced into England in 1626 by the marriage of the 7th Earl of Derby to *Charlotte* de la Trémouille, whose name is usually spelt *Charlet* in contemporary records (*Caroletta* is also found in the 17th C). The name, however, remained rare until the marriage of George III in 1761 with *Charlotte Sophia* of Mecklenburg-Strelitz, who made the name popular as her predecessor had made that of *Caroline*. The popularity of the name, with the romantically inclined, may have been partly due to its use by Goethe for the heroine of his *Sorrows of Werther* (1774), and later to the Princess

Charlotte, the daughter of George IV. The 17th-C spelling *Charlet* shows that the pronunciation of the name at that time was much the same as it is now; but there is some evidence that early in the 19th C it was sometimes made a trisyllable. In a correspondence in N & Q in 1908 Henry Bradley recalled that old people in Sheffield in his youth spoke of *Charlottē* Street; and another correspondent said he had quite recently heard a woman addressed as *Charlotty*. Great *Charlotte* Street, Liverpool, is still sometimes so pronounced. The usual abbreviation of the name is *Lottie* or *Lotty* (sometimes *Totty*), but *Charlie* is also occasionally used.

Charmian (f.) [kar'mean]: occasionally used as a christian name, being taken from Shakespeare's play of *Antony and Cleopatra*, where he gives it to one of Cleopatra's slaves. In Plutarch (Shakespeare's ultimate source) the name is χάρμιον, 'a little joy', a neuter diminutive of χάρμα 'joy'; Greek slaves were often given neuter names.

Chaunc(e)y (m.): a surname of French origin, probably from a place-name, found in England from the 13th C; it was the name of the 2nd President of Harvard, Charles *Chauncey* (1592–1672), some of whose pupils gave it to their children as a christian name, whence it has gradually come into general use as a christian name in the USA.

Cherry, see CHARITY.

Chloe (f.) [klō'ĕ]: Greek χλόη 'a young green shoot', an epithet of Demeter. St. Paul (1 Cor. i. 11) mentions a woman of Corinth named *Chloe*, and the name was adopted, like most of those which occur in the Epistles, in the 17th C. It is still a favourite with American negroes, but its main use has been by pastoral poets.

Chloris (f.): from Greek χλωρός, 'blooming', 'fresh'; given as a christian name by Lyford 1655, but there is little evidence for its use, except by poets in the 17th and 18th C.

Chris, see CHRISTABEL, CHRISTIAN(A), CHRISTOPHER.

Christabel (f.): the earliest occurrence of this name is in the Middle English romance of *Sir Eglamour d'Artois*, and it also comes in some versions (e.g. Percy's) of the *Ballad of Sir Cauline*. It was doubtless from Percy that Coleridge took it for his own poem. *Christable* occurs as a christian name in 1561, *Christabell* in 1604, *Christobelle* in 1687, *Christabel* in Cornwall in 1727; *Christobella* Lady Saye and Sele died in 1789 aet. 94. The etymology is puzzling, but it seems to be a compound of *Christus* and Latin *bella*, cf. *Dulcibel, Claribel, Rosabel*, &c. (qq.v.). Other examples of the use of *Christ* in compound names are the Old German (7th–9th C) *Cristemia, Cristehildis, Cristemberga*. The modern use of the name is probably, as a rule, consciously derived from Coleridge's poem. It is sometimes abbreviated to *Chris(sy)* or *Christy*.

Christian (m.): Latin *christianus* 'a christian'. The name is found from about 1200, but has never been common in this country. See further under CHRISTIAN(A) (f.).

Christian(a) (f.): (French, German *Christiane*): f. of Latin *christianus* 'christian'. The common noun and adjective *christian* are found in England only from the 16th C, the earlier word being the Old English *christen*. The name *Christian*, however, together with its Latin form *Christiana* (occasionally *Christiania*) are found from the end of the 12th C, and are rather commoner than *Christina* (q.v.) which is derived from the Old English *christen*. Prompt Parv 1450 gives *Kyrstyan* or *Kristyan* as the English for *Christiana*, and *Kirsty* is still used as a pet-name in Scotland. *Christian* was still common in the 17th C, but *Christiana* is now more usual, and *Christina* is commoner than either. *Christiania* is an occasional variant. The surnames *Christian, Christie, Christy, Christison* are among those derived from it. It is sometimes abbreviated to *Chrissy* or *Chris*.

CHRISTIANA Cur 1199, FA 1285, 1303, Cov 1424.
CRISTIANE Poll Tax 1379.
CHRISTIAN Cov 1424, Chester 1562.

Christina, Christine (f.): from Old English *christen*, 'christian'. The earliest example of the name noted is *Christina*, sister of

Edgar Atheling, who was born in Hungary and fl. 1086. It has been in use in England ever since but, until recently, was not as common as *Christian* (q.v.).

CRISTINA HR 1273, FA 1346.

Christmas (m., f.): this, like other names of Church festivals, was sometimes given to children born on that day (cf. *Pentecost, Easter,* &c.) and is found from the 13th C down to the present day. It gave rise to a not uncommon surname. It has now been largely replaced by *Noel* (q.v.).

Christopher (m.): (Latin *Christopherus,* French *Christophe,* Italian *Cristoforo,* Spanish *Cristoval, Cristobal,* German *Christoph*): Greek Χριστοφόρος, 'bearing Christ'. It was originally a word applied by Christians to themselves, meaning that they bore Christ in their hearts. St. *Christopher* was an early Christian martyr, to whose name was later attached the legend of a gigantic saint who carried the Christ-child across a river, and *Christopher* became an ordinary christian name. The sight of the image of St. *Christopher* was thought to be a protection from accidents and sudden death for the rest of the day ('Illa nempe die morte mala non morieris, Cristoferi sancti speciem quicumque tueris'), and it was therefore often depicted on the outside of houses and churches in Italy, Spain, and Germany. In England St. *Christopher* was, for the same reason, one of the commonest subjects for mural paintings inside churches. Always the patron of travellers, St. *Christopher* is now in Roman Catholic countries regarded as being the particular protector of motorists. Bardsley's earliest example of the name in England is of the 14th C, and he says he found none in the Hundred Rolls of 1273. There are, however, examples of the name in the Curia Regis Rolls for 1201 and 1220, though it is certainly uncommon until the 15th C when it becomes much more frequent (examples are *Christofre Crease* 1450, *Crysteffor Johnson* 1491, *Christouer Hobye* 1483). From the 16th C to the end of the 18th C the name was in fairly general use, often abbreviated to *Kester, Kit* (cf. the island of St. *Kitts*), or *Chris.* It suffered an eclipse in the 19th C, and CMY speaks as though it were little used in her time, but it has had a great revival in the present century. In Scotland the Lowland form of the name was apparently *C(h)rystal*, of which Black gives several examples. *Christopher* has often been used to render Gaelic *Gilcrist*.

CHRISTOPHERUS Cur 1201–3, 1220.
CRISTOFORUS Poll Tax 1379.
CRISTOFRE 14th-C Legendary, Linc 1450.
CHRISTOFUR St. Mary at Hill 1513.

Chrysogon (f.): Greek χρυσόγονος, 'goldborn'. St. *Chrysogonos*, a 4th-C saint, adviser of St. Anastasia, mentioned in the Canon of the Mass, was a man, and his name is found as a man's name (*Grisigion* Foule of Tenterden) in 1609. But it is more often found as a f. name, e.g. *Chrysogon* or *Grisigon* Stradling (*c.* 1550) of Co. Glamorgan, who married Anthony Porter of Aston Subedge, and whose christian name took root in the Cotswolds; later members of the Stradling family carried it to Essex and Somerset. The name is spelt variously *Chrysogon, Chrisoogone, Grisegond, Grisogonia, Grisigion, Grissecon*. It has not been noted in England earlier than the 16th C, and the reason for its use then is unknown.

Cicely, see CECILIA.

Cissy, see CECILIA.

Clara, Clare (f.): (French *Claire*, Italian *Chiara*): f. of Latin *clarus* 'bright', 'clear'; occurs in England from the beginning of the 13th C, in Latin as *Clara*, in English as *Clare*. It was apparently a f. form of *Clarus*, the name of at least two saints, a 3rd-C Bishop of Nantes and a 7th-C Norman saint; the latter gave his name to *St. Clair* in Normandy, from which came the well-known family of *St. Clair* or *Sinclair*. Later the popularity of the name was increased by St. *Clare* of Assisi (1193–1253), the friend of St. Francis and founder of the order of Poor Clares. *Clare*, though never common, is found in every century from the 13th onward. The latinized form *Clara* came into fashion in the 19th C, but both forms continued to be used.

CLARA Cur 1210, Poll Tax 1379.
CLARE Poll Tax 1379, Yorks Rec 1610, Lyford 1655.

Clarence (m.): the name of a dukedom created in 1362 for Lionel, 3rd son of Edward III, who had married the heiress of *Clare* in Suffolk. In Latin his title became *dux Clarensis* or *dux Clarenciae*. The title was later held by George, the brother of Edward IV and Richard III, and was revived for the 3rd son of George III, later William IV, and again for the elder son of Edward VII. It was probably after this last that *Clarence* came into use as a christian name at the end of the 19th C, but the hero of Maria Edgeworth's novel 'Helen' (1834) is named *Clarence* Harvey.

Claribel (f.): occurs in *The Tempest* as the name of the Queen of Tunis and appears to be formed on the analogy of *Christabel, Dowsabel, Mirabel,* &c.

Clarice (f.): apparently a French derivative of *Clara* (q.v.). It occurs in England as early as 1199 (*Claricia* in a Latin document), and was not uncommon in the 13th and 14th C in the forms *Clarice, Clarisse,* and gave rise to the surnames *Clarice, Claris, Clares,* and also, as Bardsley shows, *Clar(r)idge, Clardge, Clarges* (he gives an example of the same person referred to in a Hundred Roll of 1273 as *Claricia* and *Clarugge*). *Clarice* was popular on account of its occurrence in the romances, where it is the name of the wife of Rinaldo and sister of Huon of Bordeaux. The latinized form *Clarissa* was revived by Richardson in his novel *Clarissa Harlowe.*

CLARICIA Cur 1199, HR 1273, FA 1316, 1346, 1428.
CLARICE HR 1273.
CLARUGGE (or CLARICIA) HR 1273.
CLARISCIA Poll Tax 1379.

Clarimond (f.): Old French *Claremonde, Esclairmonde* occurs in various romances, notably in that of Huon of Bordeaux, and CMY states that *Clarimond* is found as a christian name in Devon in the 17th C. It is apparently a compound of Old German *munt* (Old English *mund*) 'protection', with Latin *clarus,* which was early borrowed by the Teutonic languages (cf. CLEREBOLD).

Clarinda (f.): this derivative of *Clare* is used by Spenser in his *Faerie Queene* and had a certain literary vogue in the 17th and 18th C. It was possibly confused with *Clorinda* which occurs in Tasso.

Clarissa, see CLARICE.

Claud(e) (m.): French, from Latin *Claudius*, the name of two famous Roman *gentes*, one patrician, the other plebeian, probably a derivative of *claudus* 'lame'. *Claude* has long been used in France, and it was adopted in the 16th C by the Hamilton family, who had French connexions, the first to bear the name being Lord *Claud* Hamilton (born 1543), Baron Paisley and ancestor of the Earls and Dukes of Abercorn, since whose time it has been used continuously in his family.

Claudia (f.): the f. form of the name of the Claudian *gens*, see CLAUD. *Claudia* is found in Lancashire in the late 16th C, probably taken from the 2nd epistle to Timothy where it occurs as the name of a Roman convert. The equivalent *Claude* has been used in France since Louis XII gave it to his daughter. The Welsh *Gladys* (q.v.) is said to be a form of the name.

Clemence, Clemency (f.): Latin *clementia* 'mildness', seems to have been used as a f. form of the man's name *Clement* (q.v.). From about 1200 *Clemence* (Latin *Clemencia*) is not uncommon in England; in the 16th C it appears as *Clemens*, later usually as *Clemency*, no doubt consciously equated with the abstract noun.

CLEMENCIA, CLEMENTIA Cur 1200, 1203, 1210, 1220.
CLEMENS Lincs 1534.
CLAMANCIA Owston Parish Reg 1676.

Clement (m.): Latin *clemens, -tis*, 'mild', 'merciful', the name of a saint, the first of the Apostolic Fathers and a disciple of St. Paul, and of many subsequent popes. St. *Clement* has over 40 church dedications in this country, and his name was a favourite one from the end of the 12th C until the Reformation; Bardsley gives some 15 surnames derived from it, including *Clement(s)*, *Clemens*, *Clemson*. The Tractarians revived the name in the 19th C, with reference rather to *Clement* of Alexandria than to the Pope. The diminutive *Clem* is found from the 13th C.

CLEMENS Cur 1199–1215.
CLEMENT HR 1273.
CLEM HR 1273.

Clementina, Clementine (f.): f. forms of *Clement* (q.v.), sometimes used in the 19th C. *Clemence* and *Clemency* (q.v.) were used earlier. *Clementine* has probably been killed by the song of that name.

Clerebold, Clarenbald (m.): this name, which was common from the 11th C to the 14th C in England, is also found in Old German in the 10th C as *Clarebald, Clarembald*. It is a compound of *klâr* (borrowed from Latin *clarus*) and *bald* 'bold'. In England it gave rise to the surnames *Claringbold, Clarabut*, &c.

CLEREBALD HR 1273.
CLERENBALD Pipe Roll 1160.

Clifford (m.): a surname derived from a place-name (there are several villages of this name). Its general use as a christian name appears to date from the last quarter of the 19th C.

Clive (m.): the surname of Robert *Clive* (1725–74), the great servant of the East India Company. The name is chiefly given as a christian name by those who have connexions with India, and was perhaps first used in this way by Thackeray in *The Newcomes* (1853–5).

Clodagh (f.): Irish, the name of a river in Tipperary; seems to have been first given as a christian name to a daughter of the Marquis of Waterford, now Lady Clodagh Anson, and has been fairly often used since.

Clorinda, see CLARINDA.

Clotilda (f.): Old German *Chlotichilda*, compound of *hloda* 'loud' and *hildi* 'battle', the name of the wife of Clovis (465–511), King of France, whom she converted to Christianity. *Clotilde* has remained in occasional use in France, and *Clotilda* is sometimes used by English Roman Catholics.

Cnut, see KNUD.

Colette (f.): French diminutive of *Nicole*, now chiefly known in this country as the pen-name of a contemporary French novelist.

but formerly not uncommon in England. It was latinized as *Coleta*
or *Colecta*, and gave rise to the surnames *Colet*, *Collett*, *Collect*.
Prompt Parv gives *Colette* as the English and *Colecta* as the Latin
form, and *Colet* is found as late as 1635 in Lincolnshire. It was
the name of the 15th-C reformer of the Poor Clares, who helped
to end the Great Schism of the West, and is much favoured in
modern Roman Catholic use.

COLETT HR 1273, Coventry Mysteries 15th C.
COLETTA FA 1316.
COLETA Poll Tax 1379.
COLLETTE Poll Tax 1379.
KALOTTE Langland *c.* 1360.

Colin (m.): French diminutive of *Col*, an abbreviation of *Nicholas*
(q.v.). *Colin* is found in England from 1200 onwards, but not
apparently as an independent name; it gave rise to the common
surnames *Collin(s)*, *Collinson*. Spenser's *Colin Clout* seems to
show that by the 16th C the name was regarded as a rustic nickname, and it gradually died out altogether. The Scottish *Colin*,
still in use (sometimes by English as well as Scots), is a different
name representing the Gaelic *Cailean*, which has been derived by
some from *coileán* a young dog, a youth, and hence a cadet. The
Irish form *Colán* has recently been revived.

COLINUS Cur 1200, HR 1273.
COLIN Poll Tax 1379.

Colum, Colm (m.): the Irish form of *Columba* (Latin 'dove'), the
name of, amongst others, St. *Columba* (521–97), the apostle of
the Picts, who was usually known as *Columcille*, 'Colum of the
Church'. See also MALCOLM.

Comfort (m., f.): occasionally used as a christian name after the
Reformation. A *Comfort* Dormer occurs in Bucks as recently as
1850.

Comyn (m.) [kŏm′in]: formerly a christian name in Ireland and
the Highlands of Scotland, but now usually a surname. It is Irish
Cuimin, a diminutive of *cam* 'crooked'.

Conal(l) (m.) [kŏn'al]: a common Irish name, derived from Old Celtic *Kuno-val-s* 'high-mighty'.

Conan (m.) [kō'nan in England, konawn' in Ireland]: probably derived from the Old Celtic root *kuno-*, 'high'. Traditionally the name of one of the early British Bishops of London, and later of several Celtic saints. One of them, *Conan* or *Kynan Meriadech*, was said to have led a band of fugitive Britons to Armorica and to have been the ancestor of the Dukes of Brittany. The name still survives in Brittany, and it was brought to England by Bretons after the Norman Conquest, and became a fairly common christian name from the 12th to 16th C, giving rise to the surnames *Conan, Con(n)ant, Connand, Conning, Connon.*

Conanus Cur 1199–1215.
Conan FF 13th C, HR 1273.
Conayn HR 1273.
Conandus FA 1428.
Conon Poll Tax 1379.

Conn, a common Irish name from Old Celtic *Kuno*.

Connie, see CONSTANCE.

Con(n)or (m.): Irish *Conc(h)ub(h)ar* 'high desire', a great name in Irish mythology, and for long a common christian name in Ireland, where it now survives mainly as a surname.

Conrad (m.): Old German *Conrad, Chonrad*, compound of *conja* 'bold' and *rad* 'counsel'. The name of a 10th-C saint, Bishop of Constance. This is essentially a German name, but has been occasionally used in England, the earliest example noted being *Conrad* Nye, rector of Foxley, Wilts, from 1436.

Constance, Constantia (f.): Latin *constantia* 'constancy'. There was a saint of the name, a daughter of Constantine the Great. The name was introduced into England at the Norman Conquest (it was borne by one of the daughters of the Conqueror, who married Alain de Bretagne), and soon became common, being anglicized as *Custance*, which is found as late as 1561. In the 16th and 17th C *Constancy* came into use among the Puritans, but was not common. In the 19th C the Latin form *Constantia* was introduced, and CMY says of it that it 'at present reigns among the favourite fancy names, scarcely less inevitable than Alice or Edith'. *Constantia* has now given way to the simpler *Constance*. It is sometimes abbreviated to *Connie*.

CONSTANCIA Cur 1199, FA 1346.
CUSTANCIA Cur 1199.
CONSTANCE HR 1273.
CUSTANCE HR 1273, Poll Tax 1379.
CUSTANS Poll Tax 1379.
CUSTINS Broughton-by-Brigg Parish Reg 1604–5.

Constant (m.): occurs as a christian name in the 17th C and was probably the common adjective, not a form of *Constantine*.

Constantine (m.): Latin derivative of *constans* 'constant', 'firm'. As the name of the first Christian Emperor, *Constantine* was early adopted as a christian name. *Constantine*, a Cornish saint, was said to have evangelized Scotland in the 6th C, and his name was borne by *Constantine* MacFergus (died 820), King of the Picts, and by three early (9th and 10th C) Scottish kings. There is one sub-tenant of the name in DB, and it was not uncommon in England as well as Scotland from the 12th to the 17th C, giving rise to the surnames *Costin*, *Costain*, *Considine*, *Constantine*, &c. *Costin* was the usual English form of the name in the Middle Ages and until the 17th C. It was particularly common in Devon and Cornwall. In Ireland it is used to render Irish *Connor* (*Conc(h)ub(h)ar*) and *Conn* (qq.v.).

CONSTANTINUS DB 1086, Cur 1200, 1205, 1210, Poll Tax 1379.
CONSTANS Cur 1200, 1213–15.
COSTIN Cur 1207.
COSTETINE Clerkenwell 1222.
COSTAINE or CONSTANTINE Keighley Reg 1586, 1597.
COSTANE, COSTAN Halifax Reg 1583, 1597.

Consuelo (f.) [konsooā′lo]: Spanish '(Our Lady of) Counsel'. Occasionally used by Roman Catholics, particularly in America (cf. MERCEDES, DOLORES). It is perhaps best known as the name of a novel by George Sand.

Cora (f.): apparently of American origin, and does not occur before the middle of the 19th C.

Coralie (f.): one of the numerous romantic names invented in France after the Revolution. It has been occasionally used in England.

Cordelia (f.): when used to-day, this name is probably always taken from *King Lear*. Shakespeare took (and slightly altered) the name from Holinshed where it appears as *Cordeilla*. It may be the same as *Cordula*, which appears in Welsh and Cornish calendars as the name of one of the companions of St. Ursula, and is found in German as *Kordula* or *Kordel*. A *Cordelia* Parker died in 1689 in Cornwall, and several examples of the name have been noted in Lancashire in the second half of the 17th C, and one in Lincolnshire (Gedney Parish Reg) in 1763.

Corinna (f.): Greek, the name of a Boeotian woman poet, possibly a derivative of κόρη 'a maiden'. It was used in 17th- and 18th-C poetry, notably by Herrick, and has sometimes also been used as a christian name. The French use *Corinne* more often, probably on account of Mme de Staël's novel of the name.

Corisande (f.): a name from medieval romance; it is borne by one of the characters in *Amadis de Gaul*, and was used as a name for Diane de Poitiers. Disraeli named one of the heroines of his *Lothair* Lady *Corisande*.

Cormac (m.): of doubtful etymology. A common name in Irish myths and legends and still sometimes used, though commoner as a surname.

Cornelia (f.): the f. form of the name of the Cornelian *gens*, made famous by the mother of the Gracchi, a daughter of Publius Cornelius Scipio. It has been used occasionally as a christian name since the 18th C. See also CORNELIUS.

Cornelius (m.): the name of a famous Roman *gens*, possibly derived from *cornu* 'a horn'. It was the name of the devout centurion (Acts x. 1) converted by St. Peter, and later of a 3rd-C

martyred pope whose relics were taken to Compiègne and later
to Rosnay in Flanders, whence the name became common in the
Low Countries. *Cornelius* de Wyrley of Hansworth, Staffs., lived
at the beginning of the 15th C. The name has not been noted
again until the 16th C; examples are *Cornelys* Smythe 1504,
Cornelius Todd, son of a Presbyterian, born 1631, and *Cornelius*,
son of Seth Wood, an ejected minister. *Cornelius* or *Corney* are
often found in Ireland, where they came into use to translate the
native *Conchubhar* (see CONNOR) or *Conn*.

Cosmo (m.): Greek κόσμος, 'order'; the name of one of the two
martyrs *Kosmas* and *Damianos* whose supposed relics were revealed in a dream to St. Ambrose, and who became the patron
saints of Milan. *Cosimo* or *Cosmo* became a favourite name in
Italy, and was adopted by the Florentine family of Medici. It was
the name of the 3rd Duke of Gordon (died 1752) whose father
was a close friend of *Cosimo* III, Grand Duke of Tuscany, and
since that time has been constantly used in the Gordon family,
who have carried it by marriage into other Scottish families.

Costin, see CONSTANTINE.

Courtenay (m.): one of the considerable number of aristocratic
surnames now often used as christian names. The family of *de
Courtenay,* famous in the West country, took its name originally
from *Courtenay* in the Île de France.

Cressida (f.): the rather complicated history of this name may
be summarized as follows. In the Iliad, Hippodamia, daughter of
Brises, is called *Briseis* (acc. *Brisëida*). Benoit de Ste Maure, the
12th-C poet who invented the story of Troilus in his *Roman de
Troie,* took the name *Briseida* for his faithless mistress, apparently
not realizing that it was simply a patronymic and could not apply
to the daughter of Calchas. When Boccaccio took Benoit's story
and refashioned it in his *Filostrato,* he presumably noted this
mistake, and substituted the name of the other captive Greek
maiden, *Chrysëis* (acc. *Chrysëida*) daughter of *Chryses* priest of
Apollo, whom Agamemnon returned to her father at the command of the god. There is a passage in Ovid which might be

misread to mean that she was in fact the daughter of Calchas. Boccaccio's *Criseida* was turned into *Criseyde* by Chaucer, and *Cressid* or *Cressida* by Shakespeare. That this name, a byword for faithlessness, should recently have been used as a christian name, is one of those aberrations of taste for which there is no accounting.

Crispin (m.): Latin *Crispinus*, a Roman cognomen, probably derived from *crispus* 'curled'. *Crispinus* and *Crispinianus*, shoe-makers of Soissons, martyred *c.* 285, were considered the patron saints of shoemakers, and both *Crispin* and *Crispi(ni)an* were used as christian names in the Middle Ages. *Crispin* survives in occasional use.

CRISPINUS Cur 1201, 1207.
CRISPIANUS HR 1273.
CRISPIAN Gedney Parish Reg 1587.

Crystal (f.): sometimes used as a woman's name in modern times, presumably on the analogy of *Ruby*, *Emerald*, &c. *Crystal* or *Chrystal* is also a Lowland Scots pet form of *Christopher*.

Cuddy, see CUTHBERT.

Curtis (m.): a common surname, originating in the nickname 'courteous' (*Curteis* is found as a personal name in 1199), and variously spelt; now sometimes used as a christian name.

Cuthbert (m.): compound of Old English *cuth* 'famous', *beorht* 'bright', a common Old English personal name, which survived the Norman Conquest, as being the name of St. *Cuthbert* (died 687), Bishop of Lindisfarne, whose body, preserved in Durham Cathedral, was said to work many miracles. There are 72 church dedications to him, mostly in the North of England where the name has chiefly flourished. It sometimes appears as *Cudbert*, and the pet-form *Cuddy* was formerly current and may have been the origin of the Scottish and Northern *cuddy*, an ass. *Cuthbert* lingered on in Yorkshire and Durham, chiefly among Roman recusants, after the Reformation, but went out of general use until it was revived by the Tractarians in the 19th C. During the War of 1914–18 *Cuthbert* was used as a slang term for an evader

of military service, and it seems now to have gone out of fashion
as a christian name.

CUDBRIHT HR 1273.
CUTHBRID Poll Tax 1379.
CUDBERT 14th C Legendary.
CUTHBERT Linc 1533, Cov 1530.
CUDDIE, CUDDY Westmorland 1587.

Cynthia (f.): one of the titles of Artemis, meaning 'of (Mt)
Cynthus', and the name of the mistress of Propertius. English
writers in the later Middle Ages, struggling to spell *Sanchia* (q.v.),
sometimes turned it into *Cynthia,* but the name was not really
used until the Renaissance. It occurs from time to time in the
17th and 18th C and Mrs. Gaskell gave it to one of the characters
in her novel *Wives and Daughters* (1866). CMY (1860) describes
it as 'name of girls in America'. About the end of the 19th C it
suddenly became fashionable in England for a time.

Cyprian (m.): Latin *Cyprianus*, 'of Cyprus', the name of a Bishop
of Carthage, one of the first great Christian Latin writers, beheaded in 258 and mentioned in the Canon of the Mass. *Ciprianus*
is found as a christian name in England at the beginning of the
13th C and at Cambridge University in the 16th and 17th C; it
was revived by the Tractarians in the 19th C.

CIPRIANUS Cur 1199, 1200, 1219.

Cyriack (m.): Greek κυριακός, 'lordly'. St. *Cyriack* or *Cyr* of
Iconium, the infant martyr son of St. Julitta, has 9 churches dedicated to him in the West of England, and *Cyriack* or *Syriack* has
sometimes been used as a christian name, the best-known example being Milton's friend *Cyriack* Skinner.

Cyril (m.): Greek κυριλλός, probably a derivative of κύριος 'lord',
'master'. There were two saints of this name, both doctors of the
Church, St. *Cyril* of Jerusalem died 387, and St. *Cyril* of Alexandria died 444. The name is first found in use in England in the
17th C (e.g. Sir *Cyril* Wyche *c.* 1620–90, named after Cyril Lukar
the patriarch), but did not become generally used until the 19th

C, when it was favoured, like other names of early Fathers of the Church, by the Tractarians. It is now a rather common name.

Cyrus (m.): Greek Κῦρος, from Persian *kuru*, 'throne'. The name of the great king of Persia occurs in the Old Testament and hence came into use among the Puritans. It has taken hold in the USA, where it is regularly used as a christian name.

D

Daisy (f.): a late-Victorian pet-name for *Margaret* (marguerite = daisy). It is sometimes used as an independent name.

Damaris (f.) [dă'maris]: the name of an Athenian woman converted by St. Paul (Acts xvii. 34), possibly a mistake for Greek *Damalis* 'a calf'. Like other New Testament names, it was adopted as a christian name by 17th-C Puritans and early examples occur at Gedney, Lincs., in 1597 and 1620.

Damian (m.): *Kosmos* and *Damianos* were brothers martyred in Syria in 303 under Diocletian. Their cult spread westward and was much increased by the supposed discovery of their relics at Milan by St. Ambrose. *Damianos* may be a derivative of Greek δαμάζω, 'to tame'. *Damian* is found in England as a christian name in 1205, and was in use for several centuries. See also COSMO.

DAMIAN Cur 1205.

Dandy, see ANDREW.

Daniel (m.): Hebrew 'God has judged'. *Daniel* is found in England before the Norman Conquest, but only as the name of monks or bishops. Its use as an ordinary christian name seems to have begun in the 12th C and it became common in the 13th and 14th C, giving rise to the surnames *Daniel(s)*, *Dann(son)*, *Dannet* (Lyford 1655 gives *Dannet* as a diminutive of *Daniel*). It was revived with other Biblical names in the 17th C and remained in general use down to the middle of the 19th C, since when it has been rare. It has been particularly common in Ireland where it is used to translate the native *Domhnall* (*Donal*), and in Wales for Welsh *Deiniol*.

DANIEL Cur 1189–1215.
DANYELL Poll Tax 1379.
DANYLL Poll Tax 1379.

Dante (m.) [dăn'tĭ]: a diminutive of the Italian *Durante* (see DURAND), the christian name of the poet Alighieri and that by which he is usually known (cf. Michelangelo, Raphael, Leonardo). The name has been long obsolete in Italy, but is occasionally used in modern times after *Dante* Alighieri, e.g. *Dante* Gabriel Rossetti.

Daphne (f.): Greek Δάφνη 'bay' or 'laurel', the name of a nymph loved by Apollo and turned into a bush. CMY says of it, 'Daphne has not subsequently been used as a name except for dogs'; but about the beginning of the 20th C it began to be used as a christian name and is now quite common.

Darby (m.): CMY says this was the form of *Diarmaid* commonly used in Limerick and Tipperary. *Darby* occurs in the Liverpool Town Books from 1560, used in the family of Ulster (presumably of Irish origin). *Darby* Braye is recorded in London in 1609. The proverbial couple *Darby and Joan* are usually supposed to originate in a set of verses printed in the *Gentleman's Magazine* for 1735 (vol. v, p. 253), though *Darby* there may be a surname.

D'Arcy (m.): a name of territorial origin, derived from either Arcy-Ste-Restitue (Aisne) or Arcy-sur-Cure (Yonne). The English family of *Darcy* or *D'Arci* was founded by *Norman d'Areci*, one of the companions of the Conqueror, who was granted large estates in Lincs. In the 14th C a branch of the family settled in Ireland, and *Darcy* was there adopted as a christian name, at first perhaps as a translation of the native Irish *Dorchaidh*.

David (m.): Hebrew, originally a lullaby word meaning 'darling', then 'friend' generally. One of the first bearers of this name in Britain was *David* or *Dewi*, Archbishop of Menevia (died 601), the patron saint of Wales. From his time the name has been a favourite one in Wales. In Scotland it was the name of two kings, *David* I 1084–1153, and *David* II 1324–71, and has also always been common. In England it is not found before the Norman Conquest, but was common in the 12th C and has been used ever since, though never a favourite name. The surnames *David(son)*, *Davy, Davi(e)s, Davison, Davitt, Davidge, Daw(es), Dawson*, and *Dawkins* are derived from *David* and its pet-forms *Davy, Davit*, and *Daw*, while *McTavish* is the Gaelic patronymic. In Ireland *David* has been used to represent Irish *Dathi*. At the present time it is enjoying a considerable degree of favour.

DAVID INTERPRES DB 1086.
DAVID Cur 1196–1220, FA 1285, Poll Tax 1379.
DAVY Cov 1471, 1494.
DAVIT HR 1273.
DAUE Poll Tax 1379.

Davina (f.): a Scottish f. form of *David*, found from the 17th C (e.g. *Davine* Dobenes 1639).

Dawn (f.): the use of this as a christian name is a 20th-C invention of novelette writers, which has sometimes been adopted in real life.

Deborah (f.) [dĕb′oră]: Hebrew 'a bee', the name of a prophetess, adopted by the Puritans in the 17th C, when it became a favourite christian name. It was borne by the youngest daughter of John Milton and, as readers of *Cranford* will remember, by the awe-inspiring Miss Jenkyns, who insisted on its being pronounced *Debōrah* in accordance with the usage of her late father. In Ireland *Deborah* is sometimes used to represent Irish *Gobnait* (cf. *Abigail*).

Decima (f.): Latin 'tenth', see DECIMUS.

DECIMA Beckingham Parish Reg 1799.

Decimus (m.): Latin *decimus* 'tenth'. This, with *Septimus*, is the commonest of the numeral christian names. CMY says: 'Decimus and Decima are now and then to be found among us in unusually large families of one sex', but they were also used for tenth children in mixed Victorian families.

Deirdre (f.) [dēr′drĕ]: the name of the heroine of 'The Sons of Uisneach', one of the Three Sorrowful Tales of Erinn, the subject of many plays and poems by modern Irish poets. The etymology of the name is doubtful. It was not known to CMY and its use as a christian name is quite recent, dating from the 'Celtic Revival' (Yeats's *Deirdre* 1907, Synge's *Deirdre of the Sorrows* 1910).

Delia (f.): an epithet of Artemis, derived from her birthplace *Delos*. It was a favourite name with pastoral poets in the 17th and 18th C. CMY mentions it as an occasional christian name, and it is still sometimes used. *Delia* or *Bedelia* is often used in Ireland by persons christened *Bridget* or *Brigid*—presumably as sounding more genteel.

Denis (m.): Latin *Dionysius*, Greek *Διονύσιος*, 'of Dionysos'; the name of the Areopagite converted by St. Paul at Athens (Acts xvii. 34), and of several saints, notably the apostle of the Gauls who was martyred near Paris in 272 and, as St. *Denys*, became the patron saint of France. There are 41 churches dedicated to him in England, where the name was introduced about the end of the 12th C and gave rise to the surnames *Den(n)is(s)*, *Den(n)ison*, *Denny*, *Dennett*, *Tennyson*. It occurs in the 15th C (*Deenys*, *Deenes* Scorchebefe) and still survived at the beginning of the 17th C, after which it went out of common use for a couple of centuries to be revived at the beginning of the 20th C. It is now in fairly frequent use. In Ireland, however, it has been used for some centuries as a substitute for the native *Donnchadh*.

DIONISIUS Cur 1200, 1221.
DYONISIUS Cur 1221.
DENES Poll Tax 1379.

Denise (f.) [děnēz']: French *Denise*, Latin *Dionysia*, f. of *Dionysius* (see DENIS). *Denise* is probably now always a conscious borrowing from the French and is pronounced in the French manner; but *Denis(e)*, with its pet-forms *Dennet* and *Diot*, was a common English girl's name from the 12th C and survived till the end of the 18th C. Lyford 1655 gives *Denis* as a girl's name. In Latin records the name appears as *Dionysia*, and a list of Yorks Recusants 1604 mentions one *Dionis* Wilden which is presumably a

E

shortened form of *Dionysia. Dionise* was borne by several members of the Markham family 1574-1631.

Dionisia HR 1273, FA 1303.
Dionycia FA 1303.
Deonysia Cov 1449.
Dionis Yorks Rec 1604.
Denote Langland *c.* 1362.

Denzil (m.): William Holles (16th C) married Anne, daughter and co-heiress of John *Denzell* Esq., of *Denzell*, Cornwall; their eldest son was named *Denzell*, and the name has been used ever since in that family and others connected with it. It is now usually spelt *Denzil*.

Deodatus, Deodonatus (m.): Latin 'given by, or to, God'. These, like *Adeodatus* and *Deusdedit*, were fairly common ecclesiastical names from the 7th C onwards, but unlike the similar Greek *Theodoros, Theodosios*, did not come into general use as christian names, though *Deodonatus* is found in England in 1205, and *Dieudonné* was sometimes used in the north of France and *Déodat* in the south.

Derek, Derrick (m.): *Diederick* or *Dirck* is the Dutch form of German *Diederich*, from Old German *Theodoric* (q.v.). *Dederick, Dyryke, Deryk* are found in England in the 15th C, borrowed, no doubt, from the Low Countries. Camden gives *Derric* as the English and *Terry* as the French forms of *Theodoric*. The name has been revived during the last 50 years; it is now oftener spelt *Derek* than *Derrick*.

Dedericus Cl 1464.
Dederic Cl 1464.

Dermot, see DIARM(U)IT.

Desdemona (f.): sometimes used as a christian name in recent times after the heroine of Shakespeare's *Othello*. Shakespeare took her name, with the story, from Cinthio (*Hecatommithi* 1565) where it appears as *Disdemona*, possibly an adaptation from Greek δυσδαιμονία 'misery'.

Desideratus (m.): Latin 'desired'. Found as a christian name (probably ecclesiastical) in England in 1200. In France *Didier* from Latin *Desiderius* (the name of the last Lombard king of Italy and of a 7th-C French saint) was not uncommon in the Middle Ages. See also DÉSIRÉE.

Désirée (f.) [dāzērā']: French *désirée* from Latin *desiderata* 'desired'. *Désirée* is nowadays sometimes used as a christian name in England, but only as a loan from the French and pronounced and accented in the French manner. In the 13th and 14th C, however, *Desiderata* and *Desirata* occur from time to time in (Latin) records, and probably represent a latinization of some English form of the name which has not survived on record.

DESIRATA, DESIDERATA Cur 1210–12, FA 1302, 1316.

Desmond (m.): Irish *Deas-Mumhain* 'South Munster', came to be used first as a surname and then as a christian name in Ireland, and has recently come into use in England also.

Diana (f.) [dīā'nă]: Latin name of the moon goddess (Greek *Artemis*), probably a derivative of *deus*. The use as a christian name was a Renaissance fashion (e.g. *Diane* de Poitiers) and it is first found in England in the 16th C, e.g. *Diana* Luttrell born 1580, *Diana* Cecil, daughter of 2nd Earl of Exeter born early in the 17th C, *Dyana* Sturdy 1618. It has never been a common name, but has been in regular use in e.g. the Manners family since the middle of the 18th C. Its comparative popularity in modern times may be due in part to Scott's *Diana* Vernon, heroine of *Rob Roy* (1817) and Meredith's *Diana of the Crossways* (1875). The abbreviation *Di* has been used since the 18th C (e.g. Lady *Di* Beauclerk (1734–1808)).

Diarm(u)it, Dermot (m.): from Old Irish *di-fharmait* 'free from envy', pronounced *dī-ormwid*. The name of the lover of Grainne. The anglicized spelling *Dermot* has lately been reinforced in Ireland by *Diarm(u)id*. See also DARBY, JEREMIAH.

Dick, see RICHARD.

Diggory (m.): this apparently goes back to the medieval romance of *Sir Degore* or *Degarre*. An early example is *Digory* Wheare (b. 1574), Master of Gloucester College, Oxford. Goldsmith used *Diggory* as the name of a serving-man in *She Stoops to Conquer* (1773). It seems to be mainly Cornish. The explanation of the name given in the romance is that the hero as a child was found by a hermit and christened *Degarre* because

> Degarre nowt elles ne is
> But thing that not neuer what hit is
> Other thing that is neg3 forlorn also.

It is presumably derived from French *égaré*, 'strayed', 'lost', though it is not clear how; possibly the *s* of the reflexive form may have been mistaken for a *d*.

Dillian (f.): Dutch *Dilliana*, perhaps a derivative of Old German *Dilli, Dillo*. It is used in a few English families.

Dilys (f.): Modern Welsh *dilys* 'certain', 'perfect', 'genuine'. First used as name in Wales in the middle of the 19th C. Now often used in England.

Dinah (f.): Hebrew 'law suit', the name of a daughter of Jacob. It came into use in the 17th C (e.g. *Dinae* Shorthose 1629) and was a favourite name with the working classes until about the end of the 19th C. It seems sometimes to have been confused with *Diana*.

Dionys(ia), see DENISE.

Dionysius, see DENIS.

Dodo, see DOROTHEA.

Dolly, see DOROTHEA and ADOLPHUS.

Dolores (f.) [dolor'es]: Spanish, short for *Maria de Dolores*, 'Mary of the Sorrows'. The name of the Blessed Virgin was formerly seldom used in Spain, but attributive names such as this are common, e.g. *(Maria de) Mercedes, (Maria de) Consuelo, (Maria) Assunta. Dolores* is sometimes used by English, more often by American, Roman Catholics.

Dominica (f.), see DOMINIC(K). The f. form *Dominica* is used from time to time.

Dominic(k) (m.): (French *Dominique*, Italian *Domenico*, Spanish *Domingo*): Latin *dominicus*, 'of the Lord'. The name may have been given originally to children born on a Sunday (*dies dominica*). In England it is found as a monk's name in Anglo-Saxon times, but did not come into use as an ordinary christian name until the 13th C, in honour of St. *Dominic* (1170–1221), founder of the Order of Preachers. It was used at first as both a m. and a f. name, sometimes appearing as *Dominick*, sometimes as *Dominy*; *Dome-nyk* occurs in the 15th C. The name was never common in England, and since the Reformation has been used almost exclusively by Roman Catholics.

Donald (m.): Gaelic *Domhnall* (pronounced *Dawnal*), from Old Irish *Domnall*, from primitive Celtic *Dubno-walos from **dubno-* 'world' and *walos 'mighty'. It is one of the commonest Highland christian names and *Donal* is much used in Ireland, often as an equivalent of *Daniel*. Early examples of the name in England are *Doneuuald*, a Yorkshire sub-tenant mentioned in DB, and a *Donaldus* Sturmyn 1346.

Donatus (m.): Latin 'given'. The name of several martyrs as well as of the famous schismatic. *Donatus* may have been used in Britain before the Anglo-Saxon period—the Welsh *Dunawd* has been derived from it, and *Donat* is found in Ireland. In the Middle Ages it is found from time to time, both m. and f. usually in the form *Donnet*, and CMY records a female *Donnet* in Cornwall as late as 1755. For the development of *Donnet* or *Donat* from *Dona-tus*, cf. the word *donet* an elementary treatise, derived from the name (Aelius) *Donatus*, the author of a popular rudimentary Latin grammar widely used in the Middle Ages.

Donnet, see DONATUS.

Dora, see DOROTHY.

Dorcas (f.): Greek δορκάς 'a roe or gazelle'. In Acts ix. 36 *Dorcas* is given as an interpretation of the Aramaic *Tabitha* (q.v.), the name of the charitable disciple raised from death by St. Paul. Both names became popular in the 17th C, and later *Dorcas* was the name given to a meeting of ladies to make clothes for the poor, in allusion to the story in Acts, where the poor are said to have wept over her, showing the coats and garments she had made for them.

Doreen (f.) [dor'ēn]: Modern Irish *Doirean*, probably an Irish adaptation of *Dorothy* (q.v.). It came into use in England about the beginning of the 20th C perhaps as a result of a novel of the name (1894) by Edna Lyall, an extremely popular writer in her day. It is now one of the commonest names among the working classes.

Dorinda (f.): an 18th-C coinage formed on the model of *Belinda* and *Clarinda* (qq.v.). It is still occasionally used.

Doris (f.) [formerly pronounced dōris]: this is a puzzling name. The first occurrence noted is *Doris* Dorcis Tabitha Mann, a New Englander, in 1819. The name is not mentioned by CMY, and seems to have leapt into sudden popularity towards the end of the 19th C. Forster, in his *Life of Dickens* (ch. xii) quotes, from a memorandum book which Dickens kept between 1855 and 1865, a list of out-of-the-way christian names taken from Privy Council Education Lists, amongst which occurs *Doris*.[1] It is the name of a character in Mrs. Oliphant's novel *Effie Ogilvie*, 1886. *Doris* is the name of a sea nymph in Greek mythology, Juvenal uses it for the mistress addressed in several of his poems, and it was the name of one of the four concubines of Agrippa the Prefect, whose conversion and martyrdom are related in the apocryphal *Acts of Peter*; but none of these seems to be a cogent reason for the sudden adoption of the name in late-Victorian England. It has been suggested that the later vogue of the name may have been helped by the actress Doris Keene (in *Romance*, 1914).

[1] I owe this reference to Professor John Butt.

Dorothea, Dorothy (f.): (French *Dorothée*, German *Dorothea*, Italian, Spanish *Dorotea*); appears to be an arbitrary inversion of the name θεοδώρα, 'gift of God', which, like the m. θεοδώρος, was apparently a christian coinage. The legend of St. *Dorothea*, a 3rd-C Cappadocian martyr, is not found very early, and the name is not found in use in England until the end of the 15th C (e.g. *Dorothy* daughter of John Markham of Sedgebrook, Lincs., born *c.* 1494). It was very common in the later part of the 16th C when it was already abbreviated to *Doll*, and throughout the 17th C, often in the forms *Doll(y)* or *Dorat(e)*. It went out of fashion in the first half of the 18th C, came back *c.* 1750–1800, and then disappeared again until *c.* 1880. The pronunciation indicated by the 17th C spelling *Dorate* apparently survived in the 18th C. Miss D. K. Broster has called my attention to a grammar published by Newbery in 1769 in which the following occurs:

'*Q*. Does *h* never lose its sound after the *t*?
A. Yes, it is quite lost in these proper names, *Esther*, *Anthony*, *Thomas*, and *Dorothy*.'

The use of *doll* for a child's plaything is first recorded in 1700 (see OED s.v.), about the time when the christian name went out of fashion. Like Jill, Parnell, Nan, and other popular names, *Doll* came to be used as a generic name for a loose woman (cf. Shakespeare's *Doll* Tearsheet and Ben Jonson's *Doll* Common), which probably accounts for its temporary disappearance. *Dorothy* has been the usual form of the name in England, but *Dorothea* was sometimes used in the 19th C (e.g. *Dorothea* Brooke in *Middlemarch*). Besides *Doll(y)* the diminutives *Dot* and *Dodo* are used. *Dora*, now an independent name, came into use at the beginning of the 19th C. *Dora* Wordsworth (1804–47), the daughter of the poet, is an early example. Although named *Dorothy* after her aunt, she was always known as *Dora* after she grew up. *Dorothy* has been used to render Gaelic *Diorbhail*.

Dougal, Dugald (m.) [doo'gal]: Old Irish *dubhgall* 'black stranger', a name originally given by the Irish to the Norwegians, which later became a common christian name. It is now chiefly used in the Highlands of Scotland. The word *dubhgall* is still used in Irish and Gaelic to indicate an Englishman and in Modern Breton for a Frenchman.

Douglas (m., f.): Gaelic *dub(h)glas*, 'dark blue'. This very common Celtic river name (e.g. *Dawlish, Devil's Water, Dowles Brook, Dulas, Divelish* in England, *Douglas* in Ireland and Scotland, and *Dulas* in Wales) became the name of a great Scottish family, and, like other such names, also a common christian name. This use is not found, however, much before the late 16th C, when it was as commonly a girl's as a boy's name. Spenser's *Daphnaïda*, for instance, was written on *Douglas* Howard, wife of Sir Arthur Gorges. Camden 1605 puts it among the women's christian names, and says of it, 'Of the Scottish surname, taken from the river *Douglas*, not long since made a Christian name in *England*'. It is now often used by people with no Scottish connexions.

Dowsabel, Dowse, see DULCIE.

Drogo (m.): Old German *Drogo*, Gothic *Draga*, a derivative of *dragen* 'to bear', 'carry'. The name was introduced into England at the time of the Norman Conquest (it was borne by several of the Conqueror's followers, notably *Drogo* de Monte Acuto, ancestor of the *Montagu(e)* and *Montacute* families), and became common, in the French form *Dru* or English *Drew*. *Drewsteignton* (Devon) was held by one *Drogo* in 1210 and is called Teyngton *Drue* in 1275; Littleton *Drew* (Wilts) was held by Walter *Drew* in 1242 and is called Littleton *Drewe* in 1316. It gave rise to the surnames *Drew(e)*, *Drews*, *Druce*, and survived as a christian name as late as the end of the 17th C; Lyford gives *Dru* in his list of names 1655, and a *Drugo* Cressener, a Hunts clergyman, died in 1679. *Drogo* was revived in the 19th C by the Montagu family (the 7th Earl of Manchester, born 1823, was christened William *Drogo*) and they have used it ever since.

DROGO DB 1086, Cur 1187–1219.
DRUET(TUS) or DROGO HR 1273.
DREW Lincs 1455.
DRUE Oseney 1460.

Dru, see DROGO.

Drusilla (f.): f. diminutive of Latin *Drusus*, a cognomen in use in the Livian *gens*, first assumed by the Livius who slew the Gaul *Drausus*. Livia *Drusilla* was the 2nd wife of Augustus, and another *Drusilla* was the daughter of Drusus Germanicus and sister and mistress of Caligula. Herod Agrippa I probably called his daughter *Drusilla* out of compliment to his patron Caligula; she is mentioned in Acts xxiv along with her husband Felix, Procurator of Judea. Like most other New Testament names, *Drusilla* was taken into use in the 17th C, and has been used from time to time since, more often in the USA than in England.

Dudley (m.): a surname derived from *Dudley* in Worcestershire, and made famous by the great family of *Dudley* which rose to power under the Tudors. Like many other aristocratic surnames, it came to be used as a christian name in the 19th C, with no reference to family connexion.

Dugald, see DOUGAL.

Dukana (f.), see MARMADUKE.

Dulcie (f.): this seems to be a modern invention, not directly connected with the medieval *Dowsabel* (Latin *Dulcibella*), but formed immediately from the Latin *dulcis* 'sweet'. An early example is to be found in *Vice Versa* (1882). *Dowsabel* or *Dowse* (French *Douce*) were common in the Middle Ages, and gave rise to the surnames *Dous, Dowse, Dowson, Duce, Dewse*, and also *Dowsett* and *Dowsing* from the diminutives *Douset* and *Dousin*. The name was latinized as *Dulcia*. *Dowsabel* was still common in the 16th C, sometimes appearing as *Dowzable, Dussabel*, &c., and it was also used as a generic name for a sweetheart. Camden 1605 gives *Douze* and *Dousabel*. In the 18th C the Latin form *Dulcibella* was sometimes used, but CMY seems to regard it and *Dowse* as obsolete. *Dowsabel* was formed in the same way as *Christabel, Mirabel*, &c. (qq.v.).

DUSSABELE, DUSZABELL Writs of Parliament *c.* 1300.
DUCE, DOUCE HR 1273.

Duncan (m.): From Old Irish *Dunecan*, with a double suffix *-ec+-an*. It is a hypocoristic form from Old Irish *Dun-chadh* 'brown warrior'. The name of two early Scottish kings, Duncan I 1034–40, Duncan II 1094–5, it has always been a fairly common name in Scotland, but has not been adopted in England as other Scottish names have been. *Donecan* occurs, however, in DB as the name of a sub-tenant in Somerset. In Ireland *Donnchadh* is usually rendered by *Denis*.

Dunstan (m.): Old English, compound of *dun* 'hill', and *stan* 'stone', the name of the great Archbishop of Canterbury, *Dunstan* son of Heorstan 924–88. His memory was held in great reverence in the Middle Ages and his name is occasionally found in use; a *Donston* Chechelly occurs in London as late as 1529, probably named after the parish of his birth. The name went out of use after the Reformation until it was revived by the Tractarians in the 19th C.

DUNSTAN, DONESTAN, DUNESTAN DB 1086.
DUNSTAN HR 1273.
DONESTAN Poll Tax 1379.

Durand (m.): apparently from Latin *durantem* 'lasting'; the French *Durand*, Italian *Durante* were common in the Middle Ages. *Durand* was introduced into England by the Normans before the Conquest; in DB there is mention of several tenants of this name who held TRE. It gave rise to various surnames, e.g. *Durand, Durant, Durrant, Durrance. Durant* Hamelyn occurs in a volume of Inquisitions as late as 1428, and *Durant* is still used as a christian name by the gipsy family of Lovell. See also DANTE, the Italian diminutive form of the name.

DURAND(US) Reg 1079–83, DB 1086, Cur 1189–1212.
DURAND HR 1273.
DURANT HR 1273.

Dwight (m.): an English surname, perhaps derived from *Diot*, a diminutive of *Dionisia*. A John *Dwight* of Dedham emigrated to New England in 1635, and was founder of a numerous family, eminent among whom was Timothy *Dwight*, President of Yale, 1795–1817. It was probably in his honour that *Dwight* first came into use as a christian name in America, where it is now common. Cf. CHAUNC(E)Y.

Dymp(h)na (f.) [dĭmf'na or dĭmp'na]: Irish *Damhnait*, possibly a formation with the suffix *-aid* from *damhna* 'one fit to be'; the name of an Irish virgin martyr, sometimes used by Irish Roman Catholics.

E

Eamon, SEE EDMUND.

Easter (m., f.): like *Christmas, Pascal, Pentecost,* &c., *Easter* was formerly used as a christian name, and still survives in some families. When used as a woman's name it was sometimes confused with *Esther*. The pet form *Eacy* is occasionally used.

Ebenezer (m.): Hebrew 'stone of help' (the name of a stone raised by Samuel to commemorate the defeat of the Philistines, 1 Sam. vii. 12); adopted as a christian name by 17th-C Puritans, sometimes in the form *Benezer* (e.g. *Benazer* Wilson born 1668, son of an ejected minister). It continued in use among Dissenters and is still used in the USA, sometimes abbreviated to *Eben*.

Eda, see EDITH.

Edborough (f.): Old English *Eadburh*, compound of *ead* 'rich', 'happy', and *burh* 'fortress', was the name of an 8th-C saint, abbess of Minster, and survived until at least the 16th C. *Edborough* Butcher is mentioned in a Somerset will of 1582.

Eden (m., f.): Hebrew 'delight'; like some other Old Testament place-names, sometimes used as a christian name in the 17th C. See also EDITH.

Edgar (m.): Old English *Eadgar*, compound of *ead* 'rich', 'happy', and *gar* 'a spear'. The first element was a distinguishing mark of the royal house of Wessex. *Eadgar* (944–75), the grandson of Alfred, was one of the most successful kings of that house; his name became a favourite among the English and survived the

Norman Conquest. It was used, though infrequently, until about the end of the 13th C. It was revived in the 18th C, along with other Old English names, by romantic writers, but the reason for its greatly increased use in the 19th C was probably that it was the name of the hero of *The Bride of Lammermoor* (1819).

EDGAR, ETGAR DB 1086.
EDGAR Cur 1200.

Edith (f.): Old English *Eadgyth*, compound of *ead* 'rich', 'happy', and *gȳð* 'war'. A fairly common Old English name which survived the Norman Conquest, probably on account of the popularity of St. *Eadgyth* (962–84), daughter of King Edgar. The marriage of Henry I to the English princess *Eadgyth* may also have helped to perpetuate the name, though she was usually known as Matilda or Mold. *Eadgyth* was sometimes confused with *Eadgifu*, compound of *ead* with *gifu* 'gift', which is also found after the Conquest, usually latinized as *Ediva*. *Edith* remained common all through the Middle Ages and never died out entirely, though it was infrequent from the 16th to 18th C. It came back into fashion in the 19th C.

The now obsolete but formerly common f. name *Ede* was from Old English *Eadu*, a f. name formed from the root *ead*. Camden 1605 says '*Ead* drawn from *Edith*', and Lyford 1655 says '*Eade* for *Edith*'; but it seems to have been an independent name earlier, was latinized as *Eda*, and often used in the diminutive form *Eden*. It gave rise to a number of surnames such as *Ede*, *Eade*, *Eadie*, *Eden*. An example of the christian name *Ede* occurs in a Notts Parish Register as late as 1765, but it seems now to be obsolete.

EADITA, EIDITA, EDGIDA, EDGED, EDIET, EDIED, EDIT, EDID DB 1086.
EDITHA Cur 1199, FA 1346.
EDITHE FA 1284.
EDA Cl 1255, HR 1273.
EDDE HR 1273.
EDDA Poll Tax 1379.
EDON HR 1273.
EDINE HR 1273.
EDDEN Poll Tax 1379.
EDAN, EDEN Poll Tax 1379.

Edmond, Edmund (m.): Old English *Eadmund*, compound of *ead* 'rich', 'happy', and *mund* 'protection'; the name of two kings of England, *Edmund* the Magnificent (922?-46), son of Edward the Elder, and *Edmund* Ironside (981?-1016), and of two saints, St. *Edmund*, King of the East Angles, martyred by the Danes in 870, and St. *Edmund* Rich (1170?-1240), Archbishop of Canterbury. It was common in the 11th C and occurs in DB. Henry III owed special devotion to SS. *Edward* and *Edmund*, and named two of his sons after them, which probably helped these names to survive at a time when many Old English names went finally out of use. *Edmund* was often written in the French form *Edmond* in the later Middle Ages. It was less common after the 15th C, but continued to be used in certain families, e.g. Courtenay, Montagu, Mortimer, Despenser, Murray, Douglas. In the 17th C *Edmund* and *Edward* were often confused. The Irish form of the name is *Eamon*, which is now also sometimes used, incorrectly, to render Edward.

EDMUND(US) DB 1086, Cur 1199–1219, HR 1273, FA 1316, Poll Tax 1379. EMOND Lincs 1450.

Edna (f.): this name occurs in various books of the Apocrypha, as the wife of Enoch, the wife of Raguel in Tobit, and twice in the book of Jubilees. Its etymology is unknown. It is not clear when it was first used as a christian name, but the first example noted is a character in C. M. Yonge's novel *Hopes and Fears* (1860). The modern vogue of the name is possibly due to the novelist '*Edna* Lyall', whose real name was Ada Ellen Bayly, of which her pen-name is a partial anagram. Her first novel *Won by Waiting* was published in 1879, and she soon became a best-seller.

Edward (m.): (Latin *Edwardus*, French *Édouard*, German *Eduard*, Italian *Eduardo*, Portuguese *Duarte*); Old English *Eadweard*, compound of *ead* 'rich', 'happy', and *weard* 'ward', 'guardian'. It was the name of one of the greatest of the West Saxon kings of England, *Edward* the Elder, son of Alfred the Great, who reigned from 901 to 924; of a saint and martyr, the son of Edgar, who reigned from 975 to 978; and of *Edward* the Confessor, the last English king of the line of Alfred. These associations were sufficient to ensure the popularity of the name in the Old English period and its survival after the Norman Conquest. It occurs in DB and is found in 12th-C records. But the reason why *Edward*, unlike most Old English names, continued in general use after the end of the 12th C was undoubtedly the fact that Henry III's devotion to SS. *Edmund* and *Edward* led him to give their names to two of his sons. From the accession of *Edward* I in 1272 there was an *Edward* on the throne of England for over a century (until 1377). From that time it has been in regular use as a christian name and has shown very little fluctuation of fashion. It is one of the very few names of English origin which have been generally adopted on the Continent. The surnames *Edward(s)*, *Edwardes* were formed from it, but *Edwardson* is surprisingly rare. The nicknames *Ned* and *Ted* have been used since the 14th C; *Eddie* is modern.

EADUUARD, ÆDUUARD, EDUUARD, EDUARD DB 1086.
EDWARDUS Cur 1187–1219.

Edwin (m.): Old English *Eadwine*, compound of *ead* 'happy', 'rich', and *wine* 'friend', the name of the first Christian king of Northumberland (585?–633), and a fairly common name in the Old English period. It survived the Norman Conquest, and is sometimes found as a surname, but seems not to have been generally used as a christian name between the 13th and the early 19th C, though it is said to have been common in Lancashire in the 16th and 17th C.

EADUIN, ÆDUUIN, ÆDUIN, EDUUIN(E), EDUIN DB 1086.
EDUINUS Cur 1200–19.

Edwina (f.): a modern f. name formed from *Edwin*.

Effie (f.), see EUPHEMIA.

Egbert (m.): compound of Old English *ecg* 'sword', and *beorht* 'bright', the name of the traditional first King of all England (died 839) and of a Northumbrian saint (639–729). It seems not to have survived the Old English period, but was revived in the 19th C.

EGBERT DB 1086.

Egelina (f.): probably a Norman version of Old German *Agilina* from the root *Agil*. It is found in England in the 13th and 14th C and gave rise to the surnames *Eglon, Eglin, Eagling, Eggling*.
EGELINA FF 1257, FA 1346.
HEGELINA Testa de Neville 13th C.

Eglentyne (f.): Old French diminutive of *aiglente* from Latin *aculenta* 'prickly', a name for the sweetbrier (later erroneously applied to the honeysuckle). The earliest example of the word in OED is 1400, but *Aiglente, Aiglentine* are common as personal names in the *chansons de geste*, and *Eglentine* occurs in England as early as 1213 (Cur). *Eglentyne* was the name of Chaucer's Prioress. It was revived in the late 19th C, but has not come into general use.

Eileen (f.): Modern Irish *Eibhlin*, pronounced *i'lēn* in Munster, but *ev'lēn* in Connaught. Also spelt *Aileen*. Often taken to be the Irish equivalent of *Helen*, but more probably an Irish development of *Evelyn* (q.v.). Often in pet-form *Eily*. Like many other Irish names it became common in England at the beginning of the 20th C.

Eithne, see AINE.

Elaine (f.): an Old French form of *Helen* (q.v.), which occurs in the *chansons de geste* and in Malory's *Morte d'Arthur*. It is not found in use as an ordinary christian name until after Tennyson's *Idylls of the King* (1859) had made familiar the story of Lancelot and *Elaine*, which he took from Malory.

Eldred (m.), see ALDRED.

Eleanor(a), Elinor (f.) [ĕ'lenor, ĕlĕänor'ă]: Provençal *Aliénor*, a form of *Helen* (q.v.), first introduced into England by *Eleanor* of Aquitaine (1122–1204), wife of Henry II, but its popularity was rather due to her descendant *Eleanor* of Castile (died 1290), queen of Edward I, in whose memory her husband erected the so-called '*Eleanor* crosses'. From the 12th to the 15th C the name usually appears as *Alienor, Eleanor, Elianor*. Its relation to *Helen* was apparently recognized as late as 1604 when a list of Yorkshire recusants calls the same person indifferently *Helen* and *Elinor*. The shorter *Elinor* came in in the 17th C, but the spelling *Elianor* also occurred, and no doubt the name was pronounced sometimes as a quadrisyllable, sometimes as a trisyllable. Its use was fairly steady in the 17th and 18th C (examples are *Elinor* (*Nell*) Gwyn 1650–87, *Elinor* Dashwood in *Sense and Sensibility* [1796] 1811). Dickens's 'Little *Nell*' (*Elinor* Trent) in *The Old Curiosity Shop* (1840) may have helped to increase the use of the name, which CMY, however, appears to have regarded as obsolete. The Italian form *Eleonora* is sometimes used. *Eleanor* is now usually so spelt and given in full, the pet-form *Nell* being used rather for *Helen*. See also LEONORA.

ALIENORA Cur 1199, 1213.
ELEANORA Cur 1205, 1207.
ELIANORA FA 1303, 1346.
ALIANORA FA 1428.
ELYENORA HR 1273.
ELINOR Yorks Rec 1604.
ELLENOR St. Michael, Cornhill 1687.
HELEANOR St. Michael, Cornhill 1690.

Eleazar (m.) [ĕlē͞ā′zar]: Hebrew 'God helped'; the name of the son of Aaron, the second chief-priest of Israel, and also of a son of Aminadab, one of David's captains. Not uncommon as a christian name in the 17th C.

Elfleda (f.): the later form of two Old English women's names, *Æthelflæd*, compound of *æthel* 'noble' and *flæd* 'beautiful', 'clean'; and *Ælflæd*, compound of *ælf* 'elf' and *flæd*. The first was the name of the most able of the daughters of Alfred, 'The Lady of the Mercians' (died 918), and the second of a famous abbess of Whitby (654–714?). Neither name long survived the Norman Conquest, but *Elfleda* was revived in the 19th C.

ÆLFLED(A), ALFLED(A), ALFLET, ELFLET DB 1086.

Elfreda (f.) [ĕlfrē′da]: Old English *Ælfthryth*, compound of *ælf* 'elf' and *thryth* 'strength'; the name of the 2nd wife of King Edgar and mother of Ethelred the Unready. She was supposed to have killed her stepson Edward the Martyr. The name did not survive the Norman Conquest but was revived in the 19th C.

Elgiva (f.): either Old English *Æthelgifu*, compound of *æthel* 'noble' and *gifu* 'a gift', or *Ælfgifu*, compound of *ælf* 'elf' and *gifu*, both common Old English names. The latter survived until the 13th C in the form *Elveva*. *Aileve*, which may represent either name, was also common in the same period. *Elgiva* is a 19th-C revival of a latinized form.

ÆILEUA, AILEUA, EILEUA DB 1086.
ÆLFGIUEE, ÆLUEUA, ALUIUA, ALUEUE, ALUEUA, ELUEUA DB 1086.

Eli (m.) [ē'lī]: Hebrew 'height'; the name of the high priest who brought up the prophet Samuel. It was taken into use as a christian name in the 17th C.

Elias [ĕlī'as], see ELIJAH.

Elihu (m.) [ĕlī'hū]: Hebrew 'God (is) he', 'he is God'; the name of one of the participants in the debate with Job, adopted as a christian name in the 17th C and still used in USA.

Elijah, Elias (m.): Hebrew 'Jehovah is God'. It was one of the most popular Old Testament names in the Middle Ages, the various vernacular forms of it being derived from the Greek form 'Ελίας. The English *Ellis*, French *Élie*, and the diminutive *Eliot* were all common in England, as is testified by the numerous surnames formed from them (e.g. *Ellis(on)*, *El(e)y*, *El(l)iot(t)*). *Ellis* gradually went out of fashion, though it is found in use as late as the end of the 15th C; in the 17th C the Puritans took to using *Elijah* (the form in which the name appears in the Authorized Version of the Old Testament). A well-known example of the name is Sir *Elijah* Impey (1732–1809), the friend and colleague of Warren Hastings. *Ellis* and *Eliot* are nowadays often found as christian names, but they are usually surnames being so used. *Élie* is still frequently used in France.

ELIS Cur 1199–1215, HR 1273.
ELYS HR 1273.
ELIAS FA 1316.
ELYAS FA 1303.
ELYE HR 1273.
ELIE QW 1292.
ELIOT Cur 1210.
ELYOT HR 1273.

Eliot, see ELIJAH.

Elisabeth, see ELIZABETH.

Elisha (m.): Hebrew 'God is generous', commonly latinized as *Eliseus*, the name of the disciple and successor of Elijah. Some of the medieval *Ellis*'s may represent this name, though most of them are undoubtedly from *Elias* (i.e. *Elijah*). *Elisha* was occasionally used as a christian name in the 17th C and later, but was never common.

Elizabeth (f.): Hebrew *Elisheba*, 'My God (is) satisfaction', the name of the wife of Aaron and of the mother of St. John the Baptist. The Greek form of the name was Ἐλίσαβετ, the Latin *Elizabetha*; in England the spelling with a *z* has been usual, on the Continent that with an *s*. It was first used as a christian name in the Eastern Church, and made its way from Russia to Germany and the Low Countries and thence to France, where it was transformed into *Isabel* (q.v.), the usual English medieval form of the name. *Elizabeth* is found in England from time to time in the 13th and 14th C, but did not become common until the end of the 15th C. The medieval use of the name, such as it was, was probably a tribute to St. *Elizabeth* of Hungary (1207–31) rather than to the mother of the Baptist. There is only one English church dedication in this name, and it has given rise to no surnames. The cause of its later immense popularity was undoubtedly the long and successful reign of *Elizabeth* Tudor, who was presumably named after her grandmother *Elizabeth* of York and her great-grandmother *Elizabeth* Woodville, wife of Edward IV. At the end of the 15th C *Elizabeth* was still a comparatively rare name; by 1560 it accounted for 16 per cent. of female baptisms, and by 1600 for over 20 per cent., a position which it held for at least 200 years. No name has been more prolific of diminutives, many of which have from time to time established themselves as independent names, a circumstance which gave rise to the old riddling rhyme:

> Elizabeth, Betsy, Betty, and Bess
> Went out one day to find a bird's nest,
> They found a nest with five eggs in it,
> They each took one and left four in it.

The chief of these are the following: *Eliza* (used of the queen by 16th-C poets, and popular in the 18th and early 19th C; Charlotte Lucas in *Pride and Prejudice* calls *Elizabeth* Bennet *Eliza*, though her family call her *Lizzy*); *Betty* (fashionable in the 18th C until it became too common, was relegated to chambermaids and the like, and gradually died out, to be restored to fashion in the 20th C); *Bess(ie)* (common in the 16th C and revived in the 19th C to take the place of *Betty*); *Betsey, Lizzie* or *Lizzy, Tetty, Tetsy, Beth*; Scottish variants are *Elspeth, Elspie*, and *Elsie*, the last of which is now often used as an independent name, *Libby* and *Tibby*. The German *Elsa, Lise, Liesl,* Italian *Bettina* and French *Élise, Lisette*, and *Babette* are all occasionally used in England. *Elizabeth* and *Isabel* were early differentiated, but were sometimes treated as the same name as late as the end of the 15th C; e.g. in 1483 there is a record of one *Ysabell* or *Elisabeth* Cutler. *Elizabella* was a 16th-C coinage. See also LIL(L)IAN.

ELIZABETH Cur 1205.
ELIZABEZ Cur 1207.
ELIZABET FA 1303.

Elkanah (m.): Hebrew 'God has created', the name of the father of the prophet Samuel. Occasionally used as a christian name in the 17th C, and later in the USA. The best-known example of the name is *Elkanah* Settle (1648–1724), the city poet.

Ella (f.): the Norman-French christian name *Ela, Ella,* or *Ala*, which was fairly common in England from the Conquest till about the middle of the 14th C, was probably derived from Old German *Alia*, a f. name from the root *alja* 'all'. It was one of the medieval names revived in the 19th C by the Pre-Raphaelite writers, and has come into general use again. It is used in Ireland as = *Ellie*, a pet-form of *Ellen*.

ELLA Cur 1196, 1200.
ELA Cur 1210–12, FA 1284, 1303, 1346.
ALA Cur 1210–12.
HELE FA 1346.
ELIA FA 1346.

Ellen (f.): the earlier English form of *Helen* (q.v.), now treated as an independent name. In medieval records *Helen* usually appears as *Elen(a)*, *Elene*, *El(l)in*, &c., and these forms, together with the diminutive *El(l)ot*, are found as late as the 17th C. *Ellen* gradually fell out of upper-class use, and CMY seems to regard it as a Scotticism; but it survived among the poorer classes in England and had some revival of popularity in the later 19th C. It is very common in Ireland.

ELENA Cur 1213–15, FA 1346.
ELENE Lincs 1529.
ELLENE Lyford 1655.
ELLYN St. Mary at Hill 1507.
ELEN, ELLIN Chester 1561.
ELOTA, ELLOTA Poll Tax 1379.

Ellis (m.): see ELIJAH and ELISHA. *Ellis* is found in the 17th C as a woman's name, but this is a corruption of *Alice* (q.v.).

Elma (f.): not uncommon in the USA where it is usually an abbreviation of *Guglielma* (q.v.) The 8th Earl of Elgin's elder daughter (born 1842) was named *Elma*, a combination of parts of the mother's names *Elizabeth Mary*, and it has continued to be used in her family.

Elmer (m.): a surname derived from the christian name *Aylmer* (q.v.). It was the name of two New Jersey brothers who played an active part in the American Revolution, and is now a common christian name in the USA. But as late as 1655 Lyford gives *Elmer* as a christian name from *Ethelmer*, and it is possible that the American use may also represent a survival of this.

Eloisa, see HELEWISE.

Elsa (f.): German diminutive of *Elisabeth* (q.v.), now sometimes used as an independent name in England, probably after the heroine of Wagner's opera *Lohengrin*.

Elsie, Elspeth, see ELIZABETH.

Eluned, Luned (f.) [ĕli'ned]: a Welsh name now occasionally used in England. See also LINNET.

Elvira (f.) [ĕlvē′ra]: this Spanish name is possibly from Old German *Alverat*, which became *Alvery* or *Aubrey* in English (see ALBREDA). It has occasionally been used in England since the beginning of the 19th C, perhaps from its associations with the Don Juan legend.

Emanuel (m.): Hebrew 'God with us', the name given to the Messiah in Isa. vii. 14, viii. 8. First used as a christian name by the Greeks (e.g. *Manuel* Comnenus), it spread westward and became particularly common in Spain and Portugal as *Manuel* or *Manoel*, with f. forms *Manuela, Manuelita*. *Manuel* and *Emanuel* are found as christian names in Cornwall in the 15th and 16th C, and *Immanuel* occurs sometimes in the 17th C, but in general the name has not been much used in England except by Jews.

Emblem, see EMMELINE.

Emerald (f.): the name of a precious stone, occasionally used in recent times as a christian name. See further under MERAUD.

Emery (m.): Old German *Emmerich*, compound of some element from the stem *Im-, Em-*, and *ric* 'ruler'; latinized as *Emericus*. *Emery* was introduced into England by the Normans and, though never common, survived both as a man's and as a woman's name until the end of the 18th C. The f. form occurs as *Emeria* in Lancashire in the 17th and 18th C. It is still used from time to time as a man's name, as also is *Emerick*.

EMERY Cur 1201.
EMERICUS FA 1284, 1316.
EMERIC HR 1273.

Emily, Emilia (f.): f. of Latin *Aemilius*, the name of a plebeian *gens*. Boccaccio's use of *Emilia* for the heroine of his *Teseide* helped to bring the name into use in the later Middle Ages, and Chaucer in his *Knight's Tale* anglicized it as *Emelye*. In FA (Heref) 1316 there occurs *Emulea* la Prys, which may be this name, and *Emerlee* is found in 1694. But it was not much used before the 18th C; George II's daughter, Princess *Amelia*, was usually called Princess *Emily*, and it was probably as a supposed equivalent of *Amelia* (q.v.) that *Emily* came into general use in the 19th C.

Emlyn (m.): a common Welsh name. It has been suggested that it is from Latin *Aemilianus*.

Emma (f.): Old German *Emma* or *Imma*, hypocoristic forms of names compounded with *ermin, irmin* 'whole', 'universal'. The name was introduced into England by *Emma*, daughter of Richard I, Duke of Normandy, who married (1) 1002 King Ethelred the Unready, and (2) 1017 King Cnut. It was a favourite Norman name, and was common from the 11th C onwards. The English form was *Em(m)*, which is found as late as the middle of the 18th C, and the diminutive *Emmot* was also common, giving rise to a number of surnames; Camden 1605 and Lyford 1655 give *Emmet* as a christian name. The form *Emma* was revived in the 18th C, probably under the influence of Prior's poem *Henry and Emma*, a paraphrase of the ballad of the 'Nut Brown Maid'.

EMMA Cur 1186–1219 *passim*, FA 1316, 1401.
EMME *Prompt Parv c.* 1440.
EMMOTE HR 1273.
EMMETE HR 1273.
EMMOT(A) Poll Tax 1379.

Emmeline (f.): Old French *Ameline, Emeline*, apparently formed from the common element *Amal-* (see AMELIA) with the diminutive suffix *-ine*. It was introduced into England by the Normans; one of the daughters of Aimeri, Vicomte de Thouars, who accompanied the Conqueror to England, was named *Ameline*. It was common throughout the Middle Ages in the forms *Emlin, Emblin*, and later *Emblem*. *Emblen* and *Imblen* occur in the 16th and 17th C, *Emlyn* in the 17th, and in Chichester Cathedral there is a memorial to *Emblem* Miller, died 1718 aet. 17. *Emblyn* Rogers, b. 1840 at Ashburton, Devon, is the latest example noted. The full form *Emmeline* was revived in the 18th C.

EMELINA Cur 1199–1219, Cl 1319.
EMELYNE QW 1292.
EMELYN Poll Tax 1379.
EMELINE Year Book 1422.
EMBLEMA Huntspill 1697, 1700.

Emrys (m.): see AMBROSE.

Ena (f.): used in Ireland as a semi-anglicization of the Irish *Eithne* (see AINE). It became popular in England on account of 'Princess *Ena*', Princess Victoria Eugénie Julia Ena, later Queen of Spain (born 1887).

Endymion (m.): Greek *'Ενδυμίων*, the name of the Latmian shepherd loved by Artemis. It was sometimes used as a christian name in the 16th and 17th C, e.g. *Endymion* Porter, the royalist (1587–1649).

Enid (f.) [ē'nid, ĕ'nid]: a Welsh name which came into use in England after the publication of Tennyson's 'Geraint and Enid' in the *Idylls of the King* (1859). It is commonly pronounced *ēnid* in England, but the Welsh pronunciation is *ĕnid*.

Enoch (m.): Hebrew 'trained', 'skilled', the name of a patriarch, father of Methuselah. It came into use as a christian name in the 17th C.

Ephraim (m.): Hebrew, possibly means 'meadows', the name of the 2nd son of Joseph. It came into use in the 17th C, and is still current in USA.

Erasmus (m.): from Greek *ἐράσμιος* 'beloved', 'desired', the name of a martyr of the Diocletian persecution and one of the 14 Holy Helpers. It is best known, however, as the name of the Dutch scholar and reformer *Desiderius Erasmus* (1465–1536). *Erasmus* came into use in England in the later Middle Ages, particularly in the Eastern counties, probably through contact with the Low Countries. Examples are *Erasmus* Paston, died 1540, Sir *Erasmus* Dryden (1553–1632) in whose family the name has been used ever since, and *Erasmus* Darwin (1731–1802) grandfather of Charles Darwin, who was named after his great-grandfather Sir *Erasmus* Earle (1590–1667).

Eric (m.): Modern Norse *Eirik*, German *Erich*.
The second element is the common Teutonic root meaning

'ruler', 'government', the first is doubtful. The name was brought to England by the Danes (there is one tenant named *Iricus* in DB), but it seems to have soon died out. Its revival in the 19th C was helped by Dean Farrar's immensely popular school-story, *Eric: or Little by Little* (1858), and it is now a fairly common name.

Erica (f.): f. of *Eric* (q.v.). CMY does not mention this name, though she gives the Swedish form *Erika*. Its use in England seems to derive from the name of the heroine of Edna Lyall's very popular novel *We Two* (1884). A correspondent to N & Q mentions it as 'a curious name' in 1898. Some users of the name now identify it with Latin *Erica*, the botanical name for heather.

Ermengarde (f.): see ERMYNTRUDE.

Ermyntrude (f.): Old German *Ermentrudis*, *Ermandrud*, compound of *ermin* 'whole', 'universal', and *drudi* 'strength'. It was used in England in the 18th and 19th C by romantic writers and sometimes as an actual christian name. *Ermegarde*, with the same first element, is still common in Germany in the form *Irmgard* and was in use in England in the 12th to 13th C in the form *Ermengarde*, though this may have been a survival of the corresponding Old English *Eormengard*, which is on record. Old English *Eormengild* also survived and is found as late as the 19th C in the form *Armigil*.

Ernest (m.): Old German *Ernust*, Modern German *Ernst*, 'vigour', 'earnestness'. The name was apparently introduced into England in the late 18th C by the Hanoverians (e.g. *Ernest* Augustus, Duke of Cumberland 1771–1851), but did not come into general use until the middle of the 19th C. The name *Ernis* or *Erneis* (Latin *Ernisius*, French *Hernays*, *Hernais*), which was common from the 11th to 13th C and gave rise to such surnames as *Harness*, was probably Old German *Arnegis* and not a form of *Ernest*. Lyford 1655 gives *Ernestus*, but specifies that it is German, and there is no evidence of its use in England at that time.

Ernestine (f.): f. form of *Ernest* (q.v.), occasionally used in the 19th C.

Esau (m.): Hebrew, etymology doubtful but possibly means 'blind'. The usual explanation 'hairy' is based on a philological error. The name of the elder son of Isaac. Occasionally used as a christian name since the 17th C.

Esmé (m., f.): the first occurrence of this name seems to be *Esmé* Stuart (1542–83), 6th Seigneur d'Aubigny and afterwards Duke of Lennox, cousin of James VI of Scotland, whose mother was French. His name, which is not found earlier in the family, and which was borne by his son and his grandson, was sometimes spelt *Aymie*, and it is possible that it is really the fairly common French name *Aimé* (see AMYAS). The name spread from the Stuarts to other Scottish families and eventually to England. It is not mentioned by CMY. It is now sometimes given to girls, probably from confusion with the old name *Ismay* (q.v.).

Esmeralda (f.): Spanish 'emerald'. It is used as a name in the romance of *Palmerin of England*, and Victor Hugo made use of it in his *Hunchback of Notre Dame*, since when it has sometimes been used as a christian name in England and France. See also EMERALD and MERAUD.

Esmond (m.): apparently Old English *Estmund*, compound of *est* 'grace', 'beauty', and *mund* 'protection' (Förstemann gives examples of names compounded with the cognate Old German *anst*). It was a rare name and died out in the 14th C. The modern use of *Esmond* as a christian name is no doubt due to the influence of Thackeray's novel *The History of Henry Esmond* (1852).

ESTMUND, ESTMOND HR 1273.
ESMOND Ass 1313–14.

Estelle (f.): a French dramatic name, possibly formed from *estoile* 'a star', used by Dickens for the heroine of *Great Expectations* (1860–1), and since then occasionally as a christian name in England.

Esther (f.) [ĕs'ter]: in the Old Testament book of this name, *Esther* is given as the Persian equivalent of the Hebrew *Hadassah* 'myrtle'; it is probably not, as usually supposed, from the Persian word for a star. In the Septuagint the name appears as 'Εσθήρ, whence Latin *Esthera*, *Hestera*. It is not found in use in England until the 17th C. Lyford 1655 gives both *Hester* and *Esther*, and the two forms were used indifferently. Racine's play gave the name some vogue in France, but it was at no time common in either country, and it is a strange coincidence that Swift's fate should have been involved with two women of this name, *Esther* Johnson and *Esther* Vanhomrigh. *Hetty* was formerly a pet-form of *Hester*. *Hadassah* was occasionally used in the 18th C.

Estrild (f.): Old English *Eastorhild*, compound of *Eastre*, the goddess of the rising sun, and *hild* 'battle'. *Estrild* survived in England until the 12th C. The Spanish *Estrella*, still sometimes used, came from the cognate Old German *Austrechildis*.

Etain (f.): Irish *Etaoin*; the name of the heroine of an Irish myth, popularized in the opera of *The Immortal Hour* (1922), since when the name has occasionally been used in England.

Ethan (m.): Hebrew 'perennial' properly applied to streams that run all the year round. The name occurs in 1 Kings iv. 31 and in the title of Psalm 89. *Ethan* Allen was a leading figure in the American Revolution, and the name has been fairly common in the USA.

Ethel (f.): *Ethel* seems not to have been an independent name in early times, though *Æthelu* occurs in Old English, corresponding to Old German *Athala*. It seems to have arisen in the 19th C as a pet-form for such names as *Ethelburg*, *Etheldred*, *Ethelinda* (qq.v.). There was a correspondence in N & Q in 1872 about *Ethel*, which was then very fashionable. Several correspondents imputed its origin to Thackeray in *The Newcomes* (1853–5); others traced it to C. M. Yonge's *The Daisy Chain* (1856), in which the heroine is called *Ethel* as an abbreviation of her full name *Etheldred*. No doubt it was the popularity of these almost contemporaneous novels which caused the spread of the name.

Ethelbert (m.): compound of Old English *aethel* 'noble', *beorht* 'bright', the name of the King of Kent (560–616) who was converted to Christianity by St. Augustine, and also of a King of England (855–65), brother of Alfred the Great. It is doubtful if it survived the Norman Conquest (but see further under ALBERT), and if it did, it was only for a short time. A solitary example occurs at Cambridge in 1564. It was revived in the middle of the 19th C, an early example being *Ethelbert* (*Bertie*) Stanhope in *Barchester Towers* (1857).

AILBERT, AILBRIHT, AILBRIC, ALBERT, ALBRICT DB 1086.

Ethelburg (f.): Old English *Æthelburh*, or *Æthelburg*, compound of *æthel* 'noble' and *burh* 'a fortress'. The survival of the name down to the 19th C in London is no doubt due to the dedication of the Church of St. *Ethelburga* in Bishopsgate. There were two saints of the name, St. *Ethelburga* (d. 676) sister of Erkenwald, Bishop of London, and St. *Ethelburga*, Abbess of Farmoutiers, sister of SS. Etheldreda, Sexburga, and Withburga.

Etheldred (f.): Old English *Æthelthryth*, compound of *æthel* 'noble', and *thryth* 'strength'. St. *Etheldred* (630?–79) was Queen of Northumbria and founder and abbess of a convent at Ely. The present Cathedral at Ely is built over her remains and there are 12 other churches dedicated to her. From the 16th C the popular corruption *Audrey* (q.v.), now an independent name, was the usual form, but Lyford 1655 gives *Etheldred* or *Ethelred*, and there is a record of one *Etheltred* Daw (born 1728), whose name was corrupted to *Theldry*. The same person is named in Market Rasen Parish Register as *Ethelia* in 1787 and *Theldred* in 1795. *Etheldred(a)* was sometimes used in the 18th and 19th C but is now supplanted by *Ethel* (q.v.).

Ethelfleda (f.): Old English *Æthelflæd*, compound of *æthel* 'noble' and *flæd* 'clean', 'beautiful'. See ELFLEDA.

Ethelinda (f.): Old German *Adallindis*, compound of *athal* 'noble' and *lindi* 'a serpent'. There appears to have been a corresponding Old English name *Æthelind*, and the name *Athelyna*, which occurs in 1346 FA may be a survival of it, though it more probably represents *Ethelwine*. *Ethelinda* is found in England from *c.* 1800 in the forms *Ethelinda, Athelinda,* and even *Earthelinda. Ethelenda* is still used by the gipsy family of Heron.

Ethelred (m.): compound of Old English *æthel* 'noble' and *ræd* 'counsel', a fairly common Old English name; one *Ethelred,* the brother of Alfred, was King of Wessex 866–71, and *Ethelred* son of Edgar was King of England 978–1016. It seems not to have survived the Norman Conquest, but was revived with other Old English names in the 19th C.

ÆTHELRÆD, ADELREDUS, EDRED, ADRED, AILRED, ALRET DB 1086.

Etta (f.): a pet-form of *Henrietta* (q.v.), occasionally used as an independent name.

Eubule (m.): Greek εὔβουλος 'he of good counsel', an epithet of Zeus. *Eubulus* occurs in 2 Tim. iv. 21 as the name of one of St. Paul's companions. It was sometimes used as a christian name in England after the Reformation (e.g. Sir *Eubule* Thelwall 1562–1630, one of the founders of Jesus College, Oxford). In the 17th C it was sometimes spelled *Ewball;* Lyford 1655 gives it as *Ybel.*

Eudo (m.): Old German *Eutha,* which Förstemann connects with Old Norse *jôdh* 'child'. It was introduced into England by the Normans and appears as *Eudes* and *Eudon* (representing Old French *cas-sujet* and *cas-régime*), and latinized as *Eudo. Udo* is found as late as 1507.

EUDO Reg 1070–7, DB 1086, Cur 1197–1219.
UDONA FA 1346.
EUDES Cur 1187–1219.

Eugene (m.) [ūjēn'] : Greek εὐγένιος 'noble', 'well-born', Latin *Eugenius.* There were four popes of this name, the first (died 657) being venerated as a saint. *Eugenio* has been fairly common in Italy, but its wider diffusion was due to the fame of Prince *Eugène* of Savoy (1663–1736), the brilliant general after whom e.g. Richard Steele's 2nd son (born 1712) was named. *Eugene* is now sometimes used in England, oftener in USA where it is often abbreviated to *Gene. Eugenius* occurs in lists of early kings of Scotland, but it then represents a Gaelic name (see EWEN). In Ireland *Eugene* has come to be the English equivalent of *Eoin*, the Old Irish form of John, later replaced by *Sean* from French *Jean*. The relationship of *Eoin* to John was almost forgotten in the 19th C.

Eugenia, Eugénie (f.) [ūjēn′ĕă, ezhā′nĕ]: Greek *Εὐγενία* 'nobility', 'excellence'; the name of a 3rd-C Roman martyr, a convert of SS. Protus and Hyacinthus. *Eugenia* is recorded in England in the 12th and 13th C. The French form of the name, *Eugénie*, was made fashionable in France by the Empress *Eugénie* (1826–1920), and is now sometimes used in England.

Eulalia (f.) [ūlā′lĕă]: from Greek *εὔλαλος* 'sweetly-speaking', an epithet of Apollo; the name of a 4th-C martyr, the patron saint of Barcelona. It is fairly common in Spain and France (*Eulalie*), and is occasionally found in England, especially in Cornwall, e.g. *Eulalia* Sarat (died 1684), *Ulalia* Moyle (married 1657), both Cornish.

Eunice (f.) [ūnī′sĕ, ū′nis]: Greek *Εὐνίκη*, compound of *εὖ* 'well' and *νίκη* 'victory'; the name of the mother of Timothy, mentioned in Acts xvi. 1 and 2 Tim. i. 5. It came into use in England in the 17th C. The spelling *Unice* is found in Lincs. in 1617 and in New England in 1804. It is often pronounced as a disyllable; as CMY says: 'A favourite with English lovers of Bible names, though unfortunately usually pronounced among the lower classes after the most ordinary English rules of spelling: Younice.'

Euphemia (f.) [ūfē′mĕă]: Greek *Εὐφημία* 'auspicious speech', hence 'worship of the gods', 'honour', or 'good repute'. The name occurs in the apocryphal Acts of Peter (*c.* 200) as that of one of the four concubines of Agrippa the prefect, who were converted and suffered death for their chastity. It was also the name of a 4th-C Bithynian martyr who has a place in the Roman Calendar. *Eufemia* or *Eupheme* is found in England from about 1200, and by the 16th C it was usually shortened to *Epham*, *Effum*, or *Effim*. Lyford 1655 gives *Eupheme*, but by his time the name was probably confined to Scotland, where it still flourishes, often in the pet-forms *Effie* or *Phemie*. One of James Boswell's daughters bore this name. A m. form *Euphemius* occurs at Cambridge in 1629.

EUFEMIA Cur 1205, 1210, 1221, QW 1292, FA 1284, 1346.
EUFEMMIA HR 1270.
EUPHEMIA FA 1346, Poll Tax 1379.
EPHAM Yorks Rec 1604.
FEMMOTA Magd. 1357.

Eusebius (m.) [ūsē'b*eus*]: from Greek εὐσεβής 'pious'; a common Greek name, the best known example being *Eusebius* of Caesarea (*c.* A.D. 264–*c.* 349), the ecclesiastical historian. It was probably after him that the name was used in the 17th C, e.g. *Eusebius* Hunt (Hunts Clergy List 1696), *Euseby* Pelsant 1642. Godstow 1450 gives *Euseby* as the English form of *Eusebius*, but there is no evidence of its use as a christian name at that date.

Eustace (m.) [ūs'tas]: there are two saints named *Eustachius* in the Roman Calendar, one of them having the same day as St. *Eustathius* in the Greek Calendar, and the two names are often supposed to be identical. But there is no trace of confusion between them at an early period, and though *Eustachius* is not easy to explain etymologically, that is no reason for confounding it with *Eustathius* (from Greek εὐστάθης 'tranquil', 'stable'). It may possibly be from εὐσταχυς 'fruitful'. The better known of the two saints *Eustachius* was a 2nd-C Roman soldier, whose legend included the story of his conversion, while hunting, by the vision of a crucifix between the horns of a stag. He was, like St. Hubert, a patron saint of huntsmen. His relics were transferred at an early date to St. Denis, and *Eustache* was a common French name. It was brought to England by the Normans and was fairly common in the 12th and 13th C. In Latin it appears as *Eustachius* or *Eustacius*, in English as *Eustace*, *Eustas* or *Ewstace*, and gave rise to the surnames *Eustace*, *Eustes*, *Eustis*. It has continued in infrequent use till the present day.

EUSTAC(H)IUS Reg 1076–84, DB 1086, Cur 1196–1215, FA 1303, 1316.
EUSTACE, EWSTACE HR 1273.

Eustacia (f.) [ūstā's*ea*]: f. form of *Eustace* (q.v.). *Eustac(h)ia* is fairly common in Latin records of the 12th and 13th C. In the vernacular the m. and f. forms of the name were doubtless identical, and in 1521 there is mention of *Eustace* wife of William Malley. The Latin form *Eustacia* was occasionally used in the 18th and 19th C.

EUSTACHIA Cur 1200, 1205, 1207, 1213.

Eva, Eve (f.): Hebrew *Chawwa*, (?) 'lively', the name of the first woman. The Jews seem not to have used it, but it is found in use in England from about the end of the 12th C, and gave rise to the surnames *Eve*, *Eaves*, &c. *Eva* is the Latin, *Eve* the vernacular form of the name. In Ireland and Scotland it was used to represent the Gaelic *Aoiffe*, Modern Gaelic *Eubha*. Its revival in England in the 19th C was no doubt partly due to the popularity of *Uncle Tom's Cabin* (1852).

EVA Cur 1199–1219, HR 1273, FA 1303, 1346.
EVE FA 1284, 1486.
EVOTA Magd. 1426.

Evadne (f.): Greek *Εὐάδνη*, the name of the wife of Capaneus, who threw herself on her husband's funeral pyre. It was used by Fletcher for the heroine of *The Maid's Tragedy*. It is now sometimes used as a christian name, such use originating, perhaps, in the name of one of the characters in Sarah Grand's popular novel *The Heavenly Twins* (1893).

Evan (m.) [ĕ′van]: Welsh form of *John* (q.v.). It is usually considered to be derived from Latin *Iohannes* by way of vulgar Latin *Iŏvannes* (cf. Italian *Giovanni*), but there are several phonological difficulties. The form *Evan* dates only from about 1500. Earlier forms were *Iefan* and *Ifan*, and in Middle English we find *Yevan*, *Zevan*.

Evangeline (f.): this name appears to have been invented by Longfellow for the heroine of his narrative poem *Evangeline* (1847), as a f. form of the noun *evangel*. It is now fairly common in the USA and is also sometimes used in England.

Eveleen (f.) [ĕvelēn′]: Irish diminutive form of *Eva* (q.v.). It is often confused with *Evelina* (q.v.).

Evelina, Evelyn (f.) [ĕvelē'na, ē'velin]: Old German *Avelina*, a hypocoristic form of *Avi* (cf. the m. name *Avila*). The Normans introduced *Aveline* into England and it was common in the 12th and 13th C, giving rise to the surnames *Aveling, Eveling, Evelyn, Eveline*, &c. *Aveline* was still used as a christian name in the 17th C and *Avaline* is found as late as 1829 in New England. The Latin form of the name, *Evelina*, was revived by Fanny Burney for the heroine of her novel of that name (1778), and has been used from that time onwards. The shorter *Evelyn*, which is now commoner than *Evelina*, and is usually pronounced *ēvelyn*, has apparently come into being through association with the m. name *Evelyn* (q.v.). See also EILEEN.

AVELINA Cur 1189, 1200, HR 1273, FF 1430.
AVELYN Poll Tax 1379.

Evelyn (m.) [ē'velin]: as a man's name this seems to date only from the 17th C and to be derived from the surname *Evelyn*. The two earliest recorded examples are *Evelyn* Pierrepont, 1st Duke of Kingston (1665-1726), and Sir *Evelyn* Alston died 1750. Both their mothers were *Evelyns* by birth. The surname probably originated in the christian name *Aveline* (see EVELINA).

Everard (m.): Old German *Eburhard*, Modern German *Eberhard*, compound of *ebur* 'a boar' and *hardu* 'hard', cognate with Old English *Eoforheard*. It was introduced into England by the Normans in the French form *Everard* and was fairly common in the 12th and 13th C, giving rise to the surnames *Everard, Everit(t)*, *Everett*, &c. It has continued in occasional use ever since, notably in the Digby family.

EBRARDUS DB 1086.
EBERARDUS Cur 1213-15.
EVERARDUS FA 1284, Cur 1196-1215, HR 1273.
EVERITT St. Jas. Clerkenwell 1619.
EVERET Gedney Parish Reg 1783.

Everild, see AVERIL.

Ewen (m.) [ū'en]: this name, now confined to Scotland, was once common in England, as may be seen by the surnames *Ewen, Ewing(s), Ewan, Ewin*, &c. It is probably the same as Irish and

Gaelic *Eoghan* 'a youth', which is frequent in Celtic legend and history. *Eoghan* is usually derived from Primitive Celtic **Esugenios* 'well-born', from which also is derived Old Welsh *Euguein* which later became Middle Welsh *Ewein, Ywein*, whence Modern Welsh *Owain, Owen* (q.v.).

Ezekiel (m.): Hebrew Y'hezqēl 'May God strengthen', the name of one of the major prophets. The English form comes from the Septuagint Greek Ἰεζεκιηλ through the Vulgate Latin *Ezechiel*. It was adopted as a christian name in the 17th C and has been common in the USA, where it is sometimes abbreviated to *Zeke*.

Ezra (m.): Hebrew 'help', the name of the author of one of the books of the Old Testament, taken into use in England in the 17th C (e.g. *Ezra* Grayle, a Presbyterian minister in 1648).

F

Fabian (m.): Latin *Fabianus* 'of *Fabius*' (the name of a Roman *gens*). *Fabius* may be derived from *faba* 'a bean', but this etymology is not certain. There was a 3rd-C Pope *Fabian* venerated as a saint and he is no doubt responsible for the survival of the name. Bardsley gives many examples of *Fabian* as a christian name in the 16th C, the earliest being in *Cocke Lorelle's Bote* 1515, but was unable to find anything earlier, though the existence of the surnames *Fabian, Fabyan* made it certain that the name was in use some centuries before. *Fabianus* does, however, occur as the name of a sub-prior of St. Albans *c.* 1200 and in a Curia Regis Roll of 1220.

Faith (f.): first used as a christian name after the Reformation. Lyford 1655 calls it 'a name commonly used'. In the 16th and 17th C it was given to boys as well as girls. Female triplets were often called *Faith, Hope*, and *Charity*. Not in CMY but now fairly common.

Fanny, see FRANCES.

Faramond (m.): Old German *Faramund*, compound of *fara* 'journey' and *mund* 'protection'. *Faramond* was the name of the legendary first King of France. It was introduced into England by the Normans and gave rise to a number of surnames, such as *Farrimond, Farman, Fairman, Fearman.* The *Ph* spelling occurs in Shakespeare's *Henry V.*

FARMAN(NUS) DB 1086.
FAREMANNE Pipe Rolls 1169.
FARMAN, FAIRMAN Writs of Parliament 1306.
FAREMAN Writs of Parliament 1316.
PHAREMAN Fines 12th C.

Farquhar (m.) [far'kar]: Gaelic *Fearchar*, from *fer* 'man' and *car* 'friendly'. The name of an early Scottish king. Still fairly common in the Highlands.

Faustus (m.): Latin *faustus* 'fortunate', 'lucky', the name of a 3rd-C Roman martyr. It was used as a christian name in the Middle Ages in Germany and Italy. In Germany it gave rise to the surname *Faust* or *Faustus*, which was borne by the 16th-C necromancer Johann *Faust*, who was the original from which the *Faust* legend arose.

Fay (f.): this name appears to be modern, first occurring in the 1890's. It may have been an abbreviation of *Faith* (q.v.) or be the word *fay* 'fairy'.

Felicia (f.): the history of this name is much confused with that of *Phyllis* (q.v.). There was a St. *Felicia* of Nicomedia of unknown date, and the name, which is a f. form of *Felicius*, a 3rd-C derivative of *Felix* (q.v.), is found in use in England from the end of the 12th C. The vernacular form of the name was *Felice* or *Felis* (cf. French *Félise*): *Felice* occurs in *Piers Plowman*; Lyford 1655 says: '*Felice* see *Felix* in Men's names.' In 1577 the name is found spelt *Phelis*, and there seems little doubt that many of the 17th-C *Phyllis's* were really *Felice's*. The name was occasionally used in the 18th C, e.g. *Felicia* Hemans (1793–1835). A writer to N & Q in 1874 says: 'I have known 3 instances of the name *Felicia* being given in Cheshire. In one case it was always shortened to *Phyllis*.' G. M. Hopkins writing to Coventry Patmore in 1883 about one of his poems says: '*Felicia*—I do not understand the name. Is it a proper name, or the neuter plural of *felix*?' Patmore replied: 'I used the name *Felicia* because it *is* a name, and suggests itself as the female of *Felix*. *Felicitas* would not have done.' At the present time *Felicity* (q.v.) is much commoner.

FELICIA Cur 1199, 1218, FA 1303, 1316, 1401.
FELICE Oseney 1460.
FELISIA Poll Tax 1379.
FELIS Poll Tax 1379.
FILISIA Poll Tax 1379.
FILLYS St. Jas. Clerkenwell 1569.

Felicity (f.): Latin *Felicitas* 'happiness'. There were two saints *Felicitas*, one a 3rd-C Carthaginian martyr, and the other a widow said to have been martyred with her seven sons, and popularly identified with the mother of the Maccabees. But the name does not seem to have been used in England until the 17th C when many abstract nouns came into use as christian names. It is spelt *Phelisstie* in 1641.

Felix (m.): Latin *felix* 'happy'. The name of four popes and several saints, notably St. *Felix* the apostle of East Anglia, after whom *Felixstowe* was named. It was used in England in the Middle Ages, but not so often as the f. form (see FELICIA). It appears as *Felis* in the *chansons de geste*, and *Felyse* is given as the English form of *Felix* in Godstow 1450. *Felix* has been commonly used in Ireland to represent the Irish *Phelim*.

Fenella (f.) [fene'lä]: Gaelic *Fionnghuala*, from *fionn* 'white' and *guala* 'shoulder'. In Ireland it has often been rendered by *Penelope* (q.v.). The name was made generally known in England by Scott in *Peveril of the Peak*. *Finola* is the usual form in Ireland to-day.

Ferdinand (m.): compound of Old German *fardi* 'journey' and *nanthi* 'risk', 'venture'. The name was never very common in Teutonic countries, but was carried south by the Goths and became very popular in Spain (it was borne by many Kings of Castille) as *Fernando*, *Hernan(do)*, and also in Italy as *Ferdinando*, *Ferrante*. *Ferrand* was not uncommon in France and England in the Middle Ages, and gave rise to the surnames *Farrand*, *Farrant*, *Farren*, &c. By the 14th C, however, the name seems to have died out. In the 16th C the Italian form *Ferdinando* suddenly came into use in England. The earliest examples noted are Sir *Ferdinando* Heybourne (born 1558), and *Ferdinando* Stanley, later 5th Earl of Derby (born 1559). From then until the end of the 17th C *Ferdinando* was not uncommon, particularly in the landed families of the Midlands; it was also used regularly by some northern families such as the Stanleys and Hudlestons. In Ireland *Ferdinand* or *Fardy* is used to represent the Irish *Feordorcha*.

FERANT HR 1273.
FERRANT HR 1273.
FERENTUS Testa de Neville 13th C.

Fergus (m.): Old Irish *Fer-gus* from *fer* 'man' and Primitive Celtic **gustus* 'choice'. Mainly Scottish and Irish but occasionally used in the North of England.

Fer(r)and, see FERDINAND.

Fer(r)y, see FREDERIC(K).

Finola, see FENELLA.

Fiona (f.): this name seems to have been invented by William Sharp (1855–1905) for his literary personality '*Fiona* Macleod'; he presumably intended it for a f. form of Gaelic *fionn*, 'fair', 'white'. It is now occasionally used as a christian name.

Firmin (m.): Latin *Firminus*, a derivative of the name *Firmius*. St. *Firminus* was a 5th-C Bishop of Metz. *Firmin* is found in England from the 12th to the 16th C and is still used in France.

FIRMIN HR 1273.
FIRMAN FF 1324.
FIRMINB FF 1552.
FYRMYN St. Dionis 1545.

Flavia (f.): f. of Latin *Flavius*, the name of a Roman *gens*, probably derived from *flavus*, 'yellow'.

Fleur (f.): French *fleur* 'flower'. Used as a christian name by Galsworthy in his *Forsyte Saga* (1926–30), and since then occasionally in real life.

Flora (f.): the name of the Roman goddess of flowers, which was adopted as a christian name in France (*Flore*) at the Renaissance, and carried thence to Scotland where it has been used ever since. *Flora* Macdonald, the Jacobite heroine, no doubt increased its popularity, and it is now often used in England, where it was formerly considered a suitable name for a spaniel but not for a woman. In the 13th and 14th C there are a few records of a name *Floria*, presumably the f. of Latin *Florius* 'of *Flora*'.

Florence (m.): Latin *Florentius*, from *florens* 'blooming'. There was a 3rd-C Roman martyr named *Florentius*, and also a Gaulish saint whose relics were preserved at Saumur. The name also occurs in the Old French romances, and was not uncommon in England in the Middle Ages. Lyford 1655 gives *Florence* as a man's name, but it does not seem to have survived the 17th C in England (Shelley's son, Percy *Florence*, was named after the city of his birth), though it has continued in use in Ireland (e.g. the inimitable '*Flurry*' Knox), where it was used to represent various native names.

FLORENCIUS Cur 1201–3, FA 1284, 1316.
FLORENCE HR 1273.

Florence (f.): Latin *Florentia* f. of *Florentius* (see man's name). *Florence* was used in the Middle Ages about equally as a man's and a woman's name, but whereas it died out as a man's it survived in use as a woman's name, e.g. *Florence* Vavzor 1621, and *Florence* Dombey in Dickens's *Dombey and Son* (1846–8). But it was rare until it was given a fresh impetus by the fame of *Florence* Nightingale (1820–1912), who herself received the name because she was born in Florence. In the 19th C it became common and was often shortened to *Florrie*, *Flo*, *Floy*, or *Flossie*.

FLORENTIA Cur 1196-1219.
FLORENCIA FA 1346.
FLORENCE Cl 1378, Lyford 1655.

Florian (m.): Latin *florianus* 'flowery', 'blooming'; the name of a 4th-C Roman saint invoked against fire and drought. It was occasionally used in the Middle Ages.

Flossie, see FLORENCE.

Flower (f.): this is found as a girl's name, occasionally, from the 17th C. Early examples are found in the parish registers of Hinton Charterhouse in 1625 and 1668.

Fortunatus (m.): Latin *fortunatus*, 'prosperous' 'lucky' a name adopted by or given to freedmen. Saints *Felix* and *Fortunatus* were martyred in 212 at Valence. Its use as a christian name has not been noted in England before the 17th C and it was probably a Puritan usage analogous to such names as *Donatus, Renatus, Desideratus,* &c. A number of examples of *Fortunatus* are cited in N & Q 192, No. 9 (3 May 1947).

Frances (f.): (French *Françoise*, Italian *Francesca*, Spanish *Francisca*, German *Franziska*): from Italian *Francesca*, f. of *Francesco* (see FRANCIS). The earliest record of the name *Francesca* seems to be *Francesca* da Rimini (died about 1288); the French *Françoise* appears about the same time. In England the name, like its m. equivalent, does not appear until the Tudor period, the earliest examples noted being *Frances*, daughter of Humfrey Cockayne, born about 1490, and Lady *Francis* Brandon (born 1517) daughter of Mary Tudor and mother of Lady Jane Grey. It was a favourite name with the aristocracy in the Elizabethan period, being spelt in the same way as the m. name and, like it, abbreviated to *Frank*. The distinctive spelling came in in the 17th C (e.g. *Francesse* Carpenter baptized at St. Giles Cripplegate 1644). Lyford 1655 says: '*Frances* see *Francis* in men's names'. The pet-form *Fanny*, from an earlier *Franny* (cf. *Biddy* from *Bridget, Kit* from *Christopher*), came in at the beginning of the 18th C, e.g. Pope's attack

(1733) on John, Lord Harvey under the name of Lord *Fanny*. *Francie* and *Frankie* are also used as diminutives of *Frances*.

Francis (m.): (French *François*, Italian *Francesco*, Spanish *Francisco*, German *Franz*): Latin *Franciscus* 'a Frenchman'. The widespread use of this name on the Continent is undoubtedly due to St. *Francis* of Assisi (1182–1226), whose baptismal name was Giovanni, *Francesco* being a nickname said to have been bestowed by his father, who was on a business journey in France at the time of his birth. But the name may have been in use earlier, for in Curia Regis Rolls of 1200 and 1207 there is mention of a certain *Franceis*, though this, too, may have been a nickname rather than a proper christian name. The surname *Francis* seems to have originated thus, for early examples are all in the form *le Franceys*, &c. The earliest examples of the christian name noted in England are *Francis* Calthorpe of Norwich (1494), and *Francis* Southwick of Norfolk (1499). It is curious that the name did not become common until the 16th C, though the Franciscans established themselves early in this country and at the Reformation had some 80 convents here. An early example is *Francis* Russell, 2nd Earl of Bedford (1527?–85), and the growing power and influence of the Russell family in the 16th C may have had a good deal to do with its spread. *Francis* Drake, for example, was a godson of this *Francis* Russell, and one of *Francis* Bacon's aunts was married to his son, Lord Russell. The name was not much used in the 17th and 18th C except in families, such as those of Russell and Drake already mentioned, where it was firmly established. It gradually came back into favour in the 19th C and is now a common name. In the 16th C *Fraunce* was sometimes used as an abbreviation, as well as the more usual *Frank*.

Frank (m.): this name is now, and has been since the 16th C, the common abbreviation of *Francis* (q.v.). But it was not uncommon in England from the time of the Norman Conquest till about the middle of the 14th C, as an independent name representing the Old German *Franco* 'a Frank'. *Franco* occurs three times in DB and *Francus* once, and *Franco, Francus, Frank, Fraunk* occur with some frequency in the records of the next three centuries.

Freda, see WINIFRED.

Fredegonde (f.): Old German *Fridegundis*, compound of *frithu* 'peace' and *gundi* 'war'. This was the name of the queen of Chilperic I, an early Frankish king, and the French form of the name, *Frédégonde*, has been used from time to time in France and, very rarely, in England.

Frederic(k) (m.): (Latin *Fredericus*, German *Friedrich*, *Fritz*, French *Frédéric*, Italian *Federigo*): Old German *Frithuric*, compound of *frithu* 'peace' and *ric* 'ruler'. There was a corresponding, rather rare, Old English name *Freodhoric* which is probably behind the *Fredericus* who appears in DB as a tenant TRE. The medieval French form *Frery* or *Ferry* is occasionally found in the 12th C, but on the whole the name was uncommon until the 17th C. Camden 1605 says: 'For *Frideric* the English have commonly used *Frery* and *Fery* which hath been now a long time a christian name in the ancient family of Tilney, and lucky to their house as they report.' (A *'Fred.* de Tilney' is recorded as early as 1360.) The real acclimatization dates from the 18th C, when the Hanoverians brought it in, e.g. *Frederick* Prince of Wales, son of George II. It very soon gained a firm footing and has for some 200 years been one of the commonest English men's names. It is usually shortened, in use, to *Fred* or *Freddy*.

Frederica (f.) [frĕderē′kă]: the f. form of *Frederick* (q.v.), coined in Germany and first used in England in the 19th C.

Frideswide (f.) [frīds′wīd]: Old English *Frithuswith*, compound of *frith* 'peace' and *swith* 'strong'. St. *Frithswith* or *Frideswide* (died 735?) is said to have been the daughter of a king of Mercia and to have fled to Oxford to preserve her virginity from a royal suitor. She founded a convent at Oxford, and the Cathedral is raised over her remains, which were in 1289 translated to a splendid shrine. Her name is found in use up to the Reformation (Godstow 1450 says *'Fryswyde* English for *Frediswitha'*) and even later. Lyford 1655 gives *Frideswid* as a woman's name, and it is found in use in 1593 (*Fridswed*), 1612 (*Fridiswid*) and 1706 (*Fridiswed*). It is now used mainly by Roman Catholics. Corruptions of this name were common: for example, it occurs in Henley church registers as *Fridayweed* and *Freadeyweed* in the early 18th C.

Frusannah (f.): this name, occasionally used in the 18th and 19th C, seems to be an artificial combination of *Frances* and *Susannah*. Cf. *Rosanna, Saranna*.

Fulbert (m.): Old German *Filibert*, compound of *filu* 'much' and *berhta* 'bright'. St. *Filibert* or *Philibert* was the 7th-C founder of the Abbey of Jumièges, and the name was introduced into England by the Normans in the forms *Filbert, Fulbert*. It gave rise to the surnames *Filbert, Philbert, Philibert*, and also to the name of the *filbert* nut, so called because it ripened about the time of St. *Philibert*'s day (22 Aug. OS). *Fulbert* is given as a christian name by Lyford 1655, and is still used in a few families.

FULBERTUS Reg 1094–9.

Fulcher, see FULK(E).

Fulk(e) (m.) [fŏolk]: Old German *Fulco*, a derivative of *Folc-* 'people'. The name was particularly common among the Burgundians and was hereditary with the Counts of Anjou. It was introduced into England at the time of the Norman Conquest, but attained its greatest popularity under the Angevins. It often appears as *Fawke* or *Fowke*, and gave rise to the surnames *Faux, Fawkes, Fowkes, Folk(es)*, &c. *Fulk(e), Fawke, Fowke* are still found as christian names in the 17th C, but the name is now apparently obsolete, except in the Greville and Markham families, which have both used it since the 16th C, and in the gipsy families of Gray and Heron, who still use the form *Fowk*.

The allied compound name *Fulcher* (Old French *Fouchier*, Old German *Folkher*) was also common in the Middle Ages, and Lyford 1655 gives it in his list of christian names.

FULCO DB 1086, Cur 1196–1220, HR 1273.
FULKE HR 1273.
FOLKE Testa de Neville 13th C.
FOLKES HR 1273.
FOWKE HR 1273.
FOLC QW 1292.
FULK or FOWKE Ox Univ Reg 1567.

G

Gabel(l), see GABRIEL.

Gabriel (m.) [gā'brēel, gă'brēel]: (Italian *Gabriele*, Russian *Gavril*): Hebrew 'God is a strong man' or 'strong man of God', the name of the Archangel of the Annunciation. Never common, it occurs sometimes in the form *Gabel* or *Gabell*, from the 12th C and has never quite died out. There are very few churches dedicated to the archangel, but it was a common dedication for bells, the angelus being rung on the *Gabriel* or *Angelus* bell.

GABRIEL Cur 1199, 1200, 1210, HR 1273, FA 1316.
GABELL HR 1273.
GABRYELL St. Mary at Hill 1480.

Gabriel(le) (f.) [gā'brēel, gă'brēel]: in the Middle Ages *Gabriel* (in Latin *Gabriela* or *Gabella*) was used as a woman's as well as a man's name. The Modern French *Gabrielle* is now sometimes used to distinguish the f.

Gaenor, see GUENEVERE.

Gaius (m.) [gī'es]: Latin *Gaius* (less correctly *Caius*) for *Gavius* (from *gaudere* 'to rejoice'). A Roman praenomen. The Welsh *Kai* or *Kay* is said to be from *Caius*. The surname of John *Caius*, founder of Caius College, Cambridge, is usually supposed to be a latinized form of the English surname Kay. Several examples of *Gaius* as a christian name have been noted in Bucks. in the 19th C, and it is still occasionally used in Wales. This use is no doubt due to the occurrence of several persons named *Gaius* in the New Testament.

Galahad (m.): the name of the spotless knight, son of Lancelot, who alone achieved the quest of the Holy Grail. The name seems to have been invented by the author of *La Queste del' Saint Graal*; *Galahad's* ancestry as given there contains several Biblical names, and it has been plausibly suggested that *Galahad*, or *Galaad* as it is spelt in the earliest MSS, represents Hebrew *Gilead*. Rhys's attempted etymology from Welsh *gwalch* 'hawk' and *hâv* or *hâf* 'summer' is unconvincing. *Galahad* has occasionally been used as a christian name since Tennyson's *Idylls of the King* made the Arthurian legends generally known.

Galfrid(us) (m.): a modern antique (cf. ALURED) formed from the medieval Latin form (*Galfridus*) of *Geoffrey* (q.v.). An early example is *Galfridus* Mann, brother of Horace Walpole's friend and correspondent, Sir Horace Mann.

Galiena (f.): this name, which occurs not infrequently in 13th-C records, always, unfortunately, in Latin, may be Old German *Gailan(a)*, a derivative of *gail* 'lofty'. It may be the origin of the surnames *Gallon*, *Gallyon* which are found as early as 1273.

GALIENA Cur 1219, 1220.
GAUNLEYA, GANLEYA, GAUNLIENA Cur 1220.

Gamaliel (m.): Hebrew *Gamlī'ēl* 'my recompense (is) God' or 'the recompense of God'; Greek Γαμαλιήλ and Latin *Gamaliel* in the Vulgate. The 'recompense' is the male child so called. The name of the teacher at whose feet Saul of Tarsus had sat. It was used as a christian name in the 17th C, e.g. *Gamaliel* Cane, a Presbyterian minister in 1648 and *Gamaliel* Chase, Rector of Wambrook, Somerset, 1621.

Gamel (m.): apparently Old Norse *gamal* (= Old English *gamol*) 'old'. It first appears in the 10th C and was apparently of Danish origin. It was common, especially in the North of England, until the end of the 13th C, and gave rise to many surnames, such as *Gamble*, *Gammel(l)*, and *Gamlin*, *Gamlen*, *Gambling* from the diminutive *Gamelin*. It has long been obsolete in England but appears to survive in the Scottish *Gemmel*.

GAMEL DB 1086, HR 1273.
GAMELINUS DB 1086.
GAMELUS FA 1303.
GAMELLUS HR 1273.
GAMMELL Lincs. Will 1669.

Gareth (m.): the name which appears as *Gareth* in Malory's *Morte d'Arthur* is *Gahariet* in his French source, and probably results from a misreading or mis-hearing of some Welsh name. *Gareth* was given to a child baptized at Wigan in 1593 and has been used from time to time since Tennyson made it generally known in his *Gareth and Lynnet*.

Garmon (m.): Welsh form of *Germanus*. See GERMAN.

Garnet (m., f.): the best-known example of this name is General Sir *Garnet* (later 1st Viscount) Wolseley (1833–1913), who had his name from his father, who had it from a great-uncle, Dr. John *Garnett*, Bishop of Clogher. The surname *Garnet(t)* came from the christian name *Garnet*, apparently a diminutive in *-et* of the common Anglo-Norman name *Guarin* (*Warren*). *Garnet* is now also sometimes a girl's name (cf. *Ruby*, *Pearl*, &c.).

Garret, see GERARD.

Gaston (m.): this name appears first among the Counts of Foix and Béarn, and was introduced to France proper by *Gaston* Duke of Orleans, son of Henry IV. It is now a common French name and is also used in other countries. The etymology is doubtful, but, since the name sometimes appears in early records as *Gascon*, it may well be that it was originally a racial designation (cf. *Norman*, *German*, *Francis*). That this phonetic change could take place is shown by 13th-C records quoted by Bardsley which refer to the same man at one time as William de *Gasconia* and at another as William de *Gaston*.

Gatty, see GERTRUDE.

Gavin [gă'vĭn], see GAWAIN.

Gawain (m.): the character who appears as *Gauvain* in French, and *Gawayne* in English medieval versions of the Arthurian cycle, is in Welsh sources named *Gwalchmai*, a compound of *gwalch* 'hawk' and *Mei* the month of May. Geoffrey of Monmouth calls him *Walganus*, and it has been suggested that *Gwalchmai* had an alternative name *Gwalchgwyn* 'white hawk', which became *Walganus* and thence *Gauvain*. Prof. Max Förster considers that *Gawain* is a genuine Welsh name corresponding to Old Breton *Gauen* found in *Uuoi-gauan* (9th C). No one seems to have noticed in this connexion the existence of an Old German name *Gawin*, a derivative of *Gavja* 'a district of land', which is found from the 7th C. Förstemann gives several examples of it, the earliest a Bishop *Gavinus* 633, another Bishop *Gavienus* (of Tours), and persons called *Gavin* and *Goin*. The English *Gawayne*, *Gawn*, *Gawin* or *Gawen*, and the French *Gauvain*, *Gavin* were fairly common in the Middle Ages and were still used at the end of the 17th C. *Gavin* has survived in Scotland where it is still quite common.

GAWYNE HR 1273.
GAWYN Poll Tax 1379.
GAWIN Lond Marr Lic 1530.
GAWEN Lancs Wills 1669, 1680, 1687.
GAVIN Yorks Rec 1604.
GAWNE Ulverston Ch 1653.

Gaynor, see GUENEVERE.

Gemma (f.) [jĕ'ma]: Italian *gemma* 'a gem'. The name occurs once in an Assize Roll for 1218. In modern times it has been borrowed from Italy and seems to have established itself as an English name, possibly helped by a modern Italian saint, *Gemma* Galgani.

Gemmel, see GAMEL.

Gene, see EUGENE.

Genevieve (f.) [jĕn'evēv]: French *Geneviève* from Gaulish *Genovefa*; the first element is *genos* 'race', the second is doubtful. St. *Geneviève*, born *c*. 422 at Nanterre, is the patron saint of Paris, and the name is a favourite one in France. It was sometimes used in England in the 19th C (e.g. the actress *Genevieve* Ward). The form *Genovefa* is still used in Germany.

Geoffrey (m.): the modern name *Geoffrey*, from Middle English *Geffrey*, Old French *Geoffroi*, *Geuffroi*, seems to represent two, if not three, Old German names, (1) *Gaufrid*, (2) *Walahfrid*, and possibly (3) *Gisfrid*. The second element in all of these is *frithu* 'peace'. The first element of *Gaufrid* is *gavja* (Modern German *gau*) 'a district of land'; the first element of *Walahfrid* (gallicized to *Gualafrid*) is *valha* 'traveller', and of *Gisfrid*, *gis* from the same root as *gisel* 'pledge'. In early medieval Latin records, traces of these origins are to be found, the name appearing in many variants of three main forms *Gaufridus*, *Galfridus*, *Goisfridus*. Later come *Geofridus*, *Joffridus*, &c., a direct latinization of the current vernacular forms. In later times the name has been further confused with *Godfrey* (*Godefridus*) (q.v.), which during the Middle Ages was a quite separate name. *Geoffrey* was common in England from the 12th to 15th C, giving rise to many surnames, e.g. *Geoffrey(s)*, *Jefferies*, *Jefferson*, &c.; *Jeeves*, *Geve*, *Jephson*, *Jepson*, &c., from the abbreviations *Jeff*, *Geve*; and *Giffen*, &c., from the abbreviation *Giff*. *Geoffrey* was rather uncommon from the 15th to 19th C. It has now once more come into favour. It seems not to have taken root in Scotland.

GOSFRIDUS, GAUFRIDUS Reg 1071–5.
GOISFRIDUS, GAUFRIDUS DB 1086.
GOFFRIDUS Reg 1087–97.
GALFRIDUS HR 1273.
GEFFREI HR 1273.
GEFFREY, GEFFRAY HR 1273, Coventry Mysteries 15th C.
GEVE HR 1273.
GEFFRAI Exch R 1306.

George (m.): (Latin *Georgius*, French *Georges*, Italian *Giorgio*, Spanish *Jorge*, German, Danish *Georg*, Russian *Yuri*, Irish *Seiorse*): Greek γεωργός 'farmer' or 'tiller of the soil'. St. *George* was a Roman military tribune martyred at Nicomedia in 303. The dragon-killing legends were attached to his name later. His cult was brought to England from the East by returning Crusaders; he was said to have come to their help under the walls of Antioch in 1089 and was then chosen as their patron by the Normans under Robert of Normandy, son of the Conqueror. There are 126 churches dedicated to him in England. But *George* as a christian name was slow in taking root. The earliest example noted is one *George* Grim at the end of the 12th C, and there are occasional occurrences in records of the 13th and early 14th C. Edward III had a particular devotion to St. *George* and in 1349, on St. George's

Day, founded the order of the Garter, which he placed under his patronage, and dedicated to him the chapel of the order at Windsor. From this time he was regarded as the patron saint of England. But even after this the name was not much used, and Edward himself gave it to none of his seven sons, the only member of the royal family to bear the name before the 18th C being his great-great-grandson, George, Duke of Clarence (born 1449). The name was used in a few families (e.g. the Villiers's, who used it from the middle of the 16th C), but was rare until the advent of the house of Hanover in 1714, when an unbroken succession of King *George*'s for 116 years at last acclimatized the name, which has now acquired an extremely English flavour. The usual Scottish and North-country pet-form is *Geordie* which is often used as a nickname for a Northumbrian (cf. *Jock* for a Scot). *Dod* is still used in the northern counties of Scotland.

GEORGIUS Cur 1199, 1203, HR 1273, FA 1303, 1346, 1428, Poll Tax 1379. JEORGIUS HR 1273. GEORGE Magd. *c.* 1270–80.

Georgi(a)na (f.): these f. derivatives of *George* (q.v.) date from the 18th C, when *George* first became common in England. CMY says: 'The first English lady on record so called was a god-child of Anne of Denmark, who caused the child to be christened *Georgia Anna*.' But this must have been an exceptional case. *Georgiana* was pronounced jorjā'na in the 18th C. *Georgina* was the commoner form in the 19th C, and was often abbreviated to *Georgie*. Another f. form of *George* is *Georgia*, which is chiefly used in the USA and is probably an adaptation of the name of the State.

Geraint (m.) [jĕrănt']: Welsh form for Old British *Gerontius*, probably borrowed from Latin *Gerontius* from Greek Γερόντιος a derivative of γέρων 'old'. A letter from St. Aldhelm, dated 705, is addressed to a Cornish King *Geruntius*, which appears in the Anglo-Saxon Chronicle as *Gerente*. The modern pronunciation with soft instead of hard *g* is the result of French influence. The story of Geraint and Enid is in the *Mabinogion*, and was the subject of one of Tennyson's *Idylls of the King* (1859), since which it has occasionally been used as a christian name.

Gerald (m.): Old German *Gairovald*, compound of *ger* 'spear' and *vald* 'rule'. It was introduced into England by the Normans and was used regularly in the Middle Ages, but was by no means so common as *Gerard* (q.v.) with which, especially in Ireland and Wales, it was often confused. It seems to have died out in England about the end of the 13th C. About the end of the 19th C it became relatively popular, probably reintroduced from Ireland where it had been kept alive by the Fitzgeralds, and it is now much commoner than *Gerard*.

GEROLDUS, GERALDUS, GIROLDUS, GIRALDUS, GIRAUDUS DB 1086.
GEROLDIN Reg ? 1086.
GEROLT Reg 1094–9.
GEROLDUS Cur 1197, 1219.

Geraldine (f.): this name seems to have been invented by the poet Surrey who, *c.* 1540, celebrated the beauty of Lady Elizabeth Fitzgerald, daughter of the 9th Earl of Kildare, under the name of 'the fair *Geraldine*' (*Geraldine* = one of the Fitzgeralds). Drayton (1597) published in his *Heroicall Epistles* one entitled 'The Lady *Geraldine* to the Earl of Surrey'. It may have been from one or other of these that Coleridge took the name for use in *Christabel* (written *c.* 1800, first published 1816). But the use of *Geraldine* as a christian name seems to antedate the publication of *Christabel*, for *Geraldine* Jewsbury, the writer and friend of Mrs. Carlyle, was born in 1812, and in the cloister of Wells Cathedral there is an inscription in memory of *Geraldina* Eugenia Wallace (born 1811, died 1820).

Gerard (m.) [je′rard]: (French *Gérard*, German *Gerhard*): Old German *Gairhard*, compound of *ger* 'spear' and *hardu* 'hard'. Probably introduced into England by the Normans shortly before the Conquest (*Girardus* and *Gerardus* occur several times in DB), *Gerard* soon became a common name and remained so for several centuries. It gave rise to many surnames, e.g. *Garrard*, *Garrett*, *Garrod*, *Jerrard*, &c. *Garrard* and *Garret* represent the usual Middle English pronunciation of the name (cf. *Barnard* and *Barnet* for *Bernard*), and *Garret* is given as a christian name by Camden 1605 and Lyford 1655; the latter seems to regard it as an independent name and confuses *Gerald* and *Gerard*. *Gerard* is not now much used. *Garret* is still used in Ireland.

GIRARDUS, GERARDUS DB 1086, Cur 1199–1219.
GERRARDUS FA 1284.
GERARD Ass 1313, Exch R 1306.
GYRERD Poll Tax 1379.
GARRETT, GARRATT 16th C Royal Accounts.
GARRAT Newcastle Epitaph 1637.
GARIT Cheshire Burials 1678.

Gerbert (m.): Old German *Gairbert*, compound of *ger* 'spear' and *berhta* 'bright'.

Gerbold (m.): Old German *Gairebold*, compound of *ger* 'spear' and *balda* 'bold'.

These two names were not uncommon in England in the Middle Ages and gave rise to the surnames *Garbett, Garbutt, Garbott*.

GERBERTUS FA 1284.
GERBALD HR 1273.
GERBOD Pipe Roll 1164.

Gerda (f.) [ger'da]: in Norse mythology the name of the wife of the god Freyr. *Gerda* has been used as a christian name in England in the present century after the little girl in Hans Andersen's story of 'The Snow Queen'.

German (m.) [jer'man]: Latin *Germanus* 'a German'. There were two saints of this name, St. *Germain* of Auxerre (*c.* 378–*c* 448) and St. *Germain* of Paris (*c.* 496–*c.* 576). It was introduced into England by the Normans, and there is one *Germanus* in DB. It was not uncommon in the 13th C and gave rise to various surnames, e.g. *German(s), Germain, Jarman, Jermyn*, &c. It has continued in infrequent use ever since.

GERMANUS DB 1086, Cur 1199, 1200, HR 1273, Poll Tax 1379.
GERMAYNE Yorks Rec 1604.
JERMAN Visitation of London 1634.

Gershom (m.) [ger'shŏm]: Hebrew 'bell', the name of sons of Moses and Levi. The Old Testament explanation 'stranger' is folk etymology. The name is now used mainly by Jews, but in the 17th C was found amongst English Puritans (e.g. *Gershom*, son of Seth Wood, an ejected minister) and survives in Scotland.

Gertrude (f.): Old German *Geredrudis, Geretrudis,* compound of *ger* 'spear' and *drudi* 'strength', the name of one of the Valkyrie. There were two saints of this name, St. *Gertrude,* Abbess of Nivelles (died 659), and St. *Gertrude,* surnamed the Great (1236–1311), a German mystic. The first of these was very popular in Brabant, and it was no doubt from the Low Countries that the name was introduced into England. It is found occasionally in the Middle Ages, and the surnames *Gatt(e), Gattie* may be derived from *Gatty,* formerly the pet-form of the name. In the 16th and 17th C the name was fairly common and it is found spelt variously *Gartrude, Gartrite, Gethrude, Garthrite.* Lyford 1655 gives it as *Gertrud.* The will of Albinia, Lady Wray 1660, mentions 'my gentlewoman *Gartrett* South'. In the later 19th C *Gertrude* became a favourite name and was often abbreviated to *Gertie.*

Gervais, Gervase (m.) [jer'vāz]: Old German *Gervas,* compound of *ger* 'spear' and the Celt stem *vass-* 'servant' (cf. *vassal*). Sts. *Gervase* and *Protase* were said to be 1st-C martyrs, whose remains were opportunely discovered at Milan by St. Ambrose. The name was introduced into England by the Normans and was common in the 12th and 13th C, giving rise to the surnames *Gervas, Gervis, Jarvis, Jarvie,* &c. It was rarer in later times, but *Jarvis* is found as a christian name in 1604, and Lyford 1655 gives *Gervasius* or *Gerfast.* Some families have continued to use it, e.g. the families of Elwes, which has used the name since the time of Sir *Gervase* Elwes (died 1615), and Markham.

GERVASIUS Cur 1199–1219.
GERVASSIUS FA 1284.
GERVAS Lincs 1456.
JARVIS Yorks Rec. 1604.

Gideon (m.): Hebrew 'having only a stump (for a hand)', the name of one of the Judges over Israel. Adopted as a christian name by the English Puritans and French Huguenots, and still current in the USA.

Giffard (m.) [gĭf'ard]: this, though long obsolete as a christian name, was common in the 11th and 12th C. It is apparently Old German *Gebahard, Gevehard,* compound of *gib* 'give' and *hardu* 'bold', 'fierce'.

GIFARDUS, GIFARTUS DB 1086.
GIFFARD HR 1273.
GYFFARD HR 1273.
GIFFORD HR 1273.

Gilbert (m.): Old German *Gisilbert,* compound of *gisil* 'pledge' and *berhta* 'bright'. The name was introduced into England by the Normans and is common in DB, though not found earlier. It was a favourite throughout the Middle Ages, as is shown by the numerous common surnames formed from it, e.g. *Gilbert(son), Gilbart, Gilson; Gibb(s), Gibson, Gibbon(s), Gibbin(s)* (from the common pet-form *Gib* and its diminutive *Gibbon*), *Gipps, Gilby, Gilpin,* &c. In the 15th C it is usually spelt *Gylbart* or *Gylbard* (cf. *Robart* for *Robert, Hubbard* for *Hubert*). It was common in Scotland from a fairly early date, being used as an equivalent of Gaelic *Gilbride,* 'servant of [St.] Bridget'. *Gib* was a common nickname for a cat (cf. Hamlet's 'from a paddock, from a bat, a gib, such dear concernings hide').

GISLEBERTUS DB 1086.
GILBERTUS Cur 1186–1220 *passim,* HR 1273.
GYLBARDE 15th C Brut.
GILEBERT HR 1273.
GILBERD Poll Tax 1379.

Gilchrist (m.): Gaelic 'servant of Christ'; now mostly a surname.

Giles (m.): Latin *Aegidius, Egidius,* derivative of Greek αἰγίδιον 'kid'. *Aegidius* became in French *Gidie, Gide* (which survives as a surname) and then *Gilles, Gile,* and *Gire*. St. *Giles* is said to have been a 6th-C Athenian who fled to France to escape the veneration aroused by the miracles he performed. He is the patron saint of cripples and beggars, and has 162 churches dedicated to him in this country. Medieval records of the name are usually of the Latin form *Egidius,* but there are a few examples of the vernacular

It was sometimes turned back into Latin as *Gilo* or *Gilius*. It was used as a woman's as well as a man's name.

EGIDIUS Cur 1199–1220, HR 1273.
GILO(NEM) Cur 1199.
GYLIS FA 1284.
EGIDIUS or GILIUS HR 1273.
EGIDIA or GILIA Cur 1201.

Gillian (f.) [jĭl'yan]: the popular English form of *Julian(a)* (q.v.); very common in the Middle Ages, especially in the diminutive forms *Gill, Jill, Gillot, Gillet* which gave rise to many surnames. *Gillot* or *Jillet* became a designation for a flighty girl, whence probably, by a process of syncopation, the word *jilt*. In the 17th C it was legally declared that *Julian* and *Gillian* were different names, like *Anne* and *Agnes* (qq.v.). *Gillian* went out of use in the 18th and 19th C, but has been revived in the 20th. *Jill* is now often given as an independent name. For forms, &c., see JULIAN(A).

Ginevra (f.) [jĭněv'rä]: the Italian form of *Guenevere* (q.v.). Occasionally used in England in the 19th and 20th C.

Gisela (f.) [jĭzěl'ä]: Old German *Gisila*, derivative of *gisl* 'pledge'. It was the name of a daughter of Charles the Simple, who married Rollo 1st Duke of Normandy. *Gisèle* is not uncommon in France and it, or *Gisela*, is sometimes used by Roman Catholics in England.

Githa, Gytha (f.) [gīth'a]: a Norse name, probably derived from *guthr* 'war'. It is found in England in the 11th C, and has recently been revived. An early example is Countess *Gytha*, a Dane, wife of Godwin, Earl of Wessex (*c.* 1054).

Gladys (f.): Welsh *Gwladys*. *Gladusa* is found in Cumberland in 1207. It is commonly said that *Gwladys* is a Welsh form of the Latin *Claudia* (q.v.), and from an early date the *Claudia* mentioned in 2 Tim. iv. 21 was supposed to be a Welshwoman, and her name identified with *Gwladys*, though Welsh Bibles do not so translate it. Camden 1605 says: '*Gladuse* (Brit) for *Claudia*'. The adoption of the name in England seems to date from the 70's of the last century and in 1877 there was an interesting correspondence on the subject in N & Q. The first letter asked 'Is Gladys a male or female name, or a name at all—at least out of a novel?' All the replies treat the name as purely Welsh, except for one which says 'I have also seen a *Gladys*, and I have frequently met with the name in fiction'. Another says that in Caernarvonshire, where *Gwladys* is common, bearers of it commonly sign their name *Claudia*. One novel in which the name occurs is Ouida's *Puck* (1870), and this may well have been the origin of its use in England, where it is now common.

Gloria (f.): Latin *gloria* 'glory'. Came into use in the late 19th C, e.g. G. B. Shaw's *You Never Can Tell* (published 1898).

Goddard (m.): Old German *Godehard* (Modern German *Gotthard*), compound of *Guda* 'god' and *hardu* 'hard'. Introduced into England at the Conquest in the Norman form *Godard*, it was common in the Middle Ages and survived in use until the 17th C. It is now used only as a surname.

GODARD Cur 1200, HR 1273.

Godfrey (m.): Old German *Godafrid*, compound of *Guda* 'god' and *frithu* 'peace'. There was a corresponding Old English *Godfrith*, but it was not common and the medieval *God(e)fry* seems to represent a Norman version of the Old German name rather than a survival of the Old English one. It was common in the 12th and 13th C and gave rise to the surnames *Godfrey*, *Godfree*, *Godfreed*, &c. In later times it has sometimes been confused with *Geoffrey* (q.v.), but was quite separate in the Middle Ages, appearing in Latin as *Godefridus* while *Geoffrey* was *Galfridus* or *Goisfridus*.

GODEFRIDUS DB 1086, Cur 1187–1220, Pipe Roll 1161.
GODFREY HR 1273.
GODEFRAY HR 1273.

Godiva (f.): Old English *Godgifu*, compound of *God* and *gifu* 'a gift'. *Godeva* is the name of a tenant in DB, and *Godefe* remained

in common use until the 13th or 14th C, giving rise to the surname *Goodeve*. The most famous bearer of the name was *Godgifu*
(*fl.* 1040–80), latinized as *Godiva*, wife of Leofric of Mercia, who
founded several monasteries and is the heroine of the well-known
Coventry legend.

GODEVA DB 1086.
GODIVA Cur 1200.
GODEFE HR 1273.
GOODIFE St. Jas. Clerkenwell 1606.

Godric (m.): Old English *Godric*, compound of *God* and *ric*
'ruler'. It seems to be a specifically Old English name, without any corresponding Old German form. It was very common
in England before the Norman Conquest. The Normans used it
as a nickname for an Englishman, and called Henry I and his
queen *Godric and Godiva*, in allusion to her English blood and
his supposedly English sympathies. It seems to have died out in
the course of the 13th and 14th C, but not before giving rise to
the surnames *Godrich, Goodrich, Goodrick, Goodridge*.

GODRIC(US) DB 1086.
GODRIGE HR 1273.
GODRICH(E) HR 1273.

Godwin (m.): Old English *Godwine*, compound of *God* and *wine*
'friend'; one of the commonest of Old English names. It survived
the Conquest and its popularity is attested by the number of surnames formed from it, e.g. *Goodwin, Godwin, Godden, Goodden,
Godding, Godin, Goding*, &c. (the last five being from the Anglo-
French form *Godin*).

GODUIN(E), GODEUUIN DB 1086, Cur 1187–1220.
GODIN HR 1273.
GODUN HR 1273.
GAUDINUS Testa de Neville 13th C, QW 1347.

Goldwin (m.): Old English *Goldwine*, compound of *gold* and
wine 'friend'. It was not uncommon in the Middle Ages, giving
rise to the surnames *Goldwin, Golden, Goulden, Goulding*, &c.,
and was still in use as a christian name as late as 1730. (The

well-known Victorian controversialist *Goldwin* Smith was named
after an uncle, Thomas *Goldwin*.)

GOLDUIN DB 1086.
GOLDWYN HR 1273.
JOLDEWIN HR 1273.
GOLDING HR 1273.
GOLDIN(E) HR 1273.
GOLDWIN St. Geo. Hanover Sq. 1730.

Goodeth (f.): Old English *Godgyth*, compound of *God* and *gyth*
'war'. *Goditha* or *Godith* was common in the 13th and 14th C,
and was sometimes confused with *Godefe* (see GODIVA). *Goodeth*
is found as late as the 17th C.

GODITHA Cur 1200, FA 1303.
GUDYTHA Poll Tax 1379.
GOODETH Somerset Wills 1597, St. Jas. Clerkenwell 1661.

Gordon (m.): the name of a large and famous Scottish family, probably derived from *Gordon* in Berwickshire. The modern use of *Gordon* as a christian name is due to the enormous popularity of General
Gordon (1833–85). It is now firmly established as a christian name.

Goronwy (m.) [gŏrŏn'wĕ]: a Welsh christian name still in use.
A London parish register of 1641 has *Granaw* Evine son of
Granawa Evine.

Grace (f.): Latin *gratia* 'grace'. *Gracia, Grecia, Gricia* occur as a
woman's name in Latin records of the 13th and 14th C and possibly represent this name, though they may be a latinization of
some name derived from Old German *grisja* 'grey'. *Grace*, like
Faith, Hope, Charity, Patience, &c., came into use as a christian
name after the Reformation, but it is also found fairly frequently
in lists of Roman recusants in the early 17th C. It was sometimes
also given to boys in the 17th C. It went out of fashion in the
18th C and its revival in the Victorian period may have been
influenced by the fame of *Grace* Darling (1815–42). In Ireland it
has been used to render the native *Grainne* (q.v.).

GRACIA Cur 1200, FA 1303, 1346.
GRECIA Cur 1213, FA 1346.
GRICIA FA 1346.
GRACE Chester 1562.

Gracilia (f.): from Latin *gracilis* 'slender'. Sometimes used as a f. christian name, probably from a mistaken derivation from *gratia*.

Graham (m.): the name of a large and famous Scottish family, originally a place-name. Its use as a christian name is comparatively recent.

Grainne, Grania (f.) [grā′nyē]: Irish *Graidhne*, the name of Diarmuit's mistress; a popular Irish name, often rendered by *Grace* (q.v.). A notable example was *Grainne* or *Grace* O'Malley, the Amazonian princess who opposed the forces of Queen Elizabeth.

Granville (m.): originally a surname derived from *Granville* in Normandy. *Grenville* is another form of it. *Granville* has been used as a christian name in the Leveson-Gower family since the early 18th C, and is now used more widely.

Gregory (m.): (Latin *Gregorius*, French *Grégoire*, Italian *Gregorio*, German *Gregor*): Greek γρηγόριος a derivative of γρηγορέω 'to be watchful'. It was the name of two fathers of the Eastern Church, St. *Gregory* Nazianzen (*c.* 325–*c.* 390) and St. *Gregory* of Nyssa (*c.* 331–*c.* 395), and of 16 Popes, beginning with St. *Gregory* 'the Great' (*c.* 540–604). The name is not found in England before the Norman Conquest, but was common in the 12th C and later. *Godstow* (1450) gives *Gregour* as the English for *Gregorius*. There are a great many surnames formed from it, e.g. *Gregory*, *Greg(g)*, *Grig(g)*, *Greggs*, *Griggs*, *Gregson*, *Grigson*, *Greig*. *Greg* and *Grig* were respectively North and South country forms of the diminutive. *McGregor* is a patronymic formed from *Gregor*, the usual Scottish form of the name.

GREGORIUS Cur 1187–1220, HR 1273, FA 1346, Cl 1386.
GREGORY HR 1273, Cl 1387.
GREG(E) HR 1273, Poll Tax 1379.
GRIGGE HR 1273.

Greta (f.): a Swedish abbreviation of *Margaret* (q.v.), sometimes also used in England in recent times. A solitary early example occurs in Assize Roll of 1218.

Griffin, Griffith (m.): Welsh *Gruffudd.* The second element is *udd* 'lord'. It was the name of several Welsh princes and has always been common in Wales, and also in the counties on the Welsh Marches, e.g. in Shropshire Feudal Aids 1428 there occur *Griffinus* Hull and *Griffinus seu Griffith* Kynaston. Lyford 1655 gives both *Griffin* and *Griffith.*

Grimbald (m.): Old English *Grimbeald.* The second element is *beald* 'bold'; the first may be either *grim* 'savage', 'fierce', or *Grima* a name for Odin (from *grima* 'a mask'). St. *Grimbald* (*c.* 820–903) was a monk at St. Omer, who was invited over to England by King Alfred to help him with his educational work. He was the first Abbot of New Minster at Winchester, and after his death was venerated as a saint. Later his name was associated with the mythical early history of Oxford University. *Grimbald* was a fairly common name in the Middle Ages and gave rise to a number of surnames, e.g. *Grimbald, Grimbold, Grimble, Grimbly, Gribble,* &c. Camden in 1605 says: 'a name most usual in the old family of Pauncefoot'.

GRIMBALD(US), GRIMBOLD, GRIMBOL, GRIMOLD DB 1086, FA 1303.
GRIMBALD, GRIMBAUD HR 1273.
GRIMALDUS FA 1284.

Griselda, Grizel (f.) [grĭzĕl′da, grĭ′zĕl]: the second element of *Griselda* or *Griseldis* seems to be Old German *hild* 'battle', 'strife', the first may be Old German *grisja* 'grey', though an Old German name *Grishild* is not actually on record. It is also possible that it represents the recorded Old German *Cristehildis,* a compound of *Christ* and *hild.* It is not found in early use as a christian name in England, and its adoption was no doubt due to the literary influence of Chaucer, who took the story of Patient *Griselda* (the Clerk's Tale) from Boccaccio. Dekker wrote a play on the subject. The name is now used mainly in Scotland where it is still quite common, usually in the form *Grizel.* Lyford 1655 gives *Grishild,* but *Grissel, Grizzel* or *Grisel* were the usual forms by that time.

Guendolen, Gwendolyn (f.): a Welsh name of which the first element is the f. of *gwyn* 'white'. The earliest form is *Guenddoleu.*

In the *Vita Merlini* it is the name of Merlin's wife and there was a saint of the name. It came into use in England in the 19th C.

Guenevere, Guinevere (f.) [gwen'evĕr]: Welsh *Gwenhwyvar*, the name of the wife of King Arthur. In Anglo-Norman the name became *Guenièvre*, and the English metrical romances give it as *Gwenore, Gonore, Ganor, Gaynore, Wannour, Wannore. Guener* and *Gueanor* occur in Lancashire at the beginning of the 17th C. In Scotland it became *Guanor, Vanora,* or *Wander. Gaenor* is still used in N. Wales, though no longer associated with *Guenevere. Gwenhevare* occurs as a christian name in Shropshire in 1431. In Cornwall the name has survived in the form *Jenifer* down to the present time. Of recent years *Jen(n)ifer* has become fashionable in the rest of England. See also WINIFRED.

Gu(g)lielma (f.): Italian f. form of *Guglielmo* (William), sometimes used in England since the 17th C., particularly by members of the Society of Friends, since it was the name of the first wife of William Penn the elder, *Gulielma* Maria Springett (*c.* 1643–93). Sometimes shortened to *Elma*.

Guiscard (m.): one of the earliest recorded bearers of this name was Robert *Guiscard*, son of Tancred de Hauteville and conqueror of Sicily. It seems to be a purely Norman name. Förstemann suggests that it is a compound of the rare root *visc* and Old German *hardu* 'bold', 'hardy'. The Normans used the name a good deal in England and it appears as *Gwychardus* (cf. the modern name of Robert *Guiscard's* birthplace, Hauteville-la-*Guichard*), *Wiscard, Wyschardus,* &c., and gave rise to the surnames *Whiskard, Whisker, Wiscar,* &c.

WISCAR, WISGARUS DB 1086.
WISCARD HR 1273.
WYSCHARDUS Testa de Neville 13th C.
WICHARD HR 1273.
GWYCHARDUS FA 1303.
GUISCHARD or WISCHARD Lyford 1655.

Gunilda (f.): Old Norse *Gunnhildr*, compound of *gunn(r)* 'war' and *hild(r)* 'battle', 'strife'. There was a corresponding Old Ger-

man *Gundichild*, but it was the Norse name which was introduced
into England by the Danes; one of the daughters of King Knut
was named *Gunhild*. The name survived the Norman Conquest,
and was in use until the 14th C, often in the Norman form
Quenild. The English form seems to have been *Gunnell*. The surnames *Quennell* and *Gunnell* are derived from these forms. The
word *gun* is probably from *Gunne*, a pet-form of *Gunhild* (see
OED s.v. *gun*); an account of munitions at Windsor Castle in 1330
mentions 'una magna balista de cornu quae vocatur domina
Gunilda', and doubtless the same nickname was later used for
cannon.

GUNILDA Cur 1200, 1210, 1213.
GUNNILDA HR 1273, Cl. 1295.
GONNILDA HR 1273.
GUNNILDE HR 1273.
GUNNELL Testa de Neville 13th C.
QWINHILD Whitby.
QUENILDA Lancs Lay Subsidy 1332.

Gunnora (f.): Old Norse *Gunnvǫr* (late Old English *Gunware*);
the first element is *gunnr* 'war'. The name was latinized by the
Normans as *Gunnora*. It was a favourite Norman name and
remained in use in England until the 14th C.

GUNORA Cur 1196–1220.
GONNORA FA 1285.
GUNNORA FA 1302.

Gunter (m.): Old German *Guntard*, compound of *gundi* 'war'
and *hardu* 'bold', 'hardy', or Old German *Gunter* a compound of
gundi and *harja* 'host'. Introduced into England by the Normans
and fairly common in the 13th and 14th C. *Gunter* is found as a
christian name as late as 1494. It gave rise to the surnames *Gunter*,
Gunther.

GUNTERIUS Reg 1086–93.
GUNTER HR 1273, Cov 1494.
GUNTARD HR 1273.

Gussie, Gussy, see AUGUSTA, AUGUSTUS.

Gustavus (m.) [gustāvus]: Old German *Chustaffus*, the second
element of which is *staf* 'staff'; the first element is doubtful,

Förstemann suggests the root *Chud*, connected with Old German *chûton* 'to meditate'. *Gustaf* (or *Gosta*) is chiefly a Swedish name, but in the 17th C the fame of the Swedish king *Gustaf Adolf* (1594–1632) (*Gustavus Adolphus*, as he is usually called) spread it over Europe (e.g. German *Gustav*, French *Gustave*). In England the latinized form *Gustavus* has occasionally been used; an early example is *Gustavus* Barratt, christened at St. Giles Cripplegate in 1638.

Guy (m.): Old German *Wido*, from the root *vid* which is common in personal names; it is doubtful whether it is the same as Old German *witu* 'wood', or *wît* 'wide'. It was introduced into England by the Normans and appears in Latin records sometimes as *Wido*, sometimes as *Guido*. The French forms of the name were *Guy* and *Guyon* (representing the *cas-sujet* and the *cas-régime*, cf. *Hue* and *Huon*), and also *Wy* and *Wyon*; the diminutives *Wyat*, *Guyat* were also common. The surnames *Guy(s)*, *Guise*, *Guyon*, *Gye*, *Wyat(t)*, *Wiatt*, &c., are derived from it. It was in common use from the Norman Conquest until the 17th C, when *Guy* Fawkes drove it out of use for some 200 years. Its revival in the 19th C may have been helped by Scott's *Guy Mannering* (1815), and later by C. M. Yonge's *Heir of Redcliffe* (1853) whose hero was named *Guy*.

WIDO DB 1086, Cur 1189, FA 1316.
GWYDO HR 1273.
GUIDO FA 1285.
GY HR 1273.

Gwladys, see GLADYS.

Gwen(da) (f.): *Gwen* is the common pet-form of *Guendolen* (q.v.) and of other Welsh f. names compounded with *gwen* (f. of *gwyn* 'white' which is used as a man's name). It is now used as an independent name in England, as is occasionally *Gwenda*.

Gwendolyn, see GUENDOLEN.

Gwyneth (f.): a name of Welsh origin now sometimes used in England.

H

Hacon (m.): Old Norse *Hakon*, modern *Haakon*, derivative of the stem *hag* 'useful', 'handy'. The name was introduced into England by the Danes and survived the Norman Conquest, *Hacun*, *Hacon* being not uncommon in the 12th C, after which it died out. It survived in Shetland, sometimes corrupted to *Hercules*.

HACUN, HACON, ACUN, DB 1086, Cur 1189, 1200.

Hadassah, see ESTHER.

Haidée (f.): from Byron's use of it in *Don Juan* (Canto ii) this is now occasionally used as a christian name in England. It is apparently a mistaken version of modern Greek *Haido*, found as a christian name in rural areas and derived from the verb *haideúo* 'to caress'.

Hal, see HENRY.

Halbert, see ALBERT.

Ham (m.): the name of the eponymous ancestor of the 'Hamites', who lived in the 'hot' (Hebrew *hām*) south (Gen. x. 6 ff.) as distinct from the Semites, whose eponymous ancestor was called Sēm (Gen. x. 21 ff.), a name of unknown meaning. *Ham* has been used occasionally as a christian name since the 17th C (cf. *Ham* Peggotty in *David Copperfield*).

Hamish (m.): an attempt to render phonetically *Sheumais*, the vocative of *Seumas*, the Gaelic form of *James* (q.v.). Scott has a *Hamish* MacTavish, but the present vogue of the name seems to be due to the novels of William Black (1841–98), very popular in their day, in several of which he makes use of the name *Hamish*. The use of this pseudo-Gaelic form is to be discouraged.

Hamo(n) (m.) [hā'mō]: Old German *Haimo* from *haimi* 'house', 'home'. The name was introduced into England by the Normans and soon became common. The two forms *Hamo*, *Hamon* represent the Old French *cas-sujet* and *cas-régime*. The diminutives

Hamelot, Hamelin, Ham(o)net were all in general use and gave rise to the surnames *Hamlet(t), Hamblet, Ham(b)lin, Hambley, Hamnet(t)*, &c. Shakespeare's only son was named *Hamnet* (after one of his godfathers). *Hamlet*, Prince of Denmark, bore a different name, the Icelandic *Amlóthi*, which appears as *Amleth* in Saxo, and was turned by English translators into the more familiar *Hamlet*. *Hamlet* and *Hamnet* survived into the 18th C (cf. *Hamlet* Winstanley, the painter, 1700–56). *Hamon* is still used in the Norfolk family of Lestrange and *Hamo* among Yorkshire gipsies belonging to one of the families of Smith. *Hamelen* is also a gipsy name. A modern example of *Hamo* is the sculptor Sir *Hamo* Thornycroft (1850–1925).

HAYMO Reg 1071–5.
HAMO DB 1086, Cur 1196–1220.
HAMMOND Cur 1200, 1210.
HAMUND HR 1273.
HAM(E)LIN DB 1086, Cur 1207, 1213.
HAMOND Exch Roll 1306.

Hannah (f.): Hebrew, a shortened form of *Hanani* and similar names, meaning 'He (= God) has favoured me'. The name of the mother of the prophet Samuel. The Greek form of the name, *Anna* (q.v.), was that in which it became acclimatized in Europe, but *Hannah* came into use at the Reformation, and was common in the 17th C. It has been in regular, though not frequent, use ever since. It is a favourite rural name in Ireland.

Hannibal (m.): Phoenician, the name of the great Carthaginian general. At a later date the name *Annibal* and its derivative *Annibalianus* were used in Rome. *Annibale* continued to be used in Italy (cf. the painter *Annibale* Caracci). *Hannibal* has been used as a christian name in Cornwall at least since the 16th C, e.g. *Hannibal* Gammon, Rector of Mawgan in Pyder 1619. It is doubtful whether this is the origin of the surnames *Hanniball, Honeyball*, &c.

Hardwin (m.): Old German *Hardwin*, compound of *hardu* 'hard', and *wine* 'friend'. It was introduced into England by the Normans,

and became very popular, usually anglicized to *Harding*. It went
out of use after the 13th C.

HARDUINUS DB 1086.
HARDWIN HR 1273.
HARDING HR 1273.

Harold (m.): Old English *Hereweald*, compound of *here* 'host',
'army', and *weald* 'power'. But the actual source of the modern
name was probably the corresponding Old Norse *Harivald*,
Modern Norse *Harald*, for it was amongst the Anglo-Danes that
it particularly flourished, the most notable bearer of it being
Harald Godwinson who contested the kingdom with William of
Normandy. The name is found from time to time in the 12th and
13th C but was not common and seems to have died out altogether.
It was revived in the 19th C.

HARALD(US), HAROLD, AROLD, HEROLD, HERALD, HERAL, ERAL, HEROULD,
HEROLT, HAIRAUD DB 1086.
HAROLDUS Cur 1201-13.

Harriet (f.): the English form of French *Henriette*, a f. derivative
of Henry (cf. *Harry* for *Henry*). *Henriette* was apparently invented
in France in the 16th C and brought to England by Charles I's
Queen, *Henriette Marie*, the daughter of Henri IV, who was
usually called Queen Mary in England (e.g. in the liturgy). Her
numerous god-daughters, however, were usually christened *Henrietta* (a latinization of *Henriette*, which became *Harriet* in speaking). *Harriet*, or *Harriot* as it was often spelt, was a very common
name in the 18th and early 19th C. It was often abbreviated to
Harry or *Hatty*.

Harry, see HENRY.

Hartley (m.): this surname, derived from the common place-
name, is now fairly often used as a christian name, one of the earliest
examples being *Hartley* Coleridge (1796-1849), the son of S. T.
Coleridge, who was named after David *Hartley* the philosopher.

Harvey (m.): this is probably from *Hervé*, the French form of
Breton *Haerveu*, the name of a favourite Breton saint and poet,

a compound of Old Breton *aer* 'carnage' and *-uiu* 'worthy'. The name was introduced into England at the Norman Conquest and soon became common. In DB there are 11 tenants of this name, including two who had held TRE, and it continued in use throughout the 12th and 13th C, giving rise to the surnames *Harvey, Hervey, Harvie, Harveson*. There is no record of its use in the 14th to 18th C, but it occurs in the 19th C (e.g. *Harvey* Goodwin, Bishop of Carlisle, 1818–91) and is still sometimes used.

HERVEUS DB 1086, Cur 1187–1215.
HARVEY HR 1273.
HERVI HR 1273.

Hatty, see HARRIET.

Hawis(e) (f.): Old German *Hadewidis*, compound of *hathu* 'battle' and *vid* 'wide'. In French it became *Ha(u)eis, Haouys*, and was introduced in this form into England in the 12th C; it was in general use until the 14th C, giving rise to the surnames *Hawes, Haweis, Hawison*.

HAWIS Cur 1189, 1203, HR 1273, Testa de Neville '13th C, Freemen of York 1326.
HAWISIA FA 1346.
HAWISE HR 1273.

Hazel (f.): apparently a late-19th-C innovation. A correspondent in N & Q 1904 mentions it as one of several flower and plant names then growing in popularity.

Heather (f.): like *Hazel* (q.v.). It is mentioned in the same article in N & Q.

Hebe (f.) [hē'bĕ]: Greek *Ήβη* 'youth', the goddess of youth and cupbearer to the gods. Sometimes used as a christian name.

Hector (m.): Greek *Έκτωρ*, the name of the heroic son of Priam; it is uncertain whether this is the same as the adjective *ἕκτωρ* 'holding fast'. In the Old French romances the name becomes *Ector*. *Hector* is found as a christian name in the 13th C, but it was only in the Highlands of Scotland that it really took root and became common; this was probably due to its being used to translate Gaelic *Eachdonn*. *Ettore* is fairly common in Italy.

HECTOR Cur 1203-5.

Helen(a) (f.): Greek ʽΕλένη, f. of ʼΕλενος 'the bright one'. The wide diffusion of the name is not due to the fame of the fateful queen of Menelaus, but to St. *Helena* (died A.D. 338), mother of the Emperor Constantine. Many legends were early attached to her name, such as that of her discovery of the true cross. There are 135 churches dedicated to her in Great Britain. She was said to have been of British origin, the daughter of a British king, the Old King Cole of the nursery rhyme. Her name was popular in Celtic countries, especially Wales, from an early date. It was not used in England in the Old English period, but is found (*Elena*) soon after the Conquest. The common English form of the name has always been *Ellen* (q.v.), but *Helen* and *Helena* came in at the Renaissance. At the present time *Helen* is probably more common than *Ellen*. For another development see ELEANOR. The *Elaine* of Arthurian romance is a gallicizing of a Welsh form of *Helen*. Like *Ellen* it is often shortened to *Nell*. The German pet-form *Lena* is also sometimes used in England.

Helewise (f.) [hĕl'ewēz]: Old German *Helewidis*, compound of *haila* 'hale', 'sound', and *vid* 'wide'. The name was apparently introduced into England by the Normans, though in DB there is a *Helewis* mentioned as having held land TRE. It is fairly common in the 12th and 13th C. The surname *Elwes* is derived from it. After this it dropped out of general use, but in the 18th C there was some use of *Eloisa*, a latinization of *Hélöise*, the French form of the name, famous for its associations with the unhappy love of Abelard.

HELEWIS DB 1086.
HEILEWIS Cur 1189.
HELEVISA HR 1273.
ELWISIA HR 1273.
HELEWYS HR 1273.
ELEWYS HR 1273.

Helga (f.): a Norse name meaning holy. *Helga, Helge, Helghi* are found in DB as the names of tenants TRE, but the name does not

G

seem to have survived in England. It has continued to be used in Scandinavia and has been carried thence to the USA where it is not uncommon. See also OLGA.

Heloise [hel'ōēz], see HELEWISE.

Henrietta (f.): this f. form of *Henry* was introduced into England by *Henriette Marie* (Latin *Henrietta Maria*) wife of Charles I. The English form *Harriet* (q.v.) quickly established itself, but *Henrietta* came back into use in the 19th C, often abbreviated to *Etta* and sometimes to *Hetty* (cf. *Hatty* from *Harriet*).

Henry (m.): (Latin *Henricus*, German *Heinrich*, *Heinz*, *Heine*, Dutch *Hendrik*, French *Henri*, Italian *Enrico*, Spanish *Enrique*); Old German *Haimirich*, compound of *haimi* 'house', 'home', and *ric* 'ruler'. This was latinized as *Henricus* and became *Henri* in French. There are five tenants of this name in DB, and the eight King *Henrys* in the 11th to 16th C are some measure of the popularity of the name in the Middle Ages, a popularity which has fluctuated very little since. *Henri* in English pronunciation became *Herry* or *Harry*, and this was the usual English form of the name until the 17th C. At the present time *Harry* is often regarded as a mere pet-form of *Henry* instead of the right English version of the name. The surnames derived from the various forms of this name are very numerous, including *Henry*, *Henryson*, *Harris(son)*, *Harries*, *Herries*, *Henderson*, *Hendry*; *Hawke*, *Hawkins*, &c., are from *Halkin*, the diminutive of *Hal*, a favourite pet-form of *Henry*; *Her(r)iot* is from the diminutive *Henriot* (English *Herriot*). The form with intrusive *d* (e.g. the surnames *Hendry*, *Henderson*, &c.) was especially common in Scotland and Wales. Other common Welsh surnames are *Penny*, *Parry*, *Perry*, from *ap Henry*, &c.

HENRICUS DB 1086, Cur 1187–1220.
HANRY HR 1273, Testa de Neville 13th C.
HENRY or HANRY Testa de Neville 13th C.
HARRY or HERRY 15th C Brut.
HRERY Lincs 1459.
HARY *Cocke Lorelle's Bote c.* 1515.
HENDRY Newcastle 1562.
HENDEREYE St. Antholin 1601.

Hephzibah (f.): Hebrew 'my delight is in her', the name of the wife of Hezekiah. It came into use in the 17th C, but has been more common in America than in England. It is often spelt and pronounced *Hepzibah*, and in the early part of this century I knew a village girl of this name who was always called *Hepsie*.

Herbert (m.): Old German *Hariberct*, compound of *harja* 'host', 'army', and *berhta* 'bright'. There was a corresponding Old English *Herebeorht*, but it was not very much used, and the wide diffusion of the name after the Norman Conquest was no doubt due to its reintroduction from the Continent. *Herbertus* occurs many times in DB, and the surnames *Herbert, Herbertson, Herbison* are derived from it. After the 13th C, however, it went out of general use, though it lingered on in remote corners. It was revived at the beginning of the 19th C, an early example being *Herbert* Southey (born 1806), the eldest son of the poet, who was named after his uncle *Herbert* Hill, born in the 1740's. It became very popular in the later part of the century, possibly by association with the noble family of *Herbert* (cf. the history of *Sidney*).

HERBERTUS DB 1086, Cur 1187–1220, FA 1303, 1346.
HEREBERT HR 1273.
HARBERT Will of Henry Condell 1625.

Hercules (m.): Greek ʿΗρακλῆς, Latin *Hercules*, of unknown etymology, the name of the son of Zeus and Alcmena. It was first used as a christian name in Italy (*Ercole*) at the time of the Renaissance, and spread to France, where *Hercule* is still sometimes used. *Hercules* is found as a christian name in England, though rarely, in the 16th and 17th C. It apparently continued to be used in Cornwall until the 19th C, but may have been confused with *Archelaus* (Matt. ii. 22). In Shetland it was used to render the Old Norse *Hakon* (see HACON).

Hereward (m.) [hĕr´eward]: Old English *Hereweard*, compound of *here* 'army' and *weard* 'guard', 'protection'. The name was made famous by *Hereward* the Wake, the last leader of Saxon resistance against the Normans. It survived until the end of the 13th C and was revived at the beginning of the 19th C by the

Wake family, which claims descent from the Saxon hero. Kingsley's novel *Hereward the Wake* (1866) helped to make the name generally known.

HEREUUARD, HERWART, HEREUUORD DB 1086.
HEREWARD Cur 1196, 1200, Testa de Neville 13th C.

Her(r)iot (m.): obsolete diminutive of *Henry* (q.v.).

Herman (m.): Old German *Hariman*, compound of *harja* 'host', 'army', and *mana* 'man'. The name was introduced into England by the Normans, and *Hermannus* occurs in DB. The French form of the name, *Armant, Armand*, also Harmand (the lichenologists of Lorraine) became in English *Armin*, which survived until recently in Norfolk. The surnames *Harman, Harmon, Armand, Arment*, &c., are derived from it. The modern German *Hermann* is occasionally used in England, usually by families of German-Jewish origin. See also ARMINEL.

HERMANNUS DB 1086, Cur 1205, 1207.
HERMAN Pat 13th C.
ARMUNDUS Testa de Neville 13th C.
ARMAND FF 1348.
HARMAN Ox Univ Reg 1549.

Hermia (f.): this is apparently a f. name formed from *Hermes* (Greek 'Ἑρμῆς), the name of the messenger of the gods. The modern use is taken from one of the characters in *A Midsummer Night's Dream*. It is not known where Shakespeare found the name.

Hermione (f.) [hermī'onĕ]: Greek 'Ἑρμιόνη, f. derivative of *Hermes*, the name of a daughter of Menelaus and Helen, the wife of Orestes. It was often used in 16th-C literature, notably by Shakespeare for the queen in *A Winter's Tale*, and it is from this that the modern use of *Hermione* as a christian name is derived. The German *Hermine* is a different name, probably a f. form of *Herman* (q.v.).

Hero (f.): Greek "Ἡρω the name of (1) a daughter of Danaus, (2) a daughter of Priam, (3) the beloved of Leander. The etymology of the word is doubtful; it is unconnected with the common noun *hero*, and may be from the name of the goddess *Hera*. The modern use of *Hero* as a christian name is the result of Shakespeare's use of it in *Much Ado about Nothing*.

Hester, see ESTHER.

Hetty, see ESTHER and HENRIETTA.

Hew, see HUGH.

Hezekiah (m.) [hĕzekī'ă]: Hebrew 'God is strength'. Brought into use by the Puritans in the 17th C.

Hilary (m., f.): late Latin *Hilarius* from *hilaris* 'cheerful'. St. *Hilarius* of Poitiers (died 368), a champion of the Church against Arianism and hence called the Athanasius of the West, was the cause of the popularity of the name (*Hilaire*) in France. It was not uncommon in England from the 13th to 16th C, and has continued in infrequent use ever since. Lyford 1655 gives it as *Hilarie*. It has become more common in recent years. In the 12th and 13th C it was also used as a woman's name (Latin *Hilaria, Illaria*, &c.), but that use seems to have died out altogether until it was revived at the beginning of the present century. CMY knows it only as a man's name.

YLLARIUS Cur 1203–5
HILLARIUS Cur 1207, FA 1346.
ILLARIUS FA 1284.
HILLARY St. Dionis Backchurch 1547, St. Peter Cornhill 1593.
ILLARIA Cur 1199.
YLLARIA Cur 1203, 1205, 1210.
HILLARIA HR 1273.

Hilda (f.): Old English *Hild*, probably a hypocoristic form of one of the names compounded with *hild* 'war', 'battle'. St. *Hild*, foundress and Abbess of Whitby (614–80), was much venerated in the Old English period and later. *Hilde, Hylde* (Latin *Hilda*) is found as a christian name until the end of the 13th C, and never died out in the neighbourhood of Whitby. The general use of the name was revived, like that of other names of Anglo-Saxon saints, by the Tractarians in the 19th C.

HILDE Cur 1201, 1203, 1210, HR 1273.
HILLDA HR 1273.
HYLDE Werburge 1513.

Hildebrand (m.): Old German *Hildibrand*, compound of *hildi* 'battle', 'strife', and *branda* 'sword'. The name was common in German medieval romances, but its general use as a christian name was probably due to St. *Hildebrand* (1000–85), Pope Gregory VII, one of the greatest of medieval popes. It was not uncommon in England in the 13th and 14th C and gave rise to the surnames *Hildebrand*, *Hildebrant*. It has occasionally been revived in modern times.

HILDEBRAND Cur 1200.
HEUDEBRAND, ODIBRAND Cur 1210.
HILDEBRANDUS HR 1273.
HILDEBRONDUS FA 1316.

Hildegard(e) (f.): Old German *Hildegard*, compound of *hildi* 'war', 'battle' and *gardi* probably a derivative of *gardan* 'to know'. St. *Hildegard*, Abbess of Bingen (died 1004) was much venerated, and her name has been used a good deal in Germany, and hence in modern times in USA. It is very rarely used in England.

Hippolyta (f.) [hĭpol'ĭtă]: Greek f. of *Hippolytus* (q.v.), the name of the queen of the Amazons, occasionally used in England in recent times, presumably on account of its occurrence in *A Midsummer Night's Dream*.

Hippolytus (m.) [hĭpol'ĭtus]: Greek Ἱππόλυτος 'letting horses loose', the name of the son of Theseus and Hippolyta, Queen of the Amazons. It was the name of a Roman saint martyred in 252. A church dedicated to him in Rome gave its name to a cardinal. *Ippolitus*, *Ypolitus* are found in the 13th C, and a 14th-C Legendary gives the name of the saint as *Ypolit*. The village of *Ippollitts* in Hertfordshire takes its name from the dedication of the church to St. *Hippolytus*, and exhibits many and strange perversions of the name, culminating in *Polledge*. Another church dedicated to this saint is that at Ryme Intrinseca in Dorset, and in 1607 a child in the neighbouring village of Holnest was christened *Epowlett*. *Hippolyte* is not uncommon in France.

YPOLITUS Cur 1200.
IPPOLITUS Cur 1207.
IPOLITUS Cur 1210, 1213.

Hiram (m.): Hebrew *Hîrām*, an abbreviated form of 'Ahiram' (Hebrew *'ăhîrām*) meaning 'my (or the) brother is high'; the reference is not to a human brother, but to the patron deity regarded as the divine 'brother' of the clan or tribe. The name of the King of Tyre who supplied cedar wood to David and his son Solomon. *Hiram* was a favourite name in the 17th C and has continued to be used in Yorkshire. It is also common in the USA.

Hob, see ROBERT.

Hodierna (f.): this name, which appears indifferently as *Hodiern(a)* and *Odiern(a)*, occurs from time to time in the 12th–14th C and was the name of the mother of Alexander Neckham and foster-mother of Richard I. Fr. Reidy has pointed out to me that on the Feast of the Epiphany the Collect in the Latin liturgy begins 'Deus qui *hodierna* die', &c., and suggests with much probability that the name may sometimes have been given to children born at that season, instead of the more usual *Theophania* (q.v.).

Hoel, see HOWELL.

Homer (m.): Greek *Ὅμηρος*, Latin *Homerus*. The name of the poet is sometimes used as a christian name in USA. A few modern examples have also been noted in England.

Honor(i)(a) (f.) [ŏn'or, hŏnōr'a, hŏnōr'ĕă]: this was a common Anglo-Norman name, a derivative of Latin *honor* 'reputation', 'beauty', though the exact etymology is doubtful. There was a St. *Honoria*, one of the companions of St. Ursula, and a St. *Honorata* (French *Honorée*), either of whom may have been the sponsor of the name, which occurs in Latin records from the 12th–14th C as *Honora, Onora, Annora. Annora,* which is the commonest form, is a regular Anglo-Norman development, cf. Middle English *annour* for *honour* (see OED s.v. *honour*). It was carried to Ireland by the Normans and became a favourite name there, giving rise to the common *Nora* (q.v.). After the Reformation *Honor* or *Honour* was adopted as a christian name in England (cf. *Faith*, &c.), and in the 16th and 17th C was used as both a man's and a woman's name. It is now always f. *Honora, Honoria* came in again in the 18th C.

ANNORA Cur 1187–1215, FA 1302, 1316, HR 1273, Testa de Neville 13th C.
ANNOR HR 1273.

Hope (m., f.): used as a christian name from the 17th C. *Faith, Hope*, and *Charity* were often given as names to triplets. *Hope* is now used only as a girl's name.

Horace, Horatio (m.) [hŏr'as, hŏrā'shĕō]: Latin *Horatius*, the name of a famous patrician *gens*, amongst whose members were the legendary three *Horatii* who fought the three Curiatii, and *Horatius* Cocles who defended a bridge across the Tiber single-handed. The chief glory of the name, however, and the reason for its survival, is the poet Horace, *Quintus Horatius Flaccus*, the son of a freedman who had adopted the name of *Horatius*. Its use as a christian name dates from the Renaissance, and seems to have started (as *Horatio*) in Italy (cf. Shakespeare's *Horatio* in *Hamlet*). The earliest example noted in England is Sir *Horatio* Vere (1563–1635), 1st Lord Vere of Tilbury. His grandson, 1st Viscount Townshend, was named *Horatio* after him, and in turn stood sponsor to one of the sons of his neighbour Sir Edward Walpole. The name was thenceforward much used by the Walpoles, sometimes written *Horatio*, sometimes *Horace*, but apparently usually called *Horace*. It was carried by marriage into the families of Suckling and Nelson. *Horatio*, 1st Viscount Nelson, received his name from his godfather and distant relative *Horatio* Walpole, 2nd Baron Walpole of Wolterton. It is a little surprising that the immense fame of the admiral did not bring his name into general use, but it remains for the most part still the peculiar property of a few families. *Horace* is rather more generally used.

Horatia (f.): f. form of Latin *Horatius* (see HORACE). Examples are Lady Anna *Horatia* Waldegrave, a grand-niece of *Horace*

Walpole, and *Horatia*, daughter of Lord Nelson and Lady Hamilton.

Hortensia (f.): Latin f. from the name of the *Hortensian gens*. The Italian *Ortensia* was taken to France by *Ortensia* Mancini, niece of Mazarin, and was acclimatized there as *Hortense*. From France it has occasionally been borrowed in England.

Hosanna (m., f.): a Hebrew word which in Greek became ὡσάννα or ὠσάννα, in Latin *Hosanna* or *Osanna*. It was an exclamation in liturgical use amongst the Jews, meaning 'save now' or 'save pray', and was shouted before Jesus on his last entry into Jerusalem. The form *Osanna* was used in England from the Old English gospels until the 16th C when the versions of Tyndale and Coverdale have *Hosanna* or *Hosianna*. It is found as a christian name for both men and women from the beginning of the 13th C, usually in the French form *Osanne* or *Ozanne*; but it did not remain in use for very long. It seems to have been revived as a man's name in the 17th C, for Lyford 1655 gives *Hosanna* in his list of men's names. An *Hosannah* Johnson has been noted in 1880, but this was a woman.

Howard (m.): the use of this surname as a christian name is quite recent and there seems no particular reason for it except that it is the name of several noble families. The origin of the surname itself is doubtful; it seems sometimes to be from the name of the manorial officer, the *hayward*, and sometimes from a personal name *Howard*, *Heward*, *Hewerald* which occurs in the 11th and 12th C. There is no Old English name corresponding to it, but Förstemann gives one example of a name *Huguard*, apparently a compound of Old German *hugu* 'heart', 'soul', and *vardu* 'ward', 'protection', which may be the source of *Howard*.

Howell (m.): Welsh *hywel* 'eminent'. The corresponding Breton name *Hoel* was occasionally used in England in the Middle Ages.

Hubert (m.): Old German *Hugubert*, compound of *hugu* 'heart', 'mind', and *berhta* 'bright'. There was a corresponding Old English *Hygebeorht*, but it was not common, and the popularity of the name in the Middle Ages was undoubtedly derived from the cult of St. *Hubert*, Bishop of Liége, the patron saint of huntsmen. The surnames *Hubert*, *Hobart*, *Hubbard* (from the usual English form of the name), *Hubbert*, &c., are derived from it and testify to its former popularity, but it seems to have died out after the 14th C, and CMY treats it as obsolete. It was revived in the later 19th C and is now not uncommon.

HUBERTUS DB 1086, Cur 1187–1220.
HUBERT Cl 1270.
HUBARD Yorks Poll Tax 1379.
HOBARD Yorks Poll Tax 1379.

Hugh, Hugo (m.): there is an Old German name *Hugi* from *hugu* 'heart', 'mind'; but *Hugh* may equally represent a hypocoristic form of any of the numerous names compounded with *hugu*. It was introduced into England by the Normans and is frequent in DB. The French forms of the name were *Hugues* and *Hugon* in the north, *Hue* and *Huon* in the south (cf. *Ives* and *Ivon*, *Guy* and *Guyon*, the medieval *cas-sujet* and *cas-régime*). *Huchon* regularly appears in Scotland in the 14th–16th C. *Huon* is found as late as the 16th C in England. The Latin form was *Hugo*. All these gave rise to English versions of the name, which are illustrated by the many surnames derived from it, such as *Hugh*, *Hughes*, *Hugget* and *Huggin(s)* (from diminutives *Hug-et*, *Hug-in*), *Hew*, *Hewes*, *Heweson* (from the Scottish and North country *Hew*), *Hewet*, *Hewit(t)* (from the diminutive *Hew-et*), *Hewlett*, *Hewlitt* (from the diminutive *Hew-el-et*), *Hewling* (from the diminutive *Hew-el-in*), *How*, *Howes*, &c., from the southern form *How*, and many others. The name was already common in the 12th C, but became still more popular in the following century in honour of St. *Hugh*, Bishop of Lincoln (1135–1200), who was venerated in the North much as St. Thomas was in the South. Later, Little St. *Hugh* of Lincoln (1246?–55), a child supposed to have been martyred by the Jews, added to the popularity of the name. In Ireland and

Scotland it has been used to render several Gaelic names, e.g.
Aodh, *Eòghann*, *Ùisdeann.*

HUGO Reg 1082, DB 1086, Cur 1199–1220.
HUGH HR 1273.
HOWE, HEWE *Prompt Parv* 1450.
HUGELIN Cur 1200, 1273.
HUGOLINUS DB 1086.
HUET HR 1273, Yorks Poll Tax 1379.
HUGLINE HR 1273.
HUELIN HR 1273.
HUGETHUN Exch R 1306.

Hulda (f.): Norse *Huldr*, 'muffled', 'covered'. Introduced into
USA by Scandinavians.

Huldah (f.): Hebrew 'weasel', the name of a prophetess (2 Kings
xxii.). Used occasionally in the 17th and 18th C.

Humbert (m.): Old German *Hunberct*, compound of *Huni* the
folk-name, which probably originally meant 'giant', and *berhta*
'bright'. The name is most common, as *Umberto*, in Italy, but is
also used in Germany, and occasionally in England by persons of
German origin.

Humphr(e)y (m.): there was an Old English *Hunfrith*, a compound of the folk-name *Huni* (see HUMBERT) and *frith* 'peace';
but the widespread use of the name in the Middle Ages was
due to the introduction by the Normans of the French *Onfroi*
from the cognate Old German *Hunfrid*. *Humfridus* or *Hunfridus* occurs some score of times in DB. Later the French
form of the name was latinized as *Onuphrius*. *Umfray*, *Humfrye*,
Humfrey are some of the English forms; the spelling with *ph*
instead of *f* is relatively modern. *Dumphry* and *Dump* were
pet-forms, and the nursery hero Humpty-Dumpty probably
contains an echo of this. *Humphrey* and *Humphries* variously
spelt are common surnames. CMY says: 'From being a noble
and knightly name, *Humphrey*, as we barbarously spell it, came
to be a peasant's appellation, and is now almost disused.' Since

then, however, it has come back into favour and fashion. See also OLAF.

HUMFRIDUS, HUNFRIDUS DB 1086.
UMFRIDUS Cur 1199–1220, FA 1346.
HUMFREDUS FA 1316.
UMFREY HR 1273.
HUNFRAY HR 1273.

Hyacinth (m.): Greek ὑακίνθος the name of a flower. St. *Hyacinthus* was a Roman martyr, brother of St. Protus. Used very occasionally. See also JACINTH.

I

Ia(i)n, see JOHN.

Ianthe (f.) [ĭăn'thĕ]: Greek Ἰάνθη (possibly a compound of ἴον 'violet' and ἄνθος 'flower'), the name of a sea-nymph, daughter of Oceanus and Tethys. In *The Siege of Rhodes* (1656) the name of the heroine is *Ianthe*, which is made to rhyme with 'dainty'. The first example noted of its use as a christian name is *Ianthe Eliza*, daughter of Shelley and Harriet Westbrook. Landor addressed some of his most pleasing poems to *Ianthe* (Sophia Jane Swift), and this may have helped to make the name known.

Ida (f.) [ī'da]: this name is found in Old German and is from the root *id-* (= Old Norse *idh* 'labour'). It was brought to England by the Normans, and *Ida* Countess of Boulogne is mentioned as a tenant-in-chief in DB. It continued to be used until at least the middle of the 14th C and was revived in the 19th C. The Old English *Ida*, a man's name, was from the same root. *Ida* has been used in Ireland as an equivalent of the native *Ita*.

IDA FB 1086, Cur 1199–1212, FA 1302, 1346.
YDA Cur 1201.

Idonea (f.) [idōn'ĕă]: this is a puzzling name, but it seems probable that it is related to the Old Norse *Idhuna*, the name of a goddess of spring, derived from the Old Norse *idh* 'work', 'labour'.

It can scarcely be (what it looks like) the Latin adjective *idonea* from *idoneus* 'suitable', for there is no trace of it in the Romance languages. Förstemann records a f. name *Idina*, which is probably the same. It was common in England from the end of the 12th C; in Latin it appears as *Idonea, Idonia*, in the vernacular as *Ideny, Idony, Edony*. Examples of the name occur in later centuries. The surnames *Edney, Idney*, and possibly *Iddon, Idden*, are derived from it.

IDONEA Cur 1201–1218, FA 1284, 1303, 1346, *Times* 4 Feb. 1882.
YDONEA Cur 1203, 1207.
IDONIA Yorks Poll Tax 1379.
EDONIA Yorks Poll Tax 1379.
IDONY HR 1273.
IDENY Beetley, Norf Reg 1644.
EDNEY Notts P Reg 1754.

Ifor, see IVOR.

Ignatius, see INIGO.

Igor (m.) [i'gor]: a Russian name of Scandinavian origin (= *Ingvarr*), sometimes used in England in recent times.

Ilbert (m.): Old German *Hildeberht*, compound of *hildi* 'strife' and *berhta* 'bright', introduced into England by the Normans in the French form *Ilbert*. It seems to have died out in the 13th C, but not before giving rise to the surnames *Ilbert, Ilberd*. There was a corresponding Old English *Hildebeorht*.

ILBERTUS DB 1086.
ILBERT Cur 1200, 1201, 1210, Pipe Roll 1159.

Imbert (m.): Old German *Isenbard*, compound of *isan* 'iron', and the folk-name *Bard*, found e.g. in *Langobardi*. Introduced into England by the Normans in the form *Isembert, Imbert*. It died out in the 14th C. *Imbart* still occurs in France.

ISENBARDUS Reg 1094–9.
IMBERT Cl 1267, 1313, Fines 1283.
ISEMBERD HR 1273.
IMBERTUS FA 1303.

Imogen (f.) [im'ojen]: this name, from the heroine of Shakespeare's play of *Cymbeline*, has been used as a christian name

during the last 50 years or so. *Imogen* appears to be a misprint in
the Folio for *Innogen*, which is how the name appears in Shakespeare's source, Holinshed. *Innogen* is also the usual form in
Geoffrey of Monmouth, who makes her the wife of Brutus.
Innogen actually appears in the Quarto *Much Ado about Nothing*
in the list of dramatis personae, as the name of the wife of Leonato,
a character who does not appear in the play. Prof. Max. Förster
suggests that *Innogen* is probably the same word as Old Irish
ingen 'daughter', 'girl', from *eni-genā, cf. Greek ἐγγόνη 'granddaughter'.

Inez (f.): Spanish form of *Agnes* (q.v.).

Ingaret, see ANCHORET.

Ingram (m.): either Old German *Angilramnus* or *Ingilramnus*
(corresponding to Old English *Engelram* and *Ingilram*). The
second element in either case is *hraban* 'raven'; the first is either
angil 'angel', or *Ingil*, a derivative of *Ingvi*, an old hero-name.
Both names were fairly common in Old German; but phonetically
the Old French *Ingelram*, later *Enguerran*, is more likely to come
from *Ingilramnus*. The name was brought to England by the
Normans, a notable example being *Ingelram* Count of Ponthieu,
brother-in-law of the Conqueror. *Enguerran* became in English
Ingran and *Ingram*, and gave rise to the surnames *Ingram, Ingra-
ham, Ingry*. It is found as a christian name as late as the 17th C.
It is sometimes found in use at the present day, but apparently
always as an adaptation of the surname.

INGELRANNUS, INGELRAMNUS, INGRANNUS DB 1086.
INGELRANDUS Reg 1094–9.
INGELRAM Cur 1196, HR 1273.
INGERAM HR 1273.
ENGERAMUS FA 1303.
INGRAM Yorks Poll Tax 1379.
INGELRAMUS Yorks Poll Tax 1379.
INGRAMUS FA 1431.

Ingrid (f.): an Old Norse name of which the first element is from
the hero-name *Ingvi* and the second *rida* 'ride'. *Ingerith* is found

in England in the 13th C, but the name, like most Norse names, died out. It has sometimes been borrowed from Scandinavia in recent years.

INGREDE DB 1086.
INGERITH Cur 1205–13.

Inigo (m.): Greek 'Iγνάτιος, of unknown etymology. It was the name of a Bishop of Antioch, martyred between A.D. 104 and 117, identified by tradition with the child whom Christ set in the midst of the disciples. He was the reputed author of epistles to the Romans, the Ephesians, Polycarp, &c., which had a wide circulation. The name was used chiefly in Russia. In the West it was confined to Spain, where it is found from the 8th C as *Ignacio*, *Iñigo*, or *Eneco*. Its wider diffusion was due to St. *Ignatius* de Loyola (*Iñigo* Lopez de Recalde, 1548–98), founder of the Society of Jesus. The Jesuits carried his name with them, and as *Ignace* in France, *Ignaz* in Germany, it became fairly common. In England it has naturally not been much used except by a few Roman Catholic families. *Inigo* Jones, the architect, was named after his father, who always signed himself *Enego*, but named his son, in his will, *Inigue*. *Jenico* has been used in the family of Preston, Viscounts of Gormanstown, since about 1430 when Christopher Preston married the daughter of Sir *Jenico* d'Artois. This is apparently a Provençal form of Spanish *Eneco*.

Iolo (m.) [ī'olō]: Welsh, probably a hypocoristic form for *Iorwerth*, a compound of *iōr* 'lord', and *-gwerth* 'worth', 'value'. It is, however, commonly supposed to be derived from *Julius*. Cf. the alleged origin of *Gladys*, *Owen*, and *Emlyn*.

Ira (m.): Aramaic 'the stallion'; the name of a priest of David. It is used extensively in the USA.

Irene (f.) [īrē'nĕ, īrēn']: Greek Εἰρήνη 'peace'. A common Byzantine name also used in Sicily. It first appears in England c. 1880 (CMY does not regard it as an English name) and is now common. The American disyllabic pronunciation is now often used in England. *Renie* is a common abbreviation.

Iris (f.): Greek *Ἶρις* 'the rainbow'. The earliest example of this name which has been noted is in a list of christian names from Privy Council Education lists compiled by Charles Dickens between 1855 and 1865, apparently on account of their oddity. A writer to N & Q 1904 gives it as one of the flower-names whose use was growing common.

Isa (f.): found chiefly in Scotland, and sometimes, at least, a pet-form of *Isabel* (cf. *Isa* Keith, cousin and correspondent of Marjorie Fleming). CMY says 'Isa is an old German feminine revived by a poetess of our own day'. She refers to *Isa* Knox (*née* Craig, 1831–1903) who contributed to the *Scotsman* over the name 'Isa'.

Isaac, Izaak (m.): Hebrew 'He (= God) may laugh', i.e. regard the bearer in a friendly light. Popular etymology connected the meaning with Sarah's laughter when she heard his conception foretold. The name of the son of Abraham and Sarah. It occurs twice in the Old English period as the name of a priest. *Isac* occurs twice in DB, and the name was used from time to time in the following centuries, sometimes, but by no means always, by Jews. The surnames *Isaac(s)*, *Isaacson*, *Isacke* are derived from it. After the Reformation it was much more commonly used. The spelling *Izaak* came in in the 17th C. The name has almost completely dropped out of use.

Isac DB 1086.
Ysaac (a Jew) Magd. 1207.
Isaac HR 1273.
Isake Lincs 1534.

Isabel(la), Isobel (f.) [Ĭz'abel, (Scottish) Ĭs'obel]: this form of *Elizabeth* (q.v.) seems to have developed in Provence, and became almost universal in both Spain and France. Camden (1605) says of it: '*Isabel*—one with *Elizabeth*; if the Spaniards do not mistake, which always translate *Elizabeth* into *Isabel*, and the French into *Isabeau*.' *Isabella* Clara Eugenia, daughter of Philip II of Spain, signed her name *Isabel*, had coins struck 'Albert and *Elisabet*' and seals with *Isabella*. The names were still interchangeable in the

16th C; for instance a Berkshire yeoman in his will, 1542, names his wife *Isabel*, but in her own will, two years later, she is named *Elizabeth*. *Isabel* first appears in England in the 12th C, and its rapid spread may have been due to its being the name of three queens, *Isabel* of Angoulême, wife of King John; *Isabel* of France, wife of Edward II; and *Isabel* of France, 2nd wife of Richard II. In the 13th and 14th C it was one of the commonest female names in England. In the 15th and 16th C it is often spelt *Issabel*, sometimes *Esabel*. It gave rise to many surnames, such as *Isabell*, *Isbell*; *Ibb(s)*, *Ibson*, *Ibbison* (from the nickname *Ib*); *Nibbs*, *Tibbs*, *Libby* (from other nicknames); *Ibbetson* (from the diminutive *Ibbot*). The English form of the name is usually *Isabel*, or the latinized *Isabella*, which came in in the 18th C. *Belle* is a common pet-form. In Scotland *Isobel*, *Isbel*, or *Ishbel* and the nickname *Tibby* are used. Borrow's *Isopel* Berners was probably a phonetic reminiscence of the Scottish *Isobel*, in which the *s* is often pronounced hard.

ISABELE Cur 1196.
ISABELLA Cur 1199, Yorks Poll Tax 1379.
ISABEL(L) Ass 1284, HR 1273.
ISSABELL Lincs 1450, 1535.
EZABELL Cov 1471.
IBOT(A) Yorks Poll Tax 1379.
IBBET Cornish Parish Reg. 1579.

Isaiah (m.) [īzī′a]: Hebrew 'Jehovah is generous', the name of one of the greatest Hebrew prophets. It has been used, infrequently, as a christian name since the 17th C.

Isidore (m.) [Iz′idōr]: Greek Ἰσίδωρος; the meaning of the first element is doubtful, the second is from δῶρον 'gift'. The name was fairly common in ancient Greece, and it was early established in Spain, where it was the name of two notable saints, St. *Isidore* of Seville (560–636), a voluminous writer, and St. *Isidore* the Ploughman, the patron saint of Madrid, who lived in the 11th or 12th C. The name was adopted by the Spanish Jews, and outside Spain is mainly a Jewish name. It has been used in the Blake family of Menlough from the mid-17th C to the present day. The f. forms *Isidora*, *Isadora* are occasionally used.

Ismay (f.): this rather rare name is found from the 13th C, spelt variously *Ysemay, Isemay, Ysmay, Isamaya,* and it gave rise to the surname *Ismay. Ismey* is found in Ireland in the 18th C, and *Ismay* has been used in England in the present century. It does not seem to be found on the Continent. There is insufficient evidence on which to base an etymology, but it may perhaps be related to *Ismenia* (q.v.).

YSEMAY HR 1273.
ISEMAY HR 1273.
YSMAY HR 1273.

Ismen(i)a (f.): this name is found from the 12th C in various forms. *Ismenia* occurs in Ireland as late as 1800. There are some signs that this and the possibly related *Ismay* (q.v.) may be of Irish provenance and possibly of Celtic origin. It is unlikely that they have anything to do with the Greek *Ismene,* although *Antigone* occurs as a christian name in the 13th C. In the 17th and 18th C *Emony, Emeny* are found as men's names, possibly a use of the surnames derived from the christian name. The gipsy family of Heron use *Emmanaia* as a woman's name.

The name *Jesmond* which was common in North Lancashire in the 16th-18th C may be the same name. Other forms of it are *Jessimond, Jesmaine, Jismond, Gismon.*

ISMENA Cur 1199, 1200, 1201.
ISMENIA Cur 1218.
ISMEINA Cur 1213.
YMEISNA, YMENIA, YSMENA Cur 1200.
YSMEINA Cur 1207.
YSMENA Cur 1210.
ISMANIA, ISMANNA FA 1303, 1346.
IMANIA QW 1294.
EMONI HR 1273.
YMANYA HR 1273.
IMANIE HR 1273.
EMAYN Poll Tax 1379.
IMAYNE Poll Tax 1379.
IMYNE Chester Wills 1594.

Isolda (f.) [ĭzŏl'da]: whether a Celtic or a German origin should be assigned to the name of the heroine of the Tristan romances is doubtful, though phonetically the German seems more likely. *Essylt* occurs early in Welsh; *Isold, Isolt*, a compound of *is* 'ice' and *vald* 'rule', occurs in Old German as early as the 8th C. It was a common christian name in the Middle Ages, owing its popularity to that of the Tristan romances. It is usually recorded in the latinized form *Isolda*, but the spoken forms of the name were derived from the French *Iseut, Isaut*. *Ysolt* occurs in 1201, *Isowde, Isolde* in the 15th C, but the usual English form of the name was *Isot* or *Izot*, which in turn was often latinized as *Isota*. Bardsley gives no fewer than 12 surnames derived from it. He also gives an example of the christian name *Izett* in Ireland as late as 1891. A writer to N & Q in 1880 stated that *Isott* was then still current in Somerset. Another N & Q correspondent in 1877 wrote: 'the name *Isolda* may be rare at the present day, but it has not fallen into disuse. I am well acquainted with a lady of that name, and I learned from her that it was an old family name in both her father's and her mother's family.' CMY, however, seems to have regarded it as obsolete. Since then the name has had some revival, probably owing to the vogue of Wagner's opera *Tristan und Isolde*.

ISOLDA Cur 1199–1313, HR 1273, FA 1346, Yorks Poll Tax 1379.
YSOLT Cur 1201.
ISOTA Yorks Poll Tax 1379.
ISOTT Cornish Reg 1576.
ISYLTE St. Jas. Clerkenwell 1612.
ISSAT Yarborough Parish Reg 1734.

Isot(t) (f.), see ISOLDA.

Israel (m.): Hebrew; the sense is much disputed, but probably 'may God prevail'. Jacob was called *Israel* after his wrestling with the Lord, and thereafter the name was applied to the whole Jewish people. It has continued to be used as a personal name among the Jews, but seems not to have been used by Christians until the Reformation. It is found among 17th-C Puritans, and continued in use, mainly among the working classes, until the end of the 19th C.

Ivo (m.): Old French *Ive(s), Ivon*. Förstemann derives it from Old German *Iv* 'yew'. The St. *Ives* who gave his name to the

Hunts. town was a legendary person, said to have come to England from Persia in the 7th C. *Yvon, Yves* was the name of one of the 12 peers who fell at Roncesvalles, and it is common in Old French romances. It was brought to England at the time of the Norman Conquest, one of the best-known examples being *Ivo* Taillebois who married an Englishwoman, sister of Edwin and Morcar. It was a favourite name with the Anglo-Normans and it, and its diminutive gave rise to many surnames, such as *Ive(s)*, *Iveson*, *Ivatt(s)*, *Ivett(s)*, *Ivens*. In the Latin form *Ivo* it has been revived in modern times. *Yves* is still used in France.

Yvo Reg 1066–71.
Ivo DB 1086.
Yvo Cur 1196, Yorks Poll Tax 1379.
Ive HR 1273.
Yvonus Testa de Neville 13th C.
Ivone, Yvone HR 1273.
Ivote HR 1273.

Ivor, Ifor (m.) [ī'vor, ē'vōr]: this name is mainly Irish, Scottish, and Welsh (there was a St. *Ivor* contemporary with St. Patrick), and is probably a borrowing of the Old Norse name *Ivarr* which was borne by several Danish Kings of Dublin in the 9th and 10th C. The Scottish surnames *MacIver, MacIvor* come from *Ivor*. *Ifor* is the Welsh spelling, and *Yfore* occurs in English records in the 13th C.

Ivy (f.): a late 19th-C invention. A writer in N & Q 1904 mentions it as one of the plant and flower names then gaining popularity.

J

Jabez (m.): Hebrew, meaning unknown. This name came into use in the 17th C and continued to be used, especially by Dissenters, until the 19th C.

Jacinth (f.): the name of a precious stone, from Old French *iacinte*, and ultimately from Greek ὑακίνθος (Hyacinth). *Jacinthe* and *Giacinta* are used respectively in France and Italy. *Jacinth* is found in use in England in the 17th C (e.g. in the Sitwell and Sacheverell families) as a man's name possibly with reference to Rev. xxi. 20 'the eleventh, a *jacinth*'.

Jack (m.): this, the commonest pet-name for *John* (q.v.), has caused a good deal of difficulty owing to the natural assumption that it must be derived from the French *Jacques* and should therefore logically represent *James* rather than *John*. The problem was cleared up by E. W. B. Nicholson in a little book entitled *The Pedigree of Jack and of Various Allied Names* (1892). He showed that there is no recorded instance of *Jack, Jak, Jacke*, or *Jakke* ever being used to represent *Jacques* or *James*, and that no statement in favour of the French connexion has been produced from any early writer. He then proceeded to elucidate and illustrate with examples the development from *Johannes* to *Jehan* and *Jan*, whence, by addition of the common suffix *-kin*, we get *Jankin*, which as a result of French nasalization becomes *Jackin*, and was finally shortened to *Jack*. There was a similar development from *Jon* to *Jock* (the Scottish form of the name). This process was complete by the beginning of the 14th C, by which time *Jack* was already established as a synonym for *man* or *boy*. The OED gives no fewer than 80 uses and compounds of *jack* as a common noun. The correctness of this derivation of *Jack* is confirmed by a passage in the *Historia Monasterii S. Augustini Cantuariensis c.* 1414: 'Mos enim est barbaricae locutionis et Saxonum, etsi non transponere, transformare tamen apocopando, et saepius syncopando: ut pro Thoma *Tomme* seu *Tomlin*; pro Johanne *Jankin* sive *Jacke*.'

Jacob (m.): Hebrew ăqōb; the meaning is much disputed. The name of the younger son of Isaac, who supplanted his elder brother Esau whence the popular explanation of the name as meaning 'he seized the heel' or 'he supplanted' (cf. Gen. xxv. 26). The name was a favourite one among the Jews, and was borne by two of the apostles. ăqōb became in Greek 'Ιάκωβος, in Latin *Jacōbus*, but in late Latin it became *Ja·cŏbus* or *Ja·cŏmus*, from the former of which developed the Italian *Jacopo, Giacobbe*, Spanish

Jaco, Jago or *Iago*, French *Jacques*, English *Jacob*, Welsh *Iago*; from the latter come Spanish *Jayme*, Italian *Iachimo, Giacomo*, Provençal *Jaume, Jacme*, Old French *James, Gemmes*, English *James, Jem, Jim*. See further under JAMES. *Jacob* is found four times in England before the Conquest, but always as the name of an ecclesiastic. After the Conquest there is little evidence of the use of *Jacob* except occasionally as the name of a Jew, though Godstow 1450 has 'St. Philip and St. *Jacob*'. *Jacobus* was, of course, the almost invariable form of *James*, &c., in Latin documents, and the surnames *Jacob, Jacobs, Jacoby*, if not of Jewish origin, are possibly from the Latin. The general use of *Jacob* as a christian name dates from the Reformation, and is due to the fact that the English translators of the Bible, while using the English form *James* for the two apostles, retained *Jacob* for the patriarch.

Jacoba, Jacobina (f.) [jakō'ba, jăkobē'na]: *Jacoba* occurs from time to time in medieval Latin records as a woman's name. Probably the women in question were actually christened and called *James*. For example, one of the three daughters of Richard Emelden who died in 1333 is called *Jacoba*. In the proof of her age, 1339, one of the witnesses said he remembered the date of her baptism because 'it seemed to him wonderful that he called her by a boy's name when she was herself a girl'. She is usually called *Joan* in later records, but after her marriage to Sir Alan Clavering there is a reference to 'Sir Alan and *James* his wife'. In the 18th C Scottish Jacobites gave the names *Jacoba* and *Jacobina* to their daughters, and *Jacobina* still survives in Scotland.

Jacqueline, Jacquetta (f.) [jăk'elēn, jakĕt'a]: French f. diminutive of *Jacques* (*James*), probably introduced to this country from Flanders and found from time to time from the 13th to 17th C. The English pronunciation of the names is preserved in the surnames *Jacklin* and *Jacket*. *Jacket* is found as a christian name as late as 1628.

JAKOLINA Cl H III.
JAKELINA Cl 1309.
JACLYN Yorks Poll Tax 1379.

Jael (f.): Hebrew *Jaalah* 'wild she-goat'. *Jael* the Kenite, who treacherously slew Sisera while he was her guest, would not seem to be an attractive person after whom to name a child, but *Jael* was a favourite Puritan name and continued in use during the 18th and early 19th C among Dissenters and in America.

James (m.): for the development of *James* from *Jacobus* and its etymology, see under JACOB and JACOBA. *Jame(s)* is found side by side with *Jacques* in Old French, the one being from *Jacomus*, the other from *Jacobus*, and it was *Jame* or *James* which took root in England where, however, it is not recorded until about a century after the Norman Conquest. The first recorded pilgrimage from England to the shrine of St. *James* in Compostella was in 1148, and the name *James* (*sic*, not *Jacobus*) occurs at the beginning of the 13th C, i.e. *James* de Houdernes and *James* de Bakepuz, so named in charters of King John. In the *Ancren Riwle c.* 1225 it is *Iame*, in the Testa de Neville *Jame*; in Chaucer's *Shipman's Tale* we find *Seynt Jame*; a 14th-C Legendary has *Seynt Iemes*, *Seynt Ieme* (cf. later vulgar *Jeames* and *Jem*), and 15th C Oseney *Jamys*. It will be noticed that most of these early examples are references to St. *James*. The saint meant is usually St. *James* the Great, the son of Zebedee, and not St. *James* the Less, the brother of our Lord; of 440 churches dedicated in this name in England, 414 are to the former and only 26 to the latter. It was the supposed tomb of St. *James* the Great which was the object of pilgrimage at Sant Jago de Compostella, the most famous shrine in Europe in the Middle Ages. The name was not very widely used in England in the Middle Ages, though it was more frequent in the North and in Scotland. The surnames *James*, *Jameson*, *FitzJames* (found in the 15th C) are, however, evidence that it was well established. The accession of *James* Stuart to the English throne in 1603 marks the beginning of the period in which it became a common English name. The usual diminutive is *Jim* or *Jimmy* (formerly *Jem* and *Jemmy*—cf. a burglar's *jemmy*), in Scotland spelt *Jamie*. The Gaelic *Seumas*, Irish *Seumus* are occasionally heard in England; more common is the monstrous pseudo-Gaelic *Hamish* (q.v.). There seems to have been a fashion for the French *Jacques*

in the 16th C, and Camden says of it: 'which some Frenchified
English, to their disgrace, have too much affected.'

JACOBUS Cur 1186–1220.
IAME Ancren Riwle c. 1225.
JAME Testa de Neville 13th C.
JAMES Magd. c. 1240.
JAMETTUS FA 1284.
JAKE, JAQUES Exch R 1306.
JACOMINUS FA 1305.
IAMES, IAME 14th-C Legendary.
JACOMYNUS FA 1428.
JAMYS Oseney 1460.
IAMES, IAMYS Lincs 1533.

Jamesina (f.) [jămzē′na]: a Scottish f. form of *James*. See also
JACOBA, JACOBINA.

Jan (m.): a dialectal form of *John* (q.v.). For a similar development, cf. *Jane* and *Joan*. It is occasionally used in Devon and
Somerset nowadays, probably on account of 'girt Jan Ridd' the
hero of *Lorna Doone*.

Jane (f.): the usual modern form of *Joan(na)* (see JOAN). It comes
from Old French *Jehane*, and is not found much before the 16th C,
Joan being the more usual medieval form of the name in England.
Jane was very common in the late 18th and early 19th C, often in
combination with other names, as *Mary Jane, Sarah Jane, Jane
Anne*. It went out of fashionable use in the middle of the 19th C
and came to be regarded as a typical maidservant's name. It has
come back into fashion in the present century. *Janey* and *Jenny*
are the usual diminutives. For *Janet* see separate article. The
Gaelic form of the name is *Sine* (phonetically rendered as *Sheena*
or *Shena*); Irish is *Séadna*.

JANE Coventry Mysteries 15th C.

Janet (f.): a diminutive of *Jane* (q.v.). *Janeta* is not uncommon in
medieval records. It is now chiefly used in Scotland and is generally
given as an independent name sometimes in the diminutive form
Netta or *Nettie*. *Jonet* and *Jennet* were other diminutives, from

Jone and *Jeanne* respectively. *Jennet* is found as late as 1660, and Lyford (1665) gives '*Jennet* diminutive from *Jeane*'. *Jonet* has been occasionally revived in recent years.

Japhet(h) (m.): Hebrew 'may he expand', the name of one of the sons of Noah. Occasionally used as a christian name in the 17th C.

Jared (m.): Arabic *ward* = Hebrew *yered, yared* = Greek ῥόδον 'rose'. Occasionally used as a christian name, especially in the USA, since the 17th C.

Jarvis, see GERVAIS.

Jason (m.): this name, occasionally used as a christian name since the 17th C, especially in USA, is not that of the Greek hero, but that of the author of the book of Ecclesiasticus and of a kinsman of St. Paul at Thessalonica who was persecuted on his account (Acts xvii. 5, Rom. xvi. 21). *Jason* was the English translators' rendering of the Greek 'Εάσων, which was no doubt a hellenizing of some Hebrew name, possibly Joshua or Jesus.

Jasper, Caspar (m.): *Jasper* is the usual English form of *Gaspar* or *Caspar*, which was the traditional name of one of the Three Kings (*Gaspar, Melchior, Balthasar*) into whom medieval legend transformed the 'wise men' who came to Bethlehem to worship the infant Christ. The Gospels say nothing of their number or their names, but the legend evidently arose early. The three kings and their names appear in an 11th-C painting. Their supposed remains were translated from Constantinople in the 12th C and were ultimately enshrined at Cologne: *Kaspar*, in consequence, became a fairly common name in Germany; and *Gaspard* in France, *Gaspar* in Spain, *Gaspare* in Italy were not uncommon. *Jasper* or *Jesper* is first found in England in the 14th C, e.g. *Jasper* Woodlock (Magd. 1370) (cf. the surnames *Jasper, Jesper*), but the name has never been popular in this country. The etymology is unknown; it is probably of eastern origin. See also BALTHASAR.

Jean (f.): the usual modern Scottish form of *Jane* or *Joan* (qq.v.).
It comes from the Old French *Jehane* (Modern French *Jeanne*)
and was formerly common in England. Lyford 1655 says '*Jeane*
see *Joane*'. The diminutive form of *Jean* was *Jennet* (see JANET).

Jedidiah (m.): Hebrew 'friend of Jehovah', one of the surnames
or epithets of Solomon. Occasionally used by English Puritans.
Still used in USA, where it is often shortened to *Jed*.

Jeffrey, see GEOFFREY.

Jehu (m.): Hebrew 'Jehovah is he'; cf. *Elihu*. Occasionally used
by English Puritans.

Jemima (f.): Hebrew 'dove'; the name of one of the three
daughters of Job, the others being *Keziah* and *Kerenhappuch*. All
three were used, though not often, in the 17th C. A natural
daughter of Charles II and Lady Shannon, born in 1650, was
christened Charlotte *Jemima* Henrietta Maria. *Jemima*, in spite of
its ugliness, became generally popular in the 19th C and was for
a time a really common name. It is possible that it was regarded
as a f. form of *James*.

Jenico, see INIGO.

Jennet, see JANET.

Jen(n)ifer, see GUENEVERE.

Jenny (f.): the usual pet-name for *Jane* (q.v.), properly pronounced *Jinny*, though a spelling pronunciation is now often
heard. In Scotland, where it is the usual pet-form of *Janet*, the
spelling pronunciation is general.

Jephthah (m.): Hebrew 'He (= God) opened (the womb for a
first-born child)' or 'may He (= God) open, release (the bearer
from harmful influences)'. Occasionally used by English Puritans.

Jeremiah, Jeremy (m.): Hebrew 'May Jehovah raise up, exalt'.
The name of one of the great Hebrew prophets. The English form

of the name, *Jeremy*, is found from the 13th C. *Jeremiah* and *Jeremias* (the Greek form) were adopted by the Puritans in the 17th C. There has been some revival of *Jeremy* in the present century. In Ireland it has been used to render the native *Diarmuit*. *Jeremiah* is particularly common in S.E. Ireland, perhaps because of the old tradition of a visit there by the prophet.

JEREMIAS Cur 1200, 1201, 1210.
JEREMY FF 1239.

Jerome (m.): Greek Ἱερώνυμος 'sacred name'. This was the name of a king of Syracuse (grandson of Hiero) and of a Rhodian peripatetic philosopher, and thirdly of St. Eusebius *Hieronymus* Sophronius (340–420) better known as St. *Jerome*, whose Latin translation of the Bible was the basis of the Vulgate. He was much reverenced in the Middle Ages and his name was used in Italy, where it became *Geronimo*, and France, where it was reduced to *Jérôme*. In England *Jeronimus*, *Geronim(us)* (variously mis-spelt) occur in Latin records from the end of the 12th C. The English pronunciation of the name is indicated by the surnames *Jerome*, *Jerram*, *Jerrems*, *Jarram*. *Ieram* occurs in 1556 and *Hierom* in 1675, but the initial *J* was usual. A f. form *Jeromia* occurs at Bury (Lancs.) in 1615.

JERONIMUS Cur 1199.
JERONIM Cur 1207.
GERONIM Cur 1200, 1201, 1210.
GEREMINUS, GERMINUS, JEREMINUM, JEREMIMUM (all the same man) Cur 1219–20.
GERONIMUS Cur 1219.

Jerry, diminutive of *Gerald*, *Gerard* or *Jeremy* (qq.v.).

Jervis, see GERVASE.

Jesse (m.) [jĕ′sĕ]: Hebrew 'Jehovah exists'. The name of the father of David; used as a christian name after the Reformation.

Jessica (f.): this name, the use of which is modern, is taken from Shakespeare's *Merchant of Venice*. It appears to be the Hebrew *Yiṣkāh* 'He beholds'. In the Authorized Version Gen. xi. 29 the name appears as *Iscah*, but in earlier translations it is *Jesca*.

Jessie (f.): a Scottish diminutive of *Janet* (q.v.), now often used as an independent name. Early examples of the name are *Jessy: or the Bridal*, a novel published in 1770, and Robert Tannahill's poem '*Jessie* the Flower o' Dunblane', which expressed his love for *Janet* Tennant (1770–1833) of Paisley. Burns in his last illness was nursed by *Jessie* Leuars. Early examples of the name in England are in Charlotte Brontë's *Shirley* (1849) and Mrs. Gaskell's *Cranford* (1853).

Jethro (m.): Hebrew 'abundance', 'excellence'. Used as a christian name after the Reformation. A notable example is *Jethro* Tull (1674–1741) the agriculturist.

Jevon (m.): Welsh *Yevan*, *Jevan*, forms of *Evan* (q.v.) or *John*. *Jevon* is still sometimes used instead of the usual *Evan*.

Jill (f.): a pet-form of *Gillian* (q.v.), now often used as an independent name.

Joab (m.) [jō′ăb]: Hebrew 'Jehovah (is a) father'. Used as a christian name after the Reformation.

Joachim (m.): Hebrew *Jehoiachim* 'May Jehovah raise up, exalt'. In apocryphal writings this was said to be the name of the father of the Blessed Virgin, and it was consequently used as a christian name, particularly in the Greek Church. *Joachim*, *Achim* or *Akim* is still fairly common in Germany and Russia. *Gioiachino* in Italy and *Joaquin* in Spain were also formerly in use. *Joachim* is recorded in England from the 13th C, but has never been in general use.
JOACHIM, JOACHIN HR 1273.
JOACHIM FA 1346.

Joan (f.): the most usual f. form of *John* (q.v.). *Jehane* or *Jehanne* became suddenly common in the 12th C in the south of France. The usual English form *Jhone*, *Johan* came into use soon after and was very common in the ensuing centuries together with its diminutive *Jonet*. By the 16th C it was the third commonest English female name and was apparently considered vulgar (e.g. Shakespeare's 'greasy *Joan* doth keel the pot') and was largely superseded by *Jane* (q.v.) which had developed from *Jehane*, whereas *Joan* came from *Johan* (cf. the parallel development of *John* and *Jan*, *Jock* and *Jack*). *Joan* was revived at the beginning of the present century (*Jane* having been overtaken by the fate which had earlier befallen *Joan*) and is once more a favourite name.

JOHANNA Cur 1189–1220, Yorks Poll Tax 1379.
JOHAN Yorks Poll Tax 1379.
JOHNE Lincs 1459.
JOHNA, JAHAN 15th-C Brut.
IONE Lincs 1535.
JONET Lincs 1450.

Jo(h)anna (f.): *Joanna* occurs in the Authorized Version of the New Testament in St. Luke's Gospel, once as the name of a man in the genealogy of Jesus, and again as the name of one of the women who ministered to Jesus. It is apparently a Greek spelling of Hebrew *Johanan* (see JOHN). It was first used as a women's christian name after the Reformation. *Johanna* was the usual medieval Latin form of *Joan* (q.v.), and was taken into use, like other medieval latinizations, in the 18th C.

Job (m.): Hebrew 'hated', 'persecuted'. The story of Job was a favourite subject of medieval plays, interludes, &c., and Bardsley would derive the surnames *Job*, *Jobson*, *Jobling*, *Jopling*, *Jupp*, *Jubs* from it. It is, however, more probable that the medieval name *Jupp* or *Job* represents an English equivalent of Old German *Joppo* (probably a hypocoristic form of *Judbert*, &c.). The Biblical name, however, came into use after the Reformation, though it was never common.

JOB, JOBBA, JOPPA, JOP HR 1273.

Jocelyn, Joscelin (m., f.): Old German *Gautelen*, *Gauzelen*, a combination of *Gauta* (from the same root as the folk-name *Goth*) and the suffix *lin* (= English *-ling*) which was not originally a diminutive. Förstemann gives many examples of the name from the 7th to the 11th C, including several in the form *Joscelin*. The name was introduced into England by the Normans (*Gozelinus* occurs 11 times and *Gos(c)elinus* 8 times in DB), and it was

common throughout the Middle Ages, giving rise to the surnames
Joslin, Josselin, Joscelyne, Gosling, and many other variants. It was
rare after the 14th C, but has never altogether died out. The use
of *Jocelyn* as a girl's name seems to be quite modern and is not
mentioned by CMY.

GOZELINUS DB 1086.
GOSCELINUS DB 1086.
GOSELINUS DB 1086.
GOSCELINUS Reg 1087-97.
JOCELIN(US) Cur 1196, HR 1273, FA 1285.
JOSCELIN Cur 1199.
GAUSELIN Cl 1292.
GOSLINUS Yorks Poll Tax 1379.

Jock, see JACK, JOHN.

Joel (m.): Hebrew 'Jehovah is God'. This name of a minor
prophet began to be used as a christian name after the Reformation.
The common medieval *Joel, Juel, Jowell,* or *Jewell,* which gave
rise to numerous surnames, is a different name, from the Breton
Judicael or *Juhel,* the name of a saint who lived as a hermit in
Ponthieu. It was introduced into England, with other Breton
names, at the time of the Norman Conquest.

John (m.): Hebrew *Johanan* (Latin *Johannes*) 'Jehovah has
favoured'. One of the commonest of Jewish names. As the name
of both the Baptist and an Evangelist (each of whom had two
festivals, the Nativity and the Decollation of St. John the Baptist,
and the Nativity of St. John the Evangelist and St. John before
the Latin Gate) *John* was marked out for popularity as a christian
name. It was rare in England in the Old English period, though
it occurs from time to time as the name of a priest or monk. In
early times its chief use was in the Eastern Church, and it did not
become common in western Europe until after the first Crusades.
The sponsor was probably more often the Baptist (who has 500
churches dedicated to him in England) than the Evangelist (181
dedications). Though *John* was a fairly common English name in
the 12-15th C, its singular predominance over all other names

came later. An analysis of names in the register of one church gives interesting results:

Period					Percentage of all males baptized John
1550–99	.	.	.	.	15½
1600–49	.	.	.	.	19
1650–99	.	.	.	.	28
1700–49	.	.	.	.	25
1750–99	.	.	.	.	19

It has been an equal favourite in other countries; French *Jean*, German *Hans* (from *Johannes*), Italian *Giovanni*, Spanish *Juan*, Russian *Ivan*, for example, are among the commonest names in their respective countries. The Welsh *Evan* and Irish *Sean*, *Shane* are noticed separately, as is also the nickname *Jack* (Scottish *Jock*). *Johnnie* is a less frequent diminutive. The Gaelic *Ian* (or better, *Iain*) is now increasingly used even in England. See also EUGENE. The number of surnames derived from *John* and its petforms is very great, e.g. *John(s)*, *Johnson*, *Jones*, *Jone*, *Jack(s)*, *Jackson*, *Jake*, *Jenkin(s)*, *Jenkinson* (from the diminutive *Jen-kin*); *Jennens*, *Jenyns*, *Jennings* (from the French diminutive *Jeanin*); *Jennett*, *Jenn(e)*, *Jennison*; *Hankin(s)*, *Hankinson*, *Hancock*, &c., from the diminutive *Hane-kin*, *Hane-cock*.

Jolyon, see JULIAN.

Jonah, Jonas (m.): Hebrew 'dove'. *Jonas* is the Greek form of the name. The story of the prophet *Jonah* was a favourite one in the Middle Ages, and *Jonas* is occasionally found in the 12th and 13th C. It became relatively popular after the Reformation, usually in the form *Jonah*, but is now seldom used.

JONAS Pipe Roll 1165, Cur 1213.

Jonathan (m.). [jŏn´athăn]: Hebrew 'Jehovah has given (i.e. a son)'. The name of the son of Saul and friend of David. *Jonathas* (the Greek form) is found as a christian name in the 13th C, but its general use is subsequent to the Reformation.

JONATHUS CUR 1213.

Jonet, see JANET.

Jordan (m.): Hebrew 'flowing down', the name of the principal river of Palestine. There was an Old German personal name *Jordanes*, probably from the same root as Old Norse *jördh* 'land'. *Jordan* is found as a christian name in England from the end of the 12th C, and the probability is that its ultimate source was the Old German *Jordanes*, but that its continued use was due to confusion with the name of the river, which would be familiar to returning Crusaders, who were in the habit of bringing back Jordan water to be used in the baptism of their children. The surnames *Jordan(s)*, *Jordanson*, *Jordison*, &c., are derived from it. Bardsley also derives the surnames *Judd*, *Judson*, *Juggins*, *Juxon*, *Jewks*, &c., from Jordan by way of the nickname *Judd*. But there is no evidence connecting *Judd* with *Jordan*, and it is more probable that it was an Old English name cognate with Old German *Judo* which is recorded.

JURDANUS Cur 1196.
JORDANUS FA 1284, 1302.
JURDAN HR 1273.
JORDAN HR 1273.
JURDI HR 1273.

Joscelin, see JOCELYN.

Joseph (m.): Hebrew 'May Jehovah add' or 'Jehovah added' (i.e. children); the Greek form was *Joses*. The name was a favourite in post-exilic Israel; in the New Testament, for instance, there are *Joseph* of Nazareth the husband of the Blessed Virgin, *Joseph* of Arimathea, *Joses* brother of James, and *Joses* surnamed Barnabas. The early use of it as a christian name, however, was probably with reference to the patriarch (cf. *Abraham*, *Isaac*, *Jacob*). It occurs once or twice before the Norman Conquest as the name of a cleric, and during the Middle Ages it was in regular though infrequent use, cf. the surnames *Joseph*, *Josephs*, *Jessop(p)*, *Jessup(p)*. The pronunciation *Jessop* may have been influenced by the Italian *Giuseppe*, introduced by Italian Jews, for there is evidence that many of the medieval *Josephs* were Jews. The general and widespread use of the name dates only from the 17th C. In England it shared in the popularity of all Biblical names (the eponym in this case being the patriarch); and in Roman Catholic countries its use was enormously increased by the growing devotion to St. *Joseph*, husband of the Blessed Virgin. Until 1624 he had had no festival dedicated to him. In Italy and Spain, particularly, *Giuseppe* (pet-form *Beppo*) and *José* (pet-form *Pepe*, *Pepito*) became very common. The usual English nickname is *Joe*.

JOSEPHUS DB 1086, Cur 1203–1321, HR 1273.
JOSEP HR 1273.

Josephine (f.): French f. diminutive of *Joseph* (q.v.). The Empress *Josephine*, who is responsible for the modern vogue of the name, was actually named *Marie Josèphe Rose*, *Josephine* being a pet-name. *Josepha* was occasionally used in the last century, when the popularity of *Joseph* was at its height.

Joshua (m.): Hebrew *Jehoshea* 'Jehovah (is) generous' or 'Jehovah (is a) help'. *Jesus* and *Jeshua* are variant transliterations of the same Hebrew name, which was a favourite in post-exilic Israel. *Joshua* came into use as a christian name in England after the Reformation. In Spain and South America *Jesus* has been used as a christian name, probably given to children born on the feast of the Sacred Name of Jesus.

Josiah (m.): Hebrew 'May Jehovah heal' (i.e. the mother at the moment of birth). The hellenized form *Josias* is sometimes used. Camden mentions this as one of the names which came in after the Reformation. It was common in the 17th C, and has continued to be used to the present day in the Wedgwood family.

Jotham (m.): Hebrew 'Jehovah is perfect'. Occasionally used in the USA.

Joy (f.): *Joia* is found as a christian name as early as 1199 and occurs from time to time in the 13th C. It looks like the ordinary word *joy* used as a christian name. It then died out, but was revived at the end of the 19th C and is now fairly common.

JOIA Cur 1199–1213.
JOHI, JOIHA Cur 1200.
JOYE FA 1285.

H

Joyce (m., f.): this common medieval name was used for both men and women in the forms *Josse, Goce,* &c. (Latin *Jodocus, Jodoca* or *Joceus, Jocea*). It is of Celtic origin, being the name of a 7th-C Breton saint, *Jodoc,* son of *Judicael,* a hermit of Ponthieu. His hermitage was at the place now called St. Josse-sur-Mer. His cult spread through North France, the Low Countries, and Southern Germany. The Dutch *Joos(t)* is a form of it. As a man's name it died out in England in the 14th C, but as a woman's name it survived, though in rare use. It has been noted in the 17th C, and in the 18th and 19th C survived in country districts. CMY says of it, 'once not uncommon amongst English ladies'. There was a correspondence on the subject in N & Q 1874 when one correspondent said: '24 years ago I used to lodge at the house of one *Joyce* Bell, at Cleator, Cumberland.' A further correspondence in 1896–7 produced evidence of the rare survival of the name in the Midlands. It was about this time that it was revived as a fashionable name, probably in part owing to Edna Lyall's use of it for the heroine of her popular historical novel 'In the Golden Days' (1885), and it is now once more in frequent use.

Jocea Cur 1167, 1200.
Juicia Cur 1210–12.
Josse HR 1273.
Jocey HR 1273.
Jossy HR 1273.

Jude (m.): Hebrew *Judah,* meaning doubtful, but possibly 'Jehovah leads' or 'He will be confessed', the name of the 4th son of Jacob and Leah. *Judas* is the hellenized form, and *Jude* an abbreviation of it. It was not used by the Jews until post-exilic times, when it became common. As the name of *Judas* Iscariot it never had a chance of being used as a christian name, in spite of the popularity in the Middle Ages of *Judas* Maccabaeus. The Authorized Version of the Bible in some places calls the apostle *Judas* ('not Iscariot'), *Jude,* and after the Reformation *Jude* was sometimes used as a christian name, as was also *Judah,* sometimes as a woman's name.

Judith (f.): Hebrew 'a Jewess', the name of the Hittite wife of Esau as well as of the slayer of Holofernes. It seems to have been

introduced into England by the marriage of Æthelwulf (died 878)
King of Wessex to *Judith* daughter of Charles the Bald. Another
early example was *Judith* Countess of Huntingdon, niece of the
Conqueror. It was not, however, until the 17th C that the name
became common. The pet-form *Judy* is now sometimes used as
an independent name, and in Ireland is also used for *Julia* (q.v.).
JUDITA DB 1086.

Julia (f.): the f. form of *Julius* (q.v.). *Julie* has been common in
France and *Giulia* in Italy since the 16th C. It is the name of a
character in *Two Gentlemen of Verona*, and Herrick used it as the
name of the mistress to whom many of his poems were addressed,
but it seems not to have been used as a christian name until the
18th C. In the 19th C *Julia* was often used in Ireland to render
Sheila (q.v.).

Julian (m.): Latin *Julianus*, a derivative of *Julius* (q.v.). There
were some 10 saints of this name, but the best known of them is
the legendary St. *Julian* the Hospitaller, the patron saint of
travellers. The name is found in England from the 13th C, and
the surnames *Julian*, *Julyan*, *Jolland*, *Jalland*, *Golland* are derived
from it. The name *Jolyon*, which Galsworthy used for several
characters in his *Forsyte Saga*, presumably derives from one of
the medieval spellings of *Julian*. *Julian* was also the usual Middle
English form of *Juliana* (q.v.).
JULIANUS FA 1285.
JOLANUS FA 1302.
JOLLANUS, JOLLAN Testa de Neville 13th C.
JOLIN HR 1273.

Julian(a) (f.): the f. form of *Julian* (q.v.). St. *Juliana* was said to
have been martyred at Nicomedia under Gallienus and her relics
were preserved at Brussels and Sablon. Her name was consequently
a favourite in the Low Countries, and it was probably from
there that it reached England towards the end of the 12th C. The
usual English form was *Julian*, *Julyan*, or *Gillian* (q.v.), together
with the diminutives *Gill*, *Jill*, *Gillot*, *Juliet*, *Juet*. It was one of the
commonest girl's names from the 12th to 15th C, and there are

many surnames derived from it, e.g. *Julian, Julien, Julyan, Jolyan, Juet, Jewett, Jowett, Gill, Gilson, Gillett, Gillott,* &c. By the 16th C *Jill* had become a synonym for a flirt or worse (cf. Shakespeare's 'flirt-gill'), and the word *jilt* comes from the diminutive *Gillot.* Another sign of the former frequency of the name is the common expression '*Jack* and *Jill*', which survives in the well-known nursery rhyme. This was no doubt the reason why the name went out of fashion in the 16th and 17th C. In the 18th C the Latin form *Juliana* came in and continued to be used in the 19th C. The older *Gillian* has been revived in the present century, and *Jill* (q.v.) is also now used as an independent name.

JULIANA Cur 1196–1220, HR 1273.
GILLIAN HR 1273.
GILLE HR 1273.
GYLLE Coventry Mysteries 15th C.
JUET HR 1273.
JELYAN *Cocke Lorelle's Bote c.* 1515.

Juliet (f.): the modern use of this name is undoubtedly taken from Shakespeare, who took it from the Italian *Giulietta* a diminutive of *Giulia* (see JULIA). But the medieval English *Julian* (q.v.) apparently had a similar diminutive, which appears as *Juet, Juetta.* There was also an occasional *Julitta* from St. *Julitta,* mother of St. Cyr.

Julius (m.): the name of a Roman *gens,* of which the most famous member was Caius *Iulius* Caesar. The Romans supposed the name to be derived from Greek ἴουλος 'downy', but there is no good evidence of this. It was first used as a christian name in Italy in the Renaissance period (*Giulio*), and the first instance recorded in England is Cesare Adelmare (1558–1636), a Venetian physician to Queen Elizabeth, who later dropped his patronymic, adopted the christian name of *Julius,* and in due course became Sir *Julius* Caesar. The family is still in existence and still uses the name *Julius.* The French *Jules* also dates from the 16th C. The Welsh name *Iolo* (q.v.) is sometimes said to be derived from *Julius.*

June (f.): the name of the month. Its use as a christian name dates from the present century (cf. *April*).

Justin (m.): a derivative of Latin *justus* 'just', the name of two Byzantine emperors, and of the writer *Justin* Martyr (died A.D. 163). The name has not been used much in England, oftener in Ireland where it is used to render some native name. The Welsh *Yestin*, *Iestin* is said to come from it.

Justina (f.) [justē′na]: f. of *Justin* (q.v.). St. *Justina* was a 4th-C martyr, the patron saint of Padua, and *Giustina* and *Justine* were current respectively in Italy and France. *Justina* is first found in England in the 18th C. A solitary example of *Justiana* has been noted in 1640.

Justinian (m.): Latin *Justinianus*, a derivative of *Justinus* (see JUSTIN), the name of the 6th-C Emperor who caused the compilation of the *corpus juris*, and also of a 6th-C Welsh saint, the confessor of St. David. Occasionally used as a christian name. An early example is *Justinian* Baldwin, a Westminster scholar in 1567.

K

Karen (f.) [kah′ren]: Danish form of *Katharine* (q.v.), which has recently come into use in England as an independent name, probably borrowed *via* the USA where it was no doubt introduced by immigrants.

Katharine, Katherine, Catharine, Catherine (f.): the name of a virgin martyr of Alexandria, died 307. The Greek form of the name was Αἰκατερίνη and the etymology is unknown. The Latin form was at first *Katerina*, later *Katharina*, with the spelling assimilated to that of καθαρός 'pure', the supposed origin of the name. Another fancied etymology was from Greek αἰκία 'torture'. The original form is preserved in the Russian *Ekaterina* (with pet-forms *Katya*, *Katinka*), and the earlier Latin form in the Italian *Caterina*. The legend of St. *Katharine*, who was said to have been broken on a wheel before decapitation, grew up in Syria, the chief centre of her cult being on Mount Sinai. It was brought to western Europe by early Crusaders, and the first reference to her in England is in a miracle play founded on her story and performed at Dunstable in 1100. In 1148 Queen Matilda founded a collegiate church and hospital of St. *Katharine* near the Tower. Her greatest popularity was in the 14th C. There are 62 English churches dedicated to her, and when bells came to be rung by wheel and rope they were often dedicated to St. Katharine, who had been broken on a wheel. The usual Old French forms of the name were *Caterine* and *Cateline* (the latter under the influence of the common diminutive suffix -*line*), and in Middle English it usually appears as *Katerine*, *Kateline*, or *Catlin* (cf. the surnames *Catlin*, *Catling*); the spelling with *th* came in about the 16th C, and in the 17th C the usual spelling is *Catherne*, *Katherne*. The name has been a steady favourite since its first introduction, changes in fashion only affecting the various pet-forms: *Kitty* seems to have been an early one, and by the end of the 16th C it had met the usual fate of common pet-names (e.g. *Jill*, *Nanny*, *Parnel*) and become a cant term for a loose woman. In the 16th and 17th C *Kate* was the common diminutive; *Kitty* came in again in the 18th and early 19th C, *Kate*, *Katie* in the late 19th C. All are now used, as well as *Cathy* and *Kay*. The Irish *Cathleen*, *Kathleen* from Middle English *Catlin*, is now often used in England. The Gaelic diminutive *Catriona* (pronounced kătrēē'onă), *Katrine*, and Danish *Karen* are also sometimes met with.

KATERINA Cur 1196–1215, HR 1273, FA 1428.
KATELINE HR 1273.
KATERINE, KATERYNE 15th-C Brut.
KATERYN Lincs 1456.
KYTTE Langland *c.* 1360, Coventry Mysteries 15th C.
KIT Yorks Poll Tax 1379.
KATE Coventry Mysteries 15th C.

Kathleen, see KATHARINE.

Katrine, see KATHARINE.

Kay (m.): this name, which has been occasionally used in recent years, is apparently taken from Hans Andersen's story of *The Snow Queen*. The name of Sir *Kay* the Seneschal in Arthurian romances is said to be from a Welsh form of Latin *Caius*. *Kay* is also used as a pet-form of *Katharine* (q.v.).

Keith (m.): a Scottish surname derived from place-name (there are several villages, &c., of this name). Its use as a christian name in England is fairly recent.

Kenelm (m.): Old English *Cenhelm* or *Cœnhelm*, compound of *cene* 'brave' and *helm* 'helmet'. *Cœnhelm* King of Mercia, who was murdered in 819, was venerated under the name of St. *Kenelm*. There are 8 churches dedicated to him. His cult was mainly confined to the Midlands, and it is there that the christian name *Kenelm* has flourished, e.g. in the Rutlandshire family of Digby, in which it is still current.

KENELM Cur 1201–3, Cov 1480.
KENHELM Lyford 1655.

Kenneth (m.): Gaelic *Cinaed*. The Welsh form of the name is found in *Cennydd* son of Gildas, a 6th-C Welsh saint. It has been a favourite name in Scotland from the time of *Kenneth* (I) Mac-Alpine (died 860), 1st King of Scotland. In recent times it has been increasingly used in England by families with no Scottish connexions. Another Gaelic name, *Coinneach*, 'comely', from which is formed the patronymic Mackenzie, was also anglicized as *Kenneth*.

Kenrick (m.): Old English *Cynric*, compound of *cyne* 'royal' and *ric* 'ruler'. *Cynric* (died 560) was traditionally the grandson of Cerdic and 2nd King of Wessex. The name was fairly common in the Middle Ages, cf. the surnames *Ken(d)rick*, *Kenrack*, *Kenwright*, *Kenwrick* (for the epenthetic *d* in *Kendrick* cf. *Hendry* for *Henry*). The christian name survived into the 17th C.

CHENRIC, KENRIC(US) DB 1086.
KENWREC Pipe Roll 1161.
KENEWREC Pipe Roll 1161.
KENDRICK Chester Wills 1602.
KENRICK Chester Wills 1613.

Kentigern (m.): Gaelic *Ceanntighern*, Welsh *Cyndcyrn* 'chief lord', the name of the patron saint of Glasgow, where it was a favourite christian name in the 16th and 17th C and is found as late as the end of the 18th.

Kenward (m.): Old English *Kenweard*, compound of *cene* 'brave' and *weard* 'guard'. It became *Kenard* in Anglo-Norman and gave rise to the surnames *Kenward, Kennard*. Now long obsolete. KENEWEARD DB 1086. KENARD FF 1282, Lyford 1655.

Kerenhappuch (f.) [kēr'en hăp'uk]: Hebrew 'horn of stibium' (eyelash paint), the name of one of the daughters of Job, the other two being *Jemima* and *Keziah* (qq.v.). It has been used from time to time since the 17th C, and in actual use is generally reduced to *Keren*.

Kester, see CHRISTOPHER.

Keturah (f.): Hebrew 'fragrance', occasionally used in USA.

Kevin (m.) [kĕ'vin]: Irish *Caomhghin*, Old Irish *Coemgen* 'comely birth'. The name of an Irish saint, common as a christian name in Ireland.

Keziah (f.) [kĕzī'a]: Hebrew 'cassia', the name of one of the daughters of Job (see also JEMIMA and KERENHAPPUCH). Used since the 17th C, especially in Evangelical circles; one of the Wesleys was named *Keziah*.

Kinborough (f.): Old English *Cyneburh*, compound of *cyne* 'royal' and *burh* 'fortress'. St. *Kyneburg* of Mercia (*c.* 657) was long venerated in the Midlands, where her name was in use as late as the 17th C. Lyford 1655 gives it as *Kinburga*. *Kimbery* Vowles occurs in a Somerset will of 1753.

Kirsty, see CHRISTIAN(A).

Kit, see CHRISTOPHER, KATHARINE.

Kitty, see KATHARINE.

Knud (m.): a common Danish name perhaps related to Old German *kint*, Saxon *kind* 'kind', 'race'. It was introduced into England by the Danes and is familiar in the form *Canute* from the

Latin version *Canutus*. It survived in use until the 13th C as *Note*, *Nute*, and the diminutive *Nutkin*, cf. the surnames *Nott*, *Nutt*, *Nute*, *Notson*.

Note HR 1273.

L

Lachlan (m.): a name much used by the McIntosh's and McLeans. It may be derived from Gaelic *laochail* 'warlike'.

Laetitia, see LETTICE.

Lalage (f.) [lăl′ajĕ]: Latin, a girl's name used by Horace, from Greek λαλαγέω 'babble'. Occasionally used as a christian name in modern times.

Lambert (m.): Old German *Landoberct*, *Landebert*, compound of *landa* 'land' and *berhta* 'bright'. There was a corresponding Old English name, but it was uncommon, and there is little doubt that the popularity of the name from the 12th to 15th C was due to Flemish influence. St. *Lambert*, a 7th-C Bishop of Maestricht, was much venerated in the Low Countries, and his name became a favourite there. In Middle English the form *Lambard* is found (cf. *Hubbard* for *Hubert*, *Robard* for *Robert*, &c.) and the diminutive *Lambin* and *Lambkin* were common. The name became rare after the 16th C but is still sometimes used.

Lambertus DB 1086, Cur 1196–1215, HR 1273.
Lambekin Cur 1213–15.
Lambard HR 1273.
Lambin HR 1273, Exch R 1306.
Lambert Cov 1574.

Lancelot (m.): this is undoubtedly a French double diminutive in *-el-ot* of the name *Lance* from the common Old German *Lanzo* from the root *landa* 'land'. Another diminutive of *Lance* was *Lancelin*. *Lance*, *Lancelot*, and *Lancelin* are found as christian names in England from the 13th C. The continued survival of

Lancelot was due to the fame of the hero of Arthurian romance, a character who does not appear in Welsh or other early sources but was apparently invented by Chrestien de Troyes. The names were often confused with *Ancel* (q.v.) and its diminutive *Ancelot* and *Ancelin*. *Lancelot* seems to have been most popular in the North of England.

LANCE Ass 1218, HR 1273.
LANCELYN HR 1273.
LANCELOT Privy Seal Warrant 1380, Yorks Rec 1604.
LAUNCELETUS FA 1428.
LAUNSELOT Lincs 1526.
LANSLET St. Anne's Blackfriars 1641.

Laura, Lauretta (f.): the history and origin of this name are somewhat obscure. *Laurencia, Lauretta, Laura,* or *Lora* are all fairly common from the end of the 12th C; *Laurencia* is evidently a Latin f. form of the popular name *Laurence,* and it is possible that *Laura* was a pet-form of it, and *Lauretta* a diminutive of *Laura*. *Laura* occurs from time to time in the 16th and 17th C, and Lyford 1655 gives *Lora, Laurana, Laurentia,* and *Laureola* all as f. christian names. *Lora* was the usual Provençal spelling, e.g. of the name of Petrarch's mistress *Lora* de Sades. *Laura* is common in Wales and has latterly come more into favour in England after being neglected for some time. The pet-form *Lolly* is sometimes used.

LAURETTA Cur 1203–15.
LAURA Cur 1210–12.
LORA HR 1273, FA 1346, Yorks Poll Tax 1379.
LAURENCIA Testa de Neville 13th C.
LORETTA Testa de Neville 13th C.
LORE Godstow 1450.

Laurence, Lawrence (m.): Latin *Laurentius* 'of *Laurentum*', the name of a city, probably ultimately derived from *laurus* 'a bay tree'. St. *Laurence* the Deacon, martyred at Rome in 258, was a favourite saint in the Middle Ages, and there are 237 churches dedicated to him in England. *Laurence* occurs in England only as a monk's name before the Norman Conquest, and there is only one *Laurentius* in DB, but it soon became common and there are a great many surnames derived from it, e.g. *Lawrence, Laurence, Lawrenson, Lawrie, Laurie, Lowrie, Lawson* (from the nickname *Law*), *Larry, Larkin*. *Laurence* has been very popular in Ireland since the time of St. *Laurence* O'Toole (1130–80), Archbishop of Dublin, whose real name was the Irish *Lorcan*. *Larry* and *Lanty* are the usual Irish nicknames, *Laurie* is Scottish.

LAURENTIUS DB 1086.
LAURENCIUS Cur 1197, 1213–15, FA 1364.
LAURENCE HR 1273.
LARANCE Yorks Visit 1563, St. Mary Aldermary 1603.
LAW Yorks Poll Tax 1379.

Lavinia (f.): the name of the daughter of Latinus, the 2nd wife of Aeneas, of unknown etymology. It seems to have come into use, like other classical names, after the Renaissance, and is found at the end of the 17th C. In the 18th C it became something of a favourite, perhaps owing to the poet Thomson, who substituted it for Ruth in his version of the Book of Ruth. It is a favourite gipsy name. In the 13th and 14th C there is occasional record of a name *Lavina, Lavena* which may possibly be a version of *Lavinia* (which would be familiar from Virgil's *Aeneid*); on the other hand it may represent some such name as Old German *Leobuina* which is on record.

LAVINA Cur 1201, 1203.
LAVENA FA 1346.

Lazarus (m.): Greek form of Hebrew *Eleazar* 'God helped', used in the Authorized Version of the Bible for the brother of Martha and Mary and for the beggar in the parable of Dives and Lazarus. It is now an exclusively Jewish name, but was used as a christian name in the 17th C.

Leah (f.): Hebrew 'cow' (cf. *Rachel* and *Rebecca*), the name of the sister of Rachel and first wife of Jacob. It was first used as a christian name in England by 17th-C Puritans.

Leila (f.) [lī′la]: Persian, the name of the heroine of the popular tale of *Leila and Majnun*. Byron used it in *The Giaour*, and thus promoted its use as a christian name in the 19th C.

Lemuel (m.): Hebrew 'devoted to God', 'Godward', the name of a king mentioned in Prov. xxxi, sometimes used as a christian name in the 17th C, e.g. *Lemuel* Tuke, an ejected minister. The name is best known from Swift's hero *Lemuel* Gulliver.

Lena, see HELEN(A).

Lenore, see LEONORA.

Leo (m.): Greek λέων, Latin *leo* 'lion'; the name of thirteen popes. *Léon* is a fairly common name in France, and *Leon* or *Lyon* is found in England in the Middle Ages, usually as a Jewish name. *Leon* is now a common Jewish name in USA and *Leo* is occasionally used in England by Roman Catholics. See also LIONEL.

LEONIDEM (acc.) Cur 1199.
LEON Cur 1213–15, Exch R 1306.
LEO HR 1273.

Leofric (m.): compound of Old English *leof* 'dear' and *ric* 'ruler'; a common Old English name. It survived the Norman Conquest and gave rise to the surnames *Leverick, Leveridge, Loveridge,* &c.

LEOFRIC(US), LEURIC, LEOURIC, LEFRIC(US), &c., DB 1086.
LEFERICH, LEVERIGE, LEFRICH, LOVERICH, LOVERICK HR 1273.

Leofwin (m.): compound of Old English *leof* 'dear' and *wine* 'friend'; a common Old English name which survived into the 13th C and gave rise to many surnames, e.g. *Lewin, Levin, Levinson, Living(s), Liven(s),* &c. *Levin* is found as a christian name as late as the 17th C.

LEOFUUIN(US), LEOUUINUS, LEFUUIN(US), LEUUINE, LEUUIN, LEWIN DB 1086.
LEFWINUS Cur 1197.
LEFWYNE, LEFFEYNE, LEWINE HR 1273.
LEWIN QW 1292.
LEVIN St. Michael Cornhill 1626.

Leonard (m.): Old German *Leonhard*, compound of *levon* (Modern German *löwe*) 'lion' and *hardu* 'hardy', 'bold'. St. *Leonhard* was a 5th-C Frankish noble, converted with Clovis, who became a hermit near Limoges and the patron saint of captives. He was a favourite medieval saint in England and France and there are 177 English churches dedicated to him. *Leonard* is found as a christian name in England from about 1200. It has remained in steady though not common use from that time (cf. the surnames *Leonard, Lennard,* &c.) until the 19th C when it gradually increased in popularity. Lyford 1655 says of it: '*Leonard,* of a churlish disposition; a name fit for another Nabal.'

LEONARDUS Cur 1200, FA 1431.
LEONARD HR 1273, Yorks Rec 1604.

Leonie (f.) [lē′onĕ]: French f. of *Léon* (see LEO) occasionally used in England in modern times. *Leonia, Leonina* are found in the 13th C, evidently f. forms of the medieval *Lion.* In 1710 one *Lioness* Lee is recorded, but that seems to be a solitary freak.

Leonora, Le(o)nore (f.): *Leonora* is the Italian, *Léonore* the French, and *Lenore* the German form of this name. Its origin is not quite clear, but it may be a form of *Eleanor* (q.v.). The various forms of the name are not found in England until the 19th C; their introduction was no doubt due to literary and musical influences, e.g. Beethoven's opera of *Fidelio* (originally called *Leonora* after the heroine), Bürger's ballad of *Lenore.*

Leopold (m.): Old German *Leudbald, Luitpold,* compound of *leudi* 'people' and *balda* 'bold'. Names in *leud-* became *leo-* under the influence of Latin and Greek names. *Leopold* was occasionally used in England in the 19th C on account of the Queen's connexions (e.g. her favourite uncle *Leopold* King of the Belgians, after whom one of her sons was named).

Lesley (f.): this is the usual spelling of *Leslie* (q.v.) when used as a girl's name.

Leslie (m., f.): a well-known Scottish surname; the family took its name from *Leslie* in Aberdeenshire; early forms of the place-name are *Lesslyn, Lescelin.* Its use as a christian name in England seems to have begun in about the last decade of the 19th C, and no explanation of it can be offered. *Leslie* is now a common man's name but is sometimes also given to girls, when it is usually spelt *Lesley.*

Lettice, Laetitia (f.): Latin *laetitia* 'gladness'. It is not clear how or when the word came to be used as a christian name, but it was in general use in England in the 12th C and remained a favourite until the 17th C. The usual English form was *Let(t)ice*, but the French *Lece* (latinized as *Lecia*) was common in the 12th and 13th C. The surnames *Lettice*, *Lett(s)*, *Letson* (from the nickname *Lett*), and possibly some of the *Leesons* (from *Lece*) are derived from it. *Lecelin* a diminutive of *Lece* is also recorded. *Lettice* went out of fashion in the 18th C and was replaced by the Latin form *Laetitia*, but it has now come back into use. *Letty* is the usual pet-form.

Leticia Cur 1199–1215.
Lecia Cur 1199–1215, HR 1273.
Lettice HR 1273, Cl 1300.
Letyce Coventry Mysteries 15th C.
Lete HR 1273.
Letia HR 1273.
Lece HR 1273.
Lecelina Cur 1220.

Levi (m.): Hebrew 'pledged' or 'attached', the name of the third son of Jacob and Leah, and father of the priestly tribe. It was also the name of St. Matthew the apostle. Occasionally used as a christian name in the 17th C.

Lewis, Louis (m.) [lo͞o′is, lo͞o′ĕ]: (Latin *Ludovicus*, French *Louis*, Italian *Luigi*, Spanish *Luis*, German *Ludwig*): Old German *Chlodovech*, compound of *hloda* from the root *hlu* 'to hear' and *viga* 'fight'. The founder of the Merovingian line of Frankish kings, *Chlodowig* I (466–511), was called in Latin *Ludovicus* or *Clovis*, and later reduction produced the French Louis. It was, perhaps, the most popular of all names in France until the Revolution and was borne by no fewer than 18 kings. It was introduced into England soon after the Norman Conquest, the English form of the name being *Lewis* or *Lowis*, and gave rise to many surnames, e.g. *Lewis*, *Lewes*, *Lowis*, *Lowes*, *Lewison*, &c. It has been used a good deal in Wales, originally as an anglicization of *Llewelyn* (q.v.). The French pronunciation is often used in Lowland Scots, e.g. Robert *Louis* Stevenson. The Provençal form of the name was

Aloys, and *Aloisio* was also sometimes used in Italy and Spain (see further ALOYSIUS). See also LODOWICK.

LEWIS Cur 1203.
LOWIS Cur 1210.
LODEWICUS FA 1428.

Liam (m.): Irish for *William* (q.v.)

Libby, see ELIZABETH.

Lil(l)ian, Lil(l)ias, Lily, Lilla(h) (f.): these names probably originated as pet-forms of *Elizabeth* (q.v.), cf. the German *Lili* for *Elisabeth. Lillian* is found as a christian name in England in the 16th C and *Lillias* at about the same time in Scotland; *Lilion* occurs as a surname as early as 1273 and looks like a diminutive in *-on* of *Lily.* Some of the many surnames *Lill(e)y, Lyly, Liley,* &c., may be from a christian name *Lily,* though it is not on record earlier than the 19th C, when it has no longer any connexion with *Lilian,* but is merely a flower-name adopted as a christian name. *Lil(l)ias* has remained principally a Scottish name. *Lillah* appears to be a 19th-C invention, perhaps a mixture of *Lily* and *Leila* (q.v.).

Lilith (f.): Assyro-Babylonian 'goddess of storms', misinterpreted as 'night-hag' from Hebrew *lail* 'night'. In Rabbinical literature the name of the first wife of Adam before the creation of Eve. *Lilith* has occasionally been used as a christian name in modern times.

Lina, see CAROLINE.

Linda (f.): this is a German name, not used in England until the end of the 19th C. It is from Old German *Lindi* or *Linda,* one of the commonest elements in Old German female names.

Linnet (f.): the medieval French form of Welsh *Eluned* (q.v.). It has sometimes been used as a christian name since it became familiar from Tennyson's *Idylls of the King.*

Lionel (m.): apparently a French diminutive in *-el* of *Leon* or *Lion* (see LEO). In the reign of Edward III (who himself named one of his sons *Lionel*) there is mention of one *Leo, Lionel,* or *Lionet* de Bradenham. The surnames *Linnell* and possibly *Lyall, Lyell* are from it. Bardsley gives many examples of the christian name *Lyell* or *Lyonel* in the North in the 16th and 17th C.

LEONEL HR 1273.
LEONEL, LYONEL 15th-C Brut.
LIELLUS FA 1428.
LYONELL Yorks Rec 1604.

Lise(tte), see ELIZABETH.

Lizzy, see ELIZABETH.

Llewel(l)yn (m.) [hlĕwĕl'ĭn]: a common Welsh name also written *Llywelyn.* The first element is probably *llyw* 'leader'. From the 13th C it is found anglicized as *Leolin(e)* and this is found as late as the 17th C (e.g. Sir *Leoline* Jenkins born 1623, Principal of Jesus College, Oxford). Camden gives it as *Lewlin,* and Lyford 1655 says: '*Lewellin* like a lion; Latin.' *Lewis* (q.v.) has also often been used as an anglicization of *Llewelyn.* The correct spelling is *Llewelyn,* but *Llewellyn* is often written, especially by English writers, who are unaware of the pronunciation of Welsh *ll.* A f. form *Leolina* occurs in Cur 1213.

Lloyd (m.): Welsh *Llwyd* 'grey', a common Welsh christian name.

Lodowick, Ludovic(k) (m.): from *Ludovicus,* the Latin form of *Lewis* (q.v.) (cf. Italian *Ludovico*); used a good deal in the Highlands of Scotland since the 17th C.

Lois (f.) [lō'ĭs]: the name of the grandmother of Timothy, mentioned in 2 Tim. i. 5. The other members of the family who are named all have Greek names, and it seems probable that *Lois* is also Greek. It presumably came into use, like other out-of-the-way Biblical names, in the 16th or 17th C (Lyford 1655 gives it in his list of women's names), and the earliest occurrence noted is in 1583 in Springthorpe, Lincs., Parish Register. It became relatively common at the beginning of the present century.

Lola (f.): sometimes used in USA and less often in England. Originally a Spanish diminutive of *Dolores* (q.v.) and of *Carlota.*

Lora, see LAURA.

Loretta (f.): a name common in Roman Catholic use, derived from Our Lady of *Loreto* in Italy, a famous place of pilgrimage. *Lourdes* is used similarly as a christian name, but usually as a second name only.

Lorna (f.): this now frequent name was invented by R. D. Blackmore for the heroine of his extremely popular novel *Lorna Doone* (1869); he apparently formed it from the title of the Marquesses of Lorne.

Lottie, see CHARLOTTE.

Louis, see LEWIS.

Louisa, Louise (f.): *Louise* is the French f. of *Louis* (see LEWIS) and was not used in England before the 17th C. The earliest example noted is *Luese* Bencon 1646. *Louisa* was the usual form in the 18th C, when the name became a popular one. *Louisa* Countess of Berkeley (born 1694) granddaughter of *Louise* de Kéroual and Charles II, is sometimes referred to in contemporary records as *Lewes. Louie* is the usual pet form.

Loveday (f.): a common medieval christian name, which later became confined to Cornwall (where it still survives), sometimes in the form *Lowdy.* The name was originally given to either boys or girls born on a *loveday,* that is, a day appointed for a meeting between enemies, litigants, &c., with a view to an amicable settlement of disputes. It is a translation of Latin *dies amoris.* The christian name *Luveday* is recorded as early as 1205, though the earliest example of the noun given in OED is *c.* 1290. It is now given only to girls.

LUVEDAY Cur 1205.
LOVEDAY HR 1273.
LOVDIE Corn Par Reg 1578.
LOWDY Corn Par Reg 1601, 1622.

Lovell (m.): this appears to have been a diminutive in -*el* of the Anglo-Norman name *Love*. Another diminutive was *Lovet*. *Love* was apparently the English form of *louve* 'wolf'. *Lovel* and *Lovet* both occur in DB. The common surnames *Lovel*(*l*), *Lowell*, *Lovet*(*t*), *Lovat* are derived from them. *Lovel* was apparently also much used for dogs, e.g. the 15th-C rhyme on the favourites of Richard III, Ratcliffe, Catesby, and *Lovel*:

> The Rat, the Cat, and Lovel our dog
> Rule all England under the hog.

These names seem to have died out in the 14th or 15th C, but *Love* (the abstract noun) was used by the Puritans in the 17th C as a christian name.

Lovel DB 1086, HR 1273.
Lovet DB 1086.
Love HR 1273.

Lucas, see LUKE.

Lucasta (f.): a name invented by the poet Lovelace, under which to address his mistress, who was possibly a member of the *Lucas* family. It has occasionally been used as a christian name since then.

Lucia, Lucy (f.): Latin f. of *Lucius* (q.v.). St. *Lucia* was a virgin martyred at Syracuse under Diocletian; she is said to have had her eyes put out, and was consequently regarded as the patroness of those suffering from diseases of the eyes. She was a popular saint in the Middle Ages and from the 12th C onwards *Lucy* or *Luce* was a favourite name in England. *Luce* continued to be used well into the 17th C. The Latin form *Lucia* came into use at the end of the 17th C. The diminutive *Lucette* (still used in France) is sometimes found in England in the Middle Ages. *Luciana*, which occurs in the 13th C, is probably a f. form of *Lucian* (q.v.), *Lucina*, also used in the 13th C, is probably another diminutive of *Lucy*. *Lucy* occurs as a man's name in some families, but in this case it is the surname used as a christian name.

Lucia Cur 1196–1215, HR 1273, FA 1428.
Lucie 14th-C Legendary.
Luce HR 1273, 15th-C Brut, Yorks Rec 1604.
Lucy Godstow 1450.
Luciana Cur 1201–3.

Lucian (m.): Latin *Lucianus* from Greek Λουκιανός; the etymology of the name is uncertain but it was probably of Asiatic origin; both *Lucian* the 2nd-C satirist, and St. *Lucian* the 3rd-C martyr, were natives of Syria, and the 2nd-C heretic of the same name was from Asia Minor. *Lucianus* occurs as a christian name in 12th- and 13th-C records, but it was never common. Since the revival of learning it has been used occasionally, with reference to the satirist rather than the saint.
Lucianus Cur 1166, 1200, 1210.

Lucilla (f.): this is apparently a diminutive derivative of Latin *Lucius*, rather than of *Lucilius* which was the name of a Roman plebeian *gens*. St. *Lucilla* was a 3rd-C Roman martyr. *Lucille* is not uncommon in France and is occasionally imported into England.

Lucinda (f.): a 17th-C poetic variation of *Lucy* (q.v.) sometimes used as a genuine christian name.

Lucius (m.): a Latin praenomen, probably derived from *lux* 'light'. St. *Lucius* was Bishop of Rome from 253-4, and there were two later popes of the name. But it seems not to have been used as an ordinary christian name until the Renaissance, when *Lucio* became common in Italy. *Lucius* is found occasionally in England, e.g. *Lucius* Cary, Viscount Falkland (1610?-43), and not infrequently in Ireland, where it has been used to render various native names.

Lucretia, Lucrece (f.): Latin, f. form of *Lucretius*, the name of a Roman *gens*. In the 15th C *Lucrezia* came into use in Italy and *Lucretia* or *Lucrece* has occasionally been used in England, probably with reference to *Lucretia*, wife of Collatinus, whose rape by Tarquin and her subsequent suicide were the immediate cause of the expulsion of the Tarquins from Rome. It was fairly common in Lancashire in the 16th-18th C.

Ludovic(k), see LODOWICK.

Luke (m.): Latin *Lucas*, Greek Λουκᾶς, of or belonging to *Lucania*: the name of the third Evangelist. Both *Lucas* and the anglicized form *Luke* or *Luck* were commonly used in the Middle Ages. The name is not found in England before the Norman Conquest, and seems to have come into use in the 12th C. There are many surnames formed from *Luke*, *Lucas* and their diminutives, e.g. *Luke(s)*, *Lucas*, *Luck*, *Luckett*, *Lucock*, *Lukin*, *Luckin*, &c.

LUCAS Cur 1196–1215, HR 1273.
LUK(E) HR 1273.

Lydia (f.): Greek *Λυδία* 'woman of *Lydia*'. *Lydia* of Thyatira is mentioned in Acts xvi, and was, in apocryphal writings, identified with a daughter of Joseph of Nazareth. The name came into use in England in the 17th C.

Lyulf, Lyulph (m.): Old English *Ligulf*, compound of *lig* 'flame, fire' and *wulf* 'wolf'. It appears in 11th-C charters as *Ligulf*, *Liulf*, *Lyolf*. It is still used in some Scottish families.

M

Mabel, Mabella (f.): the usual English form of *Amabel* (q.v.). *Mabella* is found as early as 1189; other latinized forms are *Mabilla*, *Mabilia*. The usual English forms were *Mabel*, *Mable*, or *Mably*. The surnames *Mabley*, *Mabb(s)*, *Mapp(s)* (from the nickname *Mab*), *Mabbit*, *Mabbot* (from the diminutive *Mab-et*, *Mab-ot*), *Mapson*, *Mappin* (from the diminutive *Mab-in*) are all derived from it. *Mabell* occurs in Yorkshire in 1604, and Lyford 1655 gives *Mabella*, but the name was rare from the 15th C. CMY says, 'it is still used among the northern peasantry', a remark which is left unaltered in the 2nd edition of her work (1884), though *Mabel* must by then have been returning into fashion. It was a favourite name in the last quarter of the 19th C.

MABELLA Cur 1189.
MABILLIA Cur 1196.
MABILIA HR 1273, FA 1284.
MABILLA FA 1303, 1346.
MABELL Yorks Rec 1604.
MABYLE, MABLY, MABILL, MABILE, MABLE, MABEL Godstow 1450.

Mace, see THOMAS

Madeline, Magdalen (f.): Hebrew 'woman of Magdala'. Devotion to St. *Mary Magdalene* was already growing in the 12th C, but was much increased by the supposed discovery of her relics in the 13th C when the distinctive epithet *Magdalen* was adopted as a christian name. In England the French form of the name, *Madeleine*, was further reduced to *Maudlin* and *Madlin*, which were still used in the 17th C. *Magdalen* seems to have come in after the Reformation (*Magdalen* and *Magdelne* occur in 1604), being no doubt taken directly from the Bible. Lyford 1655 gives it variously as '*Magdalene, Maudlin seu Magdalin*'.

MADELINA Ass 1221.
MAUDELEYN HR 1273.
MAWDELYN St. Jas. Clerkenwell 1562.
MAUDLIN St. Jas. Clerkenwell 1608.
MAGDALEN, MAGDELNE Yorks Rec 1604.

Madge, see MARGARET.

Madoc (m.): an old and favourite Welsh christian name, sometimes found also in the Welsh Marches. A derivative of *mad* 'fortunate'.

MADOCH DB 1086.
MADDOC Cur 1207.
MADOCUS FA 1346.

Magda (f.): German abbreviation of *Magdalena* (see MADELINE), occasionally used in England in modern times.

Magdalen, see MADELINE.

Maggie, see MARGARET.

Magnus (m.): Latin *magnus* 'great'. The first person to bear this name was *Magnus* I, King of Norway and Denmark, died 1047, son of St. Olaf. His father was a great admirer of Charlemagne, '*Carolus Magnus*', and the child is said to have been baptized by servants who thought *Magnus* was a proper name. It was subsequently borne by many kings of Norway and Denmark and

became a popular name in those countries, whence it was introduced into Shetland, Scotland, and Ireland. Bardsley says that at
the time of his writing *Magnus* was the tenth most frequent name
in Shetland, where *Magnus, Magnusson, Manson* are common
surnames. The Gaelic and Irish form of the name is *Manus* (cf.
the surname *Macmanus*).
MAGNUS Cur 1200, 1207.

Mahalah (f.): Hebrew, possibly means 'barren', but more probably the name of a city used for a person (cf. *Tirzah*). Occasionally
used in England from the 17th C and taken to America where it
was common until recently. *Mahala* occurs in Essex in 1792, and
cf. Baring Gould's novel *Mehalah*.

Máire [mār'ĕ]: Irish form of *Mary* (q.v.).

Maisie (f.): *Maisie* or *Mysie* is a Scottish diminutive of *Margaret*
(q.v.) now often used, especially in USA, as an independent
name.

Malachi (m.) [măl'akī]: Hebrew 'my messenger'; an impossible
name, probably borrowed by an editor from 'Behold! I send my
messenger' (*Mal.* iii. 1) to provide an author's name for the book.
Used as a christian name in England after the Reformation.
Malachy is common in Ireland, representing *Maelaghlin*, the
name of an Irish saint.

Malcolm (m.) [mal'kom or mah'kom]: Gaelic *maol-Columb*, 'ser-
vant' or 'disciple of Columb', a favourite Scottish name. It is
occasionally found in England in the Middle Ages. Of late years
it has come into use in England even with families who have no
close Scottish connexions.
MALCOLUM DB 1086.
MAUKOLUM Cur 1207.
MALCULMUS FA 1303, 1316, 1346.
MALCULINUS FA 1346.
MALCOLINUS FA 1316.
MALCULMS FA 1428.
MAUCOLYN Werburge 1513.

Malise (m.) [mălēz']: Gaelic *Mael-Iosa*, 'servant of Jesus'. Traditional in, amongst others, the Gordon family. *Maoliosa* is still used in Ireland.

Malvina (f.): apparently invented by Macpherson in his Ossianic poems, perhaps to represent Gaelic *maol-mhin* 'smooth brow'.

Mamie (f.): an American diminutive of *Mary* (q.v.).

Manasseh, Manasses (m.) [manăs'e, manăs'ez]: Hebrew 'one who causes to forget', the name of the first-born of Joseph. *Manasses* is, rather surprisingly, found as the name of a tenant-in-chief in DB, and again of one *Manasse* Saluernille in 1160. It has sometimes been used in Ireland to represent *Manus* (see MAGNUS). After the Reformation it was sometimes used by Puritans in England, and later in the USA.

Manfred (m.): Old German *Manifred*, compound of *mana* 'man' and *frithu* 'peace'. It was brought to England by the Normans, and there is a *Mainfridus* in DB, but it never took root here. Byron's poem of this name caused it to be used occasionally in the 19th C.

Manon, French diminutive of *Marie* (see MARY).

Manuel, see EMMANUEL.

Marah (f.) [mah'ra]: Hebrew 'bitter'. Sometimes used as a christian name in the 17th C.

Marcella (f.): f. of *Marcellus* (q.v.), the name of a Roman widow, a disciple of St. Jerome. *Marcelle* is not uncommon in France, and *Marcella* has occasionally been used in England. Lyford 1655 gives it as a diminutive of *Marcia*.

Marcellus (m.): Latin diminutive of *Marcus*; a cognomen of the Claudian *gens*. There were two saints of this name, one a 1st-C Roman martyr, the other a 4th-C Pope. *Marcello* has been used a good deal in Italy. The common French *Marcel* is one of the classical names adopted in the Revolutionary era. In England

Marcellus has been used, very rarely, since the 16th C when a good many classical names first came into use as christian names.

Marcia (f.): f. of *Marcius*, the name of a Roman *gens*, probably derived from the name of the god *Mars*. It is sometimes used as a christian name, being regarded as a f. form of *Marcus* (q.v.).

Marcus, Mark (m.): Latin *Marcus*, a common Roman praenomen, and occasionally cognomen. It was probably derived from the name of the god *Mars* from some such form as *Marticos*. Though the name of one of the four evangelists, *Mark* (which is the English form, cf. *Luke* for *Lucas*) has never been popular, but it occurs from time to time in the Middle Ages and became a little commoner in the 19th C. The Latin form *Marcus* is found once in the 17th C, and has been used occasionally since the mid-19th C.

MARCUS HE 1273, FA 1303.
MARK(E) HR 1273.

Margaret (f.): (French *Marguérite*, *Margot*, German *Margaret(h)e*, *Gretel*, *Gretchen*, Italian *Margherita*): Latin *margarita* from Greek μαργαρίτης, 'a pearl'; the ultimate origin of the word is believed to be Persian. St. *Margaret* of Antioch, one of the Fourteen Holy Helpers, was supposed to have been martyred in the 3rd C, but nothing was known of her beyond that fact and her name, until apocryphal lives were written, which represented her as having overcome a dragon. She was one of the most popular medieval saints, largely, perhaps, because her last words were reported to be: 'Hearken to my prayer, O God, and grant to every man who shall write my life or relate my works, or shall hear or read them, that his name be written in the book of eternal life, and whosoever shall build a church in my name, do not bring him to thy remembrance to punish him for his wrong-doing.' She was also regarded as the patron of women in childbirth (e.g. a daughter of Henry III was christened *Margaret* because her mother had invoked the saint during her labour). Her name appeared in English litanies as late as the 17th C. The first

recorded example of the name in England is St. *Margaret* (died
1093) sister of Edgar Atheling and wife of Malcolm III of Scotland, whose name may have been due to her Hungarian connexions (cf. *Christina*). The name soon became a favourite in both
England and Scotland, and evolved a host of nicknames, abbreviations, and diminutives such as *Margot, Magge, Magot, Madge,
Meg, Mog*. Bardsley gives more than 30 surnames derived from
them. One form of the name, *Margery* or *Marjorie* (q.v.), was
early regarded as an independent name. The nicknames *Mog*
and *Meg* later gave rise to the rhymed forms *Pog(gy)* and
Peg(gy). In Scotland the pet-forms *Maggie, Maisie*, and *Mysie*
have been chief favourites. *Maidie* is used in America. German
Greta, Italian *Rita*, French *Margot* are now sometimes used in
England. *Margaret* went somewhat out of fashion from the
16th to 18th C but regained its popularity in the later 19th
C, and is now once more one of the most generally used of
women's names.

MARGARETA Cur 1189, HR 1273.
MARGARETE, MARGARETT Lincs 1450.
MARGARETTE Lincs 1450.
MARKARET St. Mary at Hill 1494.
MARGAT Lincs 1534.
MARGYT Lincs 1540.
MERGET Oseney 1460.
MERGRET St. Mary at Hill 1498.
MAGOTE, MAGOTT HR 1273, Yorks Poll Tax 1379, Cov 1430.
MEGGOT Yorks Poll Tax 1379.
MAGGE HR 1273.
MEGGE HR 1273, Coventry Mysteries 15th C.

Margery, Marjorie (f.): *Margerie* was a French popular form of
Marguérite (see MARGARET) and it is found in England as early as
1194; *Marjorie* was a less usual spelling but is of about the same
age. *Margery* was regarded as a separate name as early as the
13th C, and all connexion with *Margaret* was soon lost. Lyford
1655 derives it from the name of the herb *marjoram*. In the 18th
and 19th C *Margery* almost disappeared except among poor
country people, but it is now general again. It is sometimes
abbreviated to *Margy*. *Marjorie* is the usual spelling in Scotland.

MARGERIA Cur 1195, HR 1273, FA 1346.
MARGERY Prompt Parv c. 1440.
MARGERYE Lincs 1529.
MARJORIA Cur 1199, 1207, 1284, Yorks Poll Tax 1379.
MARJORY Yorks Poll Tax 1379.

Maria (f.) [marī'a]: Latin form of *Mary* (q.v.); came into fashion in England in the 18th C and lasted well into the 19th C.

Mariabella (f.): a compound, formed on the model of *Christabel*, *Claribel*, &c. (qq.v.), which came into use in the early 17th C and has continued to be used to the present day in some families.

Mariamne (f.) [măriăm'nĕ]: *Miriam* (q.v.) appears as *Mariamne* in Josephus; *Mariamne* is occasionally used as a christian name.

Marian(ne), see MARION.

Marie (f.) [mah'rĕ]: French form of *Mary* (q.v.) sometimes also used in England.

Mariel (f.): Bavarian diminutive of *Mary* (q.v.) sometimes used in England recently.

Marietta (f.): common in the USA, from the name of the town of *Marietta*, Ohio, founded 1788 and named after Queen *Marie Antoinette*.

Marigold, Marygold (f.) [măr'igōld]: this flower-name is mentioned as new in N & Q 1904. It has not become common.

Marina (f.) [marē'na]: St. *Marina* of Alexandria was a virgin martyr venerated in the Greek Church and sometimes identified with St. Margaret of Antioch. The etymology of the name is doubtful, though it is usually identified with the Latin adjective *marinus* 'of the sea'. A *Marina* de Beseville is mentioned in FA 1302. The name is found at Olney in the 18th C. A writer to N & Q in 1882 said: 'There is a family in this parish [South Stoke, Wallingford] who have used the name *Marina* (abbreviated to *Rena*) for some generations. I baptized the elder daughter by that name.' *Marina* or *Mairenni* is used by Northamptonshire gipsies. The marriage of Prince George to Princess *Marina* of Greece in 1934 gave a certain vogue to the name in this country.

Marion, Marian(ne) (f.) [măr'ĕon, mărĕăn']: *Marion* was originally a diminutive in *-on* of *Mary* (q.v.). It was common in the Middle Ages and later. The spelling *Marian* led in the 18th C to the supposition that the name was really *Mary+Anne*, and *Mary Ann* was the first and chief of the double names which were so common then and in the early 19th C. The French *Marianne*, a later diminutive of *Marie*, is also sometimes used in England.

MARION Yorks Poll Tax 1379, FA 1402.

Marius (m.) [mă'rĕus]: the name of a Roman *gens*, probably derived from the name of the god *Mars*. *Marius* has been used occasionally in England since the revival of learning. *Mario* is very common in Italy, where it is apparently regarded as a masculine form of *Mary*.

Marjorie, see MARGERY.

Mark, see MARCUS.

Marmaduke (m.): fairly common in Yorkshire from the 12th C onwards, particularly in the region round Thirsk, in the families of de Arell, de Thweng, and others. In DB Wellbury, about 13 miles from Thirsk, is said to have been held TRE by Fredegist and *Melmidoc*. This looks like Irish *Maelmaedoc*, 'servant of Maedoc', which would easily become *Marmaduc* (the usual medieval spelling) in Anglo-Norman. The name has remained very much localized in its use; Camden says of it, '*Marmaduc* a name common in the North', and it is still principally used in Yorkshire, often abbreviated to *Duke*. It was used, at least from the 17 C, by a Welsh family, the Lloyds of Middleton, with a f. derivative, *Dukana*.

MELMIDOC DB 1086.
MARMADUCUS Cur 1201, 1205, 1207, FA 1431.
MARMADUC Ass 1219.
MARMEDOKE Yorks Poll Tax 1379.

Martha (f.): apparently the f. of Aramaic *mar* 'a lord'; the name of the sister of Mary and Lazarus, whom medieval legend transported with her sister to Provence, where her name became a favourite one (*Marthe*). It was not, however, used in England until after the Reformation, when it became not uncommon and evolved the nicknames *Matty* and *Patty* (cf. *Meg* and *Peg*, *Molly* and *Polly*).

Martin (m.): Latin *Martinus*, apparently a diminutive of *Martius* 'of *Mars*'. St. *Martin* of Tours was a 4th-C soldier, later Bishop of Tours and apostle of Gaul; the story of his sharing his cloak with a beggar was a favourite subject of medieval art, and St. *Martin* was a favourite saint in England and in France; there are over 170 churches dedicated to him in England. *Martin* was a common christian name from the 12th C until the Reformation, and gave rise to many surnames, e.g. *Martin(s)*, *Marten(s)*, *Martinson*, *Martel* (from the diminutive *Mart-el*), *Martlet* (from the double diminutive *Mart-el-et*), and *Martinet* (from the diminutive *Martin-et*). After the 15th C the name was less common, but never fell into complete disuse. The names of the birds *martin* and *martlet* are derived from *Martin* (cf. French *martinet* 'swift', *martin-pêcheur* 'kingfisher').

MARTINUS Cur 1196–1220, FA 1428.
MARTIN Cl 1258, HR 1273.
MARTINET Exch R 1306.
MARTYN *Cocke Lorelle's Bote c.* 1515.

Martina (f.) [martĕn'a]: f. of *Martin* (q.v.). There was a St. *Martina*, but the name when used in England and France (*Martine*) has probably usually been simply a f. form of *Martin*.

Mary (f.): (French *Marie*, Italian, German *Maria*, Russian *Marya*, *Masha*); Hebrew, probably 'wished-for child', less probably 'rebellion'. See further under MIRIAM, which is the same name. The consonants of the Hebrew word are M-R-Y-M, and when vowels were inserted in about the 7th C A.D. it became *Miryam*; the Septuagint, however, vocalized it as Μαριάμ (*Mariam*), and this is the usual form in the Greek New Testament both for the Blessed Virgin and for *Mary* sister of Lazarus, while *Mapía* (*Maria*) is most often used for the other *Marys*. The Vulgate (probably owing to a mistaken idea that *Mariam* was an accusative in -*am*) adopted *Maria* for all of them. The name of the Blessed Virgin was long held to be too sacred for common use. The Sienese, for example, would allow no woman so named to practise the calling of a prostitute. In Spain, girls whom it was wished to put under the patronage of the Blessed Virgin were given names connected with her life or attributes, e.g. *Dolores, Mercedes, Asunción*, &c. From the 12th C, however, the name *Mary* gradually came into use in western Europe, and its growing popularity reflects the growing devotion to Our Lady. It is an indication of that growth that Bede in his list of churches gives only 3 dedicated to her; such dedications increased from the 12th C onwards, and there are now twice as many of them as of the next most common, those to St. Peter. *Mary* is first found as a christian name in England at the end of the 12th C; the diminutive *Mariot* is found about the same time; its use increased slowly during the next 3 centuries, *Mary, Mariot, Marion*, and the nicknames *Mall* and *Moll* (cf. *Hal* from *Harry*) becoming moderately common and giving rise to such surnames as *Maris, Marrison, Marrian, Marriot(t), Marryat, Malleson, Mollison*, &c. *Mary* suffered an eclipse after the Reformation and was seldom used during Elizabeth's reign; it began to come back into use in the middle of the 17th C, and by the middle of the 18th C nearly 20 per cent. of female children in England were baptized in this name. In Ireland, where a quarter of the women are now called *Mary*, it was hardly used before the 17th C. In Irish, *Muire* is the form used for Our Lady, *Máire* or *Moire* being the common christian name. Several of the diminutive and pet-forms of the name are noticed separately, e.g. *Marion, Mariel. Mariot*, which was the most usual diminutive in the Middle Ages, was used in Cornwall as late as 1725. *Mally*, which was formerly much commoner than *Molly*, died out at the end of the 18th C. *Polly* is a rhyming nickname formed from *Molly* (cf. *Peg* from *Meg*). *Mamie* is a common diminutive in America. The French *Marie, Mariette, Marianne, Manon* are all occasionally used in England. For *Maria* see separate article.

May is a late-19th-C coinage. The use of *Mary* as a second name (for men as well as women) arose on the Continent in Roman Catholic countries in the 16th C, and has occasionally been adopted by English Roman Catholics.

MARIA Cur 1203–10.
MARIOTA Cur 1205, 1210, HR 1273.
MARY Prompt Parv *c.* 1440.
MALKYN Coventry Mysteries 15th C.

Matilda, Maud(e) (f.): Old German *Mahthildis*, compound of *mahti* 'might', 'strength', and *hildi* 'battle', 'strife'. It was introduced into England by the Normans (William I married *Matilda* daughter of Baldwin V of Flanders), and was a favourite in the 12th and 13th C, gradually falling into desuetude in the 14th and 15th C. The Latin forms are *Matillis* or *Matilldis* as well as *Matilda*; the French were *Mahhild, Mahault, Molde,* or *Maud,* and these were all used in England, together with the nicknames *Till, Tillot.* Many surnames are derived from them, e.g. *Madison, Maud(e), Maudson, Mawson, Moulson, Mould, Mowl(e), Moult, Till(y), Tillison, Tilson, Tillotson.* It was very rare in the 16th and 17th C, but the Latin form *Matilda* was revived in the middle of the 18th C and became a great favourite. Tennyson's poem *Maud* (1855) was probably responsible for the revival of this medieval form of the name in the later 19th C. It occurs in *John Halifax, Gentleman* (1856). The pet-forms *Matty, Tilly,* and *Tilda* were usual in the 19th C.

MATILDIS Reg 1082.
MATHILD, MATHILA, MATHELD, MATHILDIS DB 1086.
MATILDA Cur 1189–1215.
MATILLDIS FA 1284.
MATILLIS FA 1316.
MAULD Visit of Cheshire 1303.
MAUD Cl 1314.
MAUDE Godstow 1450, Lincs 1451, Cov 1486,
MOLDE, MOOLDE Godstow 1450,
MAWT Lincs 1455.
MAWDE Chester 1562.

Matthew, Matthias (m.): Hebrew *Mattathiah* 'gift of Jehovah', became Ματθαῖος or Ματθίας in Greek and *Matthaeus* or *Matthias* in Latin. The name was introduced into England by the Normans and *Mathiu seu Macy* is a tenant mentioned in DB. *Matheu* (latinized as *Matheus*) was the usual French form, together with the nickname *Mac(e)y*. From this are derived the surnames *Mayhew*, *Mayo(w)*, *Mayhow*, *Mace(y)*. *Mace* or *Macy* is sometimes found used as an independent name and latinized as *Maceus*, *Macius*. Another French diminutive was *Machin*, *Machon* which gave rise to the surnames *Machen*, *Machin*, *Machon*. *Mathew(s)*, *Mathewson*, *Matheson* (all spelt in many ways) are derived from the English *Mathew*; *Maton*, *Matkin*, *Matterson* are from the English nickname *Mat*; *Maycock* and *Maykin* from the nickname *May*, with the suffixes *-cock* and *-kin*. These surnames are only a selection of the derivatives of *Mathew* and they give some measure of its popularity in the 12th–14th C. It continued in general use, though less frequent, after the Reformation. The English versions of the Bible rendered the name variously, and in the Authorized Version *Mattathiah* is used in the Old Testament, *Matthew* for the Evangelist, and *Matthias* for the disciple who was chosen to take the place of Judas. *Matthias*, accordingly, was sometimes used in the 17th C as a christian name.

MATTHEUS DB 1086.
MATHEUS Cur 1166, HR 1273, FA 1316.
MATHIU SEU MACY DB 1086.
MATHIE, MATHEU 14th-C Legendary.
MATHEU Exch R 1306, Yorks Poll Tax 1379.
MATHEWE *Cocke Lorelle's Bote c.* 1515.
MATHY, MATHEY HR 1273.
MACIUS, MACE, MASSE HR 1273.
MAHEU HR 1273.
MAYE HR 1273.
MAYEU Writs of Parl 1300.

Matty, see MARTHA and MATILDA.

Maud(e), see MATILDA.

Mauger (m.): Old German *Malgar*, apparently a compound of *malv* from *malvjan* 'to grind' and *ger* 'spear'. The name was introduced into England by the Normans in the French form *Mauger*, which was used as a christian name until the 18th C in the Vavasour family which descended from one *Mauger* who held lands in vavasoury in the reign of Henry I. Lyford 1655 says of it: '*Maugre*, some make as it were *malgerius*, bearing evil.'

MALGERIUS DB 1086.
MALGER HR 1273.
MAUGER HR 1273, Writs of Parl 1300.
MARGRE Yorks Poll Tax 1379.

Maureen (f.) [mōr'ēn]: Irish *Máirín*, diminutive of *Máire* (*Mary* q.v.). *Maureen* has become general in England in the present century, the fashion probably coming via America.

Maurice (m.) [mŏr'ĭs]: Latin *Mauritius* 'a Moor'; the name of a martyr said to have belonged to the Theban legion and to have been martyred in Switzerland A.D. 286. The name is found in use in England from the 11th C, sometimes in the French form *Meurisse*, but more often in the English *Moris* or *Morris*. It gave rise to the surnames *Morris(s)*, *Maurice*, *Mor(r)ison*, *Morson*, *Morse*, *Morin*, and *Morcock*. *Maurice* has now replaced *Morris* as the usual spelling of the christian name. It has been used in Ireland to render the native *Moriertagh* (*Moriarty*) 'sea warrior'. The Welsh form is *Meuric*.

MAURICIUS Reg ? 1086, Cur 1196-1220.
MEURIK Testa de Neville 13th C.
MORIS FA 1346.
MORICIUS FA 1431.
MORYS Lincs 1459.
MORES Cov 1471.
MOURICE Cov 1539.
MAURIS 15th C Brut.
MERICK SEU MORRICE Lyford 1655.

Mavis (f.) [mā'vis]: an old name for the song-thrush. Marie Corelli seems to have been the first to use it as a christian name, in one of her novels, and it is now not uncommon.

Maximilian (m.): Camden gives the following account of the origin of this name: 'a new name, first devised by *Frederic* the third Emperor, who doubting what name to give his son and heire, composed this name of two worthy Romans, whom he most admired, *Q. Fabius Maximus*, and *Scipio Aemilianus*, with hope that his son would imitate their vertues (*Hieronymus Gebvilerius de familia Austriaca*).' It became a favourite name in Germany, particularly in the abbreviated form *Max*, and is occasionally used in England.

Maxine (f.): a favourite modern French girl's name, sometimes used in England and oftener in America. It is apparently a f. diminutive of *Max* (see MAXIMILIAN). *Maxencia* occurs in the 13th C, apparently a f. form of *Maxentius*, but there is no evidence of its survival.

May (f.): a 19th-C pet-form of *Margaret* or *Mary*, sometimes used as an independent name and associated with the name of the month (cf. *June, April*).

Maynard (m.): Old German *Maganhard*, compound of *magan* 'strength' and *hardu* 'hardy'. There was a similar Old English *Maegenheard*, but it was not common, and the fairly frequent use of *Maynard* after the Norman Conquest was probably due to its importation by the Normans. It appears as *Manard* in the 17th C.

MAINARD(US) DB 1086.
MAINARD Cur 1189–1203.
MAYNARD HR 1273.

Meave (f.) [māv]: Irish *Meadhbh*, the daughter of Eochaidh and heroine of many legends. In Ireland the name has often been rendered by *Mab* or *Mabel*, and it is usually stated that the English 'Queen *Mab*' is the same as the legendary Irish queen. This is, however, prima facie unlikely, and *Mab* in this case is no doubt the common abbreviation for *Mabel*.

Meg, see MARGARET.

Mehetabel (f.) [mehĕt'abĕl]: Aramaic 'God is active, treating well', a name which occurs in Gen. xxxvi. It came into use as a christian name after the Reformation and is recorded as early as 1578. It remained in use in villages until the 19th C and was transplanted to America where it is a favourite negro name.

I

Melanie, Melloney (f.) [měl′aně]: Greek μέλαινα 'black'. St. *Melania* the elder and St. *Melania* the younger were a grandmother and granddaughter, Roman ladies devoted to St. Jerome. *Mélanie* is not uncommon in France, and was probably introduced into England by Hugenot refugees. It first appears in Devon and Cornwall in the middle of the 17th C (*Melloney* 1655, *Melanie* 1660, *Melony* 1748, *Melloney* 1770). It is still used in Cornwall.

Melchior (m.): Hebrew 'King of light' or 'the King (= God) is light', the name of one of the "Three Kings' into whom medieval legend transformed the wise men from the East who visited Bethlehem. See BALTHASAR and CASPAR. *Melchior* has been used less often than the other two as a christian name. It occurs as *Melcher* at Manchester in 1592. In the 18th C it was used a good deal in Ireland, probably to represent some Irish name.

Melchisadek (m.) [melchiz′aděk]: Hebrew 'the King (i.e. God) is righteousness' or 'my King is righteous', the name of the priest-king of Salem who blessed Abraham, later taken as the type of Christ. The name was used occasionally from the 17th C.

Melesina, see MILLICENT.

Melicent, see MILLICENT.

Melior(a) (f.): this is apparently a purely Cornish name; it occurs in Assize Rolls as early as 1218 and FA in 1346 as *Meliora*, in the 17th C as *Melyear*, *Melyar*, *Mellier*, in the 18th and 19th C as *Meliora*. CMY says: '*Melior* is a Cornish name, probably an imitation of some old Keltic name. It is found as early as 1574, but is now probably ruined by Amelia.'

Melissa (f.): Greek μέλισσα 'a bee', also the name of a nymph, later used as a personal name in Greece. Italian 16th-C poets used *Melissa* as the name of a fairy, and in the 18th C it was occasionally used as a christian name in France and England.

Melloney, see MELANIE.

Melody (f.): this would seem to be the ordinary word *melody* but there is no clue to show how it came to be so used. It is recorded in Shropshire at the end of the 18th C and in Somerset *c*. 1880.

Meraud (f.): this Cornish name is usually taken to be a contraction of Middle English *emeraud* emerald, e.g. Lyford 1655: '*Meraud* perhaps by contraction from the pretious Emeraud stone.' *Esmeralda* was used as a christian name in Spain. But a *Merouda* Pygot is recorded in 1296, which is earlier than the earliest recorded occurrence of *emeraude*, and moreover there is no evidence that *emeraude* was ever shortened to *meraud*. On the whole it is probable that *Meraud* is a Cornish name, possibly a derivative of *mur* 'the sea' (cf. *Meriel* for *Muriel*).

Mercedes (f.) [mersä'dez]: Spanish elliptical for *Maria de Mercedes*, 'Mary of Mercies', an epithet of the Blessed Virgin. *Maria* was formerly seldom used as a christian name in Spain, being considered too sacred (see also DOLORES). *Mercedes* has been used a good deal in France and occasionally borrowed in England.

Mercy (f.): came into use as a christian name in the 17th C along with other similar names, e.g. *Faith, Hope, Charity*, &c.

Meredith (m.): a Welsh name (*Maredudd*), of which the second element is *iudd* 'lord'. It is still used as a christian name, though it is commoner as a surname. Lyford 1655 gives a characteristically fanciful etymology: '*Meredith*, but rather *Mere ductus* for *Mereducius*, brought together without mixing.'

Meriel, see MURIEL.

Methuselah (m.): Hebrew, first element 'man of', second element unknown. Occasionally used as a christian name in the 16th–18th C.

Micah (m.): a contraction of Hebrew *Micaiah* 'who is like Jehovah?' The name of one of the minor prophets, occasionally used as a christian name in England and USA since the 17th C.

Michael (m.): Hebrew 'Who is like the Lord?' The name of one of the archangels, the leader of the heavenly host, and hence the patron of the christian warrior. St. *Michael* and All Angels is one of the commonest church dedications (there are 687 in England and Wales) and the name was a favourite from the 12th C onwards, giving rise to a number of surnames, such as *Michell, Mitchell, Mitchelson, Mitchison*, which show that the common pronunciation was like that of the French *Michel. Mighel* was also a common medieval form of the name (cf. *Cursor Mundi* 'The sothfastenes and nothing hele, That thow hadest of seynt *Myghell*'), and this in turn was reduced to *Mihel, Miel*, or *Mial* (cf. the surnames *Mighill, Miall, Miell, Myhill*). Bardsley quotes Hudibras to show how this pronunciation persisted: 'At *Michael*'s term had many a trial, Worse than the Dragon and St. *Michael*.' The name was not used in Ireland much before the 17th C, but is now one of the commonest Irish names, often abbreviated to *Mick, Micky*, or *Mike*.

MICHAEL Cur 1196–1215, Ass 1218, FA 1303, 1346.
MICAHEL HR 1279.
MIKAEL HR 1279.
MICHELL Cov 1439, 13th C Brut.
MIHILL St. Michael Cornhill 1549.
MIGHELL St. Mary Aldermary 1598.
MYGHCHAELL St. Mary at Hill 1533.

Mildred (f.): Old English *Mildthryth*, compound of *milde* 'mild' and *thryth* 'power', 'strength'. Saints *Mildthryth* (died 700) and *Mildburh* (died 722 ?), daughters of a king of Mercia, and abbesses, were much venerated in the Middle Ages. The Middle English forms of the names were *Mildred* or *Meldred*, and *Milburh, Milbury*, or *Milborough. Milborough* survived in Shropshire till the 18th C and is still used (as *Milbrer*) by a gipsy family, the Locks. *Mildred* survived in infrequent use until the 19th C when it had a revival of popularity, and is now fairly common.

Miles (m.): Old German *Milo*, a name of doubtful etymology, possibly connected with Old Slavonic *milu* 'merciful'. The name was introduced into England by the Normans as *Miles* (*cas-sujet*) or *Milon* (*cas-régime*) and became fairly common, giving rise to the surnames *Miles, Mills, Milson*. It was less common from the

16th to 19th C but has been somewhat revived of late. In Ireland it has been used to render the native *Maolmuire* 'servant of Mary'.

MILO DB 1086, Cur 1196–1220.
MILON HR 1273.
MILES Coventry Mysteries 15th C.

Millicent, Melicent (f.): Old German *Amalasuintha*, compound of *amal* 'work' and *swintha* 'strong'; the name was current particularly among the Lombards and Burgundians, and appears early as *Malasintha*, whence *Melisenda*, the name of a daughter of Charlemagne. It was introduced into England in the French form *Melisent* at the end of the 12th C. The spelling *Milisent* occurs soon after, but *Melisent* was the more usual. *Millesant, Milicent* occur in the 15th C, and Lyford 1655 gives *Melicent*. *Millicent* is now the more usual form. In France there has been some confusion with *Mélusine*, the name of a water nymph (e.g. Maeterlinck's *Pelléas et Mélisande*). *Melesina*, a name which has been used since the 18th C in the Chenevix family and its connexions, probably derives from *Melusina* von der Schulenburg, Duchess of Kendal, whose daughter Petronella *Melusina* married Lord Chesterfield, the patron of Richard Chenevix, Bishop of Waterford. *Millicent* occurs as a man's name at Cambridge in 1584.

MELISENT Cur 1201.
MELISANT Cur 1213.
MILICENTA HR 1273.
MILLESENTA HR 1273.
MYLISANT Yorks Poll Tax 1379.

Mina (f.): pet-name for *Wilhelmina* (q.v.).

Minerva (f.): the name of the Roman goddess who was identified with the Greek Pallas Athene. It was probably of Etruscan origin and not, as is sometimes suggested, connected with *mens*. *Minerva* has occasionally been used as a christian name since the Renaissance, e.g. *Minerva* Dunn in Shropshire 1679.

Minna (f.): Old German *Minna* which may be from *minna* 'memory', 'love', or more probably from *min* 'small'. *Minna* was used in Shetland and parts of Scotland, and Scott's *Minna Troil* in *The Pirate* probably introduced it into England.

Minnie (f.): originally a Scottish pet-form of *Mary*. It became common in England in the 19th C and was often used as an independent name. Not in CMY.

Mirabel (f.) [mǐr'abel]: Latin *mirabilis* 'wonderful', 'glorious'. *Mirabella* or *Mirabilis* occurs in Latin records from the 12th C. The English form of the name was *Mirable, Mirabel,* and sometimes *Marabel* (cf. the surnames *Mirabel, Marrable*). It has not been noted between the middle of the 14th C and the beginning of the 19th C (*Maribella* Wise born 1810; *Mirabel* Saville born 1854). Congreve uses it as a man's name in *The Way of the World*. MIRABILIS Cur 1210. MIRABILLA FA 1346. MIRABLE, MIRABEL HR 1273.

Miranda (f.): Latin *miranda* 'worthy to be admired'. Apparently invented by Shakespeare for the heroine of *The Tempest,*'admired *Miranda*'. It is found at Rochdale in 1687 and in New England in 1827, and like other Shakespearian names (e.g. Cordelia, Hero, Imogen, Juliet) has been used a good deal in England in the present century.

Miriam (f.): Hebrew probably from *râma* 'high', 'longed for', 'desired', with prefixed *ma-*, hence 'wished-for child'. An alternative etymology is the accusative case of *merî*, 'rebellion', but this is less probable since this form of accusative died out very early and Semitic names are seldom if ever formed from the accusative case. For the phonology of the name see MARY. *Miriam* is the form of the name used in most versions of the Bible for the sister of Moses and Aaron. It came into use as a christian name in England after the Reformation, and is a favourite name among the Jews.

Moggy, see MARGARET.

Moira, Moyra (f.) [moy'ra]: apparently an attempt at rendering phonetically *Maire,* the Irish form of *Mary*. Not uncommon in England now.

Molly, see MARY.

Mona (f.): Irish *Muadhnait*, a diminutive of *muadh* 'noble', the name of an Irish saint. It has been used in England since the end of the 19th C, when many Irish names came into fashion.

Monday (f.): used as a christian name in the Middle Ages for children born on a *Monday*; Friday and Saturday were similarly used, cf. the surnames *Monday, Munday, Mundy*.

Monica (f.): the name of the mother of St. Augustine; the etymology is unknown; it is possibly of African origin. *Monique* is not uncommon in France. *Monica* occurs at Croston, Lancs., in *c.* 1640, and again at the end of the 18th C. It has become something of a favourite in the present century.

Montagu(e) (m.): the ancient and celebrated families of *Montacute, Montagu,* and *Montague* were founded by Drogo de *Montacute* or *Mont Aigu,* who came to England with the Conqueror and was granted lands in Somerset; he probably took his name from *Mont Aigu* near Caen. The use of *Montague* as a christian name is comparatively modern, and is paralleled by similar use of other names of noble families, e.g. *Cecil, Russell, Dudley*.

Morag (f.) [mōr'ag]: Gaelic, diminutive of *mor(a)* 'the sun'.

Mordecai (m.): Babylonian *Mardukâ* 'man of *Marduk*', i.e. a follower or worshipper of *Marduk,* the supreme god of Babylon. The name ought to be 'Mardecai', as the Septuagint's *Μαρδόχαιος* and the Vulgate's *Mardochaeus,* in agreement with the Babylonian form, show; but the Jewish scribes substituted *o* and *e* in the first two syllables as the characteristic vowels of *bōšeth* 'shame', thereby indicating their disapproval of a Jewish name containing the name of a heathen god. The name, from the Book of Esther, was used occasionally as a christian name during the 17th–19th C.

Morgan (m.): Welsh, cognate with Irish *Muirgen*. The first element is *mor* 'the sea'. It has been a favourite Welsh name from early times, and is used to render *Pelagius* in the Welsh Book of Common Prayer.

Morna (f.): Gaelic *muirne* 'beloved'.

Morris, see MAURICE.

Mortimer (m.): a surname from *Mortemer* in Normandy.

Morwenna (f.): St. *Morwenna* is the patron saint of *Morwenstow*. All that is known of her is a single mention in William of Worcester, 'Sancta *Morwinna*, virgo'; she is said to have been a daughter of St. Brychan. The name has continued to be used in Cornwall. The first element is probably *mor* 'the sea', and the name may be related to Welsh *morwaneg*, 'a wave of the sea'.

Moses (m.): the etymology of this name is obscure; it may be Egyptian rather than Hebrew. It became a favourite Jewish name after the dispersion. In Middle English it appears as *Moyse* or *Moyses* (cf. French *Moïse*), with the nickname *Moss*, and though some of the persons of this name recorded in medieval documents were Jews, it is possible that others were not. The surnames *Moyses*, *Moyse*, *Moyce*, *Moys*, *Moss* are apparently of this origin and point to the use of the name by non-Jews in the period during which surnames were coming into use. The 17th-C Puritans made use of *Moses* as a christian name, and it continued to be so used occasionally in the 18th C (e.g. the younger son of the Vicar of Wakefield).

MOYSES DB 1086.
MOSES Cur 1200, 1205, 1210.
MOSSE (a Jew) HR 1273.
MOSSEUS (a Jew) QW 1292.

Moyna (f.): an Irish name, perhaps *Muadhnait* (see MONA).

Moyra, see MOIRA.

Mungo (m.): Gaelic 'amiable', an epithet applied to St. Kentigern, and occasionally used as a christian name in Scotland, e.g. *Mungo* Park the explorer born 1771. It is most frequent in the saint's own city of Glasgow.

Murdoch (m.): Gaelic *Muireadhach* 'sea man'. Now usually a surname, but still sometimes used as a christian name. *Murdac Miles* occurs as the name of a sub-tenant in the Sussex DB. The Irish form of the name is *Murtagh*.

Muriel, Meriel (f.): this is a difficult name, probably of Celtic origin. There is an Irish name *Muirgheal*, compound of *muir* 'the sea' and *geal* 'bright'. *Mýrgjol* occurs in the Landnámabók as the name of a King of Dublin. *Muriel* is first found in Brittany and Normandy in the 11th C, when it seems to have been borne by several nuns, e.g. *Muriel* mother of Thomas of Bayeux, Archbishop of York (1070–1100), and a mysterious *Muriel*, apparently also a nun, to whom poems were addressed by Baudri de Bourgueil (1046–1130) and by Serlan de Bayeux (1050–1113). William I is said by Wace to have had a half-sister of the name. It does not appear to have been current elsewhere on the Continent, which supports the supposition that it was a Celtic name. The Normans brought it to England. *Muriel, Meriel,* and *Miriel* are common in the 12th and 13th C, giving rise to the surnames *Merrall, Merrell, Merrill, Muriel, Murrell(s)*: it was also a favourite name for English Jewesses, perhaps as a rendering of *Miriam*. Less common in later centuries, it survived in country districts; in a list of Yorkshire recusants in 1604, for instance, there are five women named *Meriall* or *Meryall,* and John Coke of Holkham in 1640 married *Meriel* Wheatley. CMY in 1863 wrote: 'an almost obsolete English name', but in her 2nd edition 1884 she altered this to 'both it and *Meriel* were once common and have lately been revived'. A correspondence in N & Q 1872–7 elicited the fact that it was then very rare. Lord Lyttelton wrote in 1874: 'The name Muriel is an eminent one in my family and my eldest daughter is so named. In our old letters it is spelt *Muriel, Meriel, Maryell.*' The revival of which CMY speaks may have been partly due to Mrs. Craik's immensely popular novel *John Halifax, Gentleman* (1856), one character in which is named *Muriel* 'after the rather peculiar name' of her father's mother. *Meriel* is still used in some families.

MURIEL Cur 1198, 1200, 1205, HR 1273.
MURIELLA Cur 1199, FA 1285.
MIRIELLA Cur 1199.
MIRIELD HR 1273.
MIRIEL, MIRIELDA Cur 1205, 1207.
MIRIALD Cur 1207.

Murtagh, see MURDOCH.

Myra (f.): this name appears to have been invented by Fulke Greville, Lord Brooke (1554–1628), who wrote love poems to a lady whom he so designated (e.g. in his poem 'I, with whose colours *Myra* dressed her hair').

Myrtle, Myrtilla (f.): the name of the shrub, first used as a christian name in the 19th C.

N

Nadine (f.) [nah′dēn]: a French version of Russian *Nadezhda* 'hope'; occasionally used in England in the present century.

Nahum (m.): Hebrew 'consoling', the name of a Hebrew prophet, sometimes used as a christian name since the Reformation, e.g. *Nahum* Tate (1652–1715), the co-author of the metrical psalms.

Nan(ny), Nancy, see ANNE.

Naomi (f.) [nā′omē]: Hebrew 'pleasaunce', the name of the mother-in-law of Ruth. It came into use as a christian name in the 17th C.

Napoleon (m.): Italian *Neapoleone* or *Napoleone*, apparently a derivative of *Neapolis* (Naples); the name of a 4th-C saint martyred at Alexandria. It was used by the Orsini and other Italian families in the Middle Ages and later, though never common. *Napoleone Buonaparte* gallicized his name as *Napoléon Bonaparte*. His name has not often been used in France, either in his lifetime or later; dictators in general seem to discourage the use of their own names, e.g. German parents were advised against calling their sons Adolf. There have been a few examples of its use in England.

Narcissus (m.): Greek νάρκισσος, the name of a flower and of the youth loved by Echo, who died for love of his own image. The name was a common one for Greek slaves. St. *Narcissus* was Bishop of Jerusalem in A.D. 195, and his name has occasionally been used in Italy. The English use of the name, which is post-Renaissance, is very rare and has reference to the Greek myth rather than to the saint.

Natalia, Natalie (f.): from Latin *natale (domini)*, i.e. Christmas Day. St. *Natalia*, wife of St. Adrian, has a place in the Calendar of the Greek Church, and *Natalia*, with its diminutive *Natasha*, is a favourite name in Russia. *Natalie* is used in France and Germany and occasionally in England.

Nathan (m.): Hebrew 'gift', the name of a prophet, occasionally used as a christian name since the 17th C, but mainly a Jewish name.

Nathanael, Nathaniel (m.): Hebrew 'God has given', the name of one of the apostles, generally known by his patronymic *Bartholomew* (q.v.). This name has only been noted once in the Middle Ages, but it became fairly common after the Reformation, often abbreviated to *Nat*.

Ned, see EDWARD.

Nehemiah (m.): Hebrew 'consolation of Jehovah', the name of one of the Hebrew prophets. A common name among the 17th-C Puritans.

Neil, see NIGEL.

Nell(y) (f.): a pet-form of *Ellen, Eleanor*, and *Helen* (qq.v.). *Nel* or *Nell* is not uncommon in medieval records, and though it is often a man's name (*Neil*), it is also sometimes a woman's. *Nell* Gwynn's name was *Eleanor*.

Nessie, Nest(a) (f.): Welsh diminutive for *Agnes* (q.v.). *Nesta* is recorded in Worcestershire and Gloucestershire as early as 1199.

Netta, Nettie (f.): Scottish diminutive of *Janet* (q.v.).

Neville (m.): this was originally a Norman surname, the family having been founded by Gilbert de *Nevil*, one of the companions of the Conqueror, who took his name from *Néville* or *Neuville* in Normandy. The family was widespread and powerful in the Middle Ages. The earliest example of its use as a christian name that has been noted is one *Nevil* or *Nevell* Kay in Lancashire at the beginning of the 17th C.

Niall, see NIGEL.

Nicholas (m.): Latin *Nicolaus* from Greek Νικόλαος, compound of νίκη 'victory' and λαός 'the people'. St. *Nicholas*, Bishop of Myra *c.* 300, is regarded as the patron saint of children, sailors, pawnbrokers, and wolves, and was much venerated in both Eastern and Western Churches. The name is found in use in England before the Norman Conquest, usually applied to a monk. DB mentions two men of the name, one of whom held TRE. In the 12th C it became a favourite, and some idea of its popularity in the Middle Ages can be gained from the number of common surnames derived from it. The usual English form of the name was *Nicol*, and Bardsley gives no fewer than 16 different spellings of the patronymic formed directly from it, in addition to the various spellings of *Nicolson*, and others formed from diminutives such as *Nicolin, Nicolet, Nick* (whence *Nixon*), *Cole* (whence *Cole(s)*, *Colley, Collis*), *Colin* (whence *Collin(s)*, &c.), *Colet* (whence *Collett,* &c.), *Colinet.* The intrusive *h* is found as early as the 12th C; *Nicholaus* occurs e.g. in *The Owl and the Nightingale.* The spelling of the name was probably influenced by medieval Latin spellings of Greek words containing χ, φ, θ, ρ, which varied between k/ch, p/ph, t/th, r/rh. *Nicholas* became much less common after the Reformation. The usual abbreviations are now *Nichol* and *Nick.* *Colin* (q.v.) is now an independent name.

NICOLAUS DB 1086, Cur 1186–1220.
NICHOLAS HR 1273.
NICOLL HR 1273.
NICHOLE HR 1273.
NICHOL Yorks Poll Tax 1379, Cl 1348.
NYCOLAS Lincs 1535.

Nicodemus (m.): Greek Νικόδημος, a compound of νίκη 'victory' and δῆμος 'the people'; the name of 'the ruler of the Jews', who came to Jesus by night (John iii. 1–21). It was evidently a Greek name adopted by the Jews (cf. *Philip*). The apocryphal 'Gospel of *Nicodemus*' was very popular in the Middle Ages and was the basis of many passion plays. *Nicodemus* was a common name in the 17th C and survived into the 19th C.

Nicola, Nicolette (f.): Italian and French f. forms of *Nicholas* (q.v.). *Nicholaa* is not infrequent in medieval Latin records, but is no doubt merely a latinization of *Nicholas* when borne by a woman, who would in the vernacular have been simply *Nicol* or *Nicolas*. *Nicole, Nicolette, Colette* are fairly common in France and are occasionally borrowed in England.

Nigel, Niall, Neil (m.): the history of this name is complicated and rather obscure, but it is probably of Irish origin, *Niul*, a derivative of *niadh* 'champion'. From Ireland it must have been introduced fairly early into Iceland, where it appears as *Njal* (e.g. the *Njalssaga*) and thence to Scandinavia, and eventually to France by the Normans, in the form *Nel* or *Nele*. It was latinized as *Nigellus* and taken to be a diminutive of *niger* 'black'. In England it was well established amongst the Danes and Norsemen before the Norman Conquest, and in DB there are many tenants of the name holding both then and TRE. *Nel, Nele, Neel* appear to have been the usual forms of the name in England; it gave rise to the surnames *Neil, Neild, Neal, Nell, Nelson, Nielson,* &c., as well as *FitzNeel*. In the 15th C there arose a back-formation from the Latin *Nigellus*, e.g. Oseney 1460 has *Nygell, Nigelle*, but Lyford 1655 gives *Neale* as still in use. *Niall* is the correct form, *Neill* being the possessive case. Both *Neil* and *Nigel* are now mainly Scottish; *Niall* is the usual modern Irish form.

NIGELLUS DB 1086, Cur 1187–1220, HR 1273, FA 1346.
NEL HR 1273.
NELL HR 1273.
NEEL Cl 1303, FA 1346.
NELE Yorks Poll Tax 1379.

Nina (f.) [ně′na]: Russian diminutive of *Anne* (q.v.) (cf. French *Ninon, Ninette*), occasionally used in England since the middle of the 19th C.

Ninian (m.): *Ninian* or *Ninias* was the name of a saint of British origin (died 432) who founded a church at Whithorn in Wigtownshire and evangelized the southern Picts. It is probably the same as *Nennius*, the name of the 8th-C British historian; the Irish *Ninidh* may be a cognate name. *Ninian* is now almost entirely Scottish, but it was formerly current in Yorkshire and Northumberland; it is, for example, frequent in early 17th-C lists of Yorkshire recusants.

Nita (f.) [ně′ta]: Spanish abbreviation of *Juanita*, itself a diminutive of *Juana* (= *Joan*). *Nita* is now occasionally used in USA and England.

Noah (m.): Hebrew 'long lived', literally 'long', being a shortened representation of the name of the Sumerian Noah, Zi-ud-sudda 'life of days long', in the Epic of Gilgamesh. It was not uncommon in the 17th C, and survived in use in the 18th and 19th C both in England and USA.

Noel (m., f.): Old French *nouel, noel* from Latin *natalis* (*dies*), used as a christian name for children of either sex born on Christmas Day. It was fairly common in the Middle Ages from about 1200, and gave rise to the surnames *Noel, Nowell. Christmas* was also sometimes used as a christian name. Cf. also *Tiffany, Pentecost, Easter, Midwinter, Loveday* which were all formerly used as christian names.
NOEL HR 1273.

Nona (f.): Latin f. of *nonus* 'ninth'. Sometimes used for a ninth child (cf. *Decima, Octavia*), but also without reference to number.

Nonie (f.): pet-form of *Nora* (q.v.).

Nora(h) (f.): Irish abbreviated form of *Honora* (q.v.), now and for long past an independent name.

Noreen (f.) [nōr'ēn]: Irish *Nóirín*, diminutive of *Nora*, now sometimes used as an independent name. *Norinna* is found in 1213.

Norma (f.): the modern use of this name seems to date from Bellini's opera *Norma* (1831), but one instance of it is recorded in 1203 (Cur). The etymology is obscure, though it may be Latin *norma* 'rule', 'precept', 'pattern'.

Norman (m.): Old English *Northman* and cognate Old German *Nordemann* were both used as christian names (cf. *German, Franco*). *Norman* was fairly common in England before the Norman Conquest, and in DB there is mention of several tenants of this name who had held land TRE. It continued in use for some centuries and gave rise to the surnames *Norman* and *Normand*, but died out in England about the 14th C, though it continued in Scotland where it is used as an equivalent of the MacLeod name *Tormond* (= Old Norse *Dormund*). CMY regards it as being in her time exclusively Scottish, and its modern revival in England may be due in part to her use of it in *The Daisy Chain* (1856).

NORMANN(US) DB 1086, HR 1273.
NORMAN HR 1273.

O

Obadiah (m.): Hebrew 'serving Jehovah', the name of one of the Hebrew prophets. It was a common christian name in the 17th C, and continued in use, particularly in America, until the 19th C.

Obedience (f.): rather common in the 17th C.

Octavia (f.): Latin f. of *Octavius* (q.v.).

Octavius (m.): Latin derivative of *octavus* 'eighth', the name of a Roman *gens*, the most famous member of which was the Emperor Augustus. It is sometimes used in England, but has naturally become somewhat rare in an age when eighth children are almost unknown.

Odette, see OTTILIA.

Odo (m.): Old German *Audo*, later *Odo* or *Otho*, derivative of *auda*, the equivalent of Old English *ead* 'rich'. It was introduced into England by the Normans, who used both *d* and *th* forms; thus in DB we find *Odo, Oddo, Otho, Otto*. The commonest form at a later date was *Otes* (the Old French *cas-sujet*). The surnames *Oddy, Oddie, Od(e)y, Odlin(g), Oat, Oat(e)s, Oatson*, and others are derived from it. Camden says '*Othes* an old name in England, drawn from *Otho*'. *Otes* is found in Cornwall as late as 1547, *Ottie* in 1597. *Odo* was used in Scotland to render the Gaelic *Aodh*. The diminutive *Odinel* was also used. *Otho* has been used in the Cooke family of Lancashire from the 17th C to the present time, and *Ot(h)i* is still used as a gipsy name. The name was revived in the form *Odo* in a few families in the 19th C. The modern German *Otto* is also now occasionally used.

ODO Reg 1067–71.
OTTO, OTHO, ODO, ODDO DB 1086.
ODO Cur 1189, FA 1346.
ODE, ODDE HR 1273.
OTES Cur 1189–1220, HR 1273, Yorks Poll Tax 1379.
HOTYS HR 1273.

Ogier (m.): Old German *Audagar, Autger*, compound of *auda* 'rich' and *ger* 'spear', so that it is the equivalent of Old English *Eadgar* (see EDGAR). It became *Oger* or *Ogier* in Old French, and was the name of one of the paladins of Charlemagne, *Ogier le Danois* or *Holger Danske*. It was introduced into England by the Normans and occurs some 7 or 8 times in DB. It was not uncommon in the 12th and 13th C and gave rise to the surnames *Odger(s)*.

OGER(I)US DB 1086.
OGER Cl 1270.
OGGERY Testa de Neville 13th C.

Olaf (m.): Old Norse *Anleifr*, of which the first element is cognate with Old German *ano* 'ancestor', and the second means 'relics', 'remains'. It was and still is a favourite name in all Scandinavian countries on account of *Olaf* Trygvasson (956–1000), King of

Norway, and St. *Olaf*, King of Norway, died 1030, who introduced
Christianity into that country. It was used by the Danes in Eng-
land, but does not seem to have survived the Norman Conquest.
In Gaelic the name became *Amhlaibh* (Aulay), whence the
Hebrides surname *Macaulay*. It is often rendered by *Humphrey*
in Ireland.

Olga (f.): a Russian name of Scandinavian origin, from Norse
helga 'holy'. Used in England in recent times like other Russian
names (cf. *Vera, Sonia*).

Olive, Olivia (f.): this is apparently Latin *oliva* 'olive', used as
a personal name. In the Roman martyrology there is a St. *Oliva*,
a virgin of Anagni of unknown date, and also a St. *Oliva*, venerated
in the place so named and the patroness of olive-trees, which looks
suspiciously as though she started life as a tutelary goddess. *Oliva*
is found in Latin records in England as early as 1203 and was not
uncommon in the 13th and 14th C, the usual English version
being *Oliff* (cf. surnames *Olive, Oliffe, Olliffe*) and the diminutives
Olivet, Ollett. *Olive* occurs in the 16th C and Lyford 1655 gives
Olive as a christian name. In the 18th C the Italian *Olivia* came
into fashion, and *Olive* survived only in rustic use, but it has now
been revived. *Olivia* has maintained its place, probably on account
of Shakespeare's *Twelfth Night*, when most of the 18th-C Italian
and Latin versions of christian names have died out.

OLIVA Cur 1203–15, HR 1273, Yorks Poll Tax 1379.
OLIF Yorks Poll Tax 1379.
OLYFFE St. Columb 1579.
OLYFF St. Columb 1581.

Oliver (m.): the name of one of the most famous of the peers of
Charlemagne and hence a favourite medieval name. The French
form was *Olivier* and it has usually been taken to be the Old
French *olivier, oliver* 'an olive-tree', from Latin *olivarius*. Alternatively it has been derived from Norse *Olaf* (q.v.). But there is no
evidence for the existence of a name *Olivarius* and almost all the
other names connected with the older versions of the Charlemagne
cycle are of Teutonic origin, whilst derivation from *Olaf* is

phonetically difficult. *Oliver* may therefore represent some such name as Old German *Alfihar* (which is on record and is the equivalent of Old English *Ælfhere* 'elf-host') adapted later to a fancied derivation from *olivarius*. For the phonetic development compare modern German *Olfert* from *Alfhard*, and *Olbrich* from *Alberich*. *Oliver* first occurs in England as the name of a sub-tenant in DB. It was moderately common in the Middle Ages (cf. the surnames *Ol(l)iver*, *Olver*, *Oliverson*; and *Ollier* from the Breton form of the name), and continued so in the 16th and 17th C. After the Restoration it went completely out of fashion owing to association with Cromwell, and it was not until the end of the 19th C that it came back into general favour. The old nickname *Noll* is now seldom heard.

OLIVERUS DB 1086, Cur 1199–1220.
OLIVER Cl 1249, HR 1273.
HOLIVER Yorks Poll Tax 1379.

Olivia, see OLIVE.

Olwen (f.): Welsh, literally 'white track'. In the Welsh tale of 'Culhwch and Olwen' it is said that 'fair white trefoils sprang up behind her wherever she went and for that reason was she called Olwen'.

Olympias (f.): Greek *'Ολυμπιάς* 'of Olympus', the name of the mother of Alexander the Great, and also of a saint, a disciple of St. Chrysostom. It was on account of the saint, no doubt, that *Olimpe* became a christian name in France. *Olimpias* occurs in England in the 13th C. Lyford 1655 gives *Olympia*, and an *Olympia* Morshead was living in 1745.

OLIMPIAS Cur 1207–15.

Oonagh, see UNA.

Ophelia (f.): probably Greek *ὠφελία* 'help', 'succour'. The name seems to have been coined by Sannazaro, in whose *Arcadia* (1504) it appears as *Ofelia*. John Rickman (born 1587) married *Ophelia* Marchant of Bath, but this appears to be an isolated example.

Shakespeare's use of *Ophelia* in *Hamlet* has led to its occasional use as a christian name in England and USA.

Oriana (f.) [ōr'ĕahna]: *Oriande, Oriante* are frequent in Old French romances, e.g. as the name of the mistress of Amadis de Gaul. It is presumably a derivative of Latin *oriri* 'to rise'. Madrigal writers applied the name *Oriana* to Queen Elizabeth, and Ben Jonson used it for Anne of Denmark 'quasi *oriens Anna*'. *Oriana* Palfreyman of W. Toynton, Lincs., was excommunicated in 1602. Tennyson's 'Ballad of Oriana' owed the name to his friend *Oriana* Reinagle, daughter of R. R. Reinagle and *Oriana*, granddaughter of Sir Mitford Crowe.

Oriel (f.): Old German *Aurildis, Orieldis*, which Förstemann considers a compound of *aur-* (= *aus* 'fire'), and *hildi* 'strife'. The name was apparently introduced into England by the Normans, and is found in the 13th C as *Oriolt, Oriolda, Oriholt, Oriel*. It does not seem to have taken permanent root, and soon died out. The recent use of the name may be a revival, but is more probably a use of the name of *Oriel* College, Oxford, which is derived from the word *oriel* 'a window', for the history of which see OED s.v.

Original (m.): used as a christian name in the 16th–18th C, usually for a first-born son.

Orlando (m.): Italian form of *Roland* (q.v.). *Orlando* was not uncommon in England in the 16th C when there was a fashion for Italian names, e.g. *Ferdinando* (q.v.). The best-known example of the name is *Orlando* Gibbons the composer (1583–1625), one of whose brothers was named *Ferdinando*.

Osanna, see HOSANNA.

Osbert (m.): Old English *Osbeorht*, compound of *os* 'a god' (a word which is not recorded except in compounds) and *beorht* 'bright'. It was principally a Northumbrian name in the Old English period and survived the Norman Conquest, being reinforced by Norman French *Osbert* from cognate Old German *Ansobert*; it was not uncommon in the 12th–14th C, is found occasionally in subsequent centuries, was revived, with other Old English names, in the 19th C, and is now fairly common again.

OSBERT(US) Reg 1066, DB 1086, Cur 1196–1220, FA 1284, 1303, 1363. HOSBERTUS FA 1285.

Osborn (m.): Old English *Osbeorn*, compound of *os* 'a god' and *beorn*, a poetical word meaning 'man' (the cognate Norse word *bjorn* means 'bear'). Both *Osbeorn* and the corresponding Norse name *Asbjorn* were in general use in England before the Norman Conquest, and were then reinforced by the Norman version. DB mentions several tenants named *Osbernus* and others who had held TRE. It remained in general use during the Middle Ages and gave rise to the common surnames *Osborn(e)*, *Osbourn(e)*, *Osbern*, *Osburn*. *Osberne* is recorded as a christian name as late as 1489, and Lyford (1655) gives it in his list.

OSBERN(US) DB 1086, Reg 1087–97.
OSEBERNE HR 1273.
OSBARN Yorks Poll Tax 1379.

Oscar (m.): Old English *Osgar*, compound of *os* 'a god' and *gar* 'spear'. Both this and the corresponding Norse *Asgeirr* were in use in England before the Norman Conquest, but do not seem to have long survived it. Macpherson in his Ossianic poems gave the name *Oscar* to the son of Ossian: the name also appears in some old Irish poems as *Osgar*, and had doubtless been carried to Ireland by the Danes. Napoleon's Ossianic enthusiasm caused him to bestow the name *Oscar* upon his godson, son of Bernadotte, who later succeeded his father as *Oscar* I, King of Sweden. The great vogue of *Ossian* on the Continent has led to the general use of the name *Oscar* there. CMY, in mentioning this, adds that with us, however, 'it has descended to dogs'. But in fact it has, since her time, been used a good deal in England and Ireland.

OSGARUS DB 1086.

Osmond (m.): Old English *Osmund*, compound of *os* 'a god' and *mund* 'protection'. Both it and the corresponding Norse *Asmundr* were in general use in England before the Norman Conquest, after which it was reinforced by the Norman version (*Osmond*).

DB gives several tenants of this name and others who held TRE. St. *Osmond* Bishop of Salisbury (died 1099) was a Norman. The surnames *Osmond*, *Osmund*, *Osman*, *Osment*, *Osmint*, *Osmon*, *Osmand* are derived from it. It became less common after the 13th C, but examples have been noted at Cambridge in the 16th and 17th C, and Lyford (1655) gives it in his list of names.

OSMUND(US), HOSMUNDUS, HOSMUNT DB 1086.
OSMUND Cur 1199–1215, HR 1273.

Oswald (m.): Old English *Osweald*, compound of *os* 'a god' and *weald* 'power'. There was a corresponding Norse name *Asvald*. St. *Oswald* (605–42), King of Northumbria, and St. *Oswald* (died 992), Archbishop of York, no doubt helped to establish the popularity of the name, which has never (like most other Old English names in *Os-*) gone out of use. The surnames *Oswald*, *Oswell*, *Oswill* are derived from it. In the 16th, 17th, and 18th C the christian name *Oswald* is found in the forms *Oswell*, *Oswall*, or *Ozwell*. It has been in regular use in the Mosley family since the end of the 16th C.

OSUUALD(US), OSUUOLD(US), OSUUOL DB 1086.
OSEWOLD Chaucer *Cant. Tales c.* 1387.
OSWOLD 14th C Legendary.
OSWELL St. Antholin 1540.
OSWALL St. Mary Aldermary 1620.
OZWELL Cant Cath Reg 1744.

Oswin (m.): Old English *Oswin*, compound of *os* 'a god' and *wine* 'friend'. It remained in use until the 14th C. and was occasionally revived in the 19th C.

Ottilia (f.): *Odala*, *Odila*, *Otila*, *Odilia* are found in Old German as a woman's name, being a derivative of *othal* 'fatherland'. The corresponding man's name *Odila* occurs in Old English. St. *Ottilia* (French *Odille*) was a 7th-C virgin who became the patron saint of Alsace. *Ottilie* is not uncommon in Germany, and *Odille* and its diminutive *Odette* are fairly common in France. They are occasionally borrowed in England.

Otto, see ODO.

Owen (m.): a common Welsh name; in Middle English romances often spelled *Owain, Owayne, Ywain*. It has been supposed to be derived from Latin *Eugenius*; cf. *Emrys* from *Ambrose, Gladys* from *Claudia*, but see EWEN.

OUEN, OUUIN, OWINE DB 1086.
OUEIN Lib Lond 10th C.
UWEN ASC 10th C.
OENUS Pipe Roll 1164.
OWEN Cur 1200, Cov 1492, HR 1273.
OWEYN HR 1273.
OWYNE Cov 1524.

P

Paddy, see PATRICIA, PATRICK.

Pagan (m.): Latin *paganus*, originally 'rustic', 'villager', later 'heathen'. Its use as a personal name appears to be late (cf. *Urbanus*). It was introduced into England by the Normans (*Edmundus fil. Pagani* occurs in DB), and it soon became common, the usual vernacular form of the name being *Payn* (cf. French *païen* 'pagan'); the surnames *Pagan, Pain(e)*, and *Payne*, and *Paynel, Paganel, Pannet* from diminutive forms, testify to its popularity. It did not, however, survive the Reformation as a christian name.

PAGANUS, PAGEN DB 1086.
PAGANUS Cur 1189-1220, FA 1303.
PAGAN Pipe Roll 1165, HR 1273.
PAYNE Cl 1249.
PAYN HR 1273.
PAGANE Godstow 1450.
PAGANEL or PAIN Writs of Parliament 1301.
PAYNEL HR 1273.

Pamela (f.) [pă'mela]: apparently invented by Sir Philip Sidney as the name of a character in his *Arcadia* (1590), and pronounced *Paměla*. Richardson adopted it for the heroine of his first novel

Pamela (1740), and the great vogue of that book led to its being sometimes used as a christian name. It is found in New England in 1812. CMY says: 'still not uncommon among the lower classes.' A writer in N & Q 1904 mentions it as an unusual name. Within the present century it has become rather fashionable. There seems to have been some doubt as to its pronunciation in the 18th C. Fielding, in *Joseph Andrews*, wrote: 'She told me that they had a daughter of a very strange name, *Paměla* or *Paměla*; some pronounce it one way, and some the other.' It is now always pronounced *Pǎ'mela*.

Parnel, see PETRONELLA.

Pascoe (m.): Middle English *Pask* 'Easter'. Both *Pask* and the adjective *Pascal* were used as christian names in the Middle Ages. *Pascal* was still used as late as the middle of the 19th C and survives as *Pascoe* in Cornwall.

PASCHE HR 1273.
PASCOWE St. Columb 1571.
PASCOW St. Columb 1542.
PASKELL St. Columb 1608.

Pat, see PATRICIA, PATRICK.

Patience (f.): Like other abstract nouns, came into use as a christian name in the 17th C, e.g. Sir Thomas Carew, Speaker of the House of Commons in the reigns of James I and Charles I, had four daughters named *Patience, Temperance, Silence,* and *Prudence*. *Patience* was in the 17th C often also a man's name. It is sometimes abbreviated to *Patty*.

Patricia (f.): f. of *Patricius* (see PATRICK). *Patricia* occurs from time to time in medieval Latin records, but then merely denotes a woman bearing the name *Patrick*. Its use as a genuine christian name seems to have begun in Scotland in the 18th C, but it was uncommon until the present century, when it became popular owing to Princess Victoria *Patricia* Helena Elizabeth of

Connaught (born 1886), usually known as Princess *Patricia*.
It is frequently abbreviated to *Pat* or *Paddy*.

Patrick (m.): Latin *patricius* 'nobleman', the name adopted by the
apostle of Ireland, whose original name was Sucat, when he was
consecrated as a missionary. It has been chiefly used in Ireland
and Scotland, but was common in the North of England from the
12th C (cf. the surnames *Patrick(son)*, *Pate(s)*, *Pat(e)y*, *Paton*,
Patten, *Patti(n)son*, *Pat(t)erson*). In Scotland *Peter* was formerly
used as a diminutive of *Patrick*, e.g. *Patrick*, Lord Robertson
(1794–1855), 'Lord *Peter*, Who broke the laws of God and man
and metre'. Black cites evidence that the two names were interchangeable in Scotland as late as 1867. In Ireland, where it is one
of the commonest men's names, the pet-forms *Pat*, *Patsy*, and
Paddy are in general use.

PATRICIUS Cur 1200–12, FA 1284, Yorks Poll Tax 1379.
PATERICK 14th C Legendary.
PATRYCKE *Cocke Lorelle's Bote c.* 1515.
PATTRIK St. Mary at Hill 1527.

Patty, see MARTHA, PATIENCE.

Paul (m.): Latin *paulus* 'small', the name of Saul of Tarsus after
his conversion. *Paul* occurs in England before the Norman Conquest only as a monk's name. St. *Paul* was not an object of particular devotion in the Middle Ages; of 326 English churches
dedicated to him, 283 are double dedications to SS. Peter and
Paul, and of the 43 remaining ones, some at least were originally
to the Celtic St. *Pol* or to St. *Paulinus*. I have found the christian
name *Paul* recorded only 4 times in the 13th C (probably the
same man in three cases), and there can be no doubt that it was a
very rare name in the Middle Ages. Bardsley, it is true, says that
it was one of the favourite names in the 13th C, but though he
derived from it many surnames (e.g. *Paul*, *Pawl(e)*, *Paulin*, *Pawley*,
Paulet, *Powell*, *Pollit*), it is significant that he does not give a single
example of it as a christian name, and he was certainly wrong
about the origin of some of these names. It was not until the
17th C that *Paul* had a certain degree of popularity, and even so

it never equalled that of many other Biblical names. It has always
been commoner in Spain (*Pablo*) and Italy (*Paolo*) and Russia
(*Pavel*) than in England, France, or Germany.

PAUL Cur 1200, 1207, 1210.
POWEL Magd. *c.* 1260.
POWLE Coventry Mystery 15th C.

Paula (f.): a German f. form of *Paul*. Occasionally used in England in recent times. It is the name of the heroine of Pinero's
popular play *The Second Mrs. Tanqueray*, which may have helped
its use in this country.

Paulina, Pauline (f.): Latin *Paulina*, f. of *Paulinus* (q.v.). St.
Paulina was a 4th-C martyr, and the name is occasionally met
with in the 12th and 13th C. It has been most common in France,
where *Pauline* is regarded as a f. form of *Paul*. *Paulina* and *Pauline*
are both occasionally used in England.

Paulinus (m.) [pawli'nus]: Latin derivative of *paulus* 'small'.
St. *Paulinus* (died 644) was one of a second mission sent to Britain
by St. Gregory to assist St. Augustine, and there are a number of
churches dedicated to him. A *Paulinus* is mentioned in DB as
having held land TRE and *Paulin* or *Pawlin* is not uncommon in
the 12th and 13th C. The latest example noted is *Paulin* Phelips
(died 1782) whose name occurs in a Hunts Clergy List.

PAULINUS DB 1086, Cur 1203, HR 1273, FA 1316.
PAULIN HR 1273.

Pearl (f.), used in recent times as a christian name (cf. *Ruby*,
Emerald), and sometimes as a pet-name for Margaret (*margarita*
= pearl).

Peg(gy), see MARGARET.

Penelope (f.) [penĕl'opĕ]: Greek Πηνελόπη, Πηνελόπεια (said to
be connected with πήνη 'a bobbin'), the name of the faithful wife
of Odysseus. It was first used as a christian name in the 16th C,
e.g. *Penelope* (1562–1607) daughter of William Devereux, Earl of
Essex, wife of Lord Rich and the *Stella* of Sir Philip Sidney.

Penelope has never been common but has been used regularly since its introduction. It is rather more frequent in Ireland where it was used to render the native name *Fionnghuala* (see FENELLA). It is sometimes abbreviated to *Pen* or *Penny*. The gipsy name *Peneli* may be a form of *Penelope*.

Pentecost (m., f.): from Greek πεντηκοστή (ἡμέρα), 'fiftieth (day)', the Greek name for Whitsuntide. *Pentecost* is found as a christian name from the beginning of the 13th C and continued in general use until the 17th C. Occasional examples occur later, and it was in use in Cornwall until the end of the 19th C. It was used indifferently for men and women.

PENTECOST Pipe Roll 1165, Cur 1200–7, Cl 1331.

Perceval, Percival (m.): this name seems to have been invented by Crestien de Troyes in the 12th C for the hero of his poem *Percevale*; it is French *perce-val* 'pierce (the) valley'. There are not many early examples of its use as a christian name, the earliest noted being Sir *Percivale* Sowdon 1375. The surname *Perceval* is found rather earlier; it was a Norman name derived from the place-name *Percheval*.

PERCYVALLUS Yorks Poll Tax 1379.
PERCYVELL, PERSIVELL Yorks Rec 1604.
PERSEFALL St. Jas. Clerkenwell 1666.

Percy (m.): this is the name of the famous family which is descended from William de *Perci*, one of the companions of the Conqueror, who took his name from the village of *Perci* near St. Lô in Normandy. The use of *Percy* as a christian name seems at first to have been confined to persons connected with the family. The earliest example noted is Lord *Percy* Seymour (died 1721), son of the 6th Duke of Somerset and Lady Elizabeth *Percy*, heiress of the Percy family. His sister Lady Catherine Seymour married Sir William Wyndham, and her 2nd son, later Earl of Thomond, was also called *Percy*. Another example was the poet *Percy* Bysshe Shelley (born 1792). The connexion between the Shelley and Percy families was very remote; the poet's grandfather married (as his second wife) the heiress of the Sidneys,

Earls of Leicester, and the 2nd Earl had in 1615 married Dorothy *Percy*, daughter of the 9th Earl of Northumberland. She was mother of Algernon Sidney, 'the patron saint of the Whigs', and it may have been Sir Timothy's Whiggism rather than his snobbishness which made him call his son *Percy*. In the course of the 19th C the name became more and more generally used, and Shelley may himself have contributed to its popularity.

Perdita (f.) [per'dĭta]: from f. of Latin *perditus* 'lost'. Shakespeare invented the name for the heroine of *A Winter's Tale*: 'and for the babe Is counted lost for ever, *Perdita* I prithee call 't.' Like other Shakespearian names, it is now occasionally used as a christian name.

Peregrine (m.) [pĕr'egrĭn]: Latin *peregrinus* 'stranger' or 'traveller', later 'pilgrim'. St. *Peregrinus* (died 643) was a hermit near Modena who was regarded as the patron of Modena and Lucca. *Peregrine* is found, though always rare, as a christian name from the 13th C; it was the name of one of the sons of Edmund Spenser.
PEREGRINUS Writs of Parliament 1291.

Perpetua (f.): f. of Latin *perpetuus* 'uninterrupted', 'perpetual'. St. *Perpetua* was a 3rd-C virgin martyred with St. Felicitas at Carthage and named in the Canon of the Mass. Her name is sometimes used by Roman Catholics.

Persis (f.): Greek Περσίς, 'Persian woman'; the name of a woman mentioned by St. Paul in Rom. xvi 'salute *Persis* the beloved'. It came into use as a christian name after the Reformation (the first example noted is 1579) and was fairly common in the 17th C.

Peter (m.): (Latin *Petrus*, French *Pierre*, Italian *Pie(t)ro*, Spanish *Pedro*, German *Peter*, Dutch *Pieter*, Norwegian *Peer*, Russian *Pyotr*): Greek πέτρος 'stone', a translation of Aramaic *Cephas*, the name given by Jesus to Simon son of Jonas. St. *Peter* appealed to the imagination of the medieval Church more than any other of the apostles (there are 1,140 churches dedicated to him in England, more than twice as many as to St. *Michael*, the next commonest); and his name was one of the commonest christian names in every country. It was introduced into England by the Normans and soon became a favourite. The usual form was the French *Piers*, which gave rise to numerous surnames such as *Piers*, *Pierce*, *Pearce*, *Pears(e)*, *Pearson*, *Pierson*; and *Perrin*, *Perkin(s)*, *Parkin(son)*, *Perrot(t)* from various diminutives. *Peters* and *Peterson* are much less common, and are usually Welsh (Welsh surnames are of later origin than English), and in fact the form *Peter* is not found before the 14th C, the earliest examples noted being *Petyr* in the alliterative *Morte Arthure* (*c.* 1355), *Petur of Westcote* mentioned in an Oseney MS of 1460, and *Petyr* which is given as the English equivalent of *Petrus* in *Promptorium Parvulorum*. From then onwards it gradually ousted the older form, though *Pearse* or *Peares* is still found in Elizabeth's reign. Lyford 1655 says '*Pierce* used for *Peter* formerly'. The Reformation struck a blow at the name which was so closely associated with the Papacy, and in the 17th and 18th C it was uncommon and regarded as rustic and old-fashioned. The sudden enormous popularity of the name in the present century is no doubt largely due to Barrie's *Peter Pan* (1904).

PETRUS DB 1086, Cur 1186–1220, HR 1273.
PETUR Oseney 1460.
PETYR *Prompt Parv c.* 1440.
PEROTE Exch R 1306.
PERES Yorks Poll Tax 1379.
PIERS 15th C *Brut*, Gedney Parish Reg 1734.
PERS *Cocke Lorelle's Bote c.* 1515.
PEARS, PEIRCE St. Columb 1641.

Petronella, Petronilla (f.): Latin f. diminutive of *Petronius*, the name of a Roman *gens*, possibly a derivative of *petra* 'stone'. The discovery of a tomb in Rome, inscribed *Filiae dulcissimae Aureliae Petronillae*, led to the belief that *Petronilla* was the name of a daughter of St. Peter, and, as St. *Petronilla*, she was invoked against fevers. The name was very common in the Middle Ages, when it was used as a convenient f. form of *Peter*. It is found in England from the 12th C and was early contracted to *Peronel*, *Pernel*, or *Parnel* (cf. the surnames *Parnall*, *Parnell*, *Parnwell*).

Pernel or *Parnel,* for some reason, came to be used as a generic name for a priest's concubine, and is so used as early as 1362 in *Piers Plowman.* Later it meant any loose woman, and survived in dialectal use until the 18th C. The christian name *Parnel* or *Peternel* survived in Cornwall and Lancashire till the 18th C.

PETRONILLA Cur 1196, HR 1273, FA 1303, 1316.
PETRONELLA Cur 1207, FA 1303.
PETRONYL Godstow 1450.
PERNEL HR 1273.
PARNELL Lincs 1529, St. Mary Aldermary 1680.
PARONEL Yorks Poll Tax 1379.
PETERNELL St. Columb 1706.
PETRONEL St. Columb 1714.

Phelim (m.) [fē'lim]: Irish *Feiolim* 'the ever good'. A common Irish name, often translated by *Felix.*

Phemie, see EUPHEMIA.

Philadelphia (f.): Greek *Φιλαδελφία* 'brotherly love', the name of a city founded by *Attalus Philadelphus,* King of Pergamus. The church at *Philadelphia* was one of the seven mentioned in the Book of Revelation, and *Philadelphia* became a favourite Puritan name (Bardsley says he found no fewer than 100 examples of it in James I's reign) and Lyford gives it as a woman's name. It was occasionally used as late as the 19th C.

Phil(i)bert, see FULBERT.

Philemon (m.) [fīlē'mŏn]: Greek *Φιλήμων,* derivative of *φίλημα* 'kiss', and a common Greek name. St. Paul's epistle to *Philemon* led to its being used as a christian name in the 17th C, and it has been retained in a few families.

Philip (m.): Greek *Φίλιππος* 'lover of horses', the name of one of the apostles. It was common in England in the Middle Ages, as is shown by the number of surnames derived from it and its nick-names; there are 8 ways of spelling the simple patronymic *Philip(s),* besides *Philipson, Philp(s), Phelip(s), Phelps, Philpot(t)(s)* (from the French diminutive *Philip-ot), Philkin, Philcox, Phipps, Philson,* and others. *Phelyp* is found as a christian name as late as the end of the 15th C, and *Philip* was used as a nickname for the sparrow. The popularity of the name waned somewhat after the reign of Mary Tudor, when *Philip* of Spain became the enemy *par excellence*. Sir *Philip* Sidney was his godson, born while he was King Consort of England.

PHILIPPUS Cur 1186–1220, HR 1273.
PHELIPPE Exch R 1306.
PHELYP St. Mary at Hill 1491.
PHELYPP Coventry Mysteries 15th C.
PHILIPOT Yorks Poll Tax 1379.
PHYLYPP *Cocke Lorelle's Bote c.* 1515.

Philippa (f.): Latin f. form of *Philip* (q.v.). *Philippa* occurs in medieval Latin records, but women so named were actually called *Philip*, e.g. in the 15th-C Brut Queen *Philippa* is *Quene Phelip*, *Philippe*, or *Phillip*, and a daughter of Henry IV is *Dame Phelyp*. Lyford 1655 in his list of women's names says '*Phil* or *Philip* see in Men's names'. The modern use of *Philippa* is quite recent. It is sometimes abbreviated to *Pippa* (an Italian form) with reference to Browning's poem *Pippa passes*.

Phillida, Phillis, see PHYLLIS.

Philomena (f.) [fĭlōmē′na] : Greek Φιλουμενα, present participle of Φιλοῡμαι 'I am loved'. There was a St. *Philomena* of unknown date, and the name was occasionally used in the Middle Ages, e.g. *Philomena* Sturdi (HR 1273). The discovery of relics in a loculus marked '*Philomena*' in Rome in 1802 revived the name in Italy (*Filomena*).

Phine(h)as (m.) [fĭn′ĕăs] : Egyptian 'the negro'. Used as a christian name in the 16th and 17th C (e.g. the two *Phineas* Fletcher's) and occasionally since.

Phoebe (f.): Greek Φοίβη, 'the shining one', an epithet of Artemis. St. Paul, in the Epistle to the Romans, recommends '*Phoebe* our sister', and the name came into use in England after the Reformation; the earliest example noted is in 1568. *Phebe* or *Phoebe* was fairly common in the 17th C, and has remained in use until the present day.

Phyllis, Phillis, Phillida (f.): Greek *Φύλλις* 'leafy', the name of a girl who hanged herself for love and was turned into a tree. *Phyllis* was used as a name in Greek and Roman pastoral poetry, and was adopted in England in the 16th C, when it became confused with *Felis*, the usual English form of *Felicia* (q.v.), so that it is often difficult to decide which name is meant. For instance, in a list of Yorkshire recusants of 1604 there are a number of cases of *Phillis, Philles, Phillice*, which almost certainly represent *Felice, Felis* rather than *Phyllis*. The 17th-C poets also used the form *Phillida*, and a *Fillida* was married at Leigh, Lancashire in 1620. *Phyllis* became almost obsolete in the 18th and 19th C, but suddenly came back into favour at the end of the 19th C, and is now common.

Phythian, see VIVIAN.

Piers, see PETER.

Pippa, see PHILIPPA.

Pleasance, Pleasant (f.): Old French *plaisance* and *plaisant* respectively (cf. *Clemency* and *Clement*); found as christian names from the 13th C onward. Dickens, who used the name for a character in *Our Mutual Friend*, noted it down in a memorandum of unusual names found in Privy Council Education List about 1855. *Pleasance* is still used in USA. *Pleasant* was a man's as well as a woman's name.

PLESENCIA Cl 1245.
PLACENCIA FA 1346.
PLESANCIA Year Book 1422.

Polly, see MARY.

Postumus (m.) [pŏst'ūmus]: Latin *postumus* 'last', 'later', applied to children born after their father's death. An erroneous idea that the word = post+humus led to the intrusive *h* in the English word *posthumous*, and it also often appears in the christian name. *Postumus* was usually given as a name to posthumous children. The first example noted is *Posthumus* Pownell born 1571, but it was more often given as a second name.

Primrose (f.): mentioned in N & Q 1904 as one of the flower-names then growing in popularity. Several examples (m. and f.) which occur in the 18th C. are no doubt cases of the use of the Scottish surname as a christian name; e.g. *Primrose* Fraser, 3rd wife of Simon Fraser, Lord Lovat, was probably named after her mother's sister-in-law, who was born *Primrose*.

Priscilla (f.): Latin diminutive of *Prisca*, the f. of the Roman cognomen *Priscus* (apparently the word *priscus* 'former'). *Priscilla* is the name of a woman mentioned in Acts xviii. 2, and was a favourite with 17th-C Puritans; the earliest example noted is *Precilla* Stevenson 1592. *Priscilla* is apparently also mentioned, in non-diminutive form, as *Prisca* in the Epistle to Timothy, and *Prisca* was also sometimes used as a christian name in the 17th C and later.

Protasia (f.): Latin f. of *Protasius*, a name of doubtful etymology. St. *Protasia* was martyred at Senlis *c*. 282 and her relics were enshrined in the cathedral *c*. 1191. It is difficult to account for the use of the name in England, which has not been noted before the late 16th C. Examples are found of various spellings, e.g. *Prothasey* at Lincoln in 1616, *Protezy* on a tombstone at Stoke-by-Nayland in the late 17th C; Sir Thomas Bodley (1545–1613) had a sister *Prothesia*, and a *Pertesia* Midwinter lived at Exeter in the reign of Elizabeth.

Prudence (f.): Latin *prudentia* 'prudence'. The name is found in use in the 13th C (cf. *Clemency, Pleasance*), and was revived, with other similar names, after the Reformation. It was rather common in the 17th and 18th C, often abbreviated to *Prue*.

PRUDENCIA Cur 1210.
PRUDENTIA Ass 1221.

Q

Queenie (f.): A pet-name, fairly common and sometimes used as an independent name in the 19th C. Dr. Johnson called Hester

Maria Thrale 'Queen Hester', which was later shortened to *'Queeney'*.

Quentin, Quintin (f.): Latin *Quin(c)tinus*, a derivative of *quinctus* 'fifth'. The town of St. *Quentin* in the north of France was the burial place of St. *Quentin*, martyred *c.* 287, and the name became common in the district and was brought to England by the Normans. It is found in the 11th to 13th C and survived in Scotland until the 17th C. It has been revived in recent times, perhaps after Scott's *Quentin Durward*.

QUINTINUS DB 1086, Cur 1199, 1200, 1213, Pat 1492.

R

Rachel (f.): Hebrew 'ewe'; a common name among the Jews, but not used as a christian name in England until after the Reformation. In the 17th C, when it was used a good deal, it was often spelt *Rachael*.

Radegund (f.): Old German *Radagundis*, compound of *radi* 'counsel' and *gundi* 'war'. St. *Radegund* was a 6th-C Queen of the Franks, wife of Clothaire I, and there are several English church dedications to her. Jesus College, Cambridge, in 1490 took over the property and dedication of the nunnery of St. *Radegund*. The name is not recorded in the Middle Ages, but the parish registers of Bengeworth, Worcs., *c.* 1580, have examples of children of both sexes being christened *Radegund*, and Lyford gives it in his list of christian names.

Ralph (m.) [rāf, rălf]: Old Norse *Raðulfr* (= Old English *Rædwulf*, compound of *ræd* 'counsel' and *wulf* 'wolf'), became *Radulf* and then *Ralf*. It was in use in England before the Norman Conquest, after which it was reinforced by Norman influence; DB mentions tenants named *Radulfus* who had held TRE, and many at the time the survey was made. It developed into *Rauf* or *Raff*, and these were the usual forms of the name until the 17th C, when *Rafe* was more usual. *Ralf* occurs in the 16th and 17th C and *Ralph* in the 18th C, but the pronunciation of the name was still

K

Rāfe. Recently, there have been signs that the spelling pronunciation *Rălf* (already general in Scotland and USA) is creeping into use. See also RAOUL.

RAUF, RAULF Reg 1066-70.
RADULF(US), RADOLF DB 1086, HR 1273.
RAFFE, RAUF HR 1273.
RAFE *Prompt Parv c.* 1440.
RAAF 15th C *Brut.*
RAUF Lincs 1455, Cov 1538.
RAFF Lincs 1533.
RAUFFE Lincs 1534.

Ranald, see RONALD.

Randal (m.): Old English *Randwulf,* compound of *rand* 'shield' and *wulf* 'wolf', was current in England before the Norman Conquest, after which it was reinforced by the corresponding Norman name derived from Norse *Ranðulfr.* The vernacular forms in the Middle Ages were *Ranulf* and *Randal,* which were latinized as *Rannulfus* and *Randulfus* respectively. The abbreviated form *Rand* and the diminutive *Rankin* were also common. The surnames *Randal(l), Randell, Randle, Rand, Randson, Rance, Ranson, Ransom, Rankin(g)* are derived from *Randal* and *Rand. Rannulf* appears to be obsolete. *Randal* was less common after the 15th C, but has never altogether died out and is also used in the gipsy families of Smith, Boss, and Lee. 18th-C antiquarianism coined the form *Randolph* from Latin *Randulfus.*

RANNULFUS, RANDULFUS DB 1086.
RANULPHUS Reg 1093-1100.
RANNULFUS Cur 1186-1220.
RANDOLPH Cur 1201.
RANULF HR 1273.
RANULPH HR 1273.
RANDLE Cheshire 1290.
RANDULL Cov 1481, Chester 1565.
RAND Yorks Poll Tax 1379.

Randolph, see RANDAL.

Raoul (m.) [rah'ōol]: French form of *Radulf* (see RALPH); not uncommon in England in the Middle Ages, especially in the diminutive forms *Raoulin, Raoulet,* whence the surnames *Rawle,*

Rawlin(gs), *Rawlinson*, *Rowlett*, &c. This form of the name died out with the use of French, but *Raoul* made its appearance again after the War of 1914–18, when it seems to have taken the fancy of British soldiers in France.

RAWLIN Exch R 1306.
RAULYN Writs of Parliament 1306.

Raphael (m.): Hebrew 'God has healed', the name of one of the archangels. It was used as a personal name among the Jews, and as a christian name in Italy in the Middle Ages. In England it seems always to be Jewish.

Ray (m., f.): usually a pet-form of *Rachel* or *Raymond* (qq.v.), but now sometimes used as an independent name. The scientist Sir *Ray* Lankester was named after John Ray, the 17th-C botanist, his father being secretary to the Ray Society.

Raymond (m.): Old German *Raginmund*, compound of *ragan* 'counsel', 'might', and *mund* 'protection'. It was introduced into England by the Normans in the form *Raimund* or *Reimund*. The surnames *Raymond*, *Reymond*, *Rayment* are derived from it.

RAIMUNDUS DB 1086, Cur 1200, 1201, 1210.
RAYMUNDUS FA 1346.
REIMOND Cl 1245.
REIMUND HR 1273.

Rayner (m.): Old German *Raganher*, compound of *ragan* 'counsel', 'might', and *harja* 'army', 'folk'. There was a corresponding Old English *Regenhere*, but it was not much used, and the common medieval *Rayner*, *Rainer*, &c., was introduced by the Normans and derived from the Old German name. It was in general use from the 12th to 14th C and gave rise to the surnames *Rayner*, *Raynor*, *Reyner*, &c.

RAINERUS, RAINERIUS, RAYNERUS DB 1086, Cur 1186–1220.
REYNER HR 1273, Cl 1320.

Rebecca, **Rebekah** (f.): Hebrew possibly 'heifer', a common Jewish name, not used as a christian name until after the Reformation. It was much used in the 17th C. Sometimes abbreviated to *Becky*; *Beck* occurs in Brome's *The Sparagus Garden* (1640).

Regina (f.) [rĕjī'na]: Latin *regina* 'queen'. Sometimes used as a christian name in the Middle Ages, probably with reference to the Blessed Virgin as Queen of Heaven. *Regina* and *Reina* occur in 13th-C Latin records. The spoken version of the name was probably the French *Reine*. *Regina* has continued to be used in Italy, Germany, and Scandinavia, and was occasionally revived in England in the 19th C.

Reginald, see REYNOLD.

René (m.) [rĕn'ā]: French, from Latin *renatus* 'born again'. St. *René* or *Renatus* was Bishop of Angers from 426, and his name became common in France. It has occasionally been borrowed in England, and *Renatus* was used in the 17th C (cf. Beatus, Desideratus, Fortunatus, &c.). The German f. name *Renate* is also sometimes used.

Renée (f.): French f. form of *René* (q.v.) sometimes used in England.

Renfred (m.): Old German *Raganfrid*, compound of *ragan* 'counsel', 'might', and *frithu* 'peace'. The name was introduced into England by the Normans and was not uncommon from the 12th to 16th C, appearing variously as *Reimfred*, *Reynfrey*, *Remfrey*, &c. *Renfry* was still used in Cornwall in the 19th C.

REIMFRED Cur 1186, 1220.
REYNFREY HR 1273.
REINFRIDUS Testa de Neville 13th C.
REMFREY St. Columb 1542, 1551.
REYNFRED Lyford 1655.

Reuben (m.): Hebrew possibly 'renewer', i.e. a child taking the place of one that has died; the name of one of the sons of Jacob and of a tribe of Israel. Its use in England dates from the 17th C.

Rex (m.): Latin *rex* 'king'. Its use as a christian name is modern and was not known to CMY. It is sometimes used as an abbreviation for *Reginald* (q.v.).

Reynard (m.): Old German *Raganhard* compound of *ragan* 'counsel', 'might', and *hardu* 'hard'. It was introduced into England by the Normans in the form *Rainard* or *Reynard*, but was never so common as *Rayner* and *Reynaud* (or *Reynold*) with which it is sometimes confused.

Reynold (m.) [rěn'old]: Old English *Regenweald*, compound of *regen* and *weald*, both of which mean 'power', 'force', 'might', was not a very common name. After the Norman Conquest it was reinforced by French *Reinald* or *Reynaud* from the corresponding Old German *Raganald*, which became a favourite name. In Middle English it is usually *Rainald* or *Reynold* (latinized as *Rainaldus*, *Reynoldus*, and occasionally *Reginaldus*). The surnames *Reynold(s)*, *Reynoldson*, *Rennell*, *Reynell*, *Rennison*, *Renaud*, *Renaut* are derived from it. In the 15th C such forms as *Raignald*, *Reignald*, *Reignolde*, *Reginalde* came into use. The reappearance of the *g* after several centuries of disuse may have been an early example of the effect of antiquarianism on names. Both *Reginald* and *Reynold* became much less common after the 15th C. Neither Camden nor Lyford gives them (though they have the German *Reinhold*), but *Reynold* has never quite died out in the West country, and *Reginald* was revived in the 19th C and is now common. See also RONALD. *Reginald* is often abbreviated to *Reg* [rěj] or *Reggy* [rěj'ě]; the earliest example of this which has been noted is in C. Reade's 'Love me Little, Love me Long' (1859).

RAINALD(US), RAGENALD, RAYNALDUS, RAYNOLDUS, REINOLD(US), RENOLDUS DB 1086.
REGINALDUS FA 1284.
REYNALD HR 1273.
REYNOLD HR 1273.
REYNAUD HR 1273.
RENAUT Testa de Neville 1379.
RAIGNALD Cov 1424.
REIGNALD Cov 1444.
REGINALDE Oseney 1460.
REGINALD or REYNOLD Oxf Univ Reg 1566.

Rhoda (f.): derivative of Greek ῥόδον 'rose'; the name of a girl mentioned in Acts xii. 13. It came into use as a christian name in the 17th C.

Rhys (m.) [rēs]: a common Welsh christian name, the origin of the surnames *Reece, Rice, Price, Preece* (= *ap Rhys*).

Richard (m.): the existence of an Old English *Richeard*, compound of *ric* 'ruler' and *heard* 'hard', is not certain, though both elements were in use. The great popularity of the name *Richard* in the Middle Ages was due to importation from the Continent, the Normans bringing in French *Richard* (from the corresponding Old German *Ricohard*). The allied name *Richer* was also common until at least the middle of the 13th C. In Latin MSS. the abbreviations *Rich.* and *Ric.* are used for *Richer* and *Ric(h)ard*, respectively. *Richard* and *Ricard* were equally common in the Middle Ages, together with many nicknames and diminutives, such as *Rich(ie)*, *Hitch, Rick, Hick, Dick, Dickon, Ricket, Hicket*, which in turn gave rise to an immense number of surnames. *Richard* has maintained its position as one of the half-dozen favourite men's names with singularly little fluctuation of fashion, though it was rather less common in the 18th C. *Richie* is still used as a pet-form in USA, but *Dick* is universal in England. *Dick* and *Hick* (now obsolete) were among the earliest of this kind of rhyming nickname (cf. *Polly* from *Molly, Bob* from *Rob, Hodge* from *Roger*), the first example noted being a record in Cur 1220 '*quidam Dicke Smith*'. *Dick*, like *Jack*, was formerly used as a colloquial term for 'man', 'fellow', &c., e.g. 'You are a gone *dick*'. The proverbial *Any Tom, Dick, or Harry* is indicative of the long-established popularity of the name. The peculiar pet-form *Hudde*, which was common in the 13th and 14th C, has long been obsolete, though its traces survive in the surnames *Hudd, Hudson*; Bardsley gives examples which prove that *Hudd* was a form of *Richard*, e.g. 'Ricardus dictus Hudde de Walkden', 'Ricardus de Knapton et Cristiana hud-wyf'.

RICARD(US) DB 1086, Cur 1186–1220, HR 1273.
RICARD Exch R 1306.
RYCHARDE *Prompt Parv c.* 1440.

Richenda, &c. (f.): *Richenda, Richarda, Richenza* are all from compounds of Old German *ric* (Modern German *reich*) 'ruler', and are recorded very early. They have occasionally been used in

England as f. forms of *Richard* (q.v.). In the 16th C the diminutive *Richardyne* is found. Other compounds are *Richolda*, recorded in the 13th C, and *Richoard*, fairly common in Devon in the 17th C. *Richenda* was used by the Gurney's in the 18th C.

Rita [rē'ta], see MARGARET.

Robert (m.): Old English *Hreodbeorht* was reinforced at the time of the Norman Conquest by French *Robert* from the cognate Old German *Hrodebert*, a compound of *hrothi* 'fame' and *berhta* 'bright'. It occurs frequently in DB, and has been a favourite name ever since. The nicknames *Rob, Hob, Dob, Nob,* and (later) *Bob*, were all commonly used, and *Robin*, a diminutive form of *Rob*, was in the 13th C more usual than *Robert* itself. In Scotland the forms *Hab* and *Rab* are found in some districts (cf. *Tam* and *Tom*). Among the many surnames derived from *Robert* and its nicknames are *Roberts(on)*, *Robins(on)*, *Robson*, *Robeson*, *Nobbs*, *Hobb(e)s*, *Hobson*, *Hopkins*, *Dobb(s)*, *Dobson*, &c. In Middle English the form *Robard* was not unusual (cf. *Hubbard* for *Hubert*), and is given in *Promptorium Parvulorum* as the English equivalent of *Robertus*. *Robin* is now sometimes used as an independent name.

RODBERTUS, ROTBERT(US), ROBERT(US) Reg 1071–5, DB 1086.
ROBERTUS Cur 1186–1220, HR 1273.
ROBIN Cur 1200, 1205, 1210, Cl 1276.
ROBYN Coventry Mysteries 15th C.
ROBARD St. Mary at Hill 1507.

Roberta, Robina (f.) [robert'a, robēn'a]: f. forms of *Robert* and *Robin* (q.v.). An early example is *Robina* Cromwell, sister of the Protector, but these forms have been used mainly in Scotland. Dickens, *c.* 1855, notes *Rubina* and *Rebinah*, which are presumably phonetic renderings of *Robina*, as occurring in Privy Council Education Lists.

Robin, see ROBERT.

Roderick (m.): Old German *Hrodric*, compound of *hrothi* 'fame' and *ricja* 'rule', was the source of Russian *Rurik* and of Spanish *Roderigo*, but has not taken deep root elsewhere. *Roderick*, however, is not infrequent in Scotland, where it is used to render the

Gaelic *Ruaidhri* 'the red' (the Irish equivalent is *Rory*). It is used particularly by the Mackenzies and McLeods. The corresponding Welsh name *Rhydderch* was rendered as *Rotheric*; *Rothericus* son of Gryfin is mentioned in FA 1303 (cf. the surname *Protheroe* = *ap Rhydderch*).

Rodney (m.): a Somerset surname, derived from the village of *Rodney Stoke*. It is now well established as a christian name, after the famous admiral, Lord *Rodney* (1719–92).

Roger (m.): Old English *Hrothgar* was reinforced at the time of the Norman Conquest by French *Roger*, from the corresponding Old German *Hrodgar*, compound of *hrothi* 'fame' and *ger* 'spear'. *Rogerus* is frequent in DB, and *Roger* was a favourite throughout the Middle Ages. Together with its nicknames *Hodge* and *Dodge*, it gave rise to a multitude of surnames, e.g. *Roger(s)*, *Rodger(s)*, *Hodge(s)*, *Dodge*, *Hodgkins*, *Hodgkiss*, *Hotchkiss*, *Hodgkinson*, &c. The colloquial use of *Hodge* to denote an agricultural labourer is an indication of the former frequency of the name. After falling into desuetude in the 18th and 19th C (though it was always used in some families), *Roger* has now regained some measure of favour.

ROGER(I)US Reg 1071–5, DB 1086, Cur 1186–1220, HR 1273, Yorks Poll Tax 1379.
ROTGERIUS Reg 1088–91.

Roland, Rowland (m.): Old German *Hrodland*, compound of *hrothi* 'fame' and *landa* 'land'. As the name of the most famous of the peers of Charlemagne, *Roland* was a favourite in the Middle Ages and was introduced into England by the Normans (*Rolland* occurs in DB), the usual English form of the name being *Rouland* or *Rowland*. *Rowland* was, indeed, the usual spelling in the 17th and 18th C, and the modern *Roland* is a piece of archaizing.

ROLLAND DB 1086.
ROLANDUS Cur 1186–1220, FA 1316, 1428.
ROULAND Testa de Neville 13th C.
ROWLAND Lincs 1529, Lyford 1655.

Rolf (m.): Old German *Hrodulf*, compound of *hrothi* 'fame' and *vulf* 'wolf' (see RUDOLF), and the cognate Old Norse *Hrólfr*, developed into *Rolf* in Normandy (cf. *Ralph* from *Raðulfr*). It was introduced into England by the Normans and survived long enough to originate the surnames *Rolf(e)*, *Rolfes*, *Rolph*, but it disappeared fairly early, perhaps on account of its likeness to the more popular *Ralf*. It has been revived of late. *Rolf* was sometimes latinized as *Rollo*, which was occasionally used as a christian name in the 19th C.

ROULF, ROLF, ROLFT DB 1086.
ROLF HR 1273.

Rollo, see ROLF.

Roma (f.): the name of the city, recently used as a christian name (cf. *Florence*).

Romola (f.) [rŏm'ola]: Italian f. of *Romolo*, Latin *Romulus*. It has occasionally been given as a christian name in England after George Eliot's novel *Romola* (1862–3).

Ronald (m.): *Ronald* and *Ranald* (Gaelic *Raonull*) are the Scottish equivalents of *Reynold* or *Reginald* (q.v.), but are derived from the Norse version of the name, *Rögnvaldr*. *Ronald* is now often used by persons of non-Scottish descent.

Rory (m.): Modern Irish form of Gaelic *Ruaidhri*, a derivative of *ruadh* 'red'. It is often rendered by *Roger*. See also RODERICK.

Rosa (f.): latinization of *Rose* (q.v.), which came into use in the 19th C.

Rosabel (f.): an 18th-C invention, formed on the model of *Christabel*, *Claribel*, &c.

Rosalie (f.) [rŏz'alĕ, rōz'alĕ]: this is apparently Latin *rosalia*, the annual ceremony of hanging garlands of roses on tombs. St. *Rosalia* was a 12th-C Sicilian recluse, patron saint of Palermo.

Her name was used in Italy and spread to France, where *Rosalie* is not uncommon. It has sometimes been borrowed and used in England.

Rosalind (f.) [rŏz'alĭnd]: Old German *Roslindis*, compound of (*h*)*ros* 'horse' and *lindi* 'serpent'. The name was carried to Spain by the Goths and took root there as *Rosalinda*. The modern use of it in England is probably owing to Shakespeare's *Rosalind* in *As You Like It*. Thackeray uses it in *The Newcomes* (1854) and Trollope in *The American Senator* (1877). *Rosaline* (e.g. in *Romeo and Juliet* and *Love's Labour's Lost*) is presumably the same name. This form has been used occasionally in recent times.

Rosamund, Rosamond (f.) [rŏz'amund]: Old German *Rosamunda*, compound of (*h*)*ros* 'horse' and *munda* 'protection'. In the Middle Ages, however, it was regarded as a Latin name *rosa+munda* = 'pure or clean rose'. It was introduced into England by the Normans, a famous example being *Rosamund* Clifford (died 1176), the unfortunate mistress of Henry II. The surnames *Roseaman, Rosomon, Rosemond, Rosamund* are derived from it. *Rosamund*, unlike many names of Germanic origin, survived the Renaissance and was fairly common in the 17th C, usually spelt *Rosamond* (the French form, cf. *Edmond* for *Edmund*), held its own in the 18th and 19th C, and is now somewhat more common than it has been for several centuries.

ROSAMUNDA Cur 1205, 1207, HR 1273.
ROSEMUNDA FA 1303.
ROSAMOND FF 1282.
ROSSAMOND Yorks Rec 1604.
ROZEMAN St. Clerkenwell 1665.

Rose (f.): although this name has, from a fairly early date, been identified with the flower-name and latinized as *Rosa*, it seems actually to be a derivative of (*h*)*ros* 'horse' (cf. *Rosalind, Rosamund*). It was introduced into England by the Normans in the form *Roese, Rohese* (Latin *Roesia, Rohesia*), which became *Royse* (latinized as *Roysia*) and *Rose* in Middle English (cf. surnames *Royce, Royse, Rose*). *Promptorium Parvulorum* gives it as *Rose,*

Latin *Rosa.*

ROESIA Cur 1199–1220.
ROHESIA, ROHEIS Cur 1164.
ROYSIA FA 1303.
ROSA FA 1316, HR 1273, Yorks Poll Tax 1379.
ROSEIA FA 1346.
ROSE FA 1316.
ROYSE Godstow 1450.
ROOS Lincs 1529.

Roseanna (f.) [rōz′ăna]: an 18th-C mixture of *Rose* and *Anna.*

Rosemary (f.) [rŏz′marĕ]: the first occurrence of this name is *Rosemary* Dacre (afterwards Lady Clerk), b. 1745 at *Rose* Castle, Cumb. The baptismal register gives her name as Mary, but her own account of her baptism gives it as *Rosemary*, and this name has been used since in the Dacre and Clerk families. It has become a fairly common name during the 20th C. For the circumstances of *Rosemary* Dacre's baptism see *Trans. of the Cumb. & West. Antiq. & Arch. Soc.* 8, 1886 (237).

Rosetta (f.): a diminutive of *Rose* (q.v.), sometimes used in the 18th and 19th C. The Spanish and Italian diminutives *Rosita* and *Rosina* are also sometimes used.

Rowena (f.) [rōē′na]: this name seems to originate with Geoffrey of Monmouth, who gives it to the daughter of Hengist, with whom Vortigern fell in love. It may be Old English *Hrōðwyn*, a compound of *hreod* 'fame' and *wine* 'friend'. Scott used it for the Saxon heroine of *Ivanhoe*, and *Rowena* (like *Cedric* (q.v.)) came into use as a result of the popularity of that novel.

Rowland, see ROLAND.

Roy (m.): originally a Gaelic name, derivative of *ruadh* 'red'. It is now fairly common in England as well as Scotland.

Ruby (f.): the name of a precious stone; its use as a christian name is modern (cf. *Diamond, Emerald, Pearl*, &c.).

Rudolf (m.): the Modern German form of Old German *Hrodulf* (see ROLF). Occasionally borrowed from Germany in recent times.

Rufus (m.): Latin *rufus* 'red-haired'; used by Jews instead of *Reuben*, and in USA sometimes by others.

Rupert (m.): Old German *Hrodebert* (see ROBERT) developed into Modern German *Rupprecht*. The name was first introduced into England by Prince *Rupprecht* of the Palatinate, the nephew of Charles I, whose name on English lips became *Rupert* (his contemporaries also often called him Prince *Robert*). It is the admiration felt for him that is responsible for the modern vogue of the name in England, which is not mentioned by CMY.

Ruperta (f.): f. form of *Rupert*, first used for a daughter of Prince *Rupert*.

Russell (m.): a surname derived from the nickname *russell* or *rousselle*, a diminutive of French *roux* 'red'. Its use as a christian name is paralleled by that of other names of famous families, e.g. *Cecil*, *Sidney*, *Mortimer*, *Montague*, and is comparatively recent.

Ruth (f.): a Hebrew or Moabitish name of doubtful etymology. First used as a christian name in England after the Reformation. *Ruthe* Evans 1589 is the earliest example noted.

S

Sabin(a) (m., f.) [săb'ĭn, sab'ĭna, săbēn'a]: Latin *Sabinus*, *Sabina* 'Sabine man or woman', a common Roman cognomen. St. *Sabinus*, a 4th-C Bishop of Spoleto, and St. *Sabina*, a Roman matron martyred under Hadrian, ensured the survival of the name. Both became *Sabin* in English, and the name is found from the 12th C, giving rise to the surnames *Sabbe*, *Sab(e)y*, *Sabin(e)*, *Saben*, &c. As a man's name it died out, but *Sabina* survived in rustic use until the 19th C and is not yet extinct.
SABINA Cur 1199–1215, FA 1303.
SABYN HR 1273, Coventry Mysteries 15th C.

Sacheverell (m.) [sashĕv′erel]: the surname of an ancient, but now extinct, family. The origin of the name is obscure; it is sometimes derived from the castle of *Saute de Chevreuil* in Normandy; but one example quoted by Bardsley from the year 1273, where it is given as *Saucheverel alias Sauzcheverel alias Saunz Cheverel*, looks like a Norman nickname '*Sans Cheverel*'; *cheverel* was Old French for a kid and for the leather made from kid-hide. In the early 18th C *Sacheverell* was often given as a christian name in honour of Dr. *Sacheverell* (1674–1724) the Tory preacher, and it is said to have survived in rural districts in the last century. The Sitwell family, who continue to use it to the present day take the name from William *Sacheverell* (1638–91) one of the founders of the Whig party.

Sadie, see SARA(H).

Saer, Sayer (m.): Old German *Sigiheri* (Old English *Sigehere*), compound of *sigu* 'victory' and *harja* 'the host' or 'people'. *Sagar, Saer,* or *Sayer* was a popular name in medieval England, and Bardsley lists some 20 or 25 surnames derived from it. It seems to have died out completely in the course of the 14th C.

SAGAR(US), SEGAR(US) DB 1086.
SAER Cur 1200.
SAERUS HR 1273.
SAYER HR 1273.
SAGARD Exch R 1306.

Salathiel (m.): Babylonian *Salti-ila* meaning 'the god is my . . .' (the meaning of the first element is unknown). This was taken over by the Hebrews as *Shaltiel* and sometimes Hebraized as *Šealtiel* 'request(ed) of God'. Both forms occur in the Book of Haggai. The Vulgate has Salathiel both there and in Matt. i. where it occurs in a genealogy as the father of Zerubbabel. It was used as a christian name from the 16th C (cf. Ben Jonson's epitaph on *Salathiel* Pavy, a child of Queen Elizabeth's chapel. *Salathiel,* son of *Salathiel* Symdsion was baptized in 1711 at Edgington, Wilts.

Sally, see SARA(H).

Salome (f.): originally Aramaic *Shalam-zion* 'peace of Zion', abbreviated to *Shalamzu*, and then hellenized as *Salome*. A favourite name in the Herod family. *Salome* was also the name of one of the women who ministered to Jesus, who was first at the sepulchre on Easter morning. It has been used as a christian name since the 17th C. It is now usually pronounced salō'mĕ, but the medieval pronunciation, according to Maurice of Kirkham (see p. xxxvii) was sal'omĕ, with a tendency to suppress the final *e*.

Sam(p)son (m.): Hebrew 'child of Shamash (the sun-god)', 'sun child', rendered in Greek as *Σαμπσών*; the name of the great champion of the Israelites against the Philistines. *Samson* was the name of a Welsh bishop (fl. 550) who crossed over to Brittany and founded the abbey of Dôl, where he was buried and later venerated as a saint. It is impossible to say whether he was named after the Biblical *Samson*, or whether his name was of Celtic origin, but there is no doubt that the prevalence of the name in Brittany and Normandy, whence it was carried to England, was due to his fame. The name was common in England from the end of the 11th C, spelt sometimes *Samson* or *Sampson*, sometimes *Sanson* or *Sansum* (from French *Sanson*). An early example is *Samson*, Bishop of Worcester, brother of Thomas, first Norman Archbishop of York. The surnames *Sam(m)s*, *Sam(p)son*, *Sansom(e)*, *Sanson*, *Sansum* testify to its popularity. In the 17th C the name was reinforced by Biblical influence, but it died out after the Restoration.

SAMPSON Reg 1074–85.
SANSON DB 1086.
SAMSON Cur 1196–1215, HR 1273, FA 1431.
SAMPSON, SANSON, SAUNSUM Testa de Neville 13th C,
SAMPSON FA 1302, 1346.
SANSUM HR 1273.

Samuel (m.): Hebrew 'name of God' or 'Shum (is) God', for there is much evidence for a god called *Shum* or *Shem*. The name of one of the greatest of the Hebrew prophets, who anointed Saul as first king of Israel. *Samuel* was rare as a christian name in the Middle Ages, though examples occur in 12th-C records, and the surnames *Samuel*, *Samwell* occur as early as 1273. Not all of these were Jewish, though some may have been. After the Reformation *Samuel* became a favourite name, an early example being *Samuel* Daniel the poet (1562–1619). It continued in general use after the Restoration, when many Biblical names went out, and is still a common working-class name, usually abbreviated to *Sam*. In Scotland it has been used to render *Somerled* (Gaelic *Somhairle*), a borrowing from Old Norse *Sumarliði*, 'summer wanderer', 'viking', which came to be used as a christian name.

Sanchia (f.): Spanish and Provençal *Sancha* or *Sanchia*, f. of *Sancho*, from Latin *sanctus* 'holy'. Introduced into England by the marriage in 1243 of Richard, Earl of Cornwall, to *Sanchia*, daughter of the Count of Provence. Her name evidently puzzled English scribes, who write it in a variety of ways, including *Cynthia*, *Scientia*, and *Science*. The name occurs during the next four centuries, variously spelt *Sens, Sence, Sense, Saints, Science, Sanche*. An example is a record in 1620 of 'James Bynde and *Sanctia* or *Sence* his wife'. Lyford (1655) gives *Sanchia* in his list of women's names. *Sence, Senses, Saint*, and *Sayntes* occur in 18th-C and early-19th-C Lincs. records. *Sanchia* is still occasionally used.

Sandra (f.): Italian diminutive of *Alessandra*, now sometimes used as a diminutive of *Alexandra* (q.v.), and recently as an independent name.

Sandy, see ALEXANDER.

Sara(h) (f.): Hebrew 'princess'. The wife of Abraham, whose name was originally *Sarai* 'contentious', was later called *Sarah*. *Sara* is the hellenized form of the name. It is found in use in England as a christian name from the 12th C, usually in the form *Sarra*, but was not really common until after the Reformation, when *Sarah* becomes the usual spelling. In the 17th C the form *Sarey* is found (cf. the vulgar 19th-C pronunciation, e.g. '*Sairey Gamp*'). In the 18th and 19th C the compound *Saranna* (*Sara+Anna*) had a certain vogue. The usual pet-form of the name is *Sally* (cf. *Mally* for *Mary*, *Hal* for *Harry*); in USA sometimes

Sadie (cf. *Maidie* for *Mary*). In Ireland *Sarah* has been used to render the native *Sorcha* and *Saraid*.
SARRA Cur 1189–1215, HR 1273, FA 1303, 1316.
SARA Yorks Poll Tax 1379.

Saul (m.): Hebrew 'asked for', the name of the first King of Israel, and later of *Saul* of Tarsus. Occasionally used as a christian name since the 17th C.

Scholastica (f.): f. of Latin *scholasticus*, Greek σχολαστικος 'scholar'. St. *Scholastica* was the sister of St. Benedict (*c.* 480–543) and the first nun of his order. Benedictine influence carried the name to England where it is found as a christian name from the beginning of the 13th C until the Reformation. A 14th-C Legendary gives *Scholace*, and Godstow (1450) gives *Scholast*, as the English form. Camden (1604) and Lyford (1655) both give *Scholastica* in their lists of women's names.
SCHOLASTICA Cur 1200, 1207, 1210, FA 1316, 1346, Salop Reg 1635.
SCHOLACE 14th C Legendary.
SCHOLAST Godstow 1450.

Sean (m.) [shawn]: Irish for *John* (q.v.), through Norman-French *Jean*. The original Irish form of the name was *Eóin* (see EUGENE.)

Sebastian (m.): Latin *Sebastianus* 'man of *Sebastia*' (a city of Pontus, from Greek σεβαστός 'venerable', modern *Sebaste*). St. *Sebastian* was a Roman legionary martyred under Diocletian. His martyrdom, by being shot with arrows, was a favourite subject of medieval art. As a christian name, *Sebastian* was particularly common in Spain, and in France where it became *Bastien*. *Bastian* and *Sebastian* have been used in Cornwall at least since the 16th C and probably earlier, for the surnames *Bastian, Bastin, Bastion*, &c., would seem to be derived from them.

Secundus (m.): Latin 'second', sometimes used as a christian name.

Selina (f.) [selē'na]: the history of this name is obscure. The first example noted is 1619 *Zelina* Gardener. *Selinah* occurs in 1687, *Sillina* in 1697. *Celina* or *Selina* Finch, born about 1680, married the 1st Earl Ferrers, and her daughter *Selina* Shirley became the Methodist Countess of Huntingdon. The name has ever since been current in the Shirley and Finch families and in other families connected with them. There is no reason to identify the name, as is sometimes done, with Greek σελήνη 'the moon', and on the whole it seems as if CMY may be right in taking it to be from French *Céline* (Latin *Coelina*, derivative of *caelum* 'heaven') the name of a 5th-C saint, mother of St. Rémy. This is borne out by occasional spellings *Celina*.

Selwyn (m.): the surname *Selwyn*, which is first recorded in the 13th C, may be from the Old English *Selewine*, a compound of *sele* 'house' and *wine* 'friend', though that name was a rare one and has not been noted after the 11th C. The current use of *Selwyn* as a christian name (particularly common in Wales) may be after George Augustus *Selwyn* (1809–78), Bishop of New Zealand and later of Lichfield, after whom *Selwyn* College, Cambridge, was named. CMY, who was a great admirer of the bishop, does not mention this name.

Septimus (m.): Latin 'seventh', often given to a seventh child in the 19th C, occasionally used without any numerical significance.

Seraphina (f.): Latin f. derivative of *seraph* (Hebrew 'noble', 'burning one'), the name of an early saint. Both it and the Spanish diminutive *Seraphita* were occasionally used in the 19th C.

Serena (f.): f. of Latin *serenus* 'calm', 'serene'. This name has been noted once in the 13th C, again in Notts in 1761, and in New England in 1830.

Serle (m.): Old English *Serlo*, Old German *Sarilo*, derivative of *sarva* 'armour'. The name was in use before the Norman Conquest, but was much commoner afterwards, being a favourite with the Normans; it died out after the 14th C. The surnames *Serle, Searl(e), Serrell, Serrill(s)* are derived from it.

SERLO DB 1086, Cur 1186–1215, FA 1346.
SERLE 15th-C Brut, HR 1273.
SERILL, SERELL Yorks Poll Tax 1379.

Seth (m.): Hebrew 'substitute', 'compensation', the name of one of the sons of Adam, born after the death of Abel. It was used as a christian name after the Reformation, the earliest example noted being *Seth* Holywell (died 1557), whose name occurs in a Hunts. Clergy List. It is now seldom used in England, but is commoner in the USA.

Seumus (m.): Irish form of *James* (q.v.).

Sewal (m.): Old English *Sigeweald*, compound of *sige* 'victory' and *weald* 'strength'. It survived as late as the 16th C.
SEWALLUS HR 1273.
SEWALE HR 1273.

Sextus (m.): Latin *sextus* 'sixth', occasionally used as a christian name for a sixth child, or a sixth son.

Shamus (m.): phonetic rendering of *Seumus*, Irish form of *James* (q.v.).

Shane (m.) [shawn]: phonetic rendering of *Sean*, Irish form of *John* (q.v.).

Sheila (f.): phonetic rendering of *Sile*, the Irish form of *Celia* from *Cecilia* (q.v.). Now extensively used in England as an independent name. In the 19th C *Sheila* was often rendered by *Julia* in Ireland.

She(e)na (f.): phonetic rendering of Gaelic *Sìne* = *Jane* (q.v.).

Shirley (f.): this is apparently a surname (derived from a place-name) used as a christian name. The first example noted is the heroine of Charlotte Brontë's novel *Shirley* (1849), who, as an only child and an heiress, was given 'the masculine cognomen' *Shirley*, a family name. I have found no clue to the modern prevalence of *Shirley* as a christian name in the Southern States of USA. It has now become a common name in England, owing to the number of children named after the child film-star, *Shirley* Temple.

Sholto (m.): this name seems to be used exclusively by the Douglas family. It was first used by them at the beginning of the 18th C, when the genealogists had derived the family from one *Sioltaich Dhu Glas, Sioltaich* meaning 'sower'.

Sibyl (f.): Greek *Σίβυλλα*, Medieval Latin *Sibilla, Sibylla, Sibulla*, the name of the women who acted as mouthpieces of the ancient oracles. From about 200 B.C. collections of alleged sibylline oracles were written and propagated by the Jews, and later by Christians. St. Augustine admits the sibyl to the City of God, and in general it was believed that the sibylline oracles represented one form of divine revelation (cf. the *Dies Irae*, 'teste David cum Sibylla'). *Sibylla*, accordingly, came to be used as a christian name, and it was introduced into England after the Norman Conquest. Robert, Duke of Normandy, son of the Conqueror, married *Sibylla* of Conversane. From the 12th C onwards the name was common. Its spelling was erratic, and the misspelling *Sybil* is common to the present day. *Sibley* was the usual Middle English form of the name and is still occasionally used in Scotland. The surnames *Sibley, Sibbs, Sibson, Sibbet* are derived from it and its abbreviation *Sib*. *Sibyl* went out of fashion after the Reformation, but never became obsolete. Its revival in the 19th C may have been partly due to Disraeli's novel *Sybil* (1845). The Latin forms *Sibylla, Sibella* are sometimes used.

SIBILLA Cur 1196–1215, FA 1316, Yorks Poll Tax 1379.
SIBILIA HR 1273, Yorks Poll Tax 1379.
SIBILIE, SIBELY HR 1273.
SYBYLE, SYBBLY, SIBBE *Prompt Parv* 1440.
SIBELL Cov 1434.
SYBILL Lincs 1455.
SYBELL Lincs 1533.
SIBOTA Yorks Poll Tax 1379.
SYBBY *Cocke Lorelle's Bote c.* 1515.
SYBYLY Coventry Mysteries 15th C.

Sidney (m.): the *Sidney* family was founded in England by William *Sidney* or *Sydney*, the Chamberlain of Henry II, who came from Anjou. The name appears regularly in Latin as *de Sancto Dionisio*, &c., and there can be little doubt that it is a reduction of *St. Denis* (cf. Semple for St. Paul, Sellinger for St. Leger, Simbarb for St. Barbe). The use of *Sidney* as a christian name was no doubt partly due to the Whig idolization of the memory of Algernon *Sidney* (1622–83); one of the earliest recorded examples of the name is *Sidney* Beauclerk, 5th son of 1st Duke of St. Albans (born 1703). *Sidney* Herbert, Lord Herbert of Lea (born 1810), was no doubt named after his ancestress Mary *Sidney*, sister of Sir Philip *Sidney*. Another early example of the name is *Sydney* Dobell, the poet, born 1824. *Sydney*, New South Wales, was named after Thomas Townshend, 1st Viscount *Sydney* (1733–1800), who was Secretary of State at the time of its foundation.

Sidney (f.): this is not uncommon as a woman's name in Ireland, and is probably a survival of *Sidony* (q.v.) rather than the family name; see above.

Sidony (f.) [sĭd'onĕ]: this name was formerly used by Roman Catholics for girls born about the date of the Feast of the Winding Sheet (i.e. of Christ), more formally alluded to as 'the Sacred *Sendon*'. *Sendon* or *Sindon* (from Latin *sindon*, Greek σινδών 'fine cloth', 'linen') was used in Middle English for a fine cloth, especially one used as a shroud. The Sacred *Sendon* is supposed to be preserved at Turin. That *Sidony* or *Sidonia* = *Sindonia* is shown by an example from Shropshire, 1793, '*Sidonia* or *Sindonia* Wilden'. *Sidonie* is not uncommon in France, and the Irish *Sidney* (q.v.) is probably really *Sidony*. No early example of the name has been found, but it seems likely that the surname *Siddons* has this origin.

Siegfried (m.): Old German *Sigifrith*, compound of *sigu* 'victory' and *frithu* 'peace'. Occasionally used as a christian name in England since the end of the 19th C, no doubt under the influence of Wagner's *Ring* (cf. *Brunhild*).

Sigrid (f.): Old Norse *Sigridhr*, compound of *sig* 'victory', and the common suffix *-ridhr*, the meaning of which is not clear. In recent times the name has sometimes been borrowed from Scandinavia, but it was also used in the 13th C, when *Sirida*, *Sierida*, *Sigerith* are recorded.

Silas (m.): apparently a shortened form of Latin *Silvanus*, the name of the god of trees. The person called *Silvanus* by St. Paul in 2 Cor. i. 19 is usually identified with the *Silas* of Acts. Neither name is found in use in England before the Reformation. *Silas* became fairly common in the 17th C, and continued to be used in Dissenting circles in the 18th and 19th C. *Silvanus* or *Sylvanus* has also occasionally been used, e.g. *Silvanus* Spencer eldest son of the poet.

Silvanus, see SILAS.

Silvester, Sylvester (m.): Latin *silvester* 'woody', 'growing or found in a wood'. It was the name of three popes, the first of whom, St. *Silvester*, was said to have baptized the Emperor Constantine, to have cured him of his leprosy, and to have received in return the 'Donation of Constantine'. The name was not uncommon in the Middle Ages (it is first noted in 1200) and gave rise to the surnames *Silvester*, *Sylvester*. Though less common since the Reformation, examples have been noted in the 16th, 17th, 18th, and 19th C; one in 1580 and one in 1623 are of *Silvester* as a woman's name.

SILVESTER Cur 1200–1215, FA 1303.
SILVESTRE HR 1273.

Silvia, Sylvia (f.): Latin f. of *Silvius*, derivative of *silva* 'wood'. *Rhea Silvia* was the name of the mother of Romulus and Remus, and it was probably from this that *Silvia* came into use as a christian name in Italy at the Renaissance. Shakespeare's use of it for one of the two heroines of *Two Gentlemen of Verona* is probably responsible for its modern use as a christian name in England, though Mrs. Gaskell's novel, *Sylvia's Lovers* probably had some influence.

Simeon (m.) [sĭm'ēŏn]: Hebrew *Shimeon* 'hearkening' (or possibly 'little hyena'). It was a common name in Israel. English versions of the Old Testament usually render it as *Simeon*, occasionally as *Shimeon*. In the New Testament, however, it is rendered as *Simon* (q.v.), except in the case of the aged *Simeon* who blessed the infant Jesus in the Temple. *Simeon* was kept separate from *Simon* in the Middle Ages, and though not a common name it is recorded from time to time and gave rise to a surname. After the Reformation it was used rather more often.

SIMEON Cur 1200.
SYMEON HR 1273.

Simon (m.) [sīmon]: the usual New Testament form of Hebrew *Shimeon* (see SIMEON). There was a Greek personal name *Σίμων*, derived from *σιμός* 'snub-nosed', and this probably influenced the later form of the name. No fewer than 8 persons of this name are mentioned in the New Testament as well as the aged *Simeon*. The great popularity of *Simon* as a christian name in the Middle Ages was due to *Simon Bar-Jonah* surnamed *Peter* (q.v.), the favourite apostle during that period. *Simon* almost rivalled *Peter* in frequency before the Reformation, and gave rise to a host of surnames, such as *Simon(s)*, *Sim*, *Sims*, *Simes*, *Syme*, *Sim(p)son*, *Simcock*, *Simcox*, *Sim(p)kin(s)*, *Simkinson*, *Sim(m)onds*, *Sinkins(on)*, *Sincox*, most of which are also found spelt with a *y*. The final *d* in *Simond* is a common development (cf. *Hammond* for *Hamon*), and *Promptorium Parvulorum* gives *Symounde* as the English form of Simon, while *Symond* is the usual spelling in the 15th and 16th C. The names *Simon*, *Simond'*, *Simund'* which occur in DB are probably not anything to do with *Simon*, but represent a Norman version of the name *Sigmund*, which existed in Old English as well as on the Continent. *Simon*, like *Peter*, went out of general use after the Reformation and has not since recovered its former popularity, though it is now more common than it has been for some centuries. The abbreviation *Sim* has been used since the 13th C. *Simon* has been used as a christian name by the Frasers of Lovat from the 12th C to the present day. In Ireland it has been used to represent the Irish *Sendn*.

SIMON Cur 1197–1215, FA 1284.
SIMOND HR 1273, Exch R 1306.
SYMOND Pat 1394, 15th-C Brut.
SYMOUNDE *Prompt Parv* 1440.
SYMKYN Cov 1480.
SYMME Coventry Mysteries 15th C.

Sis(sy), see CECILIA.

Siward (m.) [sē'ward]: Old English *Sigeweard*, compound of *sige* 'victory', and *weard* 'protection'. It was a common name before the Norman Conquest and continued in use until the 14th C, giving rise to the surnames *Seward, Seaward,* &c.
SEUUARD(US), SIUUARD(US) DB 1086.
SIWARDUS Cur 1197–1215, Pipe Roll 1159.
SYWARD(US) HR 1273.

Solomon (m.): Hebrew either 'little man of peace' or 'worshipper of (the god) Shalman', a well-known western semitic deity. *Salamon* was the usual medieval form of the name, which was not uncommon, and gave rise to the surnames *Salaman, Salmon, Salmond, Sammon, Sammond,* &c. The name died out about the beginning of the 14th C, but was revived by the Puritans in the 16th C. It is now used almost exclusively by Jews.

Somerled, see SAMUEL.

Sonia (f.) [sŏn'ya]: Russian diminutive of *Sophia* (q.v.). It came into use in England about 1920, perhaps as a result of Stephen McKenna's popular novel of that name (1917).

Sophia, Sophie (f.) [sofī'a, sŏf'ĕ]: Greek σοφία 'wisdom', was first used as a christian name in England in the 17th C (cf. *Alethea, Charis*: the youngest daughter of James I, born in 1607, who only lived for a day, was christened *Sophia*) and became common in the 18th C, being a favourite with German royal families. It was often anglicized to *Sophie* or *Sophy.* Admiral Croft, it will be remembered, wished that 'young ladies had not such a number of fine names. I should never be out, if they were all Sophys or something of that sort'. It went out of fashion during the later 19th C. *Sophia* has been used to render Gaelic *Beathag* (see BETHIA).

Stanislas (m.): Slavonic 'camp glory', the name of two Polish saints in the Roman calendar. Like another Polish name, *Casimir, Stanislas* has been used a good deal in France, and more rarely in England, chiefly by Roman Catholics.

Stanley (m.): a surname derived from a common place-name. It is not mentioned by CMY, and its use as a christian name is apparently a recent development, originally due to the popularity of the explorer Henry *Stanley* (1841–1904), whose real name was not *Stanley* but *Rowlands*. It is now a common christian name.

Stella (f.): Latin *stella* 'star'. The name was used by Sir Philip Sidney to address Penelope Rich in the sonnet sequence *Astrophel to Stella*. Later Waller also used it, and Swift bestowed it as a pet-name on Esther Johnson. The modern use of the name is doubtless often due to these literary associations, particularly those with Swift. An early example is the use of *Stella* and *Vanessa* for two of the daughters of Leslie Stephen (1832–1904). By Roman Catholics it is associated with *Stella maris*, a title of invocation of the Blessed Virgin Mary. One medieval example of the name has been noted in a Yorks Poll Tax return of 1379.

Stephanie (f.) [stĕf'anĕ]: French f. formed from Latin *Stephanus* (see STEPHEN), occasionally borrowed and used in England.

Stephen (m.): Greek Στεφανᾶς from στέφανος 'crown', a common Greek personal name, borne by the first christian martyr. *Stephanus, Stefanus* is found in England only as a monk's name before the Norman Conquest, but became a common christian name soon after. It occurs in DB. The surnames *Stephen(s)*, *Steven(s)*, *Stephenson*, *Stevenson*, *Steve(r)son, Stinson, Stim(p)son, Stenson, Steenson* are derived from it. *Stevyn* was the usual Middle English form.

STEFANUS DB 1086, Cur 1196–1220.
STEPHANUS HR 1273.
STEUEN Yorks Poll Tax 1379.
STEVEN Lincs 1450, *Cocke Lorelle's Bote c. 1515.*
STEVYN Lincs 1450, Cov 1491, *Prompt Parv* 1440.

Susan(nah) (f.): Hebrew *Shushannah* 'lily', the name of the heroine of the apocryphal Book of *Susannah and the Elders*. The name is found occasionally in the 13th C, but did not become common until the 17th C, when it often appears as *Susanney* and *Shusan(na)*. This 17th-C use probably had reference to the

Susanna mentioned in Luke viii. 3. In the 18th C it became very common, *Susan* being more usual, with *Sue* and *Sukey* as pet-forms. It was less popular in the later 19th C but is now again fashionable. The French *Suzanne* is also sometimes used.

SUSANNA Cur 1200, 1201, 1203, 1205, 1213.

Swithin, Swithun (m.): a derivative of Old English *swiþ* 'strong'. *Swithun*, Bishop of Winchester (died 852), received popular canonization and there are 35 churches dedicated to him. The name (usually in the incorrect spelling *Swithin*) is still occasionally used.

Sybil, see SIBYL.

Sylvanus, see SILAS.

Sylvester, see SILVESTER.

Sylvia, see SILVIA.

T

Tabitha (f.): the Aramaic equivalent of *Dorcas* (q.v.) 'roe' or 'gazelle'. Both names are given in Acts ix for the charitable woman who was raised up by St. Peter. *Tabitha*, like *Dorcas*, was common in the 17th C, and continued in use in the 18th and early 19th C.

Tace, Tacye (f.): this was a fairly common woman's name in the late 16th C and throughout the 17th C. Later it survived only among the Quakers. It is found (*Tacy*) as late as 1786. Lyford (1655) probably gives its origin correctly: '*Tace*, hold peace, hush! be silent, the imperative mood singular and indeed it is a fit name to admonish that sex of silence.' Camden (1605) gives much the same account of it.

Tadhgh (m.) [thīg]: Irish 'poet'. The name, a fairly common one, has been variously represented as *Teague, Thaddeus, Thady*.

Tagget, see AGNES.

Talbot (m.): this is now chiefly a surname, though occasionally used, like other surnames, as a christian name. Bardsley gives several instances of *Talebot* as a christian name in the 12th and 13th C. The famous and ancient family of *Talbot* took its name from its founder *Richard Talbot*, one of the companions of the Conqueror. The surname never appears in early records as *de Talbot*, and in the case of the original *Richard Talbot* was probably either a patronymic or (more likely) a nickname. Similar nicknames were *Taillefer* (found as a christian name as late as the end of the 13th C), and *Taillemache*, which gave rise respectively to the surnames *Telfer* and *Tollemache*. *Talbot* would be a compound of *tailler* 'to cut' and *botte* 'faggot'. At a later date *Talbot* was used (e.g. by Chaucer) as a nickname for a dog, and later still for a breed of dogs as well as (in heraldic language) for the dogs on the *Talbot* arms.

Tamasine, Tamsin, see THOMASIN.

Tancred (m.): Old German *Thancharat*, compound of *thanc* 'think' and *radi* 'counsel'. It later became *Thancred*, and in Norman French *Tancred*. In England, though not common, it gave rise to the surnames *Tancred, Tankard*.

Tanya, see TATIANA.

Tatiana (f.): the name of a martyr who suffered A.D. 225 and is venerated in the Orthodox Church. There are at least two others, as well as several saints *Tatianus*, all of whom seem to have been connected with Syria or Asia Minor and the name is possibly of Asiatic origin. *Tatiana* is a favourite Russian name, often abbreviated to *Tanya*, and is now occasionally used in England.

Ted(dy), see EDWARD, THEODORE.

Terence (m.): Latin *Terentius*, the name of a Roman *gens*, of unknown etymology. The poet, *P. Terentius*, was an African freedman, who took his name from his master. There was a 3rd-C Carthaginian St. *Terentius*, but it has not been used as a christian name, except in Ireland, where *Terence* or *Terry* is commonly used for the native *Toirdhealbhach* or *Turlough*.

Teresa, Theresa (f.) [terē'za]: (Latin *T(h)eresia*, Spanish, Italian *Teresa*, German *Theres(i)a*, French *Thérèse*). The origin of this name is obscure, and there is no real evidence for the usually accepted etymology from Greek θερίζω 'reap'. Θηρασία was the name of an island near Crete and of another near Sicily, and there may be some connexion between this and the personal name. It is first found as *Therasia*, the name of the wife of St. Paulinus, Bishop of Nola in the 5th C, who was converted by her. She was a Spaniard, and the name was for many centuries confined to the Iberian peninsula. There was a queen of Leon of this name in the 10th C, and it was firmly established in the royal house of Castile in the 11th C. It did not spread outside the Iberian peninsula until the 16th C, when the fame of St. *Teresa* of Avila (1515–82) carried it into all Roman Catholic countries. In recent times the popularity of the name in such countries has been increased by St. *Thérèse* of Lisieux (1873–97). It was not much used in England until the 18th C, when it was introduced by the admirers of the Empress Maria *Theresia* of Austria. It is now chiefly used in the abbreviated form *Tess* or *Tessa*.

Tess(a), see TERESA.

Tetty, see ELIZABETH.

Thekla (f.) [tek'la]: Greek θέκλα, an abbreviated form of θεόκλεια a derivative of θεόκλης 'god-famed'. In early legends this was the name of a convert of St. Paul, the first woman martyr. Godstow (1450) gives *Tecle* as the English of *Tecla*, but there is no evidence of its use as a christian name until the 19th C when it was occasionally borrowed from eastern Europe.

Thelma (f.): apparently invented by Marie Corelli for the Norwegian heroine of her novel *Thelma: a society novel* (1887), and frequently used as a christian name since then. Pronunciation is not there indicated, but thĕl'ma seems to be more popular than tĕl'ma, though both are used.

Theobald (m.): Old German *Theudobald*, compound of *theuda* 'folk', 'people', and *bald* 'bold'. Names compounded with *theuda* were early changed to *theo-* under the influence of such Greek names as *Theodore*. There was a corresponding Old English name *Theodbeald*, and no doubt this survived after the Normans had introduced their version of the Germanic name. There are several subtenants mentioned in DB as *Tedbaldus*, *Teodbald*, *Tetbald*, which may well represent Old English *Theodbeald*. Later *Teobaldus* or *Theobaldus* is the usual Latin form, the vernacular being *Tebald* or *Tibald*, which survives in the surnames *Tibbald*, *Tibbles*, &c. Lyford 1655 gives *Tibald* as a form of *Theobald*, and Pope pilloried Lewis *Theobald*, the editor of Shakespeare, as *Tibbald*, explaining in a note that his name was so pronounced. Cf. also *Tybalt* in *Romeo and Juliet*.

TEDBALDUS, TEODBALD, TETBALD DB 1086.
TEEBALD Cur 1196.
THEOBALDUS Cur 1199–1220, FA 1303, 1316, 1428.
TEOBALDUS FA 1428.
THEOBALD HR 1273.
TEBBE HR 1273.
TEBAUD HR 1273.
TEBALD HR 1273.
TIBBOTT Chew 1699.

Theodora (f.): f. of *Theodore* (q.v.). First found in England in the 17th C. It has never been common. Sometimes abbreviated to *Theo*.

Theodore (m.): Greek θεόδωρος 'god's gift'. There were several saints of this name, which is common in the Eastern Church. In Russia, particularly, *Fe(o)dor* is a favourite. *Theodore*, Archbishop of Canterbury (602?–690), was a native of Tarsus in Cilicia. The name has not otherwise been noted in England before the 17th C, and it remained rare until the 19th C when it was favoured by the Tractarians. But the Welsh *Tudor* or *Tewdwr* is said to be of this origin. The American diminutive is *Teddy*.

Theodoric (m.) [thĕŏd′orĭk]: Old German *Thiudoricus*, compound of *theuda* 'folk', 'people', and *ric* 'ruler'. There was a corresponding Old English name *Theodric*. It appears in DB as *Teodric*, *Theodric*, *Tedric*. The usual Middle English form was *Terry* from

Old French *Thierry*, or *Terrick*; hence the surnames *Terr(e)y*, *Ter(r)ick*. Bardsley gives an example of *Terye* as a christian name as late as 1629. *Theodoric* was occasionally revived in the 18th C. *Terry* has been used as a christian name in recent times, but apparently always with reference to the surname. See further under DEREK.

TEODRIC, THEODRIC, TEDRIC DB 1086.
TERICUS, Cur 1199.
TERRY HR 1273.
TERRICUS HR 1273, Testa de Neville 13th C.

Theodosia (f.): f. of Greek *Theodosius* 'divinely given'. It is first found in use in England in the 17th C. It is less common than *Theodora*.

Theophania (f.): Late Latin *Theophania* from Greek θεοφάνια 'the manifestation of God', another name for the Epiphany. *Theophania* became *Tifaine* in Old French, and in French folk-lore *Tifaine* was thought to be the name of the mother of the Magi. It was given to girls born at the season of Epiphany, and is found in England from about 1200. It gave rise to the surnames *Tiffany*, *Tiffen*, *Tiffin*. *Tiffeny* survived in Cornwall until the 17th C. Bardsley also records an *Epiphany* there in 1695.

TEFFANY Cur 1200.
THEOPHANIA Cur 1205.
THEFFANIA Cur 1205.
THIFANIA HR 1273.
THIPHANIA Magd. 1305.
TIFFONIA Testa de Neville 13th C.
THEOFANIA Cl 1262, FA 1346.
TIFFANY Magd. 1315.
TIFFAN Yorks Poll Tax 1379.
TEFFAN Yorks Poll Tax 1379.
TYFFANY Coventry Mysteries 15th C.

Theophila (f.) [thĕŏf'ila]: f. of *Theophilus* (q.v.). Occasionally used in the 17th C and later, e.g. *Theophila* Berkeley died 1653, and Sir Joshua Reynolds's mother *Theophila* Reynolds and his niece Mary *Theophila* Palmer (born 1757) who was usually called *Offy*.

Theophilus (m.) [thĕŏf'ilus]: Greek θεόφιλος 'loved of God', the name of the man to whom St. Luke's Gospel and the Acts of the Apostles were addressed. It was first used as a christian name in England after the Reformation, and was common in the 17th C. It has continued to be used in the Hastings family since the time of *Theophilus* Hastings, 7th Earl of Huntingdon (born 1650).

Theresa, see TERESA.

Thermuthis (f.): occasionally used as a woman's christian name in the 18th and 19th C. Josephus gives Θέρμουθις as the name of Pharaoh's daughter who adopted the infant Moses.

Thirza (f.): Hebrew *Tirzah*, possibly 'acceptance', but more probably the name of a city used for a person (cf. *Mahalah*), a name which occurs in a genealogy in the Book of Numbers. CMY says this 'was probably the origin of *Thirza*, the name of Abel's wife in Gessner's idyll of *The Death of Abel*, a great favourite among the lower classes in England, whence *Thyrza* has become rather a favourite in English cottages'.

Thomas (m.): an Aramaic word signifying 'twin'; in the Gospels the name of one of the twelve apostles, also known as *Didymus*, the Greek for a twin. Eusebius says that his real name was *Judah*, and his nickname may well have been used by his companions to distinguish him from the two other Judahs, Judah the brother of James (St. Jude), and Judah of Kerioth (Judas Iscariot). *Thomas* is found in England before the Norman Conquest only as a priest's name, but with the advent of the Normans it soon came into general use. Two of the earliest Norman Archbishops of York were so named, *Thomas* of Bayeux (died 1100) and his nephew and successor (died 1112). In the later Middle Ages *Thomas* was one of the commonest men's names, and this was owing to the fame of St. *Thomas* of Canterbury (*Thomas* Becket, 1118–70), whose martyrdom made Canterbury the greatest object of pilgrimage in the country. From the 13th C onwards *Thomas* has been one of the half-dozen commonest men's names in England (cf. the expression *Every Tom, Dick, and Harry*). Most of the church dedications in this name were originally to St. *Thomas* of Canterbury, but Henry VIII, who had a special dislike to the memory of the recalcitrant archbishop, had them altered to St. *Thomas* the Apostle. The usual medieval abbreviation of *Thomas* was *Thome*, later (from the 14th C) *Tom*. The French diminutive *Mace* or *Macey* was also used. The surnames *Thomas*, *Thom(s)*, *T(h)om(p)son*, *T(h)omlin(son)*, *T(h)om(p)kin(s)* are some of those formed from it.

Thomas DB 1086, Cur 1199–1220, HR 1273.
Thome HR 1273, Yorks Poll Tax 1379.
Thomasin, Thomelin Exch R 1306.
Tom Yorks Poll Tax 1379.
Thom Coventry Mysteries 15th C.
Mace Magd. *c.* 1200–10.

Thomasin(e) (f.): diminutive of *Thomas* (q.v.), found from the middle of the 14th C. *Thomasinus* and *Thomasina* both occur in FA 1346. *Thomas* was occasionally given to girls (*Thomasia* occurs in 14th- and 15th-C records), but the diminutive *Thomasin* soon became the usual f. form of the name. In the 16th and 17th C it appears as *Thomson*, *Tomson*, *Thomasing*, *Thomison* amongst other variants. Lyford (1655) gives it as *Thamasin* or *Thomasin*. As *Tamasine* or *Tamsin* it still survives in Cornwall.

Thomasina FA 1346.
Thomeson St. Dionis 1538.
Tomson St. Columb 1622.
Thomasin Notts P Reg 1750.

Thork(et)ill (m.): a Norse name, compounded of *Thor* the name of the god, and a second element of doubtful meaning (see ASKETIL). It was adopted into Gaelic as *Torcail*,whence *Torquil*, a favourite name with the Macleods. It was introduced into England by the Danes and survived into the 13th C, giving rise to a number of surnames, e.g. *Thurkettle*, *Thurkle*, *Thirkell*, &c.

Thorold (m.): *Thorweald*, compound of *Thor*, the Norse name of the god known in Old English as *Thunor*, and Old English *weald* 'strength'; probably a semi-anglicization of Norse *Thorvald*. It is found after, as well as before, the Norman Conquest, though it was largely supplanted by the Norman-French version of the name, *Torold* or *Turold*, which survived until the 15th C. The surnames *Thorold, Thorald, Turrell, Turrill, Terrell, Tirrell, Tyrell* are derived from it.

TUROLD(US) DB 1086, Cur 1199.
THOROLD Cur 1200, 1201, 1203.
THORALD HR 1273.
TOROLD HR 1273.

Thurstan (m.): Danish *Thorstein*, compound of *stein* 'stone' with *Thor* the god's name. It was introduced into England by the Danes and survived the Norman Conquest, often in the gallicized form *Turstan* or *Turstin*. Lyford (1655) gives '*Turstan* alias *Trustan*'. *Thurstan* has continued to be used in Lancashire. The surnames *Thurstan, Thurston, Tustin, Tustian* are derived from it.

TURSTANUS, TURSTINUS, TURSTIN, TURSTEN DB 1086.
THURSTANUS HR 1273.
THURSTANUS, THRUSTANUS Cov 1449.
THURSTAN HR 1273.
TURSTAN HR 1273.
THRYSTAN St. Dionis 1544.

Tibby, see ELIZABETH.

Tiffany, see THEOPHANIA.

Tilly, see MATILDA.

Timothy (m.): Greek τιμόθεος, compound of τιμή 'honour', 'respect', and θεός 'god'. It was the name of the convert and companion of St. Paul, to whom two of his epistles are addressed. It did not come into use in England until after the Reformation. (The common surnames *Tims, Timms,* &c., are from an Old English name cognate with Old German *Thiemmo*, which developed into *Thim* or *Tim*.) *Timothy* has been used a good deal in Ireland (usually abbreviated to *Tim*) to represent the native *Tadhgh* (q.v.). A f. form *Timothia* occurs at Burtonwood, Lancashire, in 1702.

Tirzah, see THIRZA.

Titus (m.): a common Latin praenomen, of doubtful etymology. It was the name of a disciple of St. Paul, to whom one of his epistles is addressed, and has sometimes been used as a christian name since the Reformation (e.g. *Titus* Oates 1649–1705).

Tobias, Toby (m.) [tobī′as, tō′bĕ]: Hebrew *Tobiah*, 'Jehovah (is) good'. *Tobias* is the hellenized form of the name; *Toby* was the Middle English form (cf. *Piers Plowman* 'And can tell of *Tobye*, and of twelve Apostles'). The use of *Toby* as a christian name has not been noted before the Reformation, but the existence of the surnames *Toby*, *Tobey* (which are recorded in the 13th C) and the diminutive *Tobin*, *Tobyn*, makes it probable that it was in use then. This is the more probable since the Book of Tobit (*Tobit* probably = Greek *Tobides*, 'son of *Tobias*') was a great favourite in the Middle Ages. In the 17th C it was used a good deal.

Tony, see ANT(H)ONY.

Torquil, see THORK(ET)ILL.

Tottie, see CHARLOTTE.

Tristram (m.): Celtic *Drystan* from *Drest* or *Drust* 'tumult', 'din'. The form *Tristan* was influenced by French *triste* 'sad', and the *Tristan* romances give this as the derivation of the name. *Tristan* is found as a surname in France as early as the end of the 12th C. The christian name occurs in England from 1189 in the form *Tristram*, which was the usual one in England, though it was exceptional in France. The intermediate form *Tristran* is found in one of the earliest French *Tristan* romances. The surnames *Tristram*, *Trustram*, *Triston* are derived from it.

TRISTRAM Cur 1189–1215, HR 1273.
TRYSTREM Yorks Poll Tax 1379.
TRISTIA⸱⸱ Lyford 1655.

Trix(ie), see BEATRIX.

Troth (f.): one of the many abstract nouns adopted as christian names in the 17th C. It was not uncommon during that century and continues to be used in some families. The following is an

L

example of the way in which such names were handed down; Sir
Thomas Tempest (died 1641) married *Troth* Tempest; their
daughter married John Kennett, and her daughter *Troth* Kennett
married William Bradshaw and had a daughter *Troth*.

Tryphena, Tryphosa (f.): derivatives of Greek τρυφή 'daintiness',
'delicacy'. *Tryphena* and *Tryphosa* are the names of women mentioned by St. Paul in Rom. xvi. 12, and were used a good deal as
christian names in the late 16th and 17th C. *Tryphena* is no doubt
the source of the gipsy name *Truffeni*.

Turlough (m.) [tur'lō]: Irish *Toirdhealbhach*. A common Irish
name, often represented by *Terence*, *Terry*, or *Charles* (qq.v.).

U

Uchtred, Ughtred (m.) [ū'tred]: the second element is Old
English *ræd* 'counsel', the first is obscure. It is found in the Old
English period as *Uhtred* and *Wihtred*, survived the Norman Con-
quest, and has continued to be used in a few families.

UCTRED DB 1086.
UHTRED Pipe Roll 1161.
UHREDUS Cur 1189.
UGHTRED Cur 1200, 1210, 1213, Cl 1284.
UCHTRED Cur 1203, 1205.
UCHERED Lyford 1655.

Ulick, see ULYSSES.

Ulric (m.): Old English *Wulfric*, compound of *wulf* 'wolf' and *ric*
'ruler'. It survived the Norman Conquest and gave rise to the surnames *Woolrich*, *Woolridge*, &c. The modern form, *Ulric*, is
apparently a revival of the Norman-French spelling, which occurs
in DB.

ULRICUS, ULURIC DB 1086.
WLVRICUS Cur 1199.
WULURICH HR 1273.
WLFRIC HR 1273.
WLFRICHE HR 1273.

Ulrica (f.): f. of *Ulric* (q.v.), occasionally borrowed from German.

Ulysses (m.): *Ulixes* or *Ulysses* was the Latin name for the Greek hero *Odysseus*: it was probably from Etruscan *Uluxe*. The name has been used in Ireland to represent the native names *Ulick* and *Uileos*.

Una (f.) [English ūna, Irish ōōna]: *Una* (phonetically rendered as *Oonagh*) is an ancient Irish name, still in use, but often anglicized as *Winnie* or *Winifred* or translated as *Agnes*, from a fancied connexion between *Agnes* and the Latin *agnus* on the one hand, and *Una* and the Irish *uan*, a lamb, on the other. *Juno* is yet another rendering (cf. O'Casey's play 'Juno and the Paycock'). *Una* is also sometimes used in England after *Una* in Spenser's *Faerie Queene*, where it is the f. of Latin *unus* 'one' (in distinction to the false *Duessa*).

Urania (f.): Greek *Oὐρανία*, the Muse of Astronomy (from *οὐρανός* 'the sky'). It was also an epithet of Aphrodite. Sir Philip Sidney addressed poems to *Urania*, which became a favourite poetic title in both France and England. It has been used as a christian name in some families and is still used in some gipsy families.

Urban (m.): Latin *urbanus*, 'of the town or city', like *paganus* 'a villager', came to be used as a personal name. *Urbanus* is one of those to whom St. Paul sends greetings in his Epistle to the Romans, and it was adopted by eight Popes, starting with St. Urban in the 3rd C. It was occasionally used as a christian name in the Middle Ages.

URBAN HR 1273.
URBANUS Testa de Neville 13th C.

Uriah (m.): Hebrew 'Jehovah is light' or 'Light of Jehovah'. In the case of '*Uriah* the Hittite', the Hittite *Ariya* or *Uriya* has been assimilated to the Hebrew name. Occasionally used as a christian name since the Reformation (e.g. *Uriah* Bankes 1648, a Presbyterian minister). It was never common, and if it needed a *coup de grâce*, it was given one by *Dickens* in the character of *Uriah* Heep in *David Copperfield*.

Urian, Urien (m.): this is a Welsh name, possibly derived from
Urbigenos = town born, but it is found also in England in the
Middle Ages, possibly as a result of its occurrence in the Arthurian
romances.

URIAN HR 1273.
URYENE HR 1273.
URIANUS FA 1431.
URIAN or URANIUS Lyford 1655.

Urith (f.): The name of the patron saint of the church of Chettlehampton in Devon. William of Worcester identifies this saint with
Herygh, an Irish saint, after whom he supposed the parish of St.
Erth in Cornwall to be named. But *Herygh* was a man, and there
appears to be no good reason for the identification. Camden says
of Chettlehampton:—'a small village where *Hierytha*, Kalendar'd
among the She-saints, was buried.' Nothing is known of this
Hierytha, and no suggestion can be made for the etymology of the
name, which sometimes appears locally as St. *Wurth*. The form
Urith occurs as a christian name about the beginning of the 17th C.
Early examples are *Urith*, daughter of Thomas Shapcote of Shapcote married Sir Courtenay Pole of Shute (1618–95); *Urith*,
daughter of Sir John Pole of Shute married (1693) Sir John
Trevelyan, 2nd Bart. Another John Trevelyan, High Sheriff of
Somerset in the reign of James I, married *Urith*, daughter of Sir
John Chichester of Raleigh. The name is still used in the Trevelyan
family.

Ursula (f.): Latin diminutive of *ursa* 'she-bear'. The legend of
St. *Ursula* and the 11,000 virgins was popular in the Middle
Ages, and the name was fairly common. It is also found from
time to time in the 17th–19th C, and has lately become more
frequent.

URSEL Cur 1200.
URSELL Cur 1207, HR 1273.
HURSEL HR 1273.
URCY HR 1273.
OURSE 14th C Legendary.
URSALAY, URSELEY Yorks Rec 1604.

V

Valentine (m., f.): Latin derivative of *Valens* 'strong', 'healthy' (cf. *Constantinus* from *Constans*, *Clementinus* from *Clemens*); the name of a 3rd-C Roman martyr. His feast day (14 Feb.) almost coincided with the festival of Juno Februata (15 Feb.), and the custom of drawing lots for lovers was transferred from the pagan to the christian festival. The name has never been common, but is found occasionally from the 12th C onwards. It is now used indifferently for men and women, and has been so since the 17th C.

VALENTINUS Cur 1196, 1200, 1203, 1205, FA 1284, Vis of Berks 1433.
VALANTINUS Cur 1210–12.
VALENTINE Cl 1553.

Valeria, Valerie (f.): Latin *Valeria*, f. of *Valerius*, the name of a Roman *gens*, probably derived from *valere*. St. *Valeria* was supposed to have been the wife of St. Vitalis, and mother of SS. Gervasius and Protasius, who were martyred at Ravenna in the 1st C. *Valeria* is common in Italy and *Valérie* is not uncommon in France and was imported into England as *Valerie* towards the end of the 19th C.

Valerian (m.) [valēr′ĕan]: Latin *Valerianus*, derivative of *Valerius* the name of a Roman *gens* (see VALERIA). St. *Valerianus* was a Bishop of Auxerre, and *Valérian* has had some currency as a christian name in France. It is found in England in the 13th C and has been used by the Wellesley family from the Middle Ages to the present day.

VALERIANUS Cur 1213–15.

Vanessa (f.): invented by Swift as a partial anagram of the name of Esther Vanhomrigh (cf. his *Cadenus and Vanessa*), and occasionally used as a christian name since then.

Venetia (f.): said by CMY to be a latinizing of Welsh *Gwyneth* (q.v.). Sir Kenelm Digby's wife, *Venetia*, a famous beauty, is probably responsible for its occasional use.

Vera (f.): Russian *Vjera* 'faith'. CMY does not know this as an English name. Ouida in *Moths* (1860) and Marion Crawford in *A Cigarette-Maker's Romance* (1890) both used the name, but both thought it necessary to explain it. Its popularity at the beginning of the 20th C was probably due to the second of these novels. In modern Roman Catholic use it is apparently often used as an equivalent of *Veronica* (q.v.).

Vere (m.): the name of a famous family which derived its name from *Ver* in Normandy. The *de Vere* Earldom of Oxford became extinct in the 17th C, but Lady Diana de Vere, the heiress of the last earl, married the 1st Duke of St. Albans, and their 3rd son was named *Vere* Beauclerk (later Lord Vere of Hanworth). This is the earliest example noted of the use of *Vere* as a christian name. Like other similar names, it is now often used by persons with no connexion with the family.

Verena (f.) [verē'na]: the name of a virgin martyred under Diocletian. Her cult is one of the most ancient in Switzerland and Suabia, and there are many churches and chapels dedicated to her around the Lake of Lucerne. The name *Verena* has been used in England in recent times, possibly introduced from this favourite tourist region.

Verity (f.): used as a christian name since the 17th C.

Vernon (m.): a surname of local origin (it is a very common place-name in France). Richard de *Vernon*, a companion of the Conqueror and founder of a famous family, came from *Vernon* (Eure). The use of *Vernon* as a christian name arose in the 19th C. An early example is *Vernon* Whitford in Meredith's novel *The Egoist* (1879).

Veronica (f.): from late Latin *veraiconica*, compound of f. of *verus* 'true' and *iconicus* 'of or belonging to an image'; the name given to a famous relic, a cloth supposed to retain the image of the face of Christ. Later *Veronica* was taken to be the name of the woman who had wiped His face with the cloth, and in some medieval apocryphal writings (e.g. the Acts of Pilate, the Book of Resurrection by Bartholomew) she was identified with the woman who was cured of an issue of blood. The name was also sometimes confused with *Berenice* (q.v.). *Véronique* has been used a good deal in France. Alexander Bruce, Earl of Kincardine (died 1681) married a Dutch lady, *Veronica* Sommalsdyck, and so introduced the name into Scotland; his great-grandson, James Boswell, gave the name to one of his daughters. In England it seems not to have been used until about the end of the 19th C.

Vesta (f.): the name of the Roman goddess of fire, sometimes used as a christian name in modern times.

Victor (m.): Latin *victor* 'conqueror', the name of an early Pope and of several martyrs. *Victor* is found in Curia Regis Rolls of 1200 and 1203 and a single example has been noted in 1585, but it was evidently rare in the Middle Ages, and its modern use in France seems to date from the Revolution. In England it came into general use in the later half of the 19th C, being regarded, probably, as a m. form of *Victoria*.

Victoria (f.): Latin *victoria* 'victory'. Said to occur in the Liverpool area 1617-1702, and a pauper named *Victoria* Chapman was buried at Moulton, Lincs., in 1681. Otherwise it has not been noted as a christian name in England before the 19th C. Queen *Victoria* (who was christened Alexandrina *Victoria*) was named after her German mother, Maria Louisa *Victoria*. The Queen's name was borne by her numerous godchildren and was sometimes given as a second name, but did not become generally popular and is now only rarely used. The Italian *Vittoria* and French *Victoire* are from the 3rd-C Roman martyr *Victoria*.

Viel, see VITALIS.

Vincent (m.): Latin *Vincentius*, derivative of *vincens* 'conquering'. There was a 3rd-C martyr of this name at Saragossa, whose cult was fairly extensive; and the name is found in England from the 13th C, giving rise to the surnames *Vincent, Vince, Vincey*. Later the fame of St. *Vincent* Ferrer, a 15th-C Spanish Dominican, and particularly of St. *Vincent* de Paul, the 17th-C French founder of the Vincentian Order of the Sisters of Charity, increased its use in Roman Catholic countries. It also became fairly common in England in the 19th C.

VINCENTIUS Cur 1200, 1203, 1205, 1210, Vis of Berks 1433.
VINCENT HR 1273.

Viola (f.) [vī'*ola*]: Latin *viola* 'violet'. The modern use of the name is due to Shakespeare's heroine in *Twelfth Night*. One of his possible sources has the name *Violetta*, which he may have shortened. *Viola*, however, also occurs as a name in Gower's *Confessio Amantis*.

Violet (f.): from Old French *violete*, diminutive of Latin *viola* 'violet'. *Violette* occurs as a christian name in the south of France in the Middle Ages, and there are a few instances in England, e.g. the wife of Sir John Chandos (died 1370). In the 16th C it is fairly common in Scotland, doubtless through French influence, and it has continued to be used there. It did not become general in England until the middle of the 19th C.

Virginia (f.): Latin f. of *Virginius*, earlier *Verginius*, the name of a Roman plebeian *gens*, probably cognate with *Vergilius* and of non-Latin origin. The story of *Paul et Virginie* (1786) made it popular in France. It came into use in England in the 19th C. The name arose independently in America where the first child born in America of English parentage (*Virginia* Dare, born at Roanoke, Aug. 1587) received the name of the plantation, which had been named in honour of Queen Elizabeth. It is much commoner there than in England.

Virtue (m.): used as a christian name in the 17th C and occasionally since.

Vitalis (m.): Latin *vitalis* 'of or belonging to life', 'vital'; the name of several early saints, SS. *Vitalis* of Bologna, Ravenna, and Rome. The name was introduced into England by the Normans and was not uncommon in the 12th–13th C, often in the French form, *Viel*. *Vyell* Vivian Esq. is found at Lancaster as late as 1799, but this may be a use of the surname. *Veitel* is still used in Germany.

VITALIS, FITELLUS, VITHELET, VITEL, FITEL, PHITELET DB 1086.
VITALIS Cur 1203, 1205, 1210.
VITAL Godstow 1450, Lyford 1655.
VIEL Cur 1210, 1213, HR 1273.
VITALIS or VIEL Testa de Neville 13th C.

Vivian (m.): Latin *Vivianus*, derivative of *vivus* 'alive'. St. *Vivianus* was a 5th-C martyr, who sometimes appears as *Bibianus*. The name is found in England from the 12th C, but has never been common. In the Middle Ages it was sometimes spelt *Phythian*, *Fithian*, &c.

VIVIANUS Cur 1199–1219, HR 1273.
VIVIAN St. Columb 1544.
FITHIAN HR 1273.
FITHIAN or VIVIAN Cheshire 1514.
PHYTHEON Chester Wills 1582.

Vivien (f.): Tennyson in his *Vivien and Merlin* used this form for French *Vivienne*, the name of the Lady of the Lake. The name probably originated in a misreading of MS *Ninian*, a Celtic name (see NINIAN). *Viviana*, which is found in medieval records, is a f. form of the man's name *Vivian* (q.v.).

W

Waldeve, see WALTHEOF.

Waldo, see WALTHEOF.

Wallace (m.): a Scottish surname (the equivalent of English *Welsh*, *Walsh*) used as a christian name after the famous patriot William *Wallace* (1272?–1305). This use is fairly recent and is not now confined to Scotland.

Walter (m.): Old German *Waldhar*, compound of *vald* 'rule' and *harja* 'folk'. It was a favourite with the Normans, and was introduced by them into England at the time of the Conquest. The corresponding Old English name *Wealdhere* was never common. *Walter* has been in use ever since its introduction, and gave rise to the surnames *Walter(s)*, *Watt(s)*, *Watkin*, *Watson*, *Waters*, *Gwatkin*, &c. *Wat* was the usual abbreviation until the 17th C, and apparently the full name was pronounced *Water* (cf. Shakespeare's 2 *Hen. VI*, IV. i. 31–5).

WALTER(I)US DB 1086, Cur 1196–1220.
G(U)ALTER(I)US DB 1086.
WALTER HR 1273.
WAUTER Writs of Parliament 1313, Exch R 1306.
WATER Oseney 1460, St. Dionis 1579, St. Antholin 1563.
GWALTER St. Antholin 1640.
GUALTER St. Jas. Clerkenwell 1688.

Waltheof (m.): Old English *Wealdtheof*, compound of *weald* 'power', 'rule', and *theof* 'thief'. *Waltheof* Earl of Northumbria, executed by William I in 1076, and his grandson *Waltheof*, Abbot of Melrose (died 1159), were regarded by the English as saints, and miracles were said to be worked at their tombs. The name survived in use in the North as late as the middle of the 17th C in the form *Waldeve*, *Waldive*. Bardsley would derive the name *Waldo*, still used in some families, from *Waltheof* (cf. the 11th C forms *Waltheof*, *Waldeof*, and *Waldew* for the name of the Abbot of Crowland). There was, however, an Old German name *Waldo*, from Gothic *valdan* 'to reign'.

WALDEOF, WALTHEOF, WALDEW (Abbot of Crowland at end of 11th C).
WALDIEF Pipe Roll 1161.
WALDIVE Exch Dep 1661.

Wanda (f.): a German woman's name, derivative of Old German *vand* which probably meant 'stock' or 'stem'. *Wanda* has lately been used a good deal in England, possibly taken from a novel of that name by Ouida (1883).

Warner (m.): Old German *Warinhari*, compound of the folkname *Varin* and *harja* 'folk'. It was introduced into England by the Normans in the form *Garnier*, and was fairly common in the

12th–14th C. The surname *Warner*, derived from it, is now often used as a christian name in the USA.

WARNER(I)US DB 1086, Pipe Roll 1159.
WARNER HR 1273.
WARINER HR 1273.
GERNER FF 1283.
GARNER Yorks Poll Tax 1379.

Warren (m.): Old German *Varin*, a folk-name. It was introduced into England by the Normans as *Warin* or *Guarin* and became common, giving rise to the surnames *Warren*, *Waring*, *Garnet* (from the diminutive *Guarin-et*), &c. It is rare after the 14th C, and when used as a christian name in more recent times is generally found to be a family name, e.g. *Warren* Hastings was named after his mother's maiden name. Lyford, it is true, gives *Warin* in his list of names and it is said to occur in Manchester in the early 17th C.

WARINUS DB 1086, Cur 1199–1220, Testa de Neville 13th C.
GUARINUS DB 1086, Cl 13th C.
WARRENUS Testa de Neville 13th C.
WARIN HR 1273.
GUARIN Pat 13th C.

Wendy (f.): First used by J. M. Barrie in his play *Peter Pan* (1904), and frequently used since then as a christian name. The origin of the name was a pet-name for Barrie evolved by W. E. Henley's little daughter Margaret: 'Friendy' became 'Friendy-wendy', and eventually 'Wendy'.

Wilfred, Wilfrid (m.): Old English *Wilfrith*, compound of *will* 'will', and *frith* 'peace'. St. *Wilfrith* or *Wilfrid* (*c.* 634–709), Bishop of York and one of the foremost men of his day, has some 50 churches dedicated to him. His name seems not to have survived in use after the Norman Conquest, and has not been noted before the late 16th C. It was revived by the Tractarians in the 19th C and is now common.

Wilhelmina (f.): a f. form of *Wilhelm* (see WILLIAM), borrowed from Germany in the 19th C. Sometimes abbreviated to *Mina*.

William (m.): Old German *Willahelm*, compound of *vilja* 'will' and *helma* 'helmet'. It became *Guilielm* and then *Guillaume* in French, and was introduced into England by the Normans in the 11th C, from which time it has held its place as one of the commonest men's names (from the 16th to 19th C, for instance, it averages 20 per cent. of baptismal entries in parish registers), tying with John for first place. At the present time it is (probably only temporarily) much less common. The usual abbreviation was *Will*. There is no direct evidence for the use of *Bill* as a nickname for *William* in the Middle Ages (the surnames *Bill, Bilson* may be from Old English *Bil*). There are many surnames derived from William and its diminutives, e.g. *William(s), Williamson, Wilson, Willcock, Wilcox(son), Wilmot* (from the common diminutive *William-ot*), *Wilkin(s), Wilkinson, Wilk(e)s, Wilkie,* &c. (from the pet-form *Wil-kin*), *Willis, Willet, Willin(g)s. Gill, Gillot, Gillet,* &c., are sometimes from Old French *Guille*, an abbreviation for *Guillaume*, but may also be from the girl's name *Gill* (see JULIAN). *Wilmot* was often a girl's name, and occurs as late as 1702 in the parish register of Kemble.

WILLELM Reg *c.* 1067.
WILLELMUS DB 1086, Cur 1199–1220.
WILECOC HR 1273.
WYLYMOT Poll Tax 1379.
GILLET, GILLOT(IN), GILLIAME, GUILLOT Exch R 1306.
WYLL *Cocke Lorelle's Bote c.* 1515.
GILOW, GYLAW Poll Tax 1379.
GILMYN Poll Tax 1379.

Wilmot (f.) see WILLIAM.

Winifred (f.): Welsh *Gwenfrewi*. St. *Gwenfrewi* was said to be a Welsh princess martyred by Caradoc, and her well was, and still is, regarded as miraculous. The Latin life of the saint gives the name as *Wenefreda*, which was early anglicized as *Winifred*, and was sometimes confused with the Old English man's name *Winfrith*. It has not been noted in use in England until the 16th C, and then usually with a Welsh connexion; *Wynifreed* occurs in 1585, *Winefred* 1631, *Winfrith* 1646, *Winnifred* 1704, *Winefred* 1742. It is now often abbreviated to *Winnie* and sometimes to *Freda*.

Winston (m.): used as a christian name in the Churchill family since Sir *Winston* Churchill (born 1620), father of the first Duke of Marlborough, whose mother was Sarah *Winston*, daughter of Sir Henry *Winston* of Standish in Gloucestershire. The name is derived from a hamlet near Cirencester.

Wystan (m.): Old English *Wigstan*, compound of *wig* 'battle' and *stan* 'stone'. *Wigstan*, King of Mercia, murdered in 849 while still a boy, was later revered as a saint, and his memory long survived in the Midlands.

WYSTAN FF *c.* 1190.
WISTANUS FA 1431.

Y

Yolande (f.): apparently a medieval French form of *Violante*, a derivative of *Viola* (q.v.). It has been occasionally revived in modern times.

JOLENTA FA 1289, 1302.
JOLEICIA (*sic*, the same person as in the other references) FA 1346.

Yorick (m.): Shakespeare's source for this name in *Hamlet* has been much discussed, but it was probably a phonetic rendering of *Georg* (pronounced *Yorg*) the Danish form of *George*. Sterne made use of the name *Yorick* in his *Sentimental Journey* (1768), and since then it has occasionally been used as a christian name.

Yvonne, Yvette (f.) [ēvŏn', ēvĕt']: French f. diminutive of *Yvon*, *Yve* (see IVO). *Yvonne* has become fairly common in England in the present century. *Ivetta* occurs in Cur 1167.

Z

Zacchaeus (m.): Hebrew '*Zakkai*' an abbreviated form of *Zachariah* (q.v.), latinized as *Zacchaeus* (the Greek is Ζακχιος).

It has also been explained, less probably, as identical with the Aramaic adjective *zakkai* 'pure'. *Zacchaeus* was the name of the publican of Jericho who climbed a tree in order to see Jesus pass by and later entertained him in his house (Luke 19). It was a common christian name in the 17th C.

Zacharias, Zachary (m.) [zăkarī′as, zăk′arĕ]: Hebrew 'Jehovah has remembered', the name of a king of Israel, and also of a prophet (whose name appears in the Authorized Version as *Zechariah*, a better spelling). *Zachary* seems to have been used occasionally in the Middle Ages, cf. the surname *Zachary*, which is recorded from the 16th C. It became popular with the 17th-C Puritans and lingered on in country use until recently.

Zedekiah (m.): Hebrew 'righteousness of Jehovah', the name of a king of Judah, sometimes used as a christian name in the 17th C.

Zenobia (f.): the name of a famous queen of Palmyra, probably a hellenization of some such name as *Zunab*. It was also the name of a 4th-C martyr. For some reason it came into use in Cornwall, where it occurs from about 1586. *Zenobe* Webb occurs in a Somerset will of 1694.

Zephaniah (m.): Hebrew 'Jehovah has concealed' (= 'protected') or 'stored up, treasured', the name of a Hebrew prophet, sometimes used as a christian name in the 17th C and later.

Zillah (f.): Hebrew 'shade', the name of the wife of Lamech. Occasionally used since the Reformation. It is a favourite gipsy name.

Zoë (f.): Greek ζωή 'life', used by Alexandrian Jews as a translation of the name *Eve*, and later as a christian name by the Byzantine Greeks. It was the name of a 3rd-C martyr who is in both the Greek and the Roman Calendars. Its use in England is recent. The earliest example noted is *Zoë* Skene, daughter of a British consul general at Aleppo, who in 1855 married the future Archbishop Thomson.

SOME COMMON WORDS DERIVED
FROM CHRISTIAN NAMES

Aaron's beard: kinds of plant, especially Great St. John's wort. (Reference to Ps. cxxxiii. 2.)

Aaron's rod: kinds of plant, especially Great Mullein and Golden Rod. (Reference to Num. xvii. 8.)

abigail: lady's maid. (Character in Beaumont and Fletcher's *Scornful Lady*, perhaps with reference to 1 Sam. xxv. 24–31.)

Achilles tendon: tendon connecting heel (where alone Achilles was vulnerable) with calf.

Adam: *old Adam*, unregenerate condition; *Adam's ale* or *wine*, water; *Adam's apple*, projection of the thyroid cartilage of the larynx.

Adamite: child of Adam, human being, unclothed man; name of sects who imitated Adam in this respect.

Albert: kind of watch-chain, also a frock-coat. (From Prince Albert, consort of Queen Victoria.)

Alice blue: a colour. (Named after Alice Roosevelt, daughter of President Theodore Roosevelt.)

Andrew: *Merry-andrew*, mountebank's assistant, clown, buffoon.

Ant(h)ony: *Anthony* or *Tantony*, the smallest pig of a litter; (*St.*) *Anthony's fire*, erysipelas.

Benedick: newly married man, especially confirmed bachelor who marries. (Shakespeare, *Much Ado about Nothing*.)

Benjamin: youngest child, darling. (Gen. xlii. 4.)

bertha, berthe: deep-frilling, (usually lace) collar to low-necked dress. (French *Berthe*, woman's name.)

Biddy: nickname for an Irish-woman, from the prevalence of the name Brigid in Ireland; hence *old biddy*, an old woman.

billy: (Australian) tin can used as kettle, &c., in camping out.

billy-goat: male goat. *Silly billy*, a foolish person, first used of William, Duke of Gloucester. When his cousin William IV gave the Royal Assent to the Reform Bill, Gloucester said 'Who 's silly Billy now?'

bob: (slang) a shilling. *Dry-, wet-bob, cricketing* or *boating* Etonian; *light-bob*, soldier of light infantry.

bobby: (slang) policeman. (From Sir Robert Peel, Home Secretary, 1828; cf. also *peeler*.)

Boniface: innkeeper. (Farquhar's *Beaux' Stratagem*.)

Caroline: of Charlemagne; of the time of Charles I and II of England. (From Latin *Carolus*.)

Catherine-wheel: circular spoked window or window-compartment; rotating firework; lateral somersault. (From the spiked wheel which was the instrument of St. Catherine's martyrdom.)

Charles's wain: the constellation Ursa Major. (Old English *Carles wægn*; wain of Arcturus, a neighbouring constellation, became wain of Arthur, who was confused with the other great hero of romance, Charlemagne.)

Charlotte: *apple charlotte, Charlotte Russe*, names of puddings (French).

Clarence: four-wheeled closed carriage. (From Duke of Clarence, William IV.)

cuddy: (Scottish) donkey; fool, ass; lever on tripod for lifting stones, &c. (Probably *Cuddy*, Scottish and North country diminutive of *Cuthbert*.)

dandy: (person) devoted to smartness, especially of costume; neat, smart, decorated. (Found from 1780 in Scotland, where *Dandy* is used as a pet-form of Andrew.)

Daniel: upright judge, person of infallible wisdom. (Dan. i–vi; *Merchant of Venice* IV. i. 223, 333.)

David and Jonathan: any pair of devoted friends. (1 Sam. xiii., &c.)

davit: crane at a ship's bow for hoisting anchor clear of side; one of a pair of cranes for suspending or lowering ship's boat. (Formerly also *david*, probably from the personal name.)

demijohn: bulging, narrow-necked bottle of 3–10 gal., usually cased in wicker. (Corruption of French *Dame Jeanne*.)

derrick: contrivance for moving or hoisting heavy weights; kind of crane with adjustable arm pivoted at foot to central post, deck, or floor. (Obsolete senses *hangman*, *gallows*, from the surname of a noted hangman at Tyburn, *c.* 1600.)

Diana: horsewoman, huntress. (*Diana*, goddess of the chase.)

dickens: devil, deuce. (From 1598; probably use of *Dickon* (= Richard), or the surname *Dickens*, as an alliterative substitute.)

dicky, dickey: donkey; (also *dicky-bird*) small bird; false shirt-front; pinafore or apron; driver's seat; servant's seat at back of carriage; seat at back of two-seater car. Some of these (e.g. first two) are certainly from the pet-name *Dicky* for *Richard*.

Dorcas: meeting of ladies to make clothes for the poor. (Acts ix. 36.)

doubting Thomas: incredulous person, from St. *Thomas* (John xx. 24–9).

Geordie: a nickname for a Northumbrian, from the north country form of *George*.

George: jewel forming part of Garter insignia.

gib: (obsolete) male cat. (From *Gib*, pet-form of *Gilbert*.)

Gregorian: of the plain-chant or plain-song ritual music named after Pope Gregory I; Gregorian calendar, correction by Pope Gregory XIII of the Julian calendar.

guy: effigy of Guy Fawkes burnt on 5 Nov.; grotesquely dressed person, fright.

hector: bluster(er), bully.

hick: (US colloquial) countryman, farmer, provincial. (Possibly from *Hick = Dick*, cf. *Hodge*.)

hobby: favourite subject or occupation that is not one's main business; (archaic) small horse; (hist.) early type of velocipede; *hobby-horse*, wicker horse used in morris-dance, &c., child's stick with horse's head; rocking-horse; horse on merry-go-round. (From Old French *hobin, hobi*, probably variant of the name *Robin*.)

hobgoblin: mischievous imp, bogy, bugbear. (From *Hob* for *Rob(in)*+*goblin*.)

Hodge: typical English agricultural labourer. (*Hodge* for *Roger*.)

Harry, Old: the devil.

Isabel, Isabella: greyish yellow. From the female name; history unknown, though there are several apocryphal stories attached to the word.

jack: familiar form of the name John, especially as type of the common people, as *Jack and Jill*; *every man jack*, every individual; = *jack tar*, common sailor; labourer, man who does odd jobs, &c.;

Cheap Jack, travelling hawker; *steeplejack*, man who climbs steeples, &c., to do repairs; (Cards) the Knave; machine for turning spit in roasting meat; machine for lifting heavy weights; machine for lifting axle off ground while cleaning or changing wheel; *boot-jack*, for pulling boots off; parts of various machines, &c.; pike, especially young or small one; *Jack Frost*, frost personified; *Jack-a-dandy*, dandy; *jackass*, male ass, dolt, blockhead; *laughing jackass*, Giant Kingfisher of Australia; *jack-boot*, large boot coming above the knee; *jackdaw*, thievish small crow haunting church towers; *Jack in office*, fussy official; *jack-in-the-box*, toy figure that springs out of box when opened, also kind of firework; *Jack-in-the-green*, man or boy (usually a sweep) enclosed in framework covered with leaves in Mayday sports; *jack-knife*, large clasp-knife for the pocket; *Jack of all trades*, one who can turn his hand to anything; *jack-o'-lantern*, will-o'-the-wisp; *jackplane*, for coarse work; *jack pudding*, buffoon, clown; *jack-snipe* (small species); *jack tar*, common sailor; *jack-towel* (endless, hung from roller); *jack*, a small flag flown from a *jack-staff*, whence *Union Jack*, is probably the same word.

Jack Ketch: common hangman.

Jacobean: of the reign of James I; of St. James the Less.

Jacob's Ladder: plant (*Polemonium caeruleum*) with corymbs of blue or white flowers, and leaves suggesting a ladder; (Naut.) rope ladder with wooden rungs.

Jacob's staff: surveyor's iron-shod rod; instrument for measuring distances and heights.

jacobus: English gold coin struck in reign of James I.

jane: (American slang) woman.

Jehu: furious driver. (2 Kings ix. 20.)

jemimas: (colloquial) elastic-sided boots; galoshed cloth overboots.

jemmy: crowbar used by burglars; sheep's head as a dish.

jenneting: kind of early apple. (Probably from the name *Jeannet+ing*.)

jenny: locomotive crane; *spinning jenny*, mechanism for spinning more than one strand at a time; *jenny-wren*, popular and nursery name for the wren; *Jenny donkey*, female ass.

Jeremiah: doleful prophet or denouncer of the time.

Jeroboam: wine-bottle of 8–12 times ordinary size. ('A mighty man of valour' 'who made Israel to sin'—1 Kings xi. 28, xiv. 16.)

jerry: *jerry-builder*, *-building*, builder, building of unsubstantial houses with bad materials; *jerry-built*, so built; *jerry* or *jerry-shop*, low beer-shop; (slang) chamber-pot; *Jerry* (army slang) German soldier, the Germans. (Probably familiar form of the name *Jeremiah*.)

Jezebel: impudent or abandoned woman; woman who paints her face. (Jezebel, wife of Ahab.)

Jill or Gill: *Jack and Jill*, lad and lass.

jilt: woman who capriciously casts off lover after giving him encouragement; (rarely) man who treats woman thus. (Probably from obsolete *Gillot*, diminutive of *Gill* from *Gillian*.)

Jim Crow: (USA) negro.

Job: *Job's Comforter*, one who under guise of comforter aggravates distress; *Job's tears*, seeds of a grass used as beads.

Jock: Highland soldier. (*Jock* is scottish equivalent of *Jack*.)

jockey (n.): professional rider in horse races. (From Scottish *Jocky = Jacky*.)

jockey (v.): outwit, cheat. (From preceding in obsolete sense 'cheat'.)

Joe Miller: stale joke, chestnut. (From *Joseph Miller*, comedian, died 1735.)

joey: a fourpenny-piece (first issued in 1836, at the instance of Mr. Joseph Hume, whence it for some time bore the nickname 'joey').

John: *John Barleycorn*, malt liquor personified; *John Bull*, English nation, typical Englishman; *John Chinaman*, Chinaman; *John Doe*, fictitious character in law; *John Dory*, also simply *dory*, sea fish used as food; *John Company*, the Honourable East India Company.

johnny: fellow, especially fashionable idler; *Johnny Armstrong* (nautical slang), handpower; *Johnny Raw*, novice; *johnny-cake*, cake of (USA) maize-meal or (Australia) wheat-meal. (The last, however, possibly = journey cake.)

Jonah: person who brings, or is sacrificed lest he bring, ill luck. (Jonah i. 11–16.)

Jonathan: (*Brother*) *Jonathan*, personified people of, typical citizen of, United States.

joseph: chaste man; woman's long riding-cloak of 18th C.

judas: infamous traitor; peephole in door; (of beard, &c.) *Judas-coloured*, red; *Judas kiss* (see Matt. xxvi. 48); *Judas-tree*, tree with purple flowers appearing before the leaves (from tradition that this was the tree on which Judas Iscariot hanged himself).

Julian: of Julius Caesar; *Julian calendar* (introduced by him).

Kit-cat: *Kit-cat Club*, club of Whig-politicians founded under James II; member of this; *Kit-cat* (portrait), portrait of less than half-length, but including hands. (From *Kit Cat(ling)*, keeper of of pie-house where the club met.)

Lazarus: beggar, poor man; *lazar* (archaic), poor and diseased person, especially leper; *lazar-house*, *lazaretto*, hospital for diseased poor, especially lepers; building or ship for performing quarantine in; after-part of ship's hold used for stores. (From the name *Lazarus*, Luke xvi. 20.)

louis: French gold coin of about 20 francs from Louis XIII to Louis XVI.

Lucretia: model of chastity, woman preferring honour to life.

Magdalen(e): reformed prostitute. (*Mary Magdalene* (Luke viii. 2), identified with the sinner of Luke vii. 37.)

magpie: European bird with long pointed tail, black and white plumage; variety of pigeon; (rifle shot that hits) outermost division but one of target. (*Mag*, abbreviation of *Margaret*, +*pie*.)

Marian: of the Virgin Mary, Mary Tudor, Queen of England, or Mary Queen of Scots.

marigold: kinds of plant with golden or yellow flowers. (*Mary* (the Blessed Virgin) +*gold*.)

marionette: puppet worked by strings. (From French *Marionette*, double diminutive of *Marie*.)

marry (interjection): (= the Virgin *Mary*).

martin: *St. Martin*, Bishop of Tours in 4th C; *Martinmas*, St. Martin's day, 11 Nov.; *St. Martin's summer*, fine season about this time; *martin, house-martin*, bird of swallow family (cf. French *martin-pêcheur*, the kingfisher).

martlet: the swift. (From French *martelet*, probably from *martinet*, diminutive of *Martin*.)

Mary: Australian slang for a native woman. 'Little Mary', nursery name for the belly.

maudlin: mawkishly sentimental, especially of tearful stage of drunkenness. (Middle English *Maudlin* = *Magdalen*.)

Michael: *Michaelmas*, feast of St. *Michael*, 29 Sept.

Moses: nickname for Jewish money-lender.

namby-pamby: insipidly pretty, mildly sentimental. (Formed on the name of *Ambrose Philips*, pastoral writer, died 1749.)

nanny: she-goat (cf. *billy-goat*); child's nurse.

nap: a card game, also (betting) to put all one's money on a single horse. (Abbreviation of *Napoleon*.)

Napoleon: French gold twenty-franc piece of Napoleon I; kind of top-boot; the game of *nap*.

Neddy: donkey.

nelly: largest kind of petrel. (Perhaps from the name *Nelly*.)

Noah: *Noah's ark*, child's toy, large old-fashioned trunk or vehicle, small bivalve, detached fragment of flying cloud; *Noah's nightcap*, the plant eschscholtzia (from conical bud-sheaths).

Old Nick: the devil.

Paddy: nickname for Irishman (cf. *Biddy*).

paddy(whack): a rage, fit of temper. (From the supposed irascibility of the Irish.)

Paul: *Rob Peter to pay Paul* (see PETER); *Paul Pry*, inquisitive person (character in comedy, 1825).

Pauline: of St. Paul, as *the Pauline epistles*; member of St. Paul's School in London.

peeping Tom: type of prurient curiosity (in tale of Godiva).

Penelope: chaste wife. (From *Penelope*, wife of Odysseus.)

Peter: *Rob Peter to pay Paul*, take away from one to give to another, discharge one debt by incurring another; *Blue Peter*, blue flag with white square, hoisted before sailing; *Peter's fish*, haddock

or other fish with marks supposed to have been made by St.
Peter's thumb and finger; *Peter's-penny* or *-pence*, (Hist.) annual
tax of a penny paid to the papal see.

pierrot (f. pierrette): French pantomine character; itinerant
minstrel with whitened face and loose white garment. (French
diminutive of *Pierre*.)

Poll (parrot): a nick-name for a parrot, found from about 1630.

Reynard: (proper name for) the fox; a fox. (From Old French
Renart, name of a fox in the *Roman de Renart*.)

Richard: *Richard Roe* typical name for defendant in ejectment
suit (cf. John Doe).

Robert: *herb Robert.*

robin: also *robin redbreast*, a small red-breasted bird; (with or
without epithet) kinds of American, Colonial, and Indian bird;
Robin-run-the-hedge, ground ivy; *robin's eye*, herb Robert; *Robin
Goodfellow*, a sportive goblin; *Robin Hood*, (type of) medieval
outlaw.

Roger: *the jolly Roger*, pirates' black flag. *Roger* or *Sir Roger de
Coverley*, a country-dance and tune.

Roland: *a Roland for an Oliver*, effective retort.

Sally: *Sally Lunn*, sweet light tea-cake served hot; perhaps from
name of girl hawking them at Bath *c*. 1800; *Aunt Sally*, game at
fairs, in which players throw sticks at pipe in mouth of wooden
woman's head.

Sam: *stand Sam*, bear the expense, especially of drink; *upon my
Sam*, asseveration. (Possibly the personal name.)

Sam Browne: army officer's belt and straps. (From Gen. Sir.
S. J. *Browne*.)

Sam(p)son: person of great strength, or resembling *Samson* (Judges xiii–xvi) in some respect; (Naut.) *Samson's post*, strong pillar passing through hold or between decks, post in whale-boat to which harpoon rope is attached. Hence *samsonite*, an explosive.

Sandy: nickname for a Scotsman. (The usual Scots abbreviation of *Alexander*.)

Sawney: nickname for Scotsman; simpleton. (Probably the same as *Sandy*.)

simony: buying or selling of ecclesiastical preferment. (From *Simon Magus* (Acts viii. 18.))

Sukey: (colloquial) *Sukey* or *black Sukey*, kettle. (*Sukey*, pet-form of *Susan*.)

tabby: watered fabric; brindled, mottled, or streaked cat; cat, especially female; gossiping woman, especially old maid; kinds of moth; kinds of concrete. (Some senses perhaps from *Tabitha*.)

Taffy: (colloquial) Welshman. (From Welsh *Dafydd* = *David*.)

Teddy-bear: child's toy bear (named after *Theodore* Roosevelt).

Thomism: theological doctrine and philosophy of St. *Thomas* Aquinas.

timothy, timothy grass: a fodder grass. (From *Timothy* Hanson, who introduced it into North America.)

toby: jug or mug, usually in form of old man with three-cornered hat (also *Toby Fillpot*); *toby-frill*, broad turned-down goffered collar like Punch's dog *Toby's*.

tom: *Tom, Dick, and Harry*, persons taken at random, ordinary commonplace people; male animal, especially *tom-cat*; *long tom*, (naut.) long gun, especially one carried amidships on swivel-carriage; *Old Tom*, strong kind of gin; *Tom and Jerry* (USA), rum and water beaten up with eggs, &c.; *tomboy*, romping girl, hoyden; *tomfool*, fool, trifler, *tomfoolery*, foolish trifling, foolish knick-knacks, &c.; *Tom Fool*, type of witlessness; *tomnoddy*, block-head, fool; *Tom Thumb*, a legendary dwarf, any diminutive person, dwarf variety of various plants; *Tom Tiddler's ground*, children's game, place where money can be had for the picking up; *tomtit*, kinds of small bird, especially titmouse.

tommy: *Tommy Atkins*, the British soldier, whence *Tommy* or *tommy* (slang), private in the army; (Mech.) kinds of wrench or turnscrew, (also *tommy-bar*) short bar for working box-spanners; bread, provisions, especially as given to workman in lieu of wages; this system of payment, truck system (now illegal); *tommy shop* (formerly) in which *tommy* was enforced, (now) shop in works where provisions may be bought, any baker's shop; food carried by workmen; *tommy gun* (= Thompson, from inventor); *tommy-rot*, nonsense, absurd statement or argument, foolish course, undesirable state of things; *soft tommy* (naut.), soft or fresh bread.

Uncle Sam: government, or typical citizen, of USA.

valentine: *St. Valentine's Day*, day on which St. Valentine was beheaded and on which birds were supposed to pair, 14 Feb.; sweetheart chosen on this; amatory or satirical letter or picture sent to person of opposite sex on St. Valentine's day.

veronica: kinds of herb or shrub with blue, purple, pink, or white flowers; cloth with representation of Christ's face, especially one miraculously so impressed after being used by St. Veronica to wipe sweat from Christ's face.

Victorian: of person living in the reign of Queen Victoria; *early-Victorian*, of Victoria's reign, antiquated.

victorine: woman's fur tippet with long ends. (Perhaps named from Queen Victoria.)

will-o'-the-wisp: ignis fatuus, jack-o'-lantern. (Abbreviation of *William*; *wisp* = handful of (lighted) tow, &c.)

William, Sweet: name for a common garden flower, *Dianthus barbatus*, found from 1573.